The Oyster Question

env|ronmental
h|story
and the
amer|can
south

CHRISTINE KEINER

The Oyster Question

*Scientists, Watermen,
and the
Maryland Chesapeake Bay
since 1880*

The University of Georgia Press   *Athens and London*

An earlier version of chapter 2 appeared as Christine Keiner, "W. K. Brooks and the Oyster Question: Science, Politics, and Resource Management in Maryland, 1880–1930," *Journal of the History of Biology* 31 (1998): 383–424. Earlier versions of material from chapters 2–4 appeared as Christine Keiner, "Chesapeake," in *History in Dispute*, vol. 7, *Water and the Environment since 1945: Global Perspectives*, ed. Char Miller, Marc Cioc, and Kate Showers (Detroit: St. James, 2001), 40–50.

Paperback edition, 2010

© 2009 by the University of Georgia Press

Athens, Georgia 30602

www.ugapress.org

Set in Berthold Baskerville by Graphic Composition, Inc., Bogart, Georgia

Printed digitally in the United States of America

The Library of Congress has cataloged the hardcover edition of this book as follows:
Keiner, Christine, [date]–
    The oyster question : scientists, watermen, and the Maryland Chesapeake Bay since
    1880 / Christine Keiner.
        xvi, 331 p. : ill., maps ; 24 cm. – (Environmental history and the American South)
        Includes bibliographical references and index.
        ISBN-13: 978-0-8203-2698-6 (hardcover : alk. paper)
        ISBN-10: 0-8203-2698-4 (hardcover : alk. paper)
        1. Oyster fisheries–Maryland–Management–History. 2. Oyster fisheries–
    Chesapeake Bay (Md. and Va.)–Management–History. 3. Oyster culture–Political
    aspects–Maryland. 4. Oyster culture–Political aspects–Chesapeake Bay (Md. and
    Va.) I. Title.
SH365.M3K35 2009
338.3'724409752–dc22

                                                                            2009009211

Paperback ISBN-13: 978-0-8203-3718-0
        ISBN-10: 0-8203-3718-8

British Library Cataloging-in-Publication Data available

TO MY PARENTS

CONTENTS

ILLUSTRATIONS

Figures

Table

One of the most important story lines in modern American environmental history has been the rise of the conservation state. During the field's early years, environmental historians often celebrated the coming of state conservation – national park and wilderness preservation, game and wildlife protection laws, forest and water conservation, and other statutory and administrative restrictions on resource exploitation – as an unabashedly progressive development that countered the juggernaut of capitalist expansion and protected the natural commons against individual and corporate greed. But environmental historians increasingly have come to hold a more critical view of what conservationists were doing – or thought they were doing – when they spoke for nature in the process of protecting it. In particular, scholars have shown how the rise of state conservation shifted power away from local resource users and instead invested resource management decisions in the hands of scientifically trained conservation experts. Building on the insights of Samuel Hays's formative scholarship (now more than half a century old) on progressive conservation and the "gospel of efficiency" that animated it, these historians have given us a new picture of conservation as a kind of commons enclosure that could work against those on the economic margins. As Christine Keiner puts it in this superb study of oyster management in the Maryland portion of the Chesapeake Bay, "Progressive scientific reform allied with capital-intensive industrialism . . . exerted great power on the national stage of American conservation politics."

This tradition of progressive scientific reform is a core concern of *The Oyster Question*. Keiner, whose training is in the history of science, devotes a substantial portion of this volume to the history of oyster science at Johns Hopkins University and allied institutions, highlighting the roles played by eminent scientists and scientific reformers such as William K. Brooks, Isaiah Bowman, and Abel Wolman in developing a progressive reform tradition around the oyster. Indeed, these scientists effectively defined the "oyster question": whether commercially harvested oysters ought to be a product of nature or of human culture. For these scientists, the best solution to the depletion of the oyster commons lay in a shift to privatized aquaculture, whereby oyster "planters" would own or lease their beds and raise oysters like a crop. These would-be policy advisers thus sought to engineer a shift from a public oyster-gathering commons to a privatized and enclosed system of capital-intensive cultivation. Oyster biology allowed for such agronomic methods; indeed, other coastal states saw their oyster industries move in this direction over the course of the nineteenth and twentieth centuries, often with environmental scientists leading the way. These scientific thinkers insisted that only through the careful study of oyster biology and propagation could the species be conserved as a viable and sustainable resource. Keiner's detailed discussion of more than a century of oyster science in and around the Chesapeake Bay and the impetus that such insights provided to conservation alone makes this an important study.

But something curious and unexpected happened in Maryland and its portion of the Chesapeake Bay. Bucking the national conservation trend, Maryland's state government continued to manage its oyster beds as a commons overseen by watermen working with primitive harvesting technologies and only a modicum of scientific expertise. To figure out why, Keiner turns from the history of science to social and political history. As in many other commons resource battles over the past century, proponents of science-based conservation regimes depicted commons resource users as ignorant, stubborn, and backward in their ways – as impediments to progress. But in Maryland, such political rhetoric – and the powerful alliances of scientists, packers, railroads, and urban consumers that proffered such rhetoric – did not gain sufficient political traction because watermen enjoyed a critical political advantage: Maryland operated under a county-unit system of representation that gave rural counties and their residents disproportionate political power in the state legislature. As a result, Keiner shows, Maryland's watermen resisted the urban political force behind scientific conservation and retained a remarkable degree of control over oyster management, at least until the 1960s, when the county-unit system unraveled. In its laudable attention to state politics, *The Oyster Question* provides a wonderful example of how local resource users, dependent on a natural commons, staved off the forces of modernization.

As she describes the political dimensions of these "culture wars," Keiner also provides a fascinating social history of the conflict between state conservation interests and the watermen whose habits proponents of conservation hoped to reform. Keiner suggests that these two groups had different ways of knowing the nature of the bay and understanding the issues that swirled around the oyster question. This is not, she insists, a traditional "tragedy of the commons" story in which the uninformed and undisciplined behavior of harvesters systematically depleted a resource until scientists rode to the regulatory rescue. Watermen had an understanding of the bay that science could not always capture. But Keiner also resists reflexively privileging the watermen and their ways of knowing and working with the environment. Rather, Keiner's is a story of two competing worldviews on the proper relationship between nature and culture.

The conflicts between these worldviews – usually played out in state politics but sometimes flaring up as physical violence – necessarily intersected with another set of actors in this story: oyster biology, the Chesapeake Bay environment, and a broader set of human-induced changes to both that played out over the twentieth century. As other fisheries historians have pointed out, marine ecosystems are notoriously complex and stochastic, and any efforts to conserve a resource – whether through scientific conservation or folk practices – are almost always humbled by shifting environmental baselines and confusing human legacies. Keiner's analysis is wonderfully attentive to these details of historical ecology. Moreover, as scientists and watermen sought to make sense of the Chesapeake environment and how most productively to harvest oysters from it, human activities in its watershed transformed the bay's ecology. By the late twentieth century, problems with pollution, parasitic diseases, and overdredging came together to produce a proverbial perfect storm in the Chesapeake Bay, challenging the capacity of both scientists and watermen to manage oysters sustainably and profitably. In that context, and particularly as watermen lost their disproportionate political power, unexpected new alliances and conservation suggestions emerged. Many urban and suburban environmentalists came to see watermen as "cultural indicators" of the bay's ecological health and consequently came to support their economic survival in ways that past conservationists had not. As their political advantages waned, watermen themselves became an endangered species of the sort that the new environmentalists were inclined to protect. *The Oyster Question* is an important addition not only to conservation historiography but also to a growing scholarship in marine environmental history.

What might be less apparent on the surface is how this book fits as a volume in a series on Environmental History and the American South. Although Maryland is nestled just below the Mason-Dixon Line and its colonial agricultural history clearly placed it in a southern context, the state has moved away from that southern identity over time. Indeed, Keiner shows how regionally in-between Maryland can seem. But in her insistence that this story of conflict be seen as part of a larger commons enclosure movement, she evocatively shows how southern that story often was. As Keiner inflects their history, watermen were not so different from the yeoman farmers and cattlemen who subsisted on the South's terrestrial commons until stock and fence laws and modernizing federal interventions—such as the cattle tick eradication programs that Claire Strom describes in her volume in this series—largely closed that commons to such use. But Maryland watermen, who worked in technologically primitive and labor-intensive ways and were a racially diverse lot, nonetheless had much greater success in protecting themselves against the forces of enclosure than did other southern resource users. And, ironically, that success was a product of a political system that was itself particularly southern. That said, Keiner resists seeing this as entirely a southern story. Instead, she masterfully places her story in multiple comparative contexts, providing one of the book's great virtues as a volume in this series. By examining the watery margins of the South, Christine Keiner has given us a story with broad historical and environmental implications.

Paul S. Sutter

ACKNOWLEDGMENTS

This book could not have been completed without the help of many good people. I am especially grateful to Sharon Kingsland and Paul Sutter for their wise and patient guidance. The insights of Keith Benson, John Cloud, Gerard Fitzgerald, Pamela Henson, Robert Kargon, Gabriella Petrick, Helen Rozwadowski, Jeffrey Stine, and John Wennersten have also enriched this work. I am fortunate to have such a learned circle of friends.

I also thank Mary Lou Cumberpatch (NOAA Central Library), James Gillispie (Johns Hopkins Government Publications/Maps/Law Library), Kathy Heil (Chesapeake Biological Laboratory), and all the other librarians, archivists, and interlibrary loan personnel who facilitated my research. Frank T. Gray generously provided access to documents from his personal files.

Several colleagues at Rochester Institute of Technology provided moral and/or financial support. My thanks go to Deborah Blizzard, Evelyn Bristor, Mary Lynn Broe, John Capps, Thomas Cornell, Rebecca Edwards, Lisa Hermsen, Ann Howard, Glenn Kist, Andrew Moore, Richard Newman, Richard Shearman, James Winebrake, and the College of Liberal Arts Miller Fellowship and Faculty Research Fund committees.

I must express my deep gratitude to Derek Krissoff for signing me on and to Jon Davies, Ellen Goldlust-Gingrich, two anonymous reviewers, and the rest of the University of Georgia Press team for their hard work in making this book a reality.

I thank Darren Lacey for being an all-around great guy and the teachers and professors who have helped shape my worldview.

This book is dedicated to my parents, James and Vera Keiner. Since my career took me north, they have provided a fantastic clipping service, keeping me apprised of the ongoing oyster debates in a most tangible and personal way. Most important, they gave me two wonderful siblings and a very happy upbringing in Maryland. My greatest debt will always be to them.

The Oyster Question

Introduction

Culture Wars and the Maryland Oyster

At several critical junctures since the 1880s, the Maryland oyster has found itself caught in the "culture wars" that pit modernism against traditionalism during times of swift, stressful change in the American economic and social order. Just as the forces of urbanization, industrialism, and technocracy have challenged conservative values at intervals since the late nineteenth century, radical new ideas about conserving the legendary but beleaguered oyster have sparked a series of intense debates between scientists and watermen, the traditional harvesters of the Chesapeake Bay. The story of the dying oyster fishery and the vanishing watermen is familiar to Chesapeake audiences today: scientists have been sounding the alarm for more than a hundred years, since long before the advent of environmentalism. Because oysters can be cultivated, several prominent scientists from the 1880s onward seized the opportunity of each steep harvest drop to promote what they considered the ideal solution to the "oyster question" – privatization of the oyster beds for aquaculture. But these scientists were continually thwarted by the watermen, who considered private propagation anathema and who possessed substantial clout in the state legislature. Time after time, the traditionalists beat back the modernists in the struggle to define the scope of oyster management, Maryland's first and historically most important conservation issue. Consequently, Maryland is the only one of the key oyster-producing states in the United States in which private cultivation has played only a minor role.

The process by which state entities, often in concert with elite economic interests or scientific authorities, have restricted access to common-pool resources is an important theme in the history of U.S. modernization, particularly in industries based on the extraction of natural resources. Whether benefiting private corporate interests or centralized governmental entities, enclosure processes pose hardships for those who rely on the commons for their livelihood. Although impoverished resource users' struggles to retain their local commons regimes have often failed, Maryland's oystermen historically possessed a powerful advantage because of their state's rurally biased system of legislative representation. They also benefited from the tremendous ecological resilience of the Upper Chesapeake Bay, which slowed the depletion of the oyster beds, further undermining calls for privately funded, scientifically informed aquaculture.

This book examines why the forces of progressive scientific reform, allied with capital-intensive industrialism, played such a weak role in Maryland resource management at a time when they exerted great power on the national stage. I focus on the structure of representative politics at the state rather than federal level, an analytical category grossly underrepresented in conservation historiography. In contrast to studies that have emphasized governments' overweening power in imposing environmental management regimes on local peoples, this study shows how members of a nonelite group used legal means to resist the loss of their commons and to establish a managerial framework prioritizing their needs. The ultimate result was not an open system free to be exploited at will but rather a regulated commons that coevolved through biologists' struggles to implement at least minimal publicly funded measures for sustaining production and that remained intact even after the state government changed in the 1960s in ways that should have eroded the watermen's disproportionate power base.

The political battles over oyster conservation that have cycled in and out of Maryland history over the past 130 years thus involved much more than oysters – these conflicts involved the struggle for supremacy between the rich traditions of the rural American order and the modern worldview of the ascendant urban-industrial system. The legacy of this particular version of the American culture wars remains perceptible today.[1]

The Great Shellfish Commons

Dependence on the oyster has shaped Maryland politics, culture, and commerce since the mid–nineteenth century. In the history of the state, no other topic has generated as many laws, the first of which dates to 1820.[2] After the Civil War, new rail lines transported Chesapeake oysters across the country, and for most years from the 1870s through the 1960s, Maryland's oyster industry constituted the largest in the United States and one of the largest in the world. The industry grew so powerful that in 1912, Baltimore became the first major American city to adopt a waste-treatment system and did so not primarily because of urban progressives' water-quality concerns but to protect the lucrative oyster trade from sewage contamination.[3] Oysters dominated debates over the state's proper role in managing natural resources until the mid–twentieth century.

Immense harvests in the late nineteenth century gave way to steep downturns, prompting local scientists to issue the first of many calls to evolve beyond the industry's preindustrial means of production (fig. 1). Distressed by the inefficiency of the hunter-gatherer approach and the destitution of tidewater communities, a long succession of scientists from the 1880s through the 1950s and beyond argued that the Maryland Chesapeake oyster fishery should be placed on a scientific, capital-intensive basis, as in other coastal states. Processors and railroad executives, urban conservationists, and the influential *Baltimore Sun* joined in promoting the profits from leasing submerged grounds for the scientific cultivation of the billions of oyster offspring that would otherwise perish in the struggle for existence.

William K. Brooks, the premier American morphologist of the last quarter of the nineteenth century, was the first to argue that science could play an important role in addressing the rapid depletion of the Chesapeake's most lucrative resource. A generation later, geographer Isaiah Bowman took time off from advising President Franklin D. Roosevelt on foreign policy to head commissions on restructuring Maryland's oyster management and other aspects of the natural resource bureaucracy.

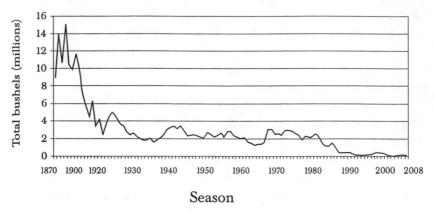

Note: Data not complete for several seasons between 1872 and 1916.

Fig. 1. Maryland oyster harvest, 1870–2008. (Graph constructed with data provided by Maryland Department of Natural Resources Shellfish Program.)

Internationally recognized sanitary engineer Abel Wolman, whose efforts to improve water quality saved countless lives over a career spanning most of the twentieth century, also advised Maryland officials on implementing more efficient seafood conservation. It was no coincidence that all three men worked for Johns Hopkins University, the first research-oriented graduate school in the United States. Not surprisingly, given the institution's conviction that scientific expertise could solve any problem and its proximity to the Chesapeake Bay, Brooks, Bowman, and Wolman believed that the salvation of the oyster industry lay in a large-scale system of "private enterprise in oyster culture."[4] Even Rachel Carson, the Hopkins zoology graduate who set in motion the modern environmental movement with her celebrated 1962 critique of the scientific-industrial establishment, *Silent Spring,* supported oyster privatization as a government biologist and aspiring science writer during the 1930s. The failures of technical experts – in this case, to influence resource management at a time when science enjoyed great cultural respect – constitute as important a part of the history of science as their successes.

The Maryland advocates of private oyster culture sought to pass laws enabling aquafarmers to cultivate individual underwater plots, just as agricultural reformers urged farmers of the postbellum New South and Great Plains to modernize by enclosing common lands long used for pasture or subsistence hunting and fishing.[5] Proponents reasoned that oyster growers would have a much greater incentive to conserve the Chesapeake's white gold than those who could mine its riches without investing in it. As Brooks asserted in 1891, Marylanders needed to stop relying on nature's bounty and instead recognize the Chesapeake Bay as one of the world's "richest agricultural regions," "adapted for producing only one crop, the oyster."[6] Consequently, this is also a story of agricultural reform and modernization efforts.

Numerous analysts of the Chesapeake oyster industry have since employed the "tragedy of the commons" thesis.[7] The phrase, popularized by biologist and human ecologist Garrett Hardin in a 1968 article, refers to the problem of common ownership of natural resources. Hardin's argument uses the case of a public pasture that ultimately becomes overgrazed as each herdsman places more cows on the commons "to maximize his gain." The hypothesis predicts that individual users will maximize short-term benefits by exploiting any common-pool resource to the point of environmental ruin. Since technical solutions cannot address the problem of common ownership, Hardin argued, users can be compelled to cease their reckless behavior only by forceful governmental policies.[8]

According to this model, it makes economic sense for an oysterman to catch all the oysters he can. Why leave a hoard of oysters on the bay floor with the expectation of later harvesting more mature, valuable specimens if they will otherwise be taken by someone else, silted over, contaminated by pollution, or killed by disease or salinity-reducing floods?[9] In an unregulated commons, individuals have little incentive to conserve resources because the costs of environmental decline are distributed among all users, who will always value immediate benefits over long-term ones. As a Crisfield, Maryland, harvester put it, "If a waterman caught the last oyster in Chesapeake Bay, he'd sell it."[10] Observers of fisheries around the world expressed such concepts long before the publication of Hardin's essay.

One solution Hardin proposed was privatization, but northern oyster industry members had long since beaten him to the punch. The belief that sustainability could be maintained by assigning exclusive rights to those willing to invest long-term capital and labor in the oyster beds influenced Connecticut, New Jersey, and other northern states in the early 1800s. Having exhausted all or some of their oyster grounds, they granted protection to those who claimed exclusive rights to oysters they "planted" on submerged tidal lands. By purchasing or taking small seed oysters and transplanting them to tidal areas for two to four years of maturation, planters could greatly increase the return on their investment, provided that the bivalves survived bad weather and predators. Oyster growing was much riskier than dry farming because of the crop's vulnerability to environmental changes and theft.

Human predation on planted oysters in New Jersey provoked several complex court cases regarding common property rights to tidal lands. As scholar Bonnie McCay explains, "Oysters and their cultivation are difficult to fit into land-based categories and philosophies of property." One particular case, tried in 1808, established what became "the sacred rule of the shellfisheries" – the common-law principle that private property claims can apply only to unproductive marine lands, not to areas where oysters grow naturally.[11] The problem of defining "natural" oyster beds became acute in the late nineteenth and early twentieth centuries, when overfishing and pollution overwhelmed the viability of many oyster beds along the mid-Atlantic coast. Maryland later developed its own definition, which privileged the views of oystermen over biologists, but the state's leasing advocates always observed the principle that private oyster culture should be limited to barren bottoms.

By raising the broad question of whether tidal waters, lands, and resources should be considered common holdings or private property, the New Jersey oyster cases helped shape an important principle in American law regarding the authority of state governments over common resources. The court rulings articulated the idea that states own the foreshore and submerged soil of all navigable and/or tidal bodies of water. The U.S. Supreme Court affirmed this concept, known as the public trust doctrine, in 1842.[12]

Although the public trust idea conveyed the state's responsibility to protect public rights to tidewater lands, later judges and legislators interpreted it to allow the enclosure of oyster commons. The New Jersey legislature's efforts to privatize natural oyster beds grew out of desperation. By the late 1870s, overfishing and urban pollution had depleted many formerly productive areas, creating a situation "dire enough to enable actors and observers to propose what was otherwise unthinkable: the creation of private property in the sacred commons of the natural beds." But the granting of riparian leases to individuals and corporations provoked violent resistance on the Delaware Bay (1893–94) and Mullica River (1907). The "oyster pirates" who challenged the new leasing system included not only poor harvesters but also small-scale planters who feared that wealthier leaseholders would monopolize areas that might still be capable of providing seed oysters (small bivalves that planters transferred to their own underwater grounds to grow into marketable products). Ensuing court cases and legislative acts reaffirmed the status of the natural oyster beds as the "natural heritage of the people." However, New Jersey's oyster industry soon faded into relative insignificance, the victim of overharvesting, pollution, and environmental change.[13]

The sacred status of the estuarine commons played just as great a role in Maryland's long-lasting oyster conservation debates. But whereas New Jersey oystermen utilized court test cases, poaching, and piracy to protect their common-use rights, their Maryland counterparts enjoyed disproportionate electoral power that enabled them to prevent the legislature from enacting laws that would enclose the public commons for the benefit of well-heeled oyster planters. Because the state Senate was apportioned by county units rather than population (as in New Jersey), and because tidewater counties outnumbered nontidal ones, watermen and their fellow shoreline residents possessed political power out of proportion to their numbers. The House of Delegates had less of a disparity between urban and rural areas because each county elected between three and six delegates based roughly on population, and Baltimore City (which was not part of any county) elected as many delegates as the most populous county. But malapportionment remained a prominent feature of the House, since the most populous county had nowhere near as many residents as Baltimore and since the 1864 constitution awarded House representation based on the number of whites in each district rather than on total population.[14] Because large numbers of Baltimoreans were African American, the city lacked its fair share of delegates. In 1898, for example, Baltimore contained almost half the state's residents and generated more than half its tax revenue but elected only three of the state's twenty-six senators and eighteen of its ninety-one delegates. Rural delegates outnumbered their Baltimore colleagues by a ratio of 3 to 1, while rural senators dominated by a ratio of 5½ to 1. A 1908 study concluded that Maryland's assembly discriminated against its main city more than any other state legislature.[15] Despite limited reapportionment efforts, by 1930, Baltimore City, which had more than 50 percent of the state's population, still held only 21 percent of the Senate seats and 22 percent of the House seats.[16] Rural lawmakers in Maryland, as in other states, especially those in the South, consistently used their disproportionate power to block efforts to establish more equitable apportionment. Because most efforts to enact scientific oyster conservation emanated from Baltimore scientists and business interests, the rurally biased Maryland legislature enabled the bay's resource users to check a powerful force associated with the rise of Progressive Era conservationism at the federal level – the expansion of state power and professional authority.

While Maryland's geographically skewed system of representation bestowed tremendous influence on watermen – and nearly all were male – the oyster workforce was not a homogenous group, nor were the oyster grounds an unregulated commons open to all.[17] The Chesapeake oyster beds functioned as "a patchwork of local commons regimes" utilized by men of different county loyalties, gear-related status, and socioeconomic aspirations.[18] By 1830, laws prevented Marylanders from taking oysters outside their own county waters, which decreased watermen's mobility and increased parochial insularities even as new transport networks expanded the national market for Chesapeake oysters.[19] The legislature also regulated access to the oyster grounds by specifying which types of gear could be used in the tributaries and in the bay's deeper main stem. Deadly battles ensued after the postbellum legalization of dredging, when deepwater dredgers used their more efficient, highly capitalized equipment to raid the shallower beds reserved for tongers. The "Oyster Wars" constitute an important chapter in the history of Chesapeake resource use, revealing the importance of place-based and technological boundaries in demarcating access to the public-domain oyster beds.

Watermen's communities also differed racially. Black oystermen have worked the Chesapeake Bay for as long as whites. Despite the discriminatory practices that prevailed on shore, racism tended to disappear on the water, "where nature held the upper hand" and exposed all human harvesters to the same risks.[20] Resistance to privatization of the oyster grounds also connected watermen across the color line despite the condescending attitudes of tidewater whites. A spokesman for the Anne Arundel County Oystermen's Protective Association epitomized both tidewater bigotry and antileasing sentiment in 1927: "The majority of oystermen in this section are Negroes. They know nothing of the [pro-privatization] conservation program and they would not understand it if it were explained to them. But when they learn what it all means, they will let out a mighty yell against it."[21] The elites who supported private cultivation viewed white watermen in exactly the same terms.

Because the Chesapeake oyster reefs encompassed the territories of two states, another set of restrictions also governed harvesters' behavior. The Maryland and Virginia legislatures established separate sets of oyster laws beginning in the early nineteenth century, largely in response to the depredations of New Englanders who had exhausted their own oyster beds. In the late nineteenth century, while Virginia instituted laws much more favorable to the development of private cultivation, both states maintained public fisheries under the protection of centralized enforcement agencies. Because each state restricted oystering to its own residents, struggles over access to the rich grounds along the murky borderline led to many bloody confrontations between Maryland and Virginia harvesters and between enforcement agents and oystermen of the opposing states. Although the Chesapeake Oyster Wars culminated in the early twentieth century, as late as 1959, the Maryland resource police fatally fired on a Virginia crew in the contested Potomac River.[22] In recent years, the nearest thing to a bistate oyster war concerned plans to introduce nonnative oysters, a controversy that underscored the important historical differences between the two states' management regimes.[23]

Despite Maryland oystermen's internal differences, whenever harvests fell low enough to embolden those seeking to lease for cultivation any part of the estuary — whether naturally productive of oysters or not — tongers and dredgers of all the tidewater counties presented a unified front in Annapolis. Although elites in other regions of the country, from southern planters to northern oyster interests, had long since prevailed on legislatures or courts to enclose commonly held resources, Maryland oystermen persuaded the General Assembly to pass only feeble leasing laws that made would-be oyster growers run a bureaucratic gauntlet. But as production of the state's dominant natural resource continued to drop, legislators felt compelled to take action. The resulting system of publicly funded cultivation, enacted in 1927, sought to boost harvests by returning empty shells to the oyster beds to provide a hard surface on which larvae could attach and develop and by transplanting immature seed oysters to more favorable growing areas. Funded by industry and state-wide taxes, Maryland's "put-and-take" oyster fishery remains in place today, though the chronic free fall of the past quarter century leaves its future in doubt.

The ways in which oystermen and their legislative allies crafted a viable alternative to private cultivation can be seen as a case of comanagement. Anthropological studies have elucidated the ways in which fishing peoples have developed "folk management" systems to conserve resources over long periods of time.[24] Maritime anthropologists argue that incorporating local folk practices and knowledge into modern fisheries management will allow community user groups and government agencies to share decision-making power in managing common property resources.[25] Comanagement has the potential to generate more sustainable production than state management alone by providing a broader knowledge base, more legitimate regulations, increased adherence to regulations by user groups, and increased management proficiency.[26] Yet despite its importance to the development of a conservation ethic, few historians have analyzed the mechanics of comanagement. More historical attention is needed to elucidate natural resource management regimes in which local knowledge played a greater role than elite scientific expertise.

Despite the positive connotations of comanagement as interpreted by anthropologists, scientists and pro-leasing business interests have often resented the watermen's influence over oyster management. As Bowman complained in 1940, legislators of the previous half century had consulted "so-called 'practical' oystermen" rather than scientists, who felt left out of the comanagement equation.[27] The Chesapeake Biological Laboratory of Solomons Island, Maryland, now takes pride in its status as the East Coast's oldest state-supported marine laboratory, but its first generation of workers struggled for respect. Tensions often flared between state biologists and oystermen as a consequence of their different understandings of nature. Scientists stressed the indispensability of their microscopic analyses of salinity, spawning, and temperature conditions, while watermen sought to rehabilitate areas known to them and their fathers as productive bars. (Reflecting the extreme localism of the tidewater region, oystermen also fought among themselves to ensure that shell- and seed-transplanting operations did not benefit other counties.) In addition, repeated calls by blue-ribbon commissions to staff the emerging resource bureaucracy with trained experts angered watermen, who argued that only "practical men" engaged in the industry could guide oyster management.

But the antidemocratic ways in which federal scientists and engineers imposed the "gospel of efficiency" on western resource management regimes during the Progressive Era had no purchase in political spheres dominated by local grassroots groups, as Samuel Hays's classic study suggests.[28] Watermen's legislative advantage prevented scientists from enacting their ideal conservation plan during the Progressive Era and for decades thereafter. Other scholars have examined state biologists' powerlessness in the context of highly industrialized, overcapitalized fisheries.[29] The Maryland oyster fishery's adherence to preindustrial methods precluded the rise of superwealthy interests, though the best-off branch, the packers, sided with scientists in the struggle for policymaking authority. Yet even when joined by a far richer lobby – railroad executives who sought to ship as many mollusks across the continent as possible – pro-privatization scientists failed to enshrine their ideal conservation plan into law.

Maryland legislators heeded scientific calls for implementing publicly funded forms of oyster repletion in 1927 only because the idea promised to revive the industry without disrupting the watermen's traditional way of life. While harvesters remained suspicious of meddling with the divinely ordained laws of nature, the Great Depression made that pill easier to swallow. The stock market crash and resultant relief policies challenged many Americans' ideas about independence and government intervention, especially in the rural South.[30] Just as southern farmers came to depend on federal New Deal programs such as acreage reduction and price stabilization, Maryland oystermen became strong supporters of state-funded repletion. The program not only seemed to aid nature and stabilize supplies but also paid oystermen to transplant shells and seed oysters, thereby providing additional income between the winter oyster and summer crab seasons. Even though this off-season employment program contradicted the waterman's cherished self-image as an independent operator, the program has endured as a fundamental part of the oyster fishery, just as other governmental subsidies still stream to groups that consider themselves indomitable individualists.[31]

Depression-era relief policies thus served as a dominant force of change for tidewater Maryland, as for other rural regions across the country. Public subsidies likewise benefited western and southern agricultural interests even after the crisis of the 1930s had passed. In those regions, however, wealthy resource users profited much more than did groups as impoverished as the Chesapeake watermen. In particular, New Deal policies benefited southern landowners by providing them with credit, which they used to mechanize and evict sharecroppers and tenants, thereby paving the way for the "rural transformation to capital-intensive farming." Conversely, the force of "government intrusion" in the form of the public oyster repletion program, combined with technological restrictions, benefited all Maryland harvesters, many of whom continued to live hand to mouth.[32] Oyster production stabilized for several decades, thereby enabling tidewater communities to subsist into the late twentieth century, when a perfect storm of parasitic diseases, pollution, and overdredging of oyster-bar habitat dealt the industry a blow from which it has not yet recovered.

The stabilization of Maryland oyster landings during the mid–twentieth century dampened technocratic arguments for capital-intensive aquaculture but did not stop proponents of leasing. Frustrated by the repletion program's dependence on insufficient tax revenues, prominent scientists renewed campaigns to liberalize the leasing laws during the 1940s and 1950s. Like their predecessors, these scientists sought to overcome oystermen's resistance by insisting that the bay bottoms be leased rather than sold outright, that barren bottoms rather than viable oyster beds be leased, and that leaseholds be granted to individuals rather than corporations. They also couched their arguments in terms of the economic benefits that leasing would generate for hard-up oystermen and their communities. But by assuming that commercial fishermen would trade their traditions of working the water for the challenges of underwater farming and by promoting a solution that overlooked either the "minimal attachment to money" or the limited access to credit that prevailed in tidewater communities, pro-leasing scientists came across as ivory-tower theorists, thereby reinforcing watermen's derision for science-based management.[33] Not until nearly the turn of the millennium did the two cultures finally acknowledge that both played crucial roles in sustaining the bay's productivity.

Writing Environmental History from Southeast to West

In his 1967 memoir, *God, Man, Salt Water and the Eastern Shore,* William Tawes compared the watermen of the Delmarva Peninsula, the tristate landmass east of the Chesapeake Bay, with the cowboys of the American West. In his view, the two groups lacked sentimentality for their ways of life: "The Creek waterman was as blind as the proverbial bat to the science and beauty of his work, and the romance of his calling meant no more to him than the long overland trails did to the old cow poke who drove his cattle over them." Yet whereas popular culture had long since immortalized the cowboy legends, Tawes observed, "the old Salts of my story have not yet had their day on the screen or in print, because they have had no champion to write about the romantic aspects of their vocation."[34] Many such champions have since emerged, often invoking the same rugged individualism that suffuses the cult of the cowboy.

Just as Westerns began popularizing cowboy culture as it was dying out, colorful accounts of the Chesapeake's commercial harvesters have increased precisely as their numbers have diminished.[35] Fascination with fading traditions has also led regional presses to produce many books on bay country culture and the estuary itself.[36] Tourist shops sell these volumes alongside knickknacks featuring the bay's "now-standard iconographic repertoire" of blue crabs, skipjacks, oysters, geese, and screwpile lighthouses, which novelist John Barth construes as "a fairly reliable sign that the way of life they vaguely symbolize . . . is passing from vigorous, unself-conscious existence into merchandisable nostalgia, or has already so passed."[37] It thus seems that the Chesapeake watermen have caught up with the western cowboys in the American imagination as "a repository for the values Americans left behind when they crossed the threshold of the modern age."[38]

The tools of environmental history reveal ironic links between watermen and other mythic groups of American history. While both cowboys and watermen personify the prized American value of individualism, the actual men engaged in rounding up cattle, crabs, and oysters in their respective public domains served as cogs in capitalist networks, mediating between the natural world and the market system "to ship meat to cities."[39] Watermen sold bay organisms to packers, who in turn dispatched the shellfish across the continent, just as the cowboys drove ungulates to urban markets from the grasslands of the Great West. Both groups, though icons of independence, were subject to economic forces over which they had little control.

Watermen shared an even closer resemblance with the Plains Indians, for both held on to their hunter-gatherer traditions in the face of rapid change. Well-meaning elites considered the cultivation of crops on private plots the quickest route to civilization and therefore spent decades trying to convince "primitive" peoples that survival in the new economic order required adopting an agrarian mind-set.[40] Of course, while oyster leasing advocates spoke of tidewater survival in symbolic terms, the idea of extinction – both cultural and actual – was all too tangible for Native Americans.

The ways in which western resource users have interacted with nature have long dominated the field of environmental history, but that trend has started to change. While there is no doubt that such classic western themes as wilderness, aridity, reclamation, and federal landownership have stimulated essential scholarship in the three decades since the field's emergence, researchers have challenged the status of the Great West as "the American environmental history Ur-region." Recent proposals for "an environmental history written from east to west rather than west to east" raise exciting new questions, as do speculations about how the field would have developed had it first focused on the South, with its deep agricultural roots.[41] While white pioneers perceived the westerly frontier as a bonanza to be exploited and abandoned, those who remained back east developed a "cultural familiarity with the land" that facilitated collective management of the resources around which life revolved. Because they could not abandon the soils, forests, fisheries, and wildlife that they consumed, eastern states developed conservation measures long before the federal government intervened to stem the wasteful pillaging of western resources during the Progressive Era. State fish commissions and other pioneering postbellum institutions emerged in the context of class struggles between groups who could or would not leave, helping to provide an understanding of the social roots of conservation policymaking. The rich record of relationships between humans and eastern settings thus offers important new insights for U.S. environmental history.[42]

Maryland is not only one of the oldest East Coast states but also has strong links to the South and thus offers an opportunity to illuminate another historiographically underrepresented region. Southern environmental history is informed to a much greater degree than are western narratives by agricultural (as opposed to wilderness or frontier) experiences. The culture of farming became so deeply woven into the South's social fabric that social and political relationships are difficult to separate from the agricultural landscapes in which they were embedded. The problem is particularly acute when examining the racist legacy of the plantation economy and the different ways in which white and black southerners have interacted with each other and the land. Such attention to how "cultivation engraved culture in the land" enriches rural social and labor history.[43]

In this volume, the "agricultural landscape" embedding social and political affairs is the Chesapeake Bay – more accurately, the bay's main stem and the many subestuaries formed by its tributary rivers (fig. 2). Celebrated writer H. L. Mencken used industrial rhetoric when he called the bay an "immense protein factory," and harvesters have long used or sought to use mechanized equipment to extract wealth from the bay's depths. But the Maryland legislature outlawed motorized harvesting in the 1860s, a ban upheld until recent years, and oystering thus for generations remained a labor-intensive endeavor. Despite the efforts of leasing advocates, the estuary never became a "cultivated environment" in the sense of a tobacco or cotton field. Nonetheless, just as the workers who grew crops shaped the South's economic, political, and cultural heritage, so did those who worked the water influence the culture of the Chesapeake.[44]

Southern farmers and Maryland oystermen prior to 1960 shared important characteristics. Both depended on muscle power rather than mechanization, eking out a living using just a few tools. Small farmers and sharecroppers often made ends meet with little more than a mule and plow, while oystermen built small sailboats and harvesting implements or traded backbreaking labor for wages crewing larger dredge boats. The other resource on which both groups drew was a fine-tuned knowledge of the local biotic conditions governing the productivity of the environment. Harvesting the Chesapeake's biological assets required an intimate relationship with the local oyster commons, a store of knowledge, experience, and awareness of place as deep and rich as that of any land-based cultivator in the preagribusiness era.

Addressing the links between agrarian and estuarine labor requires addressing Maryland's problematic status as a southern state. As the northernmost political unit south of the Mason-Dixon boundary, the Old Line State has long experienced a fractured identity. A resident with "Eastern Shore roots and Baltimore blueblood" captured this conundrum in the 1980s in her complaint, "Down South, I'm a 'Damn Yankee,' while up North, they say I have a southern accent."[45] Though

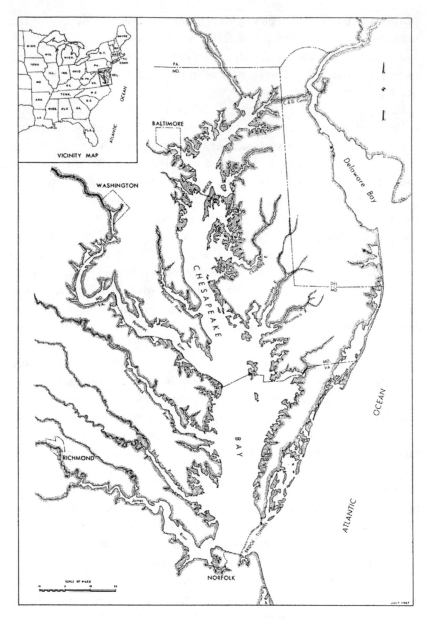

Fig. 2. The Chesapeake Bay, North America's largest and historically most productive estuary, is 190 miles long and 22 miles across at its widest. The watershed covers 64,000 square miles, including Washington, D.C., and parts of Maryland, Virginia, Delaware, Pennsylvania, New York, and West Virginia. (Courtesy of Chesapeake Biological Laboratory.)

Maryland is still part of the "Census South," historians do not place it within the Old South. While it sent soldiers to defend the Confederacy, Maryland had begun moving beyond plantation agriculture long before the Civil War, and "after 1815 no American state portrayed as vividly as did Maryland the contrast between slavery and steam power, past and future, convention and change."[46] Baltimore became the southern terminus of the U.S. manufacturing belt, generating steel, textiles, and canned goods for export via new transportation networks. The railroad was a particular boon to the oyster trade because it enabled the shipment of canned or iced mollusks over thousands of miles.[47]

Economic and demographic changes cemented Maryland's status as a "sectional netherland," and the Civil War thus caught the state in a terrible bind.[48] After a Baltimore mob attacked Union troops moving through the city in April 1861, President Abraham Lincoln imposed martial law on Maryland, whose divided loyalty persisted throughout the war.[49] Even today, the 1930s-era state song protests the specter of "northern scum" and the federal "despot's heel." Dixie's secessionist and segregationist spirit hung on deepest in the rural communities of southern Maryland and even more so the Eastern Shore (fig. 3).[50] Population densities remained low, the economy revolved around farming and fishing, and race relations festered from the 1890s through the civil rights era. As locals observed, "A hundred years ain't such a very long time on the Eastern Shore," echoing William Faulkner's famous adage that in the South, "the past is never dead. It's not even past."[51] Jim Crow policies remained in effect on the Eastern Shore, as in the rest of the state, as late as 1967, although Progressive Era efforts to deny black Marylanders the right to vote failed.[52] During the 1904 legislative session, when bills for both African American disenfranchisement and expanded oyster leasing were on the table, Democratic backers of the former got a rude awakening from tidewater Democrats who resisted the latter, and "Maryland Negroes then found that their political rights had been cast onto the weighing scales with the Maryland oyster."[53] By contrast, Virginia instituted the poll tax in 1902, which cost ex-slaves and their descendants as well as many poor whites the right to vote. Because these groups constituted the oyster industry's labor force, Virginia watermen were less able to resist the privatization of oyster grounds than their Maryland counterparts.

By the early twentieth century, Maryland, along with the rest of the South, remained within the agrarian and extraction-based periphery

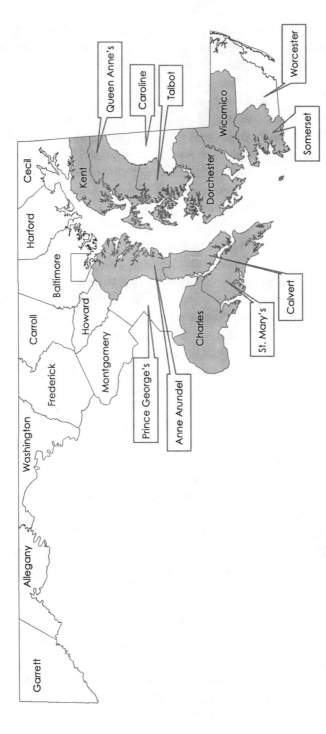

Fig. 3: Map of Maryland showing oyster-producing counties bordering the Chesapeake Bay and tributaries. (Map constructed using ArcGIS.)

of the American economy.[54] But because 60 percent of Marylanders resided in communities of at least twenty-five hundred, the Census Bureau deemed it an urban state by 1920.[55] Historians have accordingly omitted the Old Line State from analyses of twentieth-century southern modernization that show how mechanization and federal policies transformed southern agriculture starting around 1920. Although the commons lasted longer in the South than elsewhere, the shift from labor-intensive to capital-intensive enterprise culminated by 1960 and entailed the enclosure and depopulation of the southern landscape and ultimately the collapse of the rural southern way of life.[56]

As this volume shows, Maryland watermen experienced – and continue to experience – many of the same gut-wrenching changes as their southern agricultural brethren. *The Oyster Question* addresses an important though neglected part of the modernization story – how a poor yet politically savvy subculture of resource users staved off the forces of rural change, especially scientific reform and capital-intensive privatization, by manipulating a typically southern institution, the rurally biased state legislature. Although several scholars have noted how the county-based system of representation enabled oystermen and their allies to exert a disproportionately large influence in the Maryland General Assembly, none has analyzed the impacts of malapportionment and reapportionment on oyster conservation politics in particular and on science-based resource management more broadly.[57]

This book complements recent research that suggests that despite their poor economic standing, politically mobilized farmers in the South and other rural regions exerted remarkable influence on national politics during the Populist and Progressive Eras. Elizabeth Sanders provides persuasive evidence that the efforts of well-organized "periphery agrarians" to limit the excesses of corporate capitalism "provided the political muscle for enacting the progressive legislative agenda of 1909–17," which included the establishment of antitrust policy, an income tax, a publicly controlled banking and currency system, and several other important features of the modern American interventionist state. She makes the larger point that "in the territorially based American legislature, ideas had to find geographic vessels," underscoring the importance of the relationship between members of Congress and their constituencies and the legislative branch's greater responsiveness to grassroots social movements.[58]

A similar dynamic animated the Maryland General Assembly's long-running debates regarding the political football of oyster conservation. Just as the crucial votes for national economic reform policies in the Progressive Era came from the periphery regions, where farmers comprised the largest, best-organized voting blocs, antileasing advocacy radiated from the rural tidewater county legislators who outnumbered their urban counterparts and worked on behalf of their poor though organized constituents. The historical conflict between watermen and scientists for control of oyster management can thus be seen as a state-level parallel to what Sanders calls "the agrarian-capitalist duel for control of national politics."[59] This comparison has limits, since pro-leasing scientists never sought to fatten their wallets but rather intended to improve the watermen's lot. Nevertheless, for oystermen, the scientists' alliance with powerful corporate interests undermined their philanthropic rationale.

Like the politically mobilized farmers who drove Progressive Era policymaking, the watermen were not the special interest groups of today who employ professional lobbyists to obtain lucrative earmarks. By and large, they were uneducated people protecting their hand-to-mouth livelihoods not with guns but by using the political system as an agency of estuarine populism. This book thus builds on recent efforts to reveal the "hidden history of conservation" by examining the class conflicts sparked by efforts to establish centralized, science-based management of common-pool natural resources. Like other scholars, I seek to break down the boundaries between social and environmental history by elucidating the clash between subsistence resource users and affluent urbanites that underlay many conservation disputes.[60] *The Oyster Question* adds a new twist to conservation's hidden history, since unlike the country folk who resisted state regulations against hunting, fishing, and foraging by engaging in illegal acts, the resource users discussed here prevented the state from enacting many such laws. A political analysis of how nonelite groups used legal means to resist the centralization of local commons regimes further illuminates the development of state natural resource management, especially in the context of a rural legislative dominance that was distinctively, though not exclusively, southern.

The importance of state malapportionment has been obscured by environmental historians' focus on large-scale regional and federal developments at the expense of events in individual states.[61] Shifting to the local level reveals the fascinating ways in which rural resource users exploited inequalities in representation in state legislatures to control the urban-based conservation agenda. In this sense, this volume takes issue with two broad principles underlying Sanders's analysis of the roots of national economic reform. She stresses the legislature's status as "the most democratic forum" in American government and argues that because of the symbiotic economic relationship between industrial cities and their agricultural hinterlands, "the urban-rural distinction per se has limited explanatory power in American politics."[62] However, until the 1960s, many states featured systems of state-level (and congressional) representation in which numerical rural minorities possessed disproportionate political power. As one political scientist observed in 1930, "Under-represented as it is . . . Baltimore seems to be in no worse position than the other populous cities of the United States," including those of New York, Illinois, New Jersey, Missouri, Pennsylvania, and Delaware.[63] The situation was even worse in the South, where rural counties always outnumbered urban ones. Rural resource users thereby possessed a powerful means of resisting the encroachments of urban scientists and conservationists and of passing game and fish laws favorable to rural interests.[64] Sharp divisions between rural and urban and later suburban regions thus played an important role in the evolution of state environmental politics.

This book explores these changes in the context not only of southeastern environmental history but also of "the virtually nonexistent field of marine environmental history."[65] Scholars have begun to examine the changing interactions between nature and culture within watery geographies, especially the California, northwestern salmon, and Great Lakes fisheries, and to explicate the importance of estuaries as working environments.[66] As biologically rich ecosystems nourished by the perpetual mixing of fresh- and saltwater and land-borne nutrients, estuaries have provided natural wealth for eons, and the Chesapeake, North America's largest and most productive estuary, offers an excellent means for examining such environments as sites of cultural, economic, and scientific labor. Indigenous peoples subsisted on the bay's fish and shellfish for thousands of years, and white and black watermen were bartering these items by the late eighteenth century. Scientific interest in the bay dates to the 1870s, when naturalists began investigating its commercial

species. Some eight decades later, the president of the National Shellfisheries Association paid homage to the Chesapeake oyster for "spawning"
the careers of many fisheries biologists.[67]

Research on broader aspects of the bay ecosystem did not increase
substantially until after the mid–twentieth century, several decades after
ecology emerged as a distinct science addressing relationships between
organisms and their physical environment. Political circumstances often
drove the research agenda, for state governments provided more funds
when devastating shellfish diseases emerged, as did Cold War agencies
seeking to understand the movement of radioactive materials through
bombed environments.[68] In addition, coastal and watershed populations
increased rapidly during the postwar era, overwhelming bays' ability to
absorb endless inputs of sewage, sediments, toxic chemicals, and thermal
pollution from power plants. By 1970, one-third of U.S. residents lived
in estuarine environments, as did the people of seven of the world's ten
largest cities, underscoring the need for research on these underappre-
ciated ecosystems.[69] Physical oceanographers who plumbed the Chesapeake, the crown jewel of North America's 850 estuaries, developed the
classic definition of an estuary: a semienclosed body of water containing
both freshwater that streams in via tributaries and saltwater that flows in
and out with the tides at an opening to the sea.[70] The international journal *Estuaries and Coasts* started life as *Chesapeake Science* in 1960, providing further testimony regarding the influence of this particular environment on the entire scientific field of estuarine ecology.

The environmentalist revolution of the late 1960s and 1970s drew
unprecedented scientific and popular attention to the Chesapeake Bay,
but not until recent decades have its stakeholders joined forces. As scientists recognized oysters' ability to filter nutrient pollution, the bivalve
acquired a new status as an agent of improved water quality. Watermen
began meeting with environmentalists and other longtime rivals in the
1990s to work out ways to sustain both the industry and the ecological base. By that time, the harvesters had long since lost their strategic legislative advantage, a consequence of the reapportionment reforms
of the 1960s and shifts in responsibility for resource management from
the legislative to the executive branch. Nevertheless, fishery officials and
politicians ensured watermen a strong continuing role in oyster management for a complex set of reasons. The encounters between scientists and oystermen at the turn of the millennium illuminate both the

changing role of science in environmental management and the ways each group has influenced the other in the search for new solutions.

Four sets of forces have shaped the evolution of the Maryland Chesapeake oyster fishery over the past 130 years: scientific debates regarding resource management, a rurally biased state political system, the cultivation of political clout by a nonelite user group, and the ecological system of the bay itself. A fifth influence, the formation of environmentalist values, emerged in more recent decades. Despite its focus on Maryland, *The Oyster Question* is much more than a local study. Viewing these interacting forces through the lenses of the history of science, political and social history, and environmental history expands our understanding of the role of state governments in U.S. resource management.

Chapter 1 provides an ecological and cultural overview of the Chesapeake Bay, the Eastern oyster, and the watermen. Discussing the bay ecosystem in isolation from human influences is impossible because the two have always interacted. By the time the estuary formed ten thousand years ago, Native Americans had resided in the region for around three millennia. Subsequent phases of land use greatly altered the bay ecosystem, making it difficult to determine the effect of overfishing on the oyster population's long-term decline. Analysis of the multiple disturbance factors operating on land and water helps to highlight the many scientific uncertainties that came to define the "oyster problem." To shed light on the world of the watermen, the chapter examines the evolution of the regulated commons and the diverse skill set required to exact a livelihood from the bay bottoms.

The ways in which the watermen understood the workings of nature are complemented by a parallel analysis of scientists in chapter 2, which focuses on the emergence of Chesapeake science and conservation advocacy. Like the postbellum agricultural reformers who sought to revolutionize farming, Brooks and his supporters sought to modernize the Maryland oyster industry through private cultivation. After twenty years, Brooks's allies secured the passage of a 1906 law allowing limited leasing of barren bottoms rather than natural oyster bars, but the alliance that scientists forged with privatization advocates had a lasting, negative legacy for science-based conservation. Analysis of Brooks's scientific work and political involvement provides a fitting prelude for later bay policymaking debates and links the history of science with environmental history and social history.

Even the extreme downturn of the Great Depression could not diminish watermen's opposition to privatization. But continuing harvest declines demanded action, so the legislature developed a compromise solution – publicly funded repletion of degraded bars. The concurrent establishment of the state-supported Chesapeake Biological Laboratory signaled a new era in which scientists would extend the reach of the agricultural experiment station to tidewater America. But as the laboratory's founder, University of Maryland biologist Reginald V. Truitt, came to realize, doing so would not be easy. As chapter 3 demonstrates, the interwar years restructured ideas of conservation and of state aid for the fiercely independent watermen and established an enduring managerial system in which harvesters and scientists kept each other at arm's length.

On the eve of World War II, new constituencies demanded a voice in conservation policymaking, which began to encompass issues other than oyster management. The leasing question still simmered, though now in the context of a few innovative but short-lived aquaculture cooperatives. Recreational fishermen and other metropolitan residents drew attention to new problems and perceptions of the Chesapeake Bay beyond its long-standing status as a protein factory. Chapter 4 examines powerful forces that welled up within the suburbanizing bay watershed as well as the bay itself during the middle of the twentieth century. Despite immense pressures to change course, made possible by the court-ordered reapportionment of the legislature in the mid-1960s, Maryland's regulated oyster commons survived even as rural agrarian traditions disintegrated in other southern strongholds.

Chapter 5 examines two ongoing debates among three entrenched interest groups – watermen, scientists, and environmentalists. Disease reduced oyster landings to historic lows in the early 1990s, stimulating new approaches combining economic and ecological goals. Multi-million-dollar efforts to reconstruct reefs damaged by dredging and sedimentation reveal changing expectations about scientific expertise's role in solving the bay's problems. The slowness of the ecological approach soon stimulated resource users and officials to advocate a far more controversial solution – the deliberate introduction of heartier nonnative oysters to the bay. Desperate Virginia officials commenced experiments in the early 1990s, and a new gubernatorial administration put Maryland on a similar track in 2002, revealing the extent to which resource administration had shifted from the legislative to the executive realm. The issue of whether Maryland should continue to subsidize its public fishery or to expand its embryonic private aquaculture industry (with or without native bivalves) again came to the fore.

Underlying the final chapters is the question of why Maryland watermen, who now constitute a tiny minority in a booming suburban state, remain a powerful voice in estuarine policymaking. Their remarkable political endurance sheds light on the persistence of rural power in state environmental politics, and the Chesapeake Bay presents an ideal lens for exploring this theme. As a leading Chesapeake biologist lamented in 1983, just as an unprecedented multistate cleanup effort commenced, "The bay's problems are growing faster than our ability to react to them. The bay is a signal system, the country's largest, most valuable estuary. If we can't save it, we can't save any of our estuaries."[71] Now that watermen serve as a cultural indicator of the ecosystem's life-giving forces, saving the bay means saving the watermen, too.

CO

Resolving today's heated debates concerning the management of declining fisheries requires a historical understanding of the changing relationships between nature and culture. Struggles to define the cultural meanings of oysters and the ideal methods of conserving them have pervaded the oyster question since its emergence in the 1880s. Then and long thereafter, scientists and businessmen defined shellfish as a source of untold prosperity for those willing to invest in cultivation. Lacking the capital and agrarian outlook required for underwater farming, watermen considered the oyster a vehicle for earning a living on their own terms, free from the relentless ticking of the industrial time clock. In the late twentieth century, scientists and their environmentalist allies began to view the bivalve as an ecological engineer that formerly regulated the bay's overall health. For commercial fishermen, the mollusk no longer symbolized independence in quite the way it did before the state assumed a major role in maintaining the resource and before precipitous declines forced them to focus on other commodifiable organisms. Yet the promise of a revitalized oyster industry based on a foreign species, however many unknown qualities it possessed, reinforced the view of oysters as a means of economic self-determination.

In accordance with the different kinds of relationships they developed with the oyster over the course of many decades, scientists and watermen also adopted explanations of its long-term decline that suggested distinct policy outcomes. Those who considered overfishing the primary culprit often supported intensive efforts to restore and protect the native oyster reefs and to restrict harvesting, while those who believed that disease and pollution were the key stressors tended to support the introduction of a nonindigenous species capable of thriving in the altered estuarine environment. Each group supported its claims with selective historical records, thereby highlighting the need for a more comprehensive understanding of the relevance of environmental history, social history, and the history of science to current fishery-management initiatives.

A widely cited 2001 article in the prestigious journal *Science* argues that retrospective data should play a greater role in ecosystem remediation. As the authors conclude, "Historical documentation of the long-term effects of fishing provides a heretofore-missing perspective for successful management and restoration of coastal marine ecosystems. Previous attempts have failed because they have focused only on the most recent symptoms of the problem rather than on their deep historical causes."[72] Environmental historians should clearly play an important role in resolving the dilemma of the world's declining fisheries. By illuminating the ways in which stakeholders relate to nature and resource management, by showing how their attitudes have changed over time, and by clarifying the limits of previous approaches, historians can help opposing groups transcend the one-dimensional perspectives that have so often hindered effective management. Analysis of the ways in which Chesapeake oysters have linked the labor of diverse human cultures with that of nature reveals a reality much more nuanced than the stereotypes that for decades impeded dialogue.[73] While harvesters and scientists distrusted and derided each other, an array of pressures sent the Maryland oyster inching toward the abyss of extinction, a place far worse than the front line of the culture wars.

1

Chesapeake Bay

Protein Factory, Working Landscape

The Chesapeake Bay is both a work of nature that operates in accordance with physical laws and a human-dominated landscape on which we inscribe cultural practices and meanings. A recent addition to the earth's surface, the bay formed just ten thousand years ago in the drowned river valley of the Susquehanna as glaciers receded at the close of the last ice age. People inhabited the region long before the sea inundated the valley, and the bay and its many tributary branches thus share an intimate bond with human history and prehistory. Native Americans adapted well to the postglacial environmental shift, harvesting the fish and shellfish that flourished as salinity conditions stabilized. The Algonquin bestowed the name *Chesipiook,* meaning "Great Shellfish Bay," a most appropriate appellation given the oyster's long-standing importance both to other estuarine species and to human users. As environmental historians would say, the Chesapeake landscape has always embedded human relationships, making it difficult to separate its ecological and cultural components.[1] The "oyster question" and the broader history of management and conflict explored in this book cannot be understood apart from these connections.

A Watershed Transformation

The Chesapeake is one of the world's largest estuaries and Maryland's dominant physical feature. It splits the state in two and slices into the Virginia shore. The bay is about 190 miles long and 22 miles across at its widest juncture, with so many branches that its shoreline covers more than 4,600 miles.[2] The Chesapeake watershed extends far beyond Virginia and Maryland, covering parts of New York, Pennsylvania, Delaware, West Virginia, and the U.S. capital. Every drop of rain falling within this 64,000-mile expanse ends up in the bay. Nineteen rivers and four hundred creeks and streams branch off from the bay's main stem, with three massive rivers – the Susquehanna, the Potomac, and the James – accounting for 80 percent of freshwater inflows. The freshwater that feeds the bay tributaries is less dense than the saltwater that enters from the Atlantic Ocean at the bay's mouth near Norfolk, Virginia. These two layers of water identify the Chesapeake as an estuary and contribute to its immense biological productivity, as do its shallowness and expanse of land-water edge. The average depth of the estuarine system, which comprises the bay's main stem and its tributaries, is just 21 feet, and about one-fifth of the bay has an estimated depth of less than 6.5 feet. Salt- and freshwaters mix with the flow of the tides twice a day to produce a range of salinity levels, with the least saline waters at the northern head, where the Susquehanna dumps its payload, and the saltiest at the southern oceanic interface. The prized American or Eastern oyster, *Crassostrea virginica,* evolved to thrive along the Atlantic and Gulf Coasts and throughout the Chesapeake ecosystem except in the uppermost region of low salinity.[3]

Before the intensification of anthropogenic pressures, an immense variety of organisms thrived in and on the estuary's shallow waters, where sunlight reached the bottom and where nutrients flowing from the land enriched the estuarine food chain. Whereas Nile River floods left precious silt on Egyptian wheat and rice fields each year, a reverse process took place in the fertile Chesapeake watershed with every rainfall.[4] Particles of nitrogen, phosphorus, and silica that countless streams washed into bay waters facilitated the growth of phytoplankton, tiny floating plants that sustain higher bay organisms. The historic Chesapeake nurtured some two thousand species of plants and animals, including more than one hundred species of fish and two hundred species of invertebrates. Every spring and summer, the bay bottoms sprouted acres of sea-grass meadows, which trapped suspended sediments, removed excess nutrients, and provided protection or food for such delicacies as the blue crab, striped bass, hard clam, eel, shad, and of course the oyster.[5] Journalist H. L. Mencken memorialized the bay in 1940 as an "immense protein factory" out of which the citizens of Baltimore "ate divinely."[6]

Long before Baltimoreans feasted on terrapin stew and she-crab soup, the bay's bounty sustained Native Americans. The calcium-rich oyster constituted a staple of the indigenous diet by the Middle Woodland period (200 to 900 AD). Huge heaps of oyster shell middens – the largest covering almost thirty acres of land near Pope's Creek on the Potomac River – signify the bivalve's long-standing culinary importance, and archaeological investigations suggest that Chesapeake Indians used some oystering sites for thirty-five hundred years or more. Although localized depletions likely occurred, the native peoples exerted remarkably light harvest pressure overall.[7]

Until recent centuries, nonhuman predators and forces constituted the greatest threats to *C. virginica*. Though spared the plagues of starfish that prey on its brethren farther north, the Chesapeake oyster has long endured the predations of boring sponges, mud crabs, and oyster drills. Nor is it immune to storms and hurricanes, which can alter salinity levels overnight and dump loads of smothering sediment. To survive such risks, the oyster evolved remarkable reproductive capacities. Every summer, when the water reaches seventy-two degrees Fahrenheit, each sex releases enormous quantities of eggs or sperm into open water. Although many fertilized eggs fall victim to predators, survivors develop into floating larvae that feed on phytoplankton, detritus, and bacteria for two to three weeks before sinking to the bottom. The unlucky larvae that land in soft mud or sand die, but those that settle on old shells or some other hard substrate (cultch) with access to planktonic food attach themselves and metamorphose, becoming known as spat. There the oyster remains for the rest of its life, which in the absence of harvesting pressure could reach a decade.[8]

Over the millennia, generations of oysters built up structures somewhat similar to coral reefs (fig. 4). A healthy oyster reef, known also as a bar, bed, or rock, may appear lifeless but is actually a pulsating "island of intense biological activity."[9] Oysters eat low on the food chain,

Fig. 4. An oyster reef exposed at low tide near Beaufort, South Carolina, ca. 1938. The high density of the oysters indicates that the bar has not yet been subjected to heavy harvesting pressure, and it thus probably resembles the Chesapeake beds of the mid–nineteenth century. (Photo by Sean Linehan. Courtesy of Historic Fisheries Collection, National Oceanic and Atmospheric Association.)

grazing on algae and other types of phytoplankton. Depending on such physical factors as temperature and salinity, an adult oyster can filter up to sixty gallons of water a day, thereby clearing the water column of nitrogen, phosphorus, carbon, silica, and other suspended solids.[10] The resulting water clarity benefits submerged aquatic grasses, among other organisms, by allowing more light to reach the bay bottom.[11] Prior to 1870, Chesapeake oyster populations may have been able to filter the bay's entire volume in between 3 and 6 days, a sharp contrast to the late twentieth-century turnover time of 325 days.[12]

Oysters not only provide crucial ecosystem services by improving water clarity but also promote biodiversity. The dead and living bivalves that constitute each three-dimensional reef community, or biocoenose, provide habitat for barnacles, mussels, crabs, fish, sea squirts, anemones, and other creatures, which in turn attract larger predators. Oyster populations thus play a key role in the estuarine environment, both physiologically as filter feeders and structurally as ecosystem engineers.[13] As a keystone species, the oyster is thought to have disproportionately large ecological effects, though much research remains to be done.[14]

Important ecological differences govern the oyster reefs of the northern and southern portions of the bay, with major economic consequences for the postbellum fisheries of Maryland and Virginia. The high salinity levels of the Lower Bay tend to promote poor growth yet high spatfall and setting rates, resulting in abundant production of immature (seed) oysters. In particular, Virginia's James River long ranked as the world's greatest natural source of seed oysters, billions of which were exported to private planters, who grew the bivalves to market size in other estuarine bodies both in and out of state.[15] The high salt content of Virginia waters approximated that of the New England coastline and thus produced a crop pleasing to northern palates, leading one scholar to suggest that "the relationship of profitability to salinity" accounts primarily for the more favorable reception of oyster leasing in Virginia than in Maryland.[16] Although the extent to which salty oysters influenced Virginia's embrace of private property rights is debatable, high salinity levels undoubtedly facilitated the Virginia fishery's free fall in the 1960s when the pathogens MSX and Dermo invaded the Lower Bay.[17]

By contrast, until the mid-1980s, the Maryland half of the bay exhibited optimal conditions for oyster production. The region between the Chester and Potomac Rivers has historically featured salinity levels conducive to oyster growth but not to predators and pathogens. It is also far enough away from the massive Susquehanna River to resist its lethal spring floods.[18] So great was the Maryland Chesapeake's ecological superiority that its oyster bars remained viable far longer than those of other states, especially after the state resource agency began replenishing the natural beds with shell and transplanted seed oysters in the 1920s. Ecological as well as political reasons thus help explain Maryland legislatures' consistent refusal to encourage widespread leasing. The economic pressure to do so was intense, for Virginia's ecologically inferior waters and private system of production often yielded more bivalves than did its northern neighbor.[19] In 1959, however, the disease MSX struck the Lower Chesapeake, having devastated oyster populations in New York, New Jersey, and Delaware. Maryland's lower salinities protected its beds from the worst of the scourge, but only for a generation. Droughts reduced freshwater inflows during the 1980s and thus increased salinity levels, enabling the pathogens to move up the bay.[20] The state natural resource agency contributed to the spread by continuing its long-standing practice of aiding watermen by transplanting seed oysters, many of which were infected, from southern bars to more northern waters. Finally, global warming may have played a role in shifting the geographic range of MSX and Dermo as well as other species.[21] Whatever the cause, the crash of the Maryland oyster industry during the 1980s and 1990s, on the heels of Virginia's collapse, led many to question whether the Chesapeake could still support its indigenous oyster, *C. virginica*.

Such an idea would have been inconceivable three hundred years ago, when the oyster reefs were so large that they posed navigation hazards. As Swiss traveler Louis Michel wrote in 1701, "There are whole banks of them so that the ships must avoid them. A sloop, which was to land us at Kingscreek, struck an oyster bed, where we had to wait about two hours for the tide. They surpass those in England by far in size, indeed they are four times as large. I often cut them in two, before I could put them in my mouth."[22] Unlike the Indians, most colonists subsisted on oysters only during hard times, as suggested by a complaint filed in 1680 by a group of Kent Islanders who had to eat them after running out of provisions.[23] English settlers valued oysters more as a construction material, using tons for building roads, mixing mortar, and filling in wetlands. Not until the Revolutionary era did oysters gain popularity as a cheap protein source, and not until after the Civil War, when transportation and technological advances increased demand for the bivalve across the United States, did Chesapeake oystering become a lucrative vocation rather than a sideline for farmers.[24]

While native peoples had little long-term environmental impact on the Great Shellfish Bay, Europeans initiated a massive transformation of the estuary and its watershed. The first English settlers in North America landed in 1607 at Jamestown, Virginia, where they planted the seeds of the British Empire, the United States, and an addictively profitable New World crop. In clearing fields throughout the Tobacco Coast, colonists escalated the erosion of what Captain John Smith called a "fruitfull and delightsome land."[25] Erosion is a natural process in all estuaries, but farming and logging accelerated the loads of sediment that spilled into rivers with every rainfall. Archeological and historical evidence suggests that the proportion of cultivated land in southern Maryland increased from 2 percent in 1720 to almost 40 percent a century later. Erosion increased so much that several colonial harbors filled in, and sturgeon and some other fish species declined enough to elicit notice.

An even greater upsurge in erosion followed the colonial era, according to analysis of pollen grains trapped in the sediments of the bay bottoms. During the late eighteenth century, wealthy planters inspired by the Enlightenment's faith in scientific progress abandoned the agricultural traditions that their grandfathers had adapted from Native Americans. Hoes and long-fallow shifting cultivation gave way to plows and more continuous farming. Soil particles loosened by the clean-tilled fields inundated the estuary, depriving the soil of nitrogen and phosphorus, silting up navigation channels, and reducing water clarity. Agricultural inputs to bay waters intensified as antebellum farmers tried to restore lost soil fertility by applying tons of nutrient-rich guano from South America, followed by domestically manufactured chemical fertilizers.[26] Scientific agricultural reforms of the late eighteenth century thus caused much more damage than had colonial tools and techniques.[27] The history of scientific endeavors in the Chesapeake region has at times been far from benign.

Euro-American agricultural practices in the Revolutionary period initiated the process of eutrophication, the overfertilization or nutrient pollution of bay waters. The nutrients nitrogen and phosphorus are vital components of a healthy estuarine ecosystem, but in high concentrations they stimulate blooms of phytoplankton (algae), which cut off sunlight from submerged grasses and other organisms.[28] When the phytoplankton die and decompose, the bacteria that feed on them consume the oxygen that sustains life, causing hypoxia (low levels of dissolved oxygen) or anoxia (total lack of dissolved oxygen).[29] Few organisms can survive in the seasonal "dead zones" produced by anthropogenic eutrophication. Nevertheless, so great was the bay's ecological resilience that not until the early twentieth century – almost 150 years after the implementation of Enlightenment agrarian reforms – did "system-wide environmental deterioration" become apparent.[30]

At the same time, urban and industrial development augmented the waste stream of sediments, nutrients, and toxins.[31] By 1800, Baltimoreans had used their stream-powered mills and strategic location at the fall line of the Patapsco River to transform a provincial tobacco port into an international gateway linking trade among the U.S. North and South, Latin America, and Europe. Almost two hundred thousand people resided in the city at midcentury, attracted by the expanding canal and rail networks and the shipbuilding and metal-processing industries. Baltimore's canning and clothing industries boomed after the Civil War, and the population rose to half a million by the turn of the twentieth century. Because the harbor and its adjoining tributary served as the main receptacle for the masses of human and industrial waste emanating from all these activities, Baltimore also became known for its stench. By 1900, it remained the largest U.S. city without a sewer system.[32] The bay could not function indefinitely as both a waste disposal site and a thriving fishery.

But the estuary's flora and fauna tolerated and even benefited from a limited increase of sediment and nutrients. As a fisheries scientist speculated in 1908, "The denudation of our forest lands, the erosion due to faulty agriculture, the artificial fertilizers carried away from cultivated fields during periods of heavy rainfall, and the discharge of sewage rich in organic matter have undoubtedly added much to the available fertilizing content of our coastal waters, to the advantage of their microscopic vegetation."[33] Recent paleoecological and archeological studies suggest that Chesapeake oysters grew much faster during the initial phase of eutrophication, from 1760 to 1860, as a consequence of increased phytoplankton food supplies produced by overenrichment of bay waters. However, although eutrophication continued to occur, *C. virginica* growth rates slowed after 1860, a possible effect of the postbellum intensification of oyster dredging and early twentieth-century increases in hypoxia events and harmful algal blooms. The overlapping occurrences of reef degradation, reduced estuarine functioning, and decreased oyster growth around the turn of the twentieth century suggest a correlation.[34] Indeed, because they filter plankton and matter suspended in the water column, oysters and other bottom-dwelling shellfish may serve as natural eutrophication controls, a finding that has major implications for restoring the Chesapeake ecosystem.[35] More broadly, the eutrophication-fueled growth of oysters in the era preceding large-scale exploitation suggests that the resource baseline itself resulted from significant human alterations, thereby complicating efforts to assign blame for the bivalve's twentieth-century decline.

The Rise of the Oyster Industry

People have harvested the riches of the Great Shellfish Bay for thousands of years, but the oyster industry, though legendary, is a much more recent phenomenon. White farmers and black slaves began collecting shellfish for subsistence in the early eighteenth century, with a limited local market developing by the time of the Revolutionary War.[36] Chaos erupted in the early 1800s when New England dredging boats, having depleted their own resource base, raided the Chesapeake. Distressed by the brutally efficient new technology, Virginia legislators banned dredging in 1811. Nine years later, Maryland followed suit and took the further step of allowing only state residents to catch and transport oysters; later decrees established a complex set of geographical, seasonal, and gear restrictions that varied from county to county.[37] Such laws were justified as conservation measures, though the legislators who enacted them were probably just as concerned with spreading the benefits of employment to as many of their own citizens as possible.[38] New England oyster processors responded by establishing part-time residences in Maryland and by the 1860s had opened dozens of packing and canning plants in Baltimore.[39] Like other southern fisheries, the rise of the Maryland oyster industry owed much to the influx of northern capital.

One of the most important northern-financed initiatives that created a national market for Chesapeake oysters, as for so many other regional goods, was the railroad. The refrigerated rail car proved a boon to Baltimore oyster interests, just as it enabled Chicago meat packers to commodify dressed beef.[40] The Baltimore and Ohio Railroad, which made Baltimore the southern terminus of the northern capitalist network, reached St. Louis in 1857, but the greatest change came with the completion of the transcontinental railroad in 1869. To satisfy the surging demand for raw oysters, trains of thirty to forty cars left Baltimore each day during the height of the 1880 season, from Thanksgiving to Christmas.[41] Saloon patrons as far west as the Rocky Mountains feasted on bivalves that just days earlier had filtered bay waters. For more distant western, Caribbean, and European destinations, processors steamed the mollusks in the shell before shucking them and sealing them in tin cans.[42]

Another innovation that sparked the industry's phenomenal growth after the Civil War involved the practice of oystering. Forty-five years

after it banned dredging in response to the depredations of New Englanders, the Maryland legislature reversed course. An 1854 decision to allow
the use of small dredges (scrapes) in a single county had provoked jeal-
ousy among neighboring oystermen, for their tool of extraction, the
tong, could not access oysters in waters deeper than twenty-three feet.
Military operations suspended the oyster trade during the war, but high
demand for protein and thus high prices stimulated the Maryland legislature to overhaul the oyster laws in 1865. The most important change
authorized dredging in the deeper waters of the bay's main stem, a decision that transformed the region's economy. Within a generation, Maryland produced one-third of the world's oysters, more than twice the harvest of all foreign countries combined.[43]

As "the greatest oyster-producing region in the world," late nineteenth-
century Maryland employed one-fifth of the workers engaged in all
U.S. fisheries.[44] In 1879, a few years before production reached its historic peak, 23,402 of the state's 935,000 residents made their livelihood
through oysters during the September–April season, and 13,748 (59 percent) of those workers fished the oyster bars. Fifty-six hundred men
working on 700 boats worked as dredgers, while 5,148 men operating
1,825 canoes or other small boats worked as tongers and another 2,200
used dredges small enough to qualify them as a separate class, scrapers. Finally, 800 men served as runners, go-betweens who transported
oysters from the extractors to market. African Americans accounted for
about one-third of the tongers and a smaller percentage of the dredgers.[45] A masculine ethos of brute strength and bravery linked the men
who followed the water, where racist codes tended to break down in the
face of constant danger from winds, weather, and waves.[46]

After the oystermen had wrested the oysters from their watery milieu,
processors prepared them for market. Baltimore became the center of
the oyster-packing world during the Gilded Age. What is now the gleam-
ing Inner Harbor was then an area where few respectable people ven-
tured, for it housed the saloons, wharves, and warehouses that catered
to the hardened men of the oyster trade (fig. 5). Forty-five packing firms,
most owned by Connecticut Yankees who left Maryland as soon as the
season ended, processed the cargoes of almost ten thousand vessels that
arrived during the 1879–80 season, an average of thirty-seven boats per
day. Shucking the oyster was as dirty and exhausting in its own way as
working the water. Shuckers stood for hours on end at wooden troughs

Fig. 5. A mound of oyster shells outside Baltimore's C. H. Pearson and Company cannery, ca. 1890, with a line of men dumping wheelbarrows of freshly shucked shells. (Courtesy of National Archives, Records of the U.S. Fish and Wildlife Service.)

using a specialized knife and a flick of the wrist to sever the hinge muscle connecting the two halves of the oyster shell, an exceedingly repetitive task that machines have never been able to replicate. Faster workers received more pay, though the work was rarely steady. Whereas two hundred thousand bushels might arrive one week, a cold snap could reduce the catch to twenty thousand by freezing up the fleet, throwing multitudes of shuckers out of work.[47]

Shucking was a job for society's lowest economic strata. The Baltimore canneries tended to employ African American men and young white women of Bohemian or Irish heritage.[48] An observer of the trade reported in 1880 that few white native-born "girls, however poor, will consent to engage in this occupation, as in it both sexes must mingle indiscriminately, without regard to color, class, or condition."[49] African Americans of both sexes worked in the packinghouses that arose on the Eastern Shore after the Civil War, especially in Maryland's second major seafood port, Crisfield. Named for the president of the Eastern Shore Railroad, the town, located near the Virginia border, was built atop mounds of mollusk shells and featured railroad tracks that ran straight to the docks.[50] Oysters provided the literal and economic foundation of Crisfield, as was the case for many other waterfront communities in Maryland's eleven oyster counties.

Maryland experienced its all-time high oyster harvest of fifteen million bushels during the winter of 1884–85. The reasons behind this peak and especially behind successive decreases have sparked great debate. Stakeholders of the time attributed the high yield to increased consumer demand and an excellent spat set during the summer of 1883 or simply saw it as proof that the oyster beds could regenerate in the absence of conservation measures.[51] The fifteen-million mark long served as a benchmark against which to compare subsequent landings, and advocates of private oyster culture used it to argue that the cultivable bay contained immense untapped potential. Yet successive generations of harvesters scoffed at the notion of an immense unmet demand for shellfish, interpreting the spike as the consequence of increased dredging. As an oysterman explained at a 1953 legislative hearing, the fifteen million bushels had been "on the bay bottom since the year 1," long before the development of "new methods of taking oysters."[52] Although he overlooked the thousands of years during which Native Americans reaped the Chesapeake's signature crop, he underscored the problematic status of measuring the bay's productive capacity in relation to the short gold-rush period of frenzied exploitation. Fishery scholars agree that the adoption of more efficient technologies of extraction always intensifies exploitation, a view implicit in the Maryland legislature's history of mandating inefficient gear as a conservation strategy.[53]

Perhaps the most intriguing explanation for the mammoth 1884–85 harvest invokes demand from processors as opposed to consumers. The rich tidewater terrain nurtured fruits and vegetables, which provided employment for many oyster-industry workers during the summer off-season and cemented Baltimore's postbellum status as a national canning center. In a quest to profit from two regional specialties, winter oysters and summer peaches, canners may have facilitated the bivalve's historic leap. Because the spike followed the disease-induced collapse of the Eastern Shore peach industry, Baltimore canners may have driven up demand for oysters to compensate for lost fruit earnings.[54] If the timing was indeed more than coincidental, the epic figure of 1884–85 makes little sense as a meaningful benchmark.

Other caveats underlay the seemingly straightforward story of oyster landings (see fig. 1). Since 1865, Maryland has estimated its annual oyster production on the basis of processing taxes. For example, State Fishery Force inspectors collected $41,208.19 between 1 October 1916 and 30 September 1917; because the harvest tax was one cent per bushel, the official output of the 1916–17 season was registered as 4,120,819 bushels. But the actual harvest may have been higher, given that packers had financial incentives to underreport payloads.[55] Another problematic aspect of the system for calculating production became clear when officials announced that the output of the 1993–94 season was just under 80,000 bushels, the worst since the Civil War. A survey by the Maryland Watermen's Association suggested that the real figure was up to three times higher, because many oystermen had chosen not to sell to seafood dealers, thereby allowing their catch to go under the regulatory radar. Packers had to pay a state tax of a dollar per bushel, making them less likely to pay as much as restaurants and other unregulated customers.[56] Yet while watermen benefited from the higher prices paid by nondealers, the consequent drop in reported landings posed a threat, for sharp declines have always emboldened advocates of restrictive reforms.

Another reason that commercial fishermen, in the Chesapeake as elsewhere, tend to distrust the official statistical record involves their nonlinear understanding of nature. Anthropological studies have shown that whereas fishery managers construct mathematical models that express "periodic order" and linearity, industry members see the natural world in terms of "non-linear interweavings." Fishermen consider natural processes nonrandom and cyclical but unpredictable because of the immense number of atmospheric and anthropogenic conditions affecting fish abundance at any given point in time.[57] Likewise, fishery biologists and managers use graphs and the results of intermittent monitoring programs to determine when and where to impose new restrictions, but harvesters consider such "population snapshots" inappropriate because they represent only part of a longer cycle of species abundance. From the watermen's perspective, charts of data points collected at discrete moments that purport to convey the long-term status of oyster populations represent nothing more than artificial, arbitrary "cultural construc-tions."[58] Given the mutual misunderstandings and tensions spawned by such different interpretations, analysis of the ways in which scientists and watermen perceive the natural world and of historical changes in those perceptions are therefore a crucial part of forging managerial regimes acceptable to both sides.

Trying to analyze past trends based on harvest levels linked to honor-system taxes, reductionistic data sets, and other potentially unreliable indicators can leave one reeling. Yet doing so provides all the more rea-son for calling into question the idea of the Maryland oyster fishery as the embodiment of the tragedy-of-the-commons thesis. Doing so also shows the importance of analysis of multiple historical forces in under-standing the state of the fishery today. In the decades following the Civil War, new transportation networks, processing techniques, resource poli-cies, and fishing technologies introduced profound changes to the indus-try. The ways in which legislators, watermen, and scientists responded to those changes in turn illuminates ongoing controversies in resource management and the construction of environmental knowledge.

The Technology of Being an Oysterman

I tend to use the terms *watermen* and *oystermen* synonymously, though they are not quite the same. *Waterman* is an old English word for a com-mercial fisherman, reflecting the long-standing influence of seventeenth-century English settlers in the tidewater region. An oysterman is a water-man, but a waterman is not necessarily an oysterman. Since 1846, when Maryland became one of the first states to regulate the oyster season, the bivalves could be gathered legally for only part of the year, usually between September and April, when colder weather reduced spoilage.[59] Some harvesters, especially those who worked on dredge boat crews, supplemented their incomes by working for land-based agricultural interests during the spring and summer.[60] Oystermen who owned their own boats were more likely to spend the off-season maintaining their equipment, raising a few crops on personal patches of land, and/or gath-ering other species, such as blue crabs, clams, terrapins, eels, waterfowl, rockfish, and shad. Oysters constituted the most lucrative sector of the Maryland seafood industry until the mid-1980s, when disease pathogens stormed the Upper Bay. As a result, most watermen now derive their primary incomes from crabbing, and the word *oysterman* has lost its relevance as an occupational identifier over the past two decades.

The most famous tool of the Chesapeake oyster trade was the last to evolve: the skipjack, a unique boat whose design evolved as an adaptation to the economic and legislative constraints of Gilded Age Maryland. The first skipjacks of the 1890s were cheap to build, a critical factor considering the tidewater's depressed financial condition. Engineered to pull dredges under sail power, the broad-beamed, single-masted craft complied with the legislature's prohibition against steam-powered dredging.[61] By the 1960s, Maryland possessed the world's largest commercial sailing fleet, but the forty-seven skipjacks then in operation constituted a fraction of the more than nine hundred that dredged at the turn of the century. Today's working fleet can be counted on one hand. The legislature designated the skipjack the state boat during the 1980s, just as oystering became harder than ever as a consequence of MSX and Dermo.[62] The boat has subsequently emerged as a powerful symbol both of Maryland and of a thriving bay. The National Trust for Historic Preservation listed the skipjack fleet as one of the country's eleven most endangered historic resources of 2002, thereby focusing national attention on the plight of both the watermen and the oyster.[63] A few restored vessels now ferry tourists, while others serve as educational facilities to provide students a greater stake in a healthy bay. Environmentalists view such outdoor activities as essential now that so few members of American society "know nature through labor," in the words of environmental historian Richard White.[64]

The shaft or hand tong used to extract the oyster constituted the main tool of Chesapeake harvesters from its emergence around 1700 until 1865. Those living near shoreline rocks could rake the natural crops at low tide, but accessing bars further out required a simple boat and a pair of tongs as much as twenty-four feet long. Hand tongers work in the tributaries, using a scissorlike instrument with facing rakes at the bottom to retrieve oysters in water from nine to twenty feet deep (fig. 6). After feeling around the bottom with the tong and locating a promising spot, the tonger clasps a bunch of bivalves between the rakes and uses muscle power to lift the mass. (Hydraulic patent tongs, an 1880s invention utilizing ropes and a winch, enable the extraction of more oysters from deeper waters and thus have been subject to more restrictions.) If the tongs come up full of healthy, mature oysters (keepers), the tonger has had a good lick. Before the catch can be sold, the marketable oysters

Fig. 6. Having lifted the loaded tongs, tongers at Rock Point, Maryland, dump their loads onto the culling board, 1941. African American and white oystermen worked side by side on the water more often than on land. (Photo by Reginald Hotchkiss. Courtesy of Library of Congress, Prints and Photographs Division, FSA-OWI Collection.)

must be culled from the mud and trash and the undersized specimens must be thrown back onto the bar.[65]

Hand tonging traditionally required only a small investment. In the early 1880s, when the average Maryland tonger made about $225 over the eight-month season, a pair of tongs lasting a year or so cost between $3.50 and $5.00.[66] Local blacksmiths fashioned the heads, while shaft makers shaped the wooden poles, with the length depending on the depth of the particular river to be worked.[67] For tidewater residents, tonging represented an economic safety net. As a visitor to Crisfield observed in 1905, "Every dweller upon tidal water in these parts has a boat that can be used at a pinch for oystering in a small way. He can hire a boy of fifteen at 50 cents a day as a helper, buy with small outlay the necessary implements of the trade, pay the trifling tonger's license, and appear a fully equipped oysterman."[68] Nevertheless, being a successful tonger required an immense skill set, especially as the most accessible beds became depleted or silted over:

A tonger has literally to "learn" many hundreds of acres of ground in widely separated localities of quite different kinds, ground he seldom actually sees. Furthermore, what he knows one year may be of limited use the next, because of changed conditions on the bars. An oyster bar is an organic entity, subject to the fluctuations common to living organisms. On the other hand, what the tonger learned eight or ten years ago may now produce high dividends, for he has learned that it pays to remember absolutely everything he has ever known.[69]

After World War II, state fishery managers affirmed the importance of retaining the legal status of tonging: "As a matter of social policy in our tidewater communities, it appears most advantageous to maintain productive tonging bars, as they provide profitable self-employment for many individuals in a community and are in reality a most effective 'spread the work' device."[70] Of course, tonging depends on the existence of healthy oyster beds and access to them. The forces of nature and human culture control the former, while politics determines the latter.

The legalization of dredging – "drudgin'" in tidewater parlance – in 1865 created a new class of oystermen more attuned to the ethos of industrialization. Rather than working a limited area while at a standstill, dredge boats pull a metal frame with an attached mesh cage back and forth across an oyster bar for hours at a time (fig. 7).[71] Whereas a hand tonger might collect a few dozen bushels on a good day, a sailboat equipped with two dredges and four strong but otherwise unskilled crewmen could harvest five hundred bushels, and a large steam-powered boat might extract fifteen hundred bushels or more. By 1882, however, the average daily dredge boat catch had dropped to between twenty and eighty bushels per day.[72] A lowball 1880 estimate valued the average Maryland dredging boat at fifteen hundred dollars, and skippers earned almost ten times as much as tongers.[73] The huge outlay required to break into the business meant that many dredge boat captains worked at the behest of wealthy packers, for whom the dredge's superior efficiency more than compensated for its higher degree of capitalization.[74]

The dredge epitomized a technological, social, and economic divide among tidewater communities.[75] As a late nineteenth-century observer proclaimed, "There is as wide a difference between the 'tonguing-iron' and the 'dredge' as there is between the scythe of 'Old Father Time' and the McCormick reaper."[76] Dredge boat skippers indeed received much

Fig. 7. A dredge haul taken along the Atlantic coast, ca. 1938. The infestation of starfish indicates a location other than the Chesapeake Bay, whose lower salinities minimized the depredations of natural predators. (Photo by Sean Linehan. Courtesy of Historic Fisheries Collection, National Oceanic and Atmospheric Administration.)

higher remuneration than tongers did despite the fact that members of both groups used parallel bases of knowledge – of the bay bottoms, tidal flows, wind shifts, and seasonal estuarine cycles. But rationalizers overlooked the trade-offs involved in embracing modern production technology, especially the loss of control involved in outfitting such an expensive enterprise. While many watermen built or bought skipjacks and ran them as family enterprises (especially after the economic downturn of the 1890s), becoming a dredge boat captain could involve relinquishing one's independence as an owner-operator. Until the 1960s, processing plants owned dozens of boats that they leased to captains for use on particular public oyster reefs, a practice one historian terms "sharecropping the bay."[77] Corporate packers did not control the entire dredging fleet, but their ability to manipulate market conditions in such ways intensified small-scale oystermen's distrust, creating tensions that played out in the debates about privatizing the oyster beds. Long before the leasing controversy ignited in the 1880s, Maryland tongers resisted the industrialization of oystering by compelling legislators to restrain the dredging trade.[78]

Codifying the Oyster Commons

The year 1865 was a watershed for the Maryland oyster industry, as for the country at large. As the Civil War wound down, demand for cheap meat soared, and Baltimore's canning and railroad executives salivated at the prospect of mining the Chesapeake oyster beds. Dredging had been illegal for decades, and while the General Assembly could hold back no longer the floodgates of change, it acted to minimize disruptions to traditional tidewater communities. A longer closed season for dredgers during the summer months gave tongers a greater share of the market, and a statewide licensing system maintained the fishery as the province of Marylanders only. A third stipulation furthered the causes of both conservation and maximal human employment by banning steam-powered boats and equipment. In an age in which steam had long since displaced sail on the nation's commercial waterways, technological restrictions constituted a major curb on the industry's expansion by preserving arduous aspects of preindustrial fishing.

Of greatest importance to the creation of a regulated estuarine commons, the 1865 oyster code created separate domains – "state waters" and "county waters" – for dredging and tonging, respectively. Dredgers were prohibited from accessing the reefs within county limits – that is, in tributaries or bay waters within three hundred yards of the low-water mark. These shallow waters were reserved for tongers, who in turn were restricted to the waters of their own counties. Therefore, while tongers enjoyed much less mobility than dredgers, who could harvest oysters anywhere in the deeper, offshore waters of the bay proper, they possessed exclusive rights to the most accessible, sheltered oyster grounds. Such prime locations provided great temptation to desperate or dishonest dredge boat captains. The creation of local commons regimes, as embodied in the legal distinction between state and county waters, could not protect subsistence tonging communities from the depredations of illegal dredging.

Because county sheriffs failed to protect the tonging grounds, the General Assembly in 1868 created the State Fishery Force, one of the first agencies in the United States designed to safeguard natural resources.[79] Funded by dredging license fees and fines, packing taxes, and state appropriations, the "Oyster Navy" was at first no match for the faster, better-armed dredgers, who raided inshore reefs under cover of darkness or fog. Even with howitzers and rapid-fire rifles, the force's effectiveness remained limited by the huge area to be patrolled, the persistent lack of operating funds, and corruption bred by political appointees.[80] Long after the violence had subsided, a prominent citizen derided the force as a bunch of "poker-playing and whisky-drinking captains and crew."[81] Conscientious commanders faced the daily struggle of getting inspectors to enforce the laws against their relatives and neighbors.[82] At the same time, illegal dredgers benefited from loopholes, such as one that permitted inspectors to make arrests only when a boat was caught with wet oysters on deck. If a police steamer witnessed illicit dredging, a crew could easily dump the evidence overboard before the officers reached the boat.[83] And even when inspectors made arrests, county juries and judges invariably sided with those accused of violating the oyster code.[84]

Despite the legislature's regulatory efforts, gunfire erupted on the bay throughout the late nineteenth century. As investigator Richard Edmonds lamented in 1880, "Dredging in Maryland is simply a general scramble, carried on by 700 boats, manned by 5,600 daring and unscrupulous men, who regard neither the laws of God nor man."[85] The tongers, whose tools prevented them from encroaching on the deep-water dredging grounds, retaliated against illegal dredgers by firing cannonballs from shore, and Maryland tongers and dredgers fired on Virginians who crossed the invisible state boundary. Not until the turn of the century did the thirty years of "hell on the half-shell" subside, and sporadic skirmishes continued for decades longer.[86]

The Chesapeake Bay was by no means the only place in the United States where men lost their lives over oysters. At around the same time, illegal dredging provoked a series of violent battles in New Jersey, but different circumstances lay at the core of the two conflicts. In New Jersey, the poaching of oysters from privately farmed beds provoked the bloodshed, and the disputes involved two distinct groups: those who had paid for access to state tidal property for the growing of oysters, and those who, like impoverished resource users elsewhere, resisted the state-enforced enclosure of grazing and fishing grounds on which they had long relied. The New Jersey Oyster Wars thus revolved around the issue of common-property rights.[87] By contrast, Maryland oystermen possessed the political clout to preclude economic elites' efforts to privatize the oyster reefs. Their unity against those who challenged what they considered their God-given right to work the water

did not always extend to other aspects of their occupation. The Chesapeake Oyster Wars involved multiple fronts, with different classes of oystermen fighting agents of social control and each other. Only rarely did
bullets fly over clashes between concepts of private and common property, as when Marylanders looted beds leased by Virginians in waters
over which both states claimed sovereignty.[88] Within Maryland, the vast
majority of debates over leasing played out in the contentious though
nonviolent arenas of the State Capitol and local press.[89]

The Chesapeake Oyster Wars reflected the social turmoil and labor
unrest wrought by industrialization in the broader society. Like other
capital-intensive businesses employing large numbers of unskilled workers, the Gilded Age dredging fleet exacted a high toll of labor dehu-
manization. During the 1880s, when the harvest reached all-time highs,
attracting crewmen was so difficult that large boat owners paid New York
shipping agents to recruit naive immigrants willing to spend eighteen-
hour shifts at the backbreaking jobs of cranking the windlass and culling the sharp shells. The shipping agents received two dollars for each
man recruited, "whether drunk or sober, clothed or naked."[90] Closer to
home, "no man was safe around the Baltimore waterfront after dark in
the R-months," when one might be drugged, kidnapped, and forced into
dredging service.[91] Since the fleets stayed out for weeks at a time, obtaining supplies and selling their catch to middlemen known as buyboats far
from shore, crew members had little opportunity to escape. Frostbite,
broken bones, and inflamed skin (oyster hand) were common occupational hazards. Even worse, one might be left without food or clothing
on an isolated neck or "paid off by the boom" – knocked overboard into
frigid waters by the captain's abrupt turning of the tiller. Such incidents
occurred every winter, as recounted in national newspaper articles with
titles such as "Worse Than Slave-Drivers" and "Tortured on the Bay."[92]
Efforts by the Baltimore German Society to end the cruelties foundered
in the face of the strong oyster lobby. The passage of a federal antishang-
haiing law and the adoption of the gasoline-powered windlass finally
ended the practice of dredge peonage by about 1908, but tidewater inhabitants retained a long legacy of reverence for independence.[93]

Not all dredge captains persecuted their crewmen or poached on the
county commons regimes, but offenders did nothing to improve the
reputation of the Chesapeake "oyster pirates."[94] Edmonds painted a
harsh portrait of Maryland dredgers that received a wide audience in

the early 1880s when his account was reprinted in a federal survey of the nation's fisheries:

> The unscrupulousness of the captain is well assisted by the character of his men. These men, taken as a class, form perhaps one of the most depraved bodies of workmen to be found in the country. They are gathered from jails, penitentiaries, work-houses, and the lowest and vilest dens of the city. They are principally whites, many of whom are foreigners . . . unable to speak more than a few words of English. . . . With such a crew as this, who neither know nor care for laws, the captain is of course able to work wherever he desires to.

Edmonds expressed sympathy for the crew members, forced to sleep among vermin and work under freezing conditions, though he deplored their practice of spending their little pay "in debauchery, amid the lowest groggeries and dens of infamy to be found in certain portions of Baltimore."[95] His assessment of the tongers was more upbeat: "Tonging, although employing less capital and fewer men than dredging, is probably of greater value to the state than the latter, because the men engaged in it are of a better class, are better remunerated for their labor, and are less prone to evade the laws than the dredgers."[96] Even so, Edmonds expressed his annoyance that tongers also wasted money on "strong drink" and that, having secured a house with an acre of two of land on which to tend garden produce, "their ambition seems to be satisfied, and but little time or money is spent in beautifying or improving it. It is too often the case that tongers, especially many of the negroes, who comprise about one-third of the total number, will work only one or two days at a time, and then remain idle until necessity forces them again to earn a few dollars."[97] Despite his disgust at the lack of discipline he perceived in tongers, particularly African Americans, Edmonds acknowledged that nature conspired against even industrious individuals, who lost about two days every week to bad weather. Edmonds calculated that the average tonger worked only 120 of the season's 240 days, a situation that "prevents the tongers, as a class, from making any improvement in their financial condition, and upon their financial condition depends their social position." The tongers' disregard for bourgeois standards of respectability offended and bewildered would-be rationalizers of the water business.

Social differences between tongers and dredgers were reinforced by the oyster laws. The code not only imposed different geographical restrictions on oystermen but also used their license fees for different purposes. Dredge license fees went into state coffers to fund the Fishery Force, whereas after 1874 tongers' fees benefited their own communities. When a tonger visited the clerk of his county circuit court to obtain his annual license, all or most of his payment went to the county's public school commissioners. Moreover, in segregated Maryland, the law stipulated that "the sum received from white tongers shall go to white schools, and the sum from colored tongers to colored schools."[98] Whereas dredgers perceived no benefit from their license fees except in the form of social control as imposed by the Oyster Navy, tongers had more of a stake in paying up for the sake of their children's schools. Tongers also had a greater interest in ensuring the sustainability of local oyster beds because their equipment and the law limited them to the shallow waters of their home counties; they could not move on to more distant frontiers when the local reefs gave out. The county-based common property regimes of the tonging grounds were more localized than the dredgers' realm, another factor that likely accounts for what Edmonds contended were tongers' higher rates of law abidance.

Policing the Oyster Commons

In the twentieth century, political, economic, and social constraints continued to hamper efforts to enforce the oyster laws. The Oyster Navy commander's job remained thankless, with most days spent defending his actions and chastising employees. In November 1905, for example, the Baltimore Oyster Packers Association complained to the governor that Commander Thomas C. B. Howard's inspectors were enforcing the cull law (an 1890 act designed to conserve brood stock by forbidding the sale of oysters smaller than 2.5 inches across) more strictly at Baltimore than at ports down the bay, thereby driving away business.[99] In a more extreme case, the Dorchester County Democratic Campaign Committee accused the force of unspecified "treacherous" acts that led to "the mortifying result that Dorchester was the only county on the Eastern Shore to give a majority for the Republican State ticket."[100] More than half a century later, the problem persisted: the secretary of state warned the governor about an officer who was "harrassing the watermen" to such an extent that "at the present time it will be impossible for you to carry lower Dorchester County because of the damage he has done and is doing."[101] That a single inspector was seen as playing such a crucial role in electoral politics reveals the immense political strength of the watermen, even in the gubernatorial realm, where they did not enjoy the advantages accorded by the legislative county-unit system.

The perception of Oyster Navy jobs as sinecures is borne out by the almost daily letters Commander Howard sent urging his employees to arrest violators, enforce the cull law, secure licenses, file monthly reports, and convince packers to pay the oyster tax (which funded the inspectors' salaries and determined the annual official catch). Howard doubtless relied on informants, probably conscientious inspectors and oystermen who felt cheated when they observed laws being unfairly applied.[102] Not until 1959, after Maryland marine police shot and killed a Virginia dredger, did the force implement the merit system.[103] Some inspectors nevertheless retained a less-than-professional attitude – for example, by blaming superiors for the regulations that had to be enforced. An anonymous group of Cambridge, Maryland, oystermen wrote to Governor J. Millard Tawes in 1962 that

> if the watermen dont get rid of you it will be the worse winter this place has ever known. they no that you are the one Because when the inspector comes abord he tells the oysterman not to Blame us this is just handed down from the Governor. and then you expect people to vote for you. I think you have got your last vote from the waterman. peopl had no trouble at all to make a good living until you and a few more got there. You may no a lot about other things But you dont no any about the oyster Business. it is people hear now that hardly have some thing to eat just on accont of this law While you attend a dinner at $100.00. it is a disgrace to Humanity.[104]

Tawes's status as an Eastern Shoreman did not immunize him against the oystermen's rage, especially when he appeared to flout his humble origins during hard times by attending lavish campaign fund-raisers.

The Oyster Navy remained underfunded for decades. The industry taxes intended to support it often fell short, forcing the begrudging legislature and/or the governor to dip into general tax revenues. The 1947 Potomac River enforcement team epitomized the hardships of life on the force: ten poorly paid officers, some forced to live aboard their World War I–era boats, worked at all hours every day of the week, wasting entire days in court trying to get cases to trial while reluctant sheriffs delayed serving warrants on offenders. Taunting oystermen kept their illegal dredges right on the docks, since the officers could take action only if the dredge was in the boat.[105] At the same time, marine police had to avoid the perception of overzealousness. The 1959 shooting led fishery officials to eliminate the carrying of sidearms for routine patrols, a decision that elicited praise from a tidewater legislator: "It was not uncommon for an oysterman to put a bushel of oysters from his boat onto the wharf and have six, eight or ten guns staring him in the face. It tended to make all law-abiding citizens feel unnecessarily as criminals. The Rock Hall waterfront has been referred to as 'Fort Rock Hall' because there is so much artillery there."[106] The inevitable tension of enforcing laws that many resource users disregarded may well have led some inspectors to feel justified in using excessive force. The adoption of planes, cameras, and other modern surveillance equipment in the mid–twentieth century reduced violent encounters and improved enforcement, though the bay's vast commons regime still enabled many watermen to exercise what they considered their inalienable right to its bounty.

Watermen have a long-standing reputation as conservation lawbreakers, despite a strong religious orientation that dates to the spread of Methodism around the turn of the nineteenth century.[107] As observed by William Warner in his Pulitzer Prize–winning *Beautiful Swimmers,* "Watermen throughout the Bay became a devout, temperate and law-abiding people. Outsiders, however, noted one glaring contradiction. The watermen treated anything that floated, swam, crawled, or flew into their marshy domains as God-given and therefore not subject to the laws of mortal men. What the Lord provided, no landsmen should tell them how to harvest."[108] The harvesters saw the right of free plunder as divinely sanctioned. Whenever conservationists claimed that such attitudes were not conducive to the industry's long-term viability, oystermen invoked a higher authority: "God put the oysters there for a man to take."[109] Sociologist Carolyn Ellis, who lived among two Chesapeake island communities during the 1970s, confirmed that violations of water conservation and safety laws remained widespread: "Almost everyone at one time or another fished or hunted ducks out of season, used illegal methods for illegal catches in illegal places, failed to carry enough life preservers, or stole from crab pots and private oyster beds."[110] According to a 1961 study by the Department of Tidewater Fisheries, 11.8 percent of the state's more than five thousand oystermen had violated the law during the previous season, and many were repeat offenders: thirty persons concentrated in the lower Eastern Shore communities of Crisfield,

Deal Island, and Dorchester County accounted for eighty-four violations.[111] That the most southern part of the state featured the greatest concentration of conservation scofflaws is perhaps not surprising considering the Eastern Shore's long history of separatism and secessionism.

Despite their reputation for lawlessness, watermen have often advocated stricter enforcement of conservation laws as a matter of fairness. Said one Tangier Islander just before the turn of the millennium, "If [laws are] not enforced properly, it benefits the people who are going to break the law. The ones who keep it suffer."[112] Edmonds made an almost identical observation a century earlier: "An honest captain, who complies with the law by not working on Sunday, at night, or on forbidden ground, will take at least a week longer to catch a load of oysters than one who, disregarding the laws, gets his oysters whenever or wherever he can."[113] Under such circumstances, obeying the law could strike a rational resource user as foolish, especially if others were profiting through unfair competition or if his family were hungry.

Working the Water

As long as individuals did not violate communal work-control norms, locals did not perceive activities such as the taking of undersized or excessive numbers of oysters as crimes but rather as part of the challenge of deriving a livelihood from the water – in short, as part of the watermen's culture.[114] A dominant feature of that culture is the arduousness of the labor involved in extracting wealth from the bay. Harvesting oysters, whether by tong or dredge, is grueling under the best conditions, and most of the season overlaps with the dead of winter.[115] If the bay is not iced over or full of swells caused by heavy winds and waves, the oysterman's day begins at two or three o'clock in the morning and ends in the late afternoon. The historic lack of labor-saving devices requires extreme muscular endurance, but despite their vigorous image, most watermen suffer from serious health problems. Hernias, rheumatism, cataracts, skin cancer, and occupational hazards such as slipping on wet decks or falling overboard decrease life expectancy. In the words of a Smith Islander, "Ain't no glory in oysterin'. A man who doesn't want to work hard isn't going to make it in the water business." Despite all the hardships, older watermen often "believe that to stop going is to die."[116]

At the other end of the age spectrum, recent generations of watermen recount their feelings of being drawn to the water despite their fathers' efforts to make entering the trade as difficult as possible: "A man wants to follow the water, ain't neither way to keep him ashore."[117]

One of the attractions of commercial fishing relates to the independence long associated with life on the water. It is no coincidence that maritime slavery failed to become an integral part of the American South, a phenomenon historians explain as a function of slave owners' anxiety about losing control of their property: "Slavery always frayed at the water's edge, where the uncertainty of wind, weather, and labor rendered unserviceable the sorts of work routines and constant oversight practiced on plantations." Coastal slaveholders allowed a few slaves to fish, but planters feared that working on the water could promoting antislavery activism by linking otherwise isolated African American communities. Recent scholarship suggests that black watermen aided runaway slaves, fomented insurrections, and fostered a postbellum political culture of civil rights.[118] Despite its dangers, working the water provided tidewater slaves an unprecedented degree of independence from their masters and offered free blacks better opportunities than many other occupations open to them. That such oppressed groups found fishing so appealing provides strong testimony to its pull. After the Civil War, the desire to escape mainland work discipline and authority no doubt drove thousands of black and white men to follow the water.

A related core value of tidewater culture involves the deep satisfaction that watermen derive from overcoming the many risks inherent in commercial fishing, a profession more dangerous than mining or logging.[119] Meeting the daily challenges of the job requires an immense storehouse of occupational know-how. "No matter how good your muscle tone is, if you have little knowledge, or if you are unable to apply what you know, you will never make a professional waterman," explained Varley Lang, who left university life in the late 1950s to follow the water.[120] Independent fishermen developed such a specialized knowledge base that they found the prospect of having to take up other work alarming. A constituent expressed her fear of proposed new conservation regulations in a poignant 1927 letter to the governor: "I truly hope you will ask guiding from our Lord before you take any act[ion] on the part of any bills that would mean to take our livihood from us fisher wives, our husbands work hard each day that they can for a living and . . . if you would stop pound fishing or break up any of the fishing our homes would have to be sold or left and other labor to be found of which our Husbands no nothing about."[121] Yet despite the watermen's intense specialization, the ability to adapt to rapidly changing climatic and economic conditions was and remains vital to making a living on the bay.

The notion that watermen embraced the uncertainties intrinsic to the preindustrial tidewater way of life was inconceivable to professional-minded members of U.S. society on the eve of the Progressive Era. In their eyes, private oyster farming represented a crucial strategy to get commercial fishermen to engage in more steady work and to accumulate capital. Yet Maryland oystermen's keen survival abilities enabled them to resist large-scale privatization, to feed their families in hard times, and to use the regulatory system to their advantage, thereby preserving their profession long after other artisanal traditions gave way to mechanization and mass production.

Despite important differences in their occupational subcultures, outsiders perceived tongers and dredgers as sharing an economic identity. As Edmonds concluded, "It is yet an unpleasant truth that [the tongers], like all others engaged in the oyster-trade, either as catchers or shuckers, are, as a class, indolent and improvident."[122] Edmonds's assessment reflected the conventional mind-set of Victorian intellectuals and patricians and helps to explain pro-leasing scientists' belief that private cultivation would improve the oystermen's lives by inducing them to adopt such cherished goals of urban-industrial society as social mobility, sobriety, thrift, and punctuality.

The poor economic standing of both tongers and dredgers precluded their identification as an elite group, for the Chesapeake watermen of the late nineteenth century were impoverished whites and former slaves. Although they participated in the modern capitalist system by harvesting raw materials for processing and export to distant markets, commercial fishing was at best minimally profitable. The only assets tongers and independent dredge boat captains possessed were their boats, small houses, and an acre or so of land, while dredge boat crewmen usually had even less. In 1915, the *Baltimore Sun* called crew members "human flotsam and jetsam" who drifted between oyster seasons doing odd jobs and whose "most valuable possession is their political franchise." Continued the paper, "Scarcely an election contest or investigation of 'stuffing' ballot boxes occurs in tidewater counties in which they do not figure.

The class includes probably more negroes than white men."[123] Poverty was so widespread on the Eastern Shore that most communities did not obtain electricity and running water until the 1930s or later.[124] Even as they participated in the national markets made possible by the influx of northern capital in the form of railroads and processing infrastructure, oystermen did not accumulate money and invest in modern innovations or at least did not do so as quickly as rationalizers might have liked.

Of course, the degree of capital accumulation varied throughout tidewater, as Ellis's ethnographic study of two Chesapeake settlements during the 1970s suggests. Though the two communities shared outwardly similar religious, economic, and ecological settings, work and success were valued in very different ways. Residents of "Fishneck" (an isolated Virginia peninsula) lived in deteriorating houses, disdained upward mobility, used small skiffs, and turned to wage labor or harvested other species when oysters and crabs became scarce or unprofitable. By contrast, inhabitants of "Crab Reef" (Smith Island, Maryland) kept their lawns mowed and houses painted, invested in larger boats and equipment suited only to crabbing and oystering, and disrespected working for others.[125] Crab Reefers made more money but also had to work harder than Fishneckers, who struggled on a day-to-day basis yet also retained greater flexibility in the face of market fluctuations. According to Ellis, religious institutions lay at the heart of these different work values and patterns. In Crab Reef, a strong central church stressed "hard work on the water and for the community," whereas in Fishneck, small, sectarian local churches emphasized supporting family members. The church also mediated the greater concern for capital accumulation that prevailed among Crab Reef watermen, who adhered to a communal code of egalitarianism rather than mainland conceptions of competition and mobility, thereby limiting individual levels of production.[126]

Ellis looked back in time to explain why Crab Reef's economic base changed from subsistence and barter by the mid–nineteenth century while Fishneck's did not. The differences in the degree of the institutionalization of the Methodist Church shaped the response of the two communities to a fateful economic opportunity. In the early 1800s, a renowned missionary trained Crab Reef leaders to spread the Gospel in his absence, but Fishneckers encountered preachers only on an intermittent basis. When New Englanders offered to buy all the available oysters, Crab Reefers, infused with a work ethic reinforced by frequent sermons, responded to the new market by constructing larger boats and expanding their work activity to meet the demand but did not do so beyond the level of family enterprise. In contrast, Fishneckers, lacking exposure to social institutions promoting work-related values, reacted "by turning the markets into marginal money, a resource useful only for expanding purchasing power, not capital accumulation." Even during the boom years of World War II, when demand and prices for fish and shellfish soared as a consequence of meat rationing, Fishneckers' "minimal attachment to money" and refusal to patronize financial institutions perpetuated their subsistence economy.[127] A recent archeological investigation of the material culture of two other nineteenth-century oystering communities corroborates the role of social institutions in influencing the extent to which members invested in more industrialized equipment, infrastructure, and ideologies.[128]

The Ecology of Oystering

Just as the Maryland legislature, the Oyster Navy, the Methodist Church, and other institutions of social control affected tidewater communities' and individuals' choices regarding their occupational subcultures, the technologies of oystering have had major impacts on the oyster beds. Since the 1880s, conservation-minded scientists have implicated oystermen in the decline of oyster populations, assigning varying levels of liability to the extractive tool of choice. Tonging is labor-intensive, slow going, and less efficient than dredging and thus is often recognized as less damaging to the reef habitat. As an outsider who embraced the tonging way of life argued in 1961, "A hundred years of hand tonging alone have not depleted a single natural bed, whereas dredging has destroyed some of the finest bars in the Bay."[129] The assessment echoed that of a Maryland shellfish culturist who announced in the late 1940s that tributary bars remained relatively robust, whereas oysters in the bay's main stem – the dredgers' domain – were virtually extinct.[130] Scientific studies have since documented how long-term dredging, even when conducted under sail rather than mechanized power, ground down the three-dimensional reefs that had built up over thousands of years. While the flattening of the reefs removed navigation obstacles, it probably exacerbated major declines in water quality over the course of the twentieth century by removing large numbers of filter-feeding mollusks.[131]

Conversely, defenders of dredging have long argued that it facilitates the growth of oysters. As early as 1843, a writer announced that the Delaware Bay oyster grounds had expanded over the past generation: "This fact, strange to the mind of many, is said to be imputable to the great use of the dredging-machines, which, by dragging over a greater surface, clears the beds of impediments, and trails the oysters beyond their natural position, and thus increases the boundaries of the field." Dredging produced a less competitive, crowded environment by spreading out the bivalves and freeing them from smothering sediments: "It is said to be a false kindness to oysters to let them alone, as they did in New York to their famous 'Blue Points,' by a protecting law, which served only to have them so covered with mud as to actually destroy them."[132] Private culturists in northern states subsequently utilized dredges to stir up their beds prior to the spawning season to produce a cleaner shell surface for spat attachment.[133] In the late twentieth century, the Maryland natural resources agency adopted a version of this practice known as "bagless dredging" that leaves the oysters on the bay floor after breaking up the clumps.[134]

Generations of dredgers have viewed themselves as cultivators, an intriguing choice of words given the Maryland oystermen's rejection of private oyster farming. One captain provided a classic example of such rhetoric in 1938 when the state fishery force arrested him for taking shellfish from a prohibited area undergoing public repletion activities. The man contested the state's authority to close reserve areas by asserting that proper growth required the assistance of the dredge: "I can prove that any rock, if it is not worked, oysters never will get large. We are simply cultivating the rocks."[135] In the early twenty-first century, dredgers convinced lawmakers to permit mechanized power a few days a week by arguing that such work was needed to rescue reefs that would otherwise be buried under the loads of silt unleashed by shoreline development.[136]

The decision horrified scientists, who have often warned that excessive dredging destroys beds by removing the brood stock. Indeed, the English, French, and German oyster fisheries provided a cautionary tale for early conservationists. The rise of the European rail network fueled new demand for fresh oysters, thereby intensifying harvesting pressure: "As the best-stocked and most productive beds of Europe were quickly destroyed by unrestricted dredging, so may the hitherto seemingly exhaustless beds of the Chesapeake bay be depleted, if the present rate of dredging is continued," worried Edmonds.[137] By the 1940s, conservationists perceived the virtual disappearance of oysters from the dredging grounds of the bay bars that lay outside the tributaries as tragic testimony to the ruinous impact of the loss of brood stock. Dredgers disagreed, arguing, like commercial fishermen elsewhere, that oysters followed cycles of boom and bust according to the will of Nature and God, who provisioned the bay's species for human use.

This argument thus takes the sense of the God-given "right of free plunder" and mediates it with locally generated norms in tight-knit communities. As Ellis's study shows, "The expressed attitude concerning the water in both communities was to 'get by with whatever one can' within the limits of family responsibility and ties in Fishneck and community rules in Crab Reef."[138] Subsequent research by maritime anthropologists suggests that members of localized fishing communities the world over observe complex behavioral codes that operate to limit exploitation of common-pool assets.[139] That is not to say that the Chesapeake's "indigenous" commercial fishermen have been model conservationists or that such community norms have always operated throughout the Maryland oyster commons. But it does complicate the notion of a tragedy of the commons.

This idea also challenges a long-standing perception, held by scientists, sport fishermen, environmentalists, and other groups that claimed a stake in the bay after declines in its bounty became evident, that watermen's work is the enemy of nature. Critical analysis of this notion is important, argues White, because it undermines respect for environmentalist concern among those who make their living from nature and overlooks the reality that every type of work has environmental consequences: "There are clearly better and worse technologies, but there are no technologies that remove us from nature." Environmentalists might wish that nature remain beyond the reach of human labor, but every resident of the watershed has an inevitable impact on the air, land, and water feeding the bay.[140]

If all work inevitably embeds humans in nature, then the social fabric of the watermen's culture is interwoven with the bay and its ecology. Like their postbellum southern counterparts who labored on the land, Chesapeake watermen shared a dependence on and deep knowledge of the cyclic rhythms of the natural world, a profoundly religious outlook, and a nominal interest in capital accumulation. In petitions to state entities regarding the fishing laws, oystermen even referred to themselves as "yeomen."[141] Above all, members of both groups resisted efforts to enclose common-pool resources that sustained their livelihoods.

The comparison is not absolute, for watermen were not tied to the water in the same way that sharecroppers and tenants were bound to the soil. While state-imposed restrictions on mobility and gear restricted the oystermen's sphere, the oyster laws were not akin to the ways in which the southern debt peonage system locked practitioners into a difficult way of life.[142] Unlike disenfranchised sharecroppers, Maryland oystermen benefited from the rural domination of state legislatures that tended to prevail in southern states. The actions of Maryland legislators preserved preindustrial work patterns for commercial fishermen, regardless of race, long after the forces of industrialization reshaped the agrarian systems of the rest of the country.

Even so, the Chesapeake watermen are not a static group, frozen in time since their ancestors began following the water three centuries ago. Despite their retention of significant preindustrial features and mainstream portrayals of them as a relic group whose traditions and speech patterns hark back to the colonial era, tidewater fishing communities have adapted to technological, political, and social challenges, just as the Chesapeake Bay has evolved over the past ten millennia in response to changing geological and climatological conditions. The influx of New Englanders in the early 1800s, followed by the emergence of a national market and of large-scale dredging after the Civil War, presented great challenges to the stability of subsistence fishing and farming communities. The subsequent Oyster Wars pitted competing classes of oystermen against each other and against agents of state control. Against this bloody backdrop, the seeds for long-lasting conflicts between commercial fishermen and conservation-minded scientists were sown in the 1880s with the initiation of an intensive modernization campaign to increase oyster production and watermen's productivity. Consequently, the cultural beliefs and values of today's watermen cannot be fully explicated without an appreciation of the ways in which their fathers, grandfathers, and great-grandfathers dealt with challenges to their understanding of the bay as a working landscape.

Culture Shock

Progressive Era Science, Tidewater Tradition, and the Oyster Privatization Debate

When watermen and Chesapeake scientists first looked at each other in the late nineteenth century, they did so from opposite sides of the Industrial Revolution.[1] Scientists and their technocratic allies stood on the cutting edge of the urban-industrial frontier, whereas watermen struggled to remain rooted in the world of laissez-faire agrarianism. Most features of the older system – individualism, self-sufficiency, dependence on seasonal rhythms – did not suit the new order, which demanded professionalized punctuality, mass markets, and centralized efficiency. The effects of this clash were felt first in the cities of the North, as a new business entity, the corporation, consolidated its economic control over the manufacturing sector by exploiting unskilled workers and automating production. To produce food and raw materials for the voracious urban centers, agricultural areas became increasingly commercialized.[2] Scientists played important roles in both spheres of industrialization, whether by quantifying time-motion studies on the factory floor or by demonstrating the latest fertilizers, seed varieties, and breeding techniques at the county agricultural experiment station. Scholars have shown how the latter endeavors aided farmers yet also diminished their traditional expertise and control over the marketplace.[3] Both directly and indirectly, scientists contributed to the complex of forces underlying the integration of rural society into the modern economy.

By the time researchers came on the Chesapeake scene in the late 1870s, oystermen were already enmeshed in the new commercial networks of the industrial age. The widespread adoption of the dredge, the rise of the refrigerated railroad car, and the expansion of Baltimore's packinghouses – all made possible by northern capital – had transformed oystering from a subsistence or secondary pursuit into a full-time profession for thousands of men during the eight-month season. Although oystermen shared more in common with farmers than with urban laborers vis-à-vis contact with nature, the two classes of oyster harvesters corresponded roughly with the workers on either side of the industrial divide. Tongers were analogous to skilled independent artisans or semi-independent craft workers, the groups most threatened by mechanized manufacturing. At the other extreme, the large dredge boats, with their unskilled, immigrant crewmen and absentee owners (Baltimore or New England processing firms), replicated the separate labor and management functions of the mass-production wage system. As discussed in chapter 1, dredgers often invaded the tongers' state-sanctioned local commons regimes, prompting the two groups to battle for access to the richest reefs. But when conservation-minded scientists threatened to eradicate the most vital vestige of the preindustrial order by promoting private aquaculture, self-employed oystermen of all stripes joined forces to defeat what they perceived as the packers' efforts to control the entire estuary-based economy.

For William K. Brooks and other fishery experts, oyster leasing offered an opportunity to enrich all Marylanders by systematizing the mayhem of the harvest and precluding an "oyster famine."[4] Nature need not be exhausted, as demonstrated by the fish-culture movement, and the oyster was especially suited to artificial increase because of its immobility. Northern states and European countries that had long since overharvested their shellfish had developed new industries based on the fattening of small seed oysters taken from elsewhere (as practiced in New England) or aiding spat attachment by laying collectors beneath spawning oysters (as in France). Both methods relied on the presence of thriving natural beds, but Brooks believed that the tools of reproductive biology could be used to decrease reliance on the vagaries of nature. By controlling fertilization in the laboratory and transferring the resulting young to the rich waters of the Chesapeake, aquafarmers could reap billions of bushels. Because of the high cost of propagating bivalves and protecting them from predators, he argued that the bay states should transfer tracts of the submerged public domain to people or companies willing to invest in them. As a professor of biology at the innovative, research-oriented Johns Hopkins University, Brooks worked to convince Maryland's decision makers that private oyster farming would help his adopted state pull up the last of its decaying southern roots and enter the industrial age. He broke ground not only as a scientific policy adviser but also as a scientist-advocate for conservation in its original sense of efficient resource development. Brooks's decision to become a spokesperson for the controversial cause would affect Chesapeake scientists for decades thereafter.

Instituting private oyster culture would not be as easy as it had been in places such as Connecticut and Cancale, France. Maryland had more extensive and abundant oyster beds and a system of legislative representation that favored the oystermen. The ecological resilience of the Upper Chesapeake Bay allowed it to yield wild oysters long after other estuaries succumbed to overharvesting and pollution. As long as the protein factory kept producing without human manipulation, the incentive to sink capital into private farming ventures remained muted.

Furthermore, legislative malapportionment enabled watermen to control oyster policy through their representatives, thereby protecting themselves from the scientific and corporate forces that threatened to stamp out crucial components of their traditional way of life. Malapportionment was not unique to Maryland: well into the twentieth century, many U.S. states featured political systems in which rural residents enjoyed disproportionate power relative to urbanites. Well-organized blocs of farmers benefited greatly from the widespread use of the county as the legislative district and the numerical domination of rural counties. But commercial fishermen could benefit only in states where the number of rural waterfront counties exceeded inland jurisdictions, as in baycentric Maryland. Geographic and political circumstances thus benefited the Old Line State's oystermen at a time when scientific, economic, and political forces weakened their counterparts in Virginia and other East Coast states.

Cultivating Fish, Conserving Fish

For nineteenth-century Americans, the word *culture* conjured up images of agricultural improvement rather than our current understanding of highbrow sophistication or group-mediated traditions. For generations, human cultivation of the soil had enhanced the land by generating food and fiber. As the nation industrialized, practitioners of an exciting new realm of knowledge, the life sciences, sought to breed better plants, animals, and even humans.[5] New public and private institutions, from agricultural colleges and experiment stations to research universities and laboratories, emerged to fulfill American biology's promise of an unprecedented degree of progress. Fish culture gained popularity and prestige in the postbellum era as the aquatic adjunct to agricultural science. As several historians have argued, the fish-culture movement helped forge a conservation ethic.[6]

Pisciculturists acted on the unshakable belief that releasing vast quantities of young finfish, mollusks, and crustaceans would counteract the damage inflicted on the nation's fish stocks by dams, pollution, erosion, and overharvesting. The art and science of fish culture grew out of amateur and academic experiments in propagating fry within hatcheries or otherwise protected environments for eventual release into depleted waterways. Such goals complemented traditional agrarian attitudes regarding human ingenuity's power to restore the balance of nature and feed the nation.[7]

Having experienced fishery declines long before the later-settled regions of the country, New Englanders pioneered the hatchery movement. To restore salmon and shad runs destroyed by industrialization and thereby replenish a rural staple, northeastern states formed the nation's first permanent fish commissions and established systematized laws and enforcement regimes to protect the resulting stocks. They thus deserve credit, argues Richard Judd, for launching the conservation movement in the 1860s, a decade to a generation earlier than previous historians have suggested.[8] Moreover, the New Hampshire, Vermont, and Massachusetts legislatures initiated statewide fishery management in response to the demands of rural citizens, whose practical concerns regarding the preservation of fishing traditions often trumped scientific concerns.

As other regional fisheries became capitalized and exploited after the Civil War, declining fish populations became impossible to ignore. Thirty states, among them Maryland, had established fishery agencies by 1880. The federal government got in on the act in 1871 as a consequence of pressure regarding the decline of offshore southern New England fisheries and from the recently formed American Fish Cultural Association (later renamed the American Fisheries Society).[9] In creating the U.S. Fish Commission (USFC) to "look into the cause of depletion" and otherwise aid the fisheries, Congress made the groundbreaking acknowledgment "that the North American frontier was not, after all, boundless."[10] The USFC's first director, Smithsonian Institution assistant secretary Spencer Fullerton Baird, sponsored wide-ranging biological and ecological studies of commercial species, thereby helping to advance fish culture beyond the realm of tinkerers. His assistant, ichthyologist George Brown Goode, stressed the agency's scientific credibility at the 1883 International Fisheries Exhibition in London: "Pure and applied science have laboured together always in the service of the Fish Commission, their representatives working side by side in the same laboratories; indeed, much of the best work both in the investigation of the fisheries and in the artificial culture of fishes has been performed by men eminent as zoologists."[11] For the taxpaying public, however, the USFC's prestige flowed from its practical results in stocking streams and lakes with native and nonnative species, especially game fish. So popular were the fish-cultural operations that constituents in every corner of the country besieged their congressmen for hatcheries.[12] Artificial propagation and the introduction or "acclimatization" of exotic fish eclipsed the bureau's ecological and biological research, especially after Baird's death in 1883.

Fish culture emerged in 1850s New England in the context of a regional farm reform movement. Neither agricultural nor fisheries reformers saw any limit to humans' ability to transform the natural world and thereby achieve "a moral balance between nature and culture." The first fish commissioners also drew inspiration from "an agrarian vision of the democratic commons" as a source of food for the masses, though by the late twentieth century that egalitarian view had given way to the much narrower goal of enhancing recreational opportunities for wealthy anglers.[13] In any case, the practice of fish culture failed to replicate the agricultural processes of plowing, hoeing, and otherwise preparing the soil. Artificial propagation aimed merely to increase the number of fish to a level representing an acceptable balance between industrial and natural forces, not to improve fish habitats degraded by dams and pollution.[14] As a USFC official put it, hatchery work sought to counteract the effects of the "improvidence" of commercial fishermen; he made no mention of the damage to fish stocks and habitat caused by other human activities.[15] Pisciculture offered a simple, intuitive, technical solution that required much less political will to implement than did the fundamental changes required to reverse the root causes of fishery depletion.[16]

Proponents of oyster culture shared many of the optimistic expectations – and experienced many of the inherent limitations – of the fish-culture movement. Both groups employed agrarian analogies, with oyster conservation advocates viewing the organism's immobility as the key to authentic underwater farming. Just as yeomen cultivated the soil before they could expect crops to grow, sowing seeds only after ascertaining the suitability of the microclimate, successful oyster "planters" would have to prepare the submerged beds each season, paying attention to the condition of the bottoms, tides, temperature, and salinity gradients. (After oyster-borne typhoid outbreaks began undermining consumer confidence in the 1890s, oyster cultivators also had to heed new pollution standards.) And just as Americans have always perceived a close relationship between agriculture and landownership, oyster culturists sought to expand the U.S. legal system's protection of riparian rights.[17] If the artificial propagation of migratory fish blurred the border between settled agriculture and frontier hunting and gathering, oyster cultivation promised to shift the balance toward the more civilized – more "cultured" – end of the scale.

Farming Oysters

As the northern New England states pioneered inland fish culture, their coastal neighbors played an important role in advancing the art of oyster growing. Having depleted their natural bars by the early nineteenth century, dredge boats financed by rich seafood dealers steamed south, first to Delaware Bay and then to the Chesapeake. The dredgers returned home each spring with hundreds of thousands of bushels of undersized oysters in the shell for "bedding" in nearby salty waters for between one summer and a few growing seasons. Scientific observers argued that this process did not represent true cultivation since it produced no new organisms; it was but "a device of trade to get fresh oysters and increase their size and flavor, which adds proportionate profit in selling," analogous to the fattening of livestock.[18] Nevertheless, the procedure became known as one of the branches of oyster culture.[19] The antebellum northern oyster industry represented an imperialist enterprise, with southern estuarine states supplying the raw materials. Northern dredge boat owners evaded the Maryland and Virginia laws banning nonresidents by breaking them, by living in the state during the season, or simply by buying from local tongers. Trillions of Chesapeake oysters thus enriched Yankee capitalists by restoring, for a time, the productiveness of their industry if not their actual reefs.[20]

Oyster cultural operations raised difficult questions regarding property rights. Because seed- and shell-transplanting operations incurred significant expense, cultivators pressured their legislators for exclusive rights to the submerged lands in question, thereby challenging the traditional common-property status of tidal waters. Despite vehement protests from fishermen who had always relied on the public domain, Massachusetts, Rhode Island, Connecticut, New York, and New Jersey granted bottom leases for oyster planting by 1855.[21] However, all participants recognized the value of maintaining a common fishery by excluding natural oyster beds from private property claims. The "sacred rule of the shellfisheries" – the principle that the public should retain the right to grounds on which oysters could grow unaided by humans – acquired legal standing in New Jersey following an 1808 court case brought by harvesters accused of stealing planted oysters.[22] Other coastal states subsequently adopted this standard.[23]

Scientific efforts to improve on nature's output of oysters first attracted governmental interest on the other side of the Atlantic, in 1850s France.[24] Harvesting regulations had been on the books for almost a century, yet poor enforcement facilitated overharvesting. Threatened by France's loss of status as Europe's largest oyster producer, Emperor Napoleon III turned to naturalist Victor Coste of the College of France. Coste embarked on a fact-finding trip to Lake Fusaro, an Italian Mediterranean estuary where the locals still cultivated oysters as in the ancient Roman era. They surrounded the oyster beds with bundles of branches (fascines) to provide a surface for spat attachment during the spawning season and after two years "picked the fruits of these artificial clusters" for a short sojourn in salty water for further flavoring.[25] This method differed from the long-standing French practice of transferring eighteen-month-old oysters caught on the public sea beds to claires (artificial basins engineered to receive saltwater during spring tides), which were operated by private individuals known as *amareilleurs*. Although their work spawned no new oysters, *amareilleurs* considered themselves farmers who had to prepare the soil and maintain the claires during the two to four years of fattening and flavoring.[26] Inspired by his 1853 excursion to Fusaro and armed with scientific knowledge of the astonishing procreative powers of marine invertebrates, Coste believed that the French could do better by cultivating spawn on hard substrate and thus engaging in true oyster culture – that is, generating new organisms rather than maturing seed from elsewhere. A similar practice utilizing oyster shells had apparently been under way in New York City's East River since the 1830s or 1840s. Regardless, Coste and the French government played a pioneering role in the scientific study and publication of oyster culture efforts both in France and in other nations and sponsored the first comprehensive study of the U.S. oyster industries in 1862.[27]

To convince the *amareilleurs* and other potential cultivators of the wisdom of investing in the expensive, time-consuming process of cultivating embryonic oysters, Coste urged the emperor to initiate a grand demonstration project, restocking the depleted natural beds of the Bay of Saint-Brieuc by transplanting seed oysters to mud-free bottoms and laying down an extensive system of spat collectors. Only government could bring such an experiment to fruition, "for the domain of the seas is common property."[28] Napoleon III, an oyster aficionado, gave Coste the go-ahead, and naval personnel transplanted three million oysters from the still-thriving beds of Cancale, on the northern French coast (fig. 8).

The 1858 trials appeared to be a great success, for the fascines sprouted "bouquets of oysters" in just six months and the work revealed the importance of utilizing shells as substrate.[29] The 1858 efforts also stimulated the granting of government leaseholds (concessions) to private individuals, who set up "oyster parks" along the coastlines for artificial reproduction.[30] But despite well-publicized successes, storms destroyed the artificial beds of Saint-Brieuc during the 1860s, and the private parkers experienced "numerous and bitter disappointments," in the words of Coste's collaborator, M. de Bon, a naval officer and oyster culture

Fig. 8. Highly engineered oyster plots, Cancale, France, ca. 1890s. (Courtesy of Underwood & Underwood Glass Stereograph Collection, Archives Center, National Museum of American History, Behring Center, Smithsonian Institution.)

enthusiast. De Bon attributed the parkers' failures to their inexperience and ignorance of the natural laws governing oyster abundance. He also stressed the molluscan equivalent of the cardinal rule of real estate (location, location, location): "The artificial breeding of oysters can scarcely be successful excepting in the neighborhood of natural spawning-beds." As he looked back in 1875, when French interest in private oyster culture was picking up again as a result of the development of better methods and the adoption of nonnative species (see chapter 5), de Bon expressed cautious optimism that it would be possible "at some future time" to utilize the oyster's huge untapped quantities of progeny without relying on the natural reefs.[31]

Across the ocean, another naturalist was ready to take up that challenge. W. K. Brooks's first efforts on behalf of private oyster culture were

Fig. 9. Professor William Keith Brooks, ca. 1900. (Author's collection.)

supported not by the government but rather by his academic employer. Beginning with Brooks (fig. 9), Johns Hopkins University played a unique role in the Maryland oyster question almost from the institution's 1876 founding. "The Hopkins" was neither a traditional academy nor part of the new public land-grant college movement oriented toward agriculture and the mechanical arts. In shaping what one of its chroniclers called "the greatest adventure as yet undertaken in higher education in the United States," its first president, Daniel Coit Gilman, used the fortune amassed by merchant banker Johns Hopkins to establish a private, graduate-focused institution based on the German research model.[32] Seeking top-notch faculty, Gilman appointed Brooks on the recommendation of illustrious Harvard naturalist Louis Agassiz, under whom Brooks had completed his doctorate.[33] Brooks is known to historians of biology for his pioneering morphological research on tunicates and coelenterates and for his crucial influence on America's first biology graduate program.[34] Accordingly, some observers have viewed his practical interest in oyster cultivation as anomalous.[35] But Gilman and the Hopkins Board of Trustees would not have supported Brooks's work if it failed to advance the fledgling institution's interests.

Research on oysters and oyster culture served the university in ways both obvious and subtle. First, it advanced basic knowledge of the cutting-edge fields of experimental embryology and physiology, thereby boosting the school's reputation for world-class research. It also promoted science-based shellfish culture at a time when both national governments and prestigious scientific associations called for increasing the supply of food fish as a scientific commitment to humanity. Third, Brooks's oyster work promoted the new university as a benefactor of the state's economy, thereby generating favorable exposure in the local press and community. Finally, it demonstrated the institution's relevance to what might be called its first corporate sponsor, the Baltimore and Ohio Railroad. Johns Hopkins himself donated fifteen thousand shares of company stock to endow the school, and the railroad's longtime president, John Garrett, and his family were major contributors.[36] Oysters represented valuable cargo for the B&O; thus, when its chief attorney joined Brooks in promoting privatized oyster culture in the late 1880s, many oystermen suspected that the two institutions had hatched a plan to take over the Chesapeake's best oyster grounds.

Brooks found such ideas shocking, for like other professionalizing scientists of the Darwinian era, he sought to show the public the importance of secular research, especially in biology. To that end, he wrote for popular science journals and lectured to local lay audiences on controversial issues regarding evolution, heredity, and development.[37] Given his interest in popularization, it is not surprising that Brooks sought to apply his expertise to a major economic problem facing his adopted state. Although he was under no obligation to conduct applied research of economic importance (a primary goal of agricultural scientists employed by land-grant colleges and experiment stations), Brooks considered it his duty to contribute "to the welfare of society by doing the best possible as a trained specialist."[38]

As a researcher, Brooks's work bridged the transition between the descriptive natural history studies of the nineteenth century and the dynamic, experimental biology that would become "the most active, the most relevant" science of the twentieth century.[39] A former student eulogized in 1908 that "Brooks was not an experimenter" but rather "a recorder of nature and a philosophic reasoner about the outside universe as it appeared to his consciousness."[40] But even if Brooks failed to meet the standards of experimentalism that had come to prevail in academic biology by the early twentieth century, he was no slouch when it came to manipulating and controlling nature. A deep appreciation for the value of experimentalism pervaded his oyster work as well as his teaching. Several of his graduate students became leaders in their fields, in both applied shellfisheries biology and in the more prestigious university-based life sciences.[41]

While experiencing great success as a scientific popularizer and professor, Brooks never lost the desire to modernize the oyster industry. As his former student Edwin G. Conklin recalled, "His absorption in this work was so complete that he talked oysters in season and out of season. The story is current that at a university reception a society woman attempted to engage him in small talk; he listened mutely for a while, and then was heard to say, 'Madam, the Maryland oyster is being exterminated.'"[42] Another student, Ethan Allen Andrews, reminisced that Brooks "became so determined to see the state enter upon the enjoyment of the fruits of his labors that the oyster question and its ultimate solution played no small part" in keeping him from accepting enticing offers elsewhere, including the high-status directorship of the Marine Biological Laboratory in Woods Hole, Massachusetts.[43] Andrews perceived his former professor as "temperamentally more at home in the non-nervous community of his adoption than in the bustle of the strenuous life of denser populations," a polite way of saying that the slower pace of Maryland living suited the easygoing, tobacco-chewing Ohioan.[44]

Brooks may have identified the oyster problem as a key issue for southern progressivism, which encompassed several reform movements promoting economic development and social uplift.[45] Because Johns Hopkins University became an intellectual gateway for southern go-getters, Brooks probably encountered many faculty members and students grappling with the challenges facing the New South. The Hopkins history department in particular gained fame for producing a generation of southern intellectuals that promoted economic modernization and sectional reconciliation yet also denounced Reconstruction as a case study in overbearing federal authority.[46] Somewhat similar themes pervaded

Brooks's approach to the oyster question, which featured a decades-long educational campaign, as he called it, to convince Marylanders of the wisdom of cultivating the Chesapeake's untapped reserves of "imbedded wealth" via private rather than governmental enterprise.[47]

Science Comes to the Chesapeake

Inspired by Agassiz's famous command to "study nature, not books," Brooks inaugurated the Chesapeake Zoological Laboratory (CZL) in the summer of 1878.[48] The CZL was not a fixed facility but rather an annual outing of graduate students and faculty eager to escape Baltimore's stifling humidity and obtain fresh marine creatures that would shed light on evolution and taxonomy.[49] Brooks's model was the summer school founded by Agassiz on Cape Cod's Penikese Island, the first U.S. seaside laboratory, which operated from 1873 to 1898.[50] Despite its name, the only Chesapeake locales in which the CZL convened during the decade of its existence were Fort Wool, Virginia (1878 and 1879), and Crisfield, Maryland (1879 and 1883). Other sessions took place in North Carolina, Bermuda, and Jamaica, where participants studied a range of estuarine and oceanic organisms.[51] The CZL fulfilled both institutional and individual missions for Brooks, attracting students to the fledgling Hopkins biology department and providing him with material for studies that inspired several of his books. The Hopkins researchers probably had only minimal interactions with Eastern Shore locals, as evidenced by Brooks's later advocacy of private oyster propagation, which disregarded tidewater hostility to both aquaculture and the withdrawal of the public domain.

Frustration filled the CZL's first session, though all was not lost. In a makeshift lab in the unfinished military base at Fort Wool, Brooks and his collaborators searched in vain for pregnant oysters. They had assumed that the species inhabiting the Atlantic coastline of North America resembled its French/British/Dutch cousin, *Ostrea edulis,* in which fertilization and early development took place within the parental shell. Try as they might, however, the Baltimore embryologists could not duplicate findings regarding the European flat oyster. Yet their work caught the attention of the Maryland Fish Commission, a new agency charged with augmenting the state's declining fish populations through artificial propagation.[52] Eager to ascertain the food requirements and growth rates of the renowned Chesapeake shellfish, the commissioners offered better facilities and some funds in return for a commitment to continue the research the following summer. It was a great deal for Brooks, who made the emerging seafood center of Crisfield the locale for the CZL's second session in 1879.

Despite Crisfield's proximity to the rich oyster reefs of Tangier and Pocomoke Sound, what most excited Brooks was the Fish Commission's well-equipped barge floating in the harbor. There he spent two months conducting unprecedented experiments in the artificial fertilization of oysters and examining more than a thousand adult specimens without finding a single fertilized egg or embryo anywhere inside the shell. Though the swampy town's brutal mosquitoes forced him to cut short the academic session, Brooks's results suggested a crucial difference between the European flat oyster and the species indigenous to the East and Gulf Coasts. The eggs of the American Atlantic species underwent development not within the parental shell but rather in open water, which made the process of fertilization much more amenable to human manipulation.[53] Fertilized eggs could be created simply by mixing the sex cells of spawning oysters in a watch glass, and the resulting embryos could be reared to viability in the protected environment of the lab, as opposed to the violent world of Darwinian nature, where the majority of spawn lost out in the cruel struggle for existence. Brooks failed to keep larvae alive beyond six days, for he always wound up throwing out the baby oysters with the rancid water, no matter how fine the straining cloth. But he presumed that that technological glitch would soon be overcome and later hailed his work on artificial oyster fertilization as "one of the most important discoveries of the last fifty years."[54] While self-aggrandizing, the statement demonstrated Brooks's absolute conviction in the power of science to improve human well-being.

Others agreed with Brooks's grandiose assessment, viewing his discovery through the lens of outrageous nationalism. Delegates at the 1883 International Fisheries Exhibition in London spoke of the "more adventurous" character of the young American oyster. The *New York World* praised the upstart species for refusing "to be tied to its mother's apron strings, as the European oyster is tied." Hopkins physiologist H. Newell Martin provided the most jingoistic judgment, blaming his colleague's initial failure on his "too great reliance upon the natural history of the oyster of the effete monarchies of the Old World."[55] The popular and scientific reaction to Brooks's discovery and his claim regarding misleading European research revealed a deep American desire to play a commanding role on the world scientific stage.[56]

Despite its anti-European slant, Brooks's report, "Development of the American Oyster," sparked international acclaim. France's Société d'Acclimation, a scientific society dedicated to domesticating exotic animals and plants, awarded Brooks its 1881 medal. Ernest Ingersoll of the U.S. Fish Commission quoted long sections of the report in his series on the nation's fisheries, completed in conjunction with the 1880 census. Such exposure established Brooks as a world authority on oyster development and opened new doors at home.[57] The ecstatic Maryland fish commissioners publicized his work to the governor and funded studies in artificial oyster breeding at public hatching stations for several years thereafter.[58] While Brooks did not participate in these investigations, he accepted an appointment from the General Assembly to chair a commission investigating recent allegations of overdredging made by Lieutenant Francis Winslow II of the U.S. Coast and Geodetic Survey. The decision both altered Brooks's life and established important patterns for the relationships governing ensuing generations of Chesapeake scientists and watermen.

The Oyster Commission

As Brooks and his team struggled to find oyster embryos during the first CZL session, a bigger study was under way nearby. In response to concerns that the 1865 legalization of dredging had already eroded many of the Tangier and Pocomoke Sound reefs straddling the Maryland-Virginia border, the U.S. Coast and Geodetic Survey agreed to apply its topographical expertise to the problem. Charged with aiding navigation by charting the nation's coastal waters, the agency played a crucial role in the development of privatized oyster fisheries. Because oyster-producing states restricted private cultivation to barren bottoms, accurate maps distinguishing productive areas soon became "a *sine qua non* of oyster culture."[59] But that was not the goal of this first survey. Lieutenant Winslow and his team interviewed industry members and made painstaking measurements to ascertain the reefs' limits, productiveness, and ability to withstand dredging and environmental changes. For each bed, they dragged a dredge across the bottom to determine the number of oysters per square yard, the ratio of living oysters to empty shells, and the ratio of mature to immature oysters. Winslow concluded from this painstaking work that the beds had been fished beyond their capacity to reproduce and that their total failure was thus "but a question of time."[60] The journal *Science* praised the team for establishing baseline figures and a quantitative means for measuring "future decrease."[61] The Winslow method remained the dominant means of determining oyster abundance until the turn of the millennium.[62]

The Winslow report worried Maryland legislators enough to appoint an expert to look into the problem, but that concern did not translate into financial support. This presented Brooks and his fellow commissioners, Oyster Navy captain James Waddell and tidewater politician William Henry Legg, with a serious problem. Even in 1882, hiring inspection crews, boats, and assistants was an expensive proposition. The resources needed to complete the job came from the governor, who tapped his emergency fund, and Hopkins administrators, who granted Brooks two summers of paid leave, prompting him to call the commission work "a gift from the University to the State."[63] Like many bureaucratic bodies, the state legislature had done the minimum necessary to appease critics and appear proactive: it appointed a blue-ribbon committee to write a report with nonbinding recommendations.

The legislature's stinginess precluded a full survey of the Maryland oyster grounds. It had taken Winslow nearly two years just to survey the Tangier-Pocomoke region, so Brooks and his partners settled for a hurried inspection of fifty-nine of the largest bars, a fraction of the more than nine hundred that would eventually be mapped.[64] Following Winslow's protocol, the commission's unnamed laborers dredged and measured 30,000 oysters from 326 dredge hauls that covered 121,000 square yards of bottom. The data revealed an average of 1 oyster per 4.25 square yards, as opposed to Winslow's figure of 1 per 3 square yards. As the report's chief author, Brooks concluded that the Maryland reefs had lost a staggering 39 percent of their value within three years, thereby justifying "the worst forebodings" of destruction.[65]

Yet he did not blame overharvesting. Unlike Winslow (and Coste a generation earlier), Brooks viewed overfishing as a symptom of a basic economic imbalance. In his blunt words, "THE DEMAND HAS

OUTGROWN THE SUPPLY." Because consumer demand had taxed the beds "far beyond their natural productive powers," he saw only one solution: to increase their yield by artificial means.[66] Science-based private cultivation would resolve the disparity between supply and demand, modernize the fishery, and bestow the fruits of capitalism on the impoverished tidewater region.

Maryland had had oyster-leasing laws on the books as far back as 1830, though few people profited from those measures. The most recent act, passed in 1867, allowed individuals to appropriate five acres of barren bottom. Most of the leaseholders chose inshore areas close to their homes, which tended to be in rivers where the water did not flow fast enough to distribute larvae. Lacking scientific guidance and the patience or means to try out other microenvironments, many lease-holders assumed that cultivation on anything but a natural bed was futile and thus allowed their leases to lapse. Poaching was another huge disincentive, for oystermen rejected the idea that private property rights applied to the bay, and the Oyster Navy had its hands full policing the public domain.[67] Rather than highlighting the reasons for those failures, Brooks sought to win over tidewater residents by pointing to the success of northeastern states that had provided more extensive legal protections for private oyster planting.

Connecticut offered the most impressive case of leasing success. In 1855, the state began granting two submerged acres of unproductive bottom to individuals. Applicants evaded the antimonopoly spirit of the law by taking out grants in the names of friends and family members and eventually realized that artificial beds could be created by distributing shells and mature oysters. When no more lots remained in the vicinity of New Haven Harbor, packer Henry C. Rowe, flush with the fortune he had earned by shipping three thousand bushels of Chesapeakes to oyster-starved London in 1872, "inaugurated a new era in American oyster culture" by reshelling several dozen acres in the deep waters of Long Island Sound.[68] Despite violent opposition from public-domain oystermen, the powerful Rowe convinced the 1881 legislature to allow both resident individuals and corporations to obtain and sell an unlimited number of acres, though the state retained the common-property status of areas that had harbored natural beds within the past ten years. The ensuing expansion of private operations produced so many seed oysters that growers no longer had to rely on southern imports. In 1879,

Brooks had proposed the same measures to Maryland lawmakers, but, he complained, "the recommendation met with no attention, as it was looked upon as the *unpractical* view of a student." In the wake of Connecticut's success, he hoped, "our people may perhaps be able to learn from the *practical* example of Connecticut what they would not learn on the authority of a scientific paper."[69] Brooks was not the only scientist awed by the success of the deep-water cultivators. During the mid-1880s, Connecticut attracted national attention for "putting into practice the best system of oyster-culture in the world," as Goode asserted in a not-so-subtle swipe at the French.[70]

For Brooks, as for other reformers in the decades after Reconstruction, the northern states provided a model for the New South. Connecticut Yankees had demonstrated their superior commercial and intellectual fitness by applying modern agricultural techniques to the oyster fishery. By contrast, Chesapeake harvesters remained stuck in the past, impoverishing themselves by exporting valuable seed oysters for immediate gain. In a critique exemplifying the ideology of Social Darwinism, Brooks contended that adhering to the old tidewater ways would render Marylanders as pitiable as the vanquished Native Americans:

> It is not in the spirit of harsh criticism, but in the hope that our people may be awakened to their own interest, that we point out the similarity between the views of our people and their legislators and the opinions of savage races. We live in a highly civilized age, and if we fail to grasp its spirit we shall go to the wall before the oyster cultivators of the Northern States, just as surely as the Indians have been exterminated by the whites. We cannot resist the progress of events, but we can control it if we will be wise in time.[71]

Brooks employed sharp rhetoric to shake up the complacency he perceived outside his circle. If the industry did not adapt to changing conditions – excess demand and insufficient supply – Maryland would lose its status as the nation's top oyster producer.

Brooks recognized that the shift to greater private property rights could not occur overnight, though his caution did not necessarily arise out of concern for the stress that such a radical change would impose on the oystermen and their communities.[72] For one thing, no one knew the monetary value of the oyster grounds, which had yet to be surveyed in their entirety; therefore, he noted, the state would be unwise to "part with the public property without a proper return." Moreover,

Marylanders lacked aquacultural experience. To address both deficiencies, he called on the legislature to establish a state oyster farm, similar to Coste and Napoleon III's French restocking project, to be maintained for five years in a highly visible place, the waters bordering Annapolis, the state capital. In the interim, Maryland should close exhausted beds to give them a rest, compel packers and oystermen to return shells to the bay (and preferably to the beds from which they were taken), prohibit the sale of immature bivalves, professionalize the marine police force, and do a better job of enforcing the license laws, among other actions. Of course, these were but temporary expedients. The only long-term "remedy for the evil" of undersupply, Brooks insisted, was private cultivation.[73]

While Brooks looked to the legislature to enact his recommendations, he emphasized the government's inability to act as a permanent oyster-farming overseer. Publicly funded organizations such as the Maryland Fish Commission could undertake scientific management of migratory fish that ignored political boundaries, Brooks thought, "because it is not within the power of individuals to improve [such fish], or increase their numbers or value." But oysters were immobile and therefore "as subject to improvement by cultivation as a potato." Hence, "the common right to the beds must in time give way to private enterprise, just as surely as the common right to the natural products of the soil has given way before the progress of civilization." The most effective way to develop the industry was by redefining the commons as private real estate, since he considered "personal interest . . . the strongest motive which can exist to prevent the needless destruction of property."[74] Dividing up the oyster grounds into private holdings would both increase production and obviate the need for protective laws and the expensive Oyster Navy by encouraging practitioners to practice conservation of their own volition.

Brooks made one concession to the drawbacks of privatization when he admitted that private interests lacking "sound education" had failed to conserve stocks of eastern timber.[75] Indeed, the exploitation of North American forests sparked outrage during the 1870s and 1880s, both among preservationists such as John Muir who wanted to safeguard scenic wilderness landscapes from development and among Gifford Pinchot and his fellow utilitarian conservationists who sought to use the country's resources on a more efficient, equitable basis. Whereas western homesteaders opposed efforts to restrict the disposal of public lands, scientific foresters, often with corporate backing, perceived stricter government regulation as the key to reversing the social, economic, and environmental damage wrought by private entities concerned only with short-range profits. In the 1890s and early 1900s, Congress established a nationwide system of forest reserves to promote science-based management, which included fire suppression, tree planting, and long-term timber sales.[76] Accordingly, by advocating the withdrawal of oyster grounds from the Chesapeake commons, Brooks and other fishery experts went against the grain of the broader utilitarian conservation movement and its core message that comprehensive resource development required financial and organizational means that only governments could provide.

Private oyster culture thus both upheld and contradicted aspects of the Progressive Era conservation ethic. It espoused the ideals of efficiency, legislative remedies for social problems, and technical expertise over political efficacy, but it also undercut Progressive ideals by elevating private over public solutions, promoting the concentration of wealth at the expense of the greatest good for the greatest number, and rejecting government involvement at precisely the time that state and federal agencies intensified their commitment to implementing forest management, reclamation, and other broad-scale conservation projects.

One of the most revolutionary recommendations of Brooks's report was buried in the back. Brooks proposed eliminating a revered principle of the public trust doctrine as observed in most oyster-producing states of the northeastern United States and Western Europe – the idea that the public's access to natural beds should be safeguarded, while private entities should be allowed to gain title only to nonproductive tidal bottoms.[77] He justified breaking with the standard in the name of pragmatism. Reefs in other coastal bodies, like the Connecticut portion of Long Island Sound, covered less ground than those of the Chesapeake Bay – fifty-seven hundred acres versus some two hundred thousand. Moreover, whereas the Connecticut beds were clustered together, Maryland's were so diffuse that "there is scarcely a spot where some oysters have not at some time existed," especially since dredging had extended the reefs by breaking up and dispersing shells and oysters.[78] Environmental forces, from storm surges to erosion, could also shift the limits of the beds. Therefore, adhering to the old distinction between natural and artificial beds would impede the beneficial work of private cultivators by requiring endless rounds of surveying, during which the natural beds of the public domain would continue their inevitable descent into ruin.

The shifting boundaries of the oyster beds made it difficult to apply land-based notions of property to oyster bottoms.[79] In an 1881 court case from Dorchester County, on Maryland's lower Eastern Shore, Judge Charles Goldsborough tried to resolve the legal ambiguity regarding the definition of a natural bed by ruling that areas containing only "moderate" numbers of oysters—too few to be profitable to commercial fishermen yet capable of being increased by cultivators—could not be considered natural: "Land cannot be said to be a natural oyster bar or bed merely because oysters are scattered here and there upon it, and because, if planted, they will readily live and thrive there; but wherever the natural growth is so thick and abundant that the public resort to it for a livelihood, it is a natural bar or bed . . . and cannot be . . . appropriated by an individual."[80] The Goldsborough definition, which relied on "the history of the bar [as relayed by oystermen] rather than upon a scientific determination of its present condition," would enjoy long standing in Maryland tidewater county courts, which used it to support protests of proposed leaseholds.[81] In Connecticut, the 1881 legislature modified the definition to appease both the leasing lobby and the oystermen struggling to maintain the commons: "In order that no grievance may lie with the 'natural-growthers' [public-domain oystermen], no ground in Connecticut can be designated that has at any time for 10 years previous been a natural bed in the sense of the above-mentioned decision."[82] Brooks took exception to such a long interval because the area would lose its value; he believed that it would be better to "throw open" the natural beds to private cultivators before overfishing took its toll. However, because doing so might be politically impossible, he offered a fallback plan: "If public sentiment condemns this course, the next best plan is to construct . . . maps showing the areas which are to be legally regarded as natural beds, and to permit private oyster culture on all other areas."[83] In the interim, the educational campaign to wear down resistance to the sacred shellfisheries rule of the public trust doctrine would have to continue.

Brooks recognized a public interest in maintaining some state control over the resource and in preventing monopolization. The submerged grounds should be leased rather than sold outright, at least in the early stages, but "the chief danger which is to be avoided is the monopoly by a few persons of the oyster area." Though Brooks glossed over the consolidation of capital in the Connecticut deep-water oyster farming industry, an 1889 study outlined its rapid transformation: "Fifteen years ago it is said there were few persons engaged in this fishery who were possessed of $10,000. Now one would scarcely be classed as a successful cultivator the value of whose oyster property alone does not reach $20,000." At a time when the average oysterman made $300 a year, seventeen Connecticut firms had more than $10,000 invested in oyster property, eighteen had invested more than $20,000, fifteen topped $50,000, several exceeded $200,000, and one had more than $400,000.[84] Corporate mergers and acquisitions soon inundated lesser players. By 1894, Rowe, the most successful Connecticut planter, had amassed fifteen thousand acres in Long Island Sound and employed three steamers capable of harvesting four thousand bushels a day. As he boasted at a pro-leasing conference convened by the Richmond, Virginia, Chamber of Commerce, "When I made my first purchases [of deep-water lots], my neighbors were wont to call me a **** fool; since then, they have changed their views and use the epithet of **** monopolist."[85]

So how could robber barons be kept off the Chesapeake? Brooks's solution to avoiding monopolies was to allow every Marylander to hold a five-acre lot for small-scale farming in the shallows, an enterprise he asserted would require little capital.[86] In this way, everyone could hypothetically share in the profits of aquaculture, though he provided no details on how to implement this plan or whether uninterested parties should be compensated. Perhaps he included this inchoate idea to offer a veneer of equity, for another of his proposals seemed destined to replicate the rise of big business in the industrializing economy. Brooks urged the legislature to implement legal protections for cultivating the mollusk in the farthest depths of the bay. This was, of course, the key feature of the highly capitalized and consolidated Connecticut industry. Although he did not dwell on this point, Brooks admitted that deep-water cultivation could be carried out on a large scale only by individuals or corporations willing to invest "great sums of money."[87] For tidewater residents, any sum was too much.

Tidal Waves of Backlash

Only one of the other two members of the Oyster Commission agreed with Brooks. The third member, Legg, a legislator from the tidewater county of Queen Anne, offered an outraged minority report that disavowed his colleagues' conclusions, articulating what became the two main criticisms lodged by the antileasers or antiplanters. According to Legg, "The oysters of the State belong to the people of the State, and the true policy of the State is to guard and protect our oyster grounds for the benefit of the citizens." His language echoed that of the Populists and Progressives who sought to curb the corporate excesses and injustices of the Gilded Age:

> The citizens of the State have the right to ask and expect that legislation be in the interest of the many, not of the few; in the interest of the weak rather than the strong, and to demand that this vast public domain – the oyster grounds – shall be held now and for all time to come, as it ever has been held, as a great commons, to be used in common by the citizens of the State under such rules and regulations as the State may prescribe, and not sold to a few capitalists, thereby making the rich richer and the poor poorer.

Oystermen rejected both the privatization of the oyster grounds and the opposite extreme on the scale of property rights, a laissez-faire commons. Instead, they favored a regulated, state-defined commons regime in which all harvesters played on a level field. Legg's claim that leasing violated the rights of Marylanders echoed the main argument that oystermen would make for decades thereafter: the natural oyster beds belonged to the people, not to corporate monopolies.[88]

The Chesapeake equivalent of the robber barons, the business leaders who exerted so much control over the Gilded Age economy, were the seafood packers. Northern processing firms, especially those from Connecticut, were responsible for the hundreds of dredge boats that raided the Lower Chesapeake Bay in the early 1800s. To squeeze extra profit from the imported seed oysters, they pioneered simple forms of oyster culture. Packers also stored mature oysters on underwater plots to wait until prices improved, such as after gluts subsided or during cold snaps that froze in the fleet. Above all, processors sought a more stable, predictable supply.[89] Investing in the development of submerged areas for artificial cultivation thus made perfect sense to well-capitalized packing firms. It came as no surprise that they joined scientists as prominent advocates of private oyster culture and that when Maryland allowed limited leasing in the early twentieth century, packers became its dominant practitioners.

Small-scale harvesters perceived private oyster culture as a threat because it would enable packers to exert even more control over the tidewater economy. The largest packing firms built up vertically integrated empires to control the source of raw materials, the processing and distribution of the final product, and the workers themselves. Rowe, "the powerful oyster pasha who controlled the fate of thousands with the ease and ruthlessness of an Ottoman prince," extended his reach into Maryland in 1880 and soon controlled about a hundred dredge boats with seven hundred crewmen.[90] Another firm, the Tilghman Packing Company of Avalon Island, Maryland, owned a cannery, a fish meal operation, a machine shop, farmland (to grow vegetables that could be canned when oysters were out of season), the homes and general store where the company's shuckers lived and shopped, and an ice machine, fuel station, and rental slips for supplying the community's watermen. Recalled one old-timer, "If you didn't get your gas from them, they wouldn't buy your catch from you."[91] William Valliant of Bellevue, Maryland, presided over a comparable empire in which "the money went around in a circle" from his wallet to the local shuckers and oystermen and back to his grocery store and gas station.[92]

The largest Baltimore-based packinghouses possessed their own dredging fleets. During the 1892–93 season, for example, only 324 of Maryland's 719 licensed dredge boats were owned entirely or largely by their captains.[93] The rest were skippered by men who lacked the means to build or buy their own vessels, as in the impoverished community of Deal Island.[94] Captains who owned their own skipjacks were most likely to live in relatively prosperous communities with strong religious and social institutions that valued hard work.[95] But even self-employed tongers and dredgers had to buy gas and groceries, leaving them vulnerable to dealers' demands.

The idea of dredge boat captains as packinghouse employees is difficult to reconcile with the Chesapeake watermen's venerable image as the personification of independence. But in the oyster industry's heyday, processing firms functioned as the crucial link in the commodity chain that connected the bottom of the bay with the raw-bar saloons of the urban North, West, and Midwest. The packer's century ended only in the 1970s, when the Chesapeake seafood distribution system shifted to one in which many watermen sold their catch at the docks to truckers, who in turn sold the mollusks to processors and restaurants.[96] Until then, as oystermen saw it, packers wielded far too much power even without an aquacultural industry biased toward their interests.

Harvesters thus were greatly relieved when the Oyster Commission's proposals imploded. As is often the case, major policy change became most feasible in the wake of a dramatic disaster that fixed public attention on a particular issue.[97] But the harvest following the publication of the Brooks report was anything but unfortunate. The 1884–85 season yielded fifteen million bushels, the highest in Maryland history. Assuming that the bay had thrown down a triumphant rebuke to Brooks's claim that the Maryland oyster faced "imminent danger of complete destruction," state legislators felt no need to act on the suggestions they had requested three years earlier.[98] As Brooks student Caswell Grave sarcastically observed years later, "The *patient* was thought to have completely recovered from its slight indisposition, and the *doctor* was dismissed without thanks for his diagnosis."[99] Privatization advocate John K. Cowen claimed that the report was "too advanced, too bold, too thorough for our rulers, and [so] they quietly pigeon-holed it."[100] But considering the oystermen's opposition to leasing and their disproportionate legislative influence, it would have been impossible for the assembly to act on Brooks's radical proposals following such an upswing. Even the strong-arm packer-planters of the northern states obtained favorable legislation only after the prolonged declines of their fisheries.

Having devoted two summers to the thankless work of the commission, Brooks must have been happy to resume the CZL expeditions far from the actual Chesapeake. But he still sought to prove the feasibility of artificial oyster propagation. One vexing question involved the difficulty of rearing embryos past the earliest stages of development, a problem his team eventually solved by adding macerated shell, which provided calcium carbonate for faster growth and extended survival.[101] A French naturalist beat him to the next challenge. Using the Portuguese oyster, which like the American species underwent fertilization in open waters rather than the parental shell, G. Bouchon-Brandeley developed a practical method of rearing oysters from artificially fertilized eggs in claire ponds.[102] Despite an article in the American journal *Science* claiming that "most scientific men harbor a little distrust of French work," Brooks was thrilled.[103] As he enthused in the CZL report, "Our own share of the work is therefore exactly what we should wish: the discovery of a new scientific truth, which has, in the hands of practical economists, contributed to the welfare of mankind."[104] Brooks's language conveyed the message that his findings would enrich neither him nor his institution.

Yet beneath the surface lurked a deeper ambivalence about the propriety of practical work. In a letter to Hopkins president Gilman, Brooks noted his hope "that some one will have energy enough to put . . . into practical use" the results of his 1885 experiments with floating oyster culture devices during the 1885 CZL session in Beaufort, North Carolina. Stressing his proper duties as a university researcher, he continued, "I shall write and publish my results this fall, and if no one else takes it up I shall repeat my experiments next year, and rear a few oysters for the market, keeping a strict account of the dollars and cents. I think though that the advantages of the plan will be so obvious that I shall not need to do this myself."[105] In the official report, however, Brooks adopted a sterner tone: "Engagement in business projects is no part of the office of a university, and I feel that the experiments of the past summer have brought the subject of oyster culture to a point where its further development should be left to the people who are most interested."[106] Victorian propriety demanded that academic scientists not profit from commercial applications of their knowledge.

To Brooks's relief, nonscientific men did take up the cause, though not quite as he envisioned. Maryland's hostile political climate prevented entrepreneurs from investing in the new technologies needed for such a venture and especially in shellfish hatcheries. However, an up-and-coming player threw himself into the effort to bring about the legislative changes needed to foster an aquaculture industry. At the time he became involved in the oyster question, Cowen had served for several years as the general counsel for the Baltimore and Ohio Railroad.[107] In his quest to secure legislation favorable to the B&O, Cowen had spent countless hours in the halls of Annapolis. During the 1890s, he parlayed this experience into a term in the U.S. Congress (giving up his seat to become president of the B&O) and used his power and fund-raising skills to help the Republican Party win the governorship and Baltimore mayorship for the first time since the Civil War.[108] "There are many men in the State who consider John K. Cowen the intellectual superior of any man who ever lived in Maryland," wrote *Baltimore Sun* political analyst Frank Kent, who seemed to agree that had Cowen desired, he could have become the president of the United States.[109] Leasing advocates no doubt welcomed him to the cause.

However, despite Cowen's famous resurrection of the Republicans in a fiercely Democratic state, even he could not overcome the antileasing forces. In fact, his participation did irreparable damage to the cause. Operating with little government oversight, the Gilded Age railroads personified the worst of big business, alienating "a remarkable range of Americans" through their manipulative practices. The B&O in particular stoked the flames of working-class resentment by cutting wages and using trigger-happy troops to restore order during the strikes of 1877.[110] In an era in which railroads benefited tremendously from lobbyists such as Cowen, he was bound to be a target. The fact that railroads played an instrumental role in the growth of the oyster industry only heightened the oystermen's suspicion that big corporations had sinister plans to transform the bay commons into vast underwater plantations.

Cowen made a splashy entrance onto the stage of oyster politics in 1889. Why he decided to do so is not clear, especially since the late 1880s were a period of financial and organizational turmoil for the B&O. Four years had passed since the state's huge harvest had made Brooks look like a fool. But landings were again dropping. Cowen wrote a long, eloquent harangue published on the front page of the *Baltimore Sun,* a privilege for which he probably paid. The letter was then reprinted in booklet form with the catchy title *The Maryland Oyster and His Political Enemies.*[111]

Cowen's impassioned essay linked the practice of private oyster culture with the theme of civilization. He attacked the state's oyster policy as "economic barbarism" in need of a shot of scientific enlightenment, arguing that "every civilized State" that had eliminated public ownership of at least part of its oyster fishery had profited. When the Maryland oysterman acquiesced, "he will have passed from the precarious life of the 'trapper' and 'hunter' to that of civilized man, with his own vine and fig tree." Cowen extended his critique to the ban on dredging in county waters, which he compared to outlawing the reaper and self-binder in favor of the sickle and hand rake, emblems of hopeless backwardness. Rather than legislating technological inefficiency, the General Assembly should develop the oyster supply through leasing. Cowen also defended Brooks against the charge that he was "only a scientific student and not a 'practical man' – simply a 'theorist.'" In reality, the state legislature needed more men like Brooks: "I would like to see a few people among our leaders who did not know anything about winning elections, and did know something about the elementary principles of political economy."[112] Such calls for experts in governmental affairs became a hallmark of the era of professionalization.

Legislators ignored Cowen's critique, but as harvests continued to drop, some kind of action had to be taken. Like previous assemblies, the 1890 legislature sought to arrest depletion through restrictive measures. But it did so in a novel way, passing one of the nation's first laws requiring harvesters to return immature oysters to the beds from which they came. The cull law required that specimens less than two and a half inches wide (about two and half years old) be thrown back immediately to serve another year or two as brood stock. Although such small oysters generated much less profit than the plump "selects" demanded by the raw-bar trade, they fueled the growth of the northern seed-planting industry. Oystermen facilitated the loss of brood stock by selling them to planters for peanuts, which Brooks likened to "mowing down young wheat to make hay."[113] With the return of mediocre harvests, the cull law offered a way for politicians to appear proactive without challenging the fishery's common-property status. Maryland was a pioneer in this matter simply because it made no sense for states with extensive private planting to protect undersized oysters, since they would be bedded until they reached market size.[114] Committed to the common fishery yet refusing to authorize public repletion efforts, the Old Line State had to find other remedies.

But stemming declines required that any law be enforced, and enforcement remained grossly inadequate. As Cowen asked, how could the fifteen-ship Oyster Navy police eight thousand tonging boats, eight hundred large dredging vessels, and twelve hundred small dredge boats?[115] Oystermen had few incentives to conserve brood stock because picking out undersized oysters took extra time and demand for them remained strong. Even petite mollusks, while not suitable for the raw bar trade, could be canned for use in soups, stews, and stuffing.[116] "If anyone doubts this, let him go to the piles of shells around the steam packing-houses," wrote a veteran oysterman to the *Baltimore American* several months after the law's passage; there "he will find millions of shells under two-and-one-half inches."[117] Nor did it make economic sense for packers without leaseholds to return the shucked shells to serve as spat collectors, since they could be sold to the lime, chicken grit, and road-building industries.[118]

The packers provoked oystermen by convening a mass meeting headlined by Brooks and Cowen. The harvest had fallen so much that packinghouses were shutting down or importing product from as far away as North Carolina.[119] "Is it reform or ruin?" asked the *Baltimore American.*[120] To answer the question, more than two dozen Baltimore packing firms invited four distinguished advocates of private oyster culture to speak on 18 March 1891 at the Academy of Music.[121] The palatial hall was not neutral ground, since it served as the unofficial auditorium for Johns Hopkins University. Fifteen years earlier, Thomas Henry Huxley, a brilliant English scientist and notorious Darwinian, had delivered the new institution's first public lecture without benefit of an introductory prayer, sparking cries that Hopkins was a den of irreligiousness, a memory that no doubt riled devout residents of tidewater Maryland who read newspaper accounts of the conference.[122]

The meeting provided a forceful reiteration of the pro-privatization agenda. Cowen praised Brooks and his hosts for perceiving the truth despite the darkness enveloping the oystermen and their allies: "The danger apparent to the distinguished scientist twelve years ago, is the danger realized by the practical oyster packer of to-day." But the attendees did not adopt Brooks's perspective on the root cause of declining harvests. Rather than citing a disparity between supply and demand, they placed the sole blame on "the defective condition of our laws relating to oysters, which do nothing to encourage their artificial propagation."[123] Accordingly, the packers joined scientists in calling for a liberalization of the leasing provisions.

Opponents organized a rally in the Baltimore port neighborhood of Canton on 30 April 1891. "If it be barbaric to insist upon these bottoms remaining public property, it is rank favoritism to parcel them out to the exclusion of the general public," declared Colonel Henry Page, who turned Brooks's analysis on its head: "Nor does science demand it. Professor Brooks says the failure in supply does not result from the methods of taking, nor the seasons, but from an inexhaustible demand. A natural bed needs only protection" through well-enforced measures such as the cull law. Eliminating the commons would destroy a principle enshrined in the Magna Carta and abolish the oysterman's independence by making him the "the hired employee of more highly favored citizens or strangers," in Page's words. The end of the commons would also undermine the oysterman's masculinity, and as another attendee argued, "preserving American manhood" transcended the goal of increasing oyster production.[124] Gendered arguments shaped national politics in this period, when conservative critics linked the specter of expanding federal power to the threatened loss of men's authority over the home and family order, a recurring theme of later culture wars in American society.[125]

Others at the Canton meeting framed the debate as a conspiracy between scientists and corporate cartels to swindle the people of Maryland. Cowen's railroad connections presented an obvious target. As "the ablest corporation lawyer in the State," he doubtless had ulterior motives: "Behind all he says looms the dark cloud of a corporation hand to grab not only the deep-water lots, but with them to scoop in the shallow water lots" that Brooks had proposed for ordinary citizens. Another speaker mocked Cowen and Brooks as arrogant con artists: "The promoter sees everything distorted by his desires. He assures us that an industry which gives employment to upward of 55,000 people, and indirectly contributes to the support of 220,000 more, which keeps 8,800 boats working in our oyster fisheries, and which yielded 9,650,000 bushels of edible oysters to the pack of last season, is going to suddenly dry up and die out unless the 'professor' steps in and lends the helping hand of science to old 'Dame-Nature.'" A third speaker twisted Brooks's utopian vision of enriching all Marylanders. The loss of the free fishery would destroy thousands of jobs by replacing watermen with steam-powered dredges, thereby plunging the tidewater region into an "eclipse which this generation will not see lightened."[126] While this speaker overlooked the possibility of regulating leaseholders' equipment—a solution that Virginia later embraced—he articulated the palpable threat that industrialism posed to artisanal fishing communities.

The Canton rally's most well-known attendee, Delegate Legg, stressed the futility of applying agricultural concepts to watery environs, asserting that none of his open-minded friends who had tried private planting under the 1867 Five-Acre Law had ever made "a cent profit."[127] The failure of these attempts challenged the idea that oysters could be induced to grow on barren bottoms, providing powerful proof of the apparent folly of trying to improve an environment governed by divine laws. The bay yielded many fish and shellfish in some years, few in others; so went the cycle of nature. Religious convictions about the shifting bounty meted out by Providence played an important role in undermining the idea that science could aid the fisheries.

Some leasing opponents did not reject the idea of underwater farming, however. At a forum held the same week by the Nationalist Club of Baltimore City, the anti-immigration group's chair, George Wrightson, affirmed the importance of oyster culture while demanding to know why it required private management: "Is the spreading of oyster shells upon our bay and river bottoms such a stupendous undertaking that only private enterprise or privileged monopolies can hope to attain proficiency in it? Are oyster shells or other hard bodies only to be attracted by the magnetic influence of private capital? Is it a fact that the oyster will positively refuse to propagate except upon private beds?" By outsourcing the important work of repletion to private firms, he argued, the northeastern states had ceded control of their oyster grounds to the capitalists of Philadelphia, New York, and Boston and robbed American workers of their "natural heritage." Far from enriching the populace, private cultivation had replaced "the independent tongman working for himself" with "the imported Italian or Hungarian."[128] But Maryland's public-domain fleet also featured many foreigners; an 1892 study showed that more than half the dredge boat crewmen were immigrants, primarily German and Irish.[129] In fact, Brooks believed that private cultivation would offer greater incentives to native-born Americans. Because locals knew that signing on to a dredge boat with an unfamiliar captain was a good way to get hurt, swindled, or killed, owners relied on gullible immigrants. Allowing leaseholders to operate steam-powered dredges, Brooks believed, would "improve the dredger's life" enough to make it "attractive to Marylanders," thereby precluding the need for "the cheaper labor of foreigners."[130] Despite their different analyses, the fact that both Wrightson and Brooks interpreted cheap, unskilled immigrant labor as a problem for the oyster industry revealed how out of touch they were with broader trends of the corporate-dominated, industrializing economy.

The Professor Strikes Back

Brooks took the attacks with a grain of salt. Though he had stopped experimenting with artificial oyster fertilization, he capped his advocacy work with *The Oyster* (1891). Long before interdisciplinary thinking became fashionable, he laid out the biological, economic, and political case for private oyster culture. Most of the content was recycled, except for a chapter posing an amusingly didactic conversation between a

Baltimore packer and a farmer on the wisdom of private oyster culture. Another new bit revealed Brooks's self-deprecating yet sardonic sense of humor regarding his role in the debate:

> I speak on this subject with the diffidence of one who has been frequently snubbed and repressed; for while I am myself sure of the errors of the man who tonged oysters long before I was born, it is easier to acquiesce than to struggle against such overwhelming ignorance, so I have learned to be sub-missive in the presence of the elderly gentleman who studied the embryology of the oyster when years ago as a boy he visited his grandfather on the Eastern Shore, and to listen with deference to the shucker as he demonstrates to me at his raw-box, by the aid of his hammer and shucking-knife, the fallacy of my notions of the structure of the animal.

As to the charge of being "a mere theorist," Brooks pointed to his experience dredging in "every part of the bay," tonging in five states, and even "wading over the sharp shells which cut the feet like knives."[131] By defending the legitimacy of his expertise with respect to his bodily labor, Brooks acknowledged that understanding the bay's secrets required a physical connection with nature as well as a scientific approach.

Beyond his hands-on qualifications, Brooks invoked scientific expertise against his opponents. Oystermen lacked a crucial perspective on the oyster: "As its world is chiefly microscopic, no one can penetrate into the secrets of its structure and history without training in the technical methods of the laboratory; and business contact with the oyster cannot possibly, with any amount of experience, give any real insight into its habits and mode of life."[132] In other words, resource users could not appreciate the oyster's capacity for artificial increase because they had no understanding of its anatomy and physiology, which led them to explain shellfish abundance or decline as a function of divine will and natural cycles, neither of which could be controlled by mere humans. Like other late nineteenth-century professionals in the social and hard sciences who sought to use their knowledge to address modern problems, Brooks applied to oystermen an urban, secular standard of value that contrasted sharply with what anthropologist Michael Paolisso calls their "cultural models."[133]

Not surprisingly, Brooks's influence among his professional peers was strong. Prominent fishery experts who joined his campaign included Lieutenant Winslow; Marshall McDonald, who promoted fish culture at the expense of biological research as head of the U.S. Fish Commission from 1888 to 1895; and Lieutenant James B. Baylor, who supervised the charting of Virginia's oyster grounds from 1892 to 1896.[134] McDonald and Baylor disagreed with the idea of privatizing natural beds, but few other members of the rising fisheries bureaucracy questioned Brooks's basic assumptions in print. A major exception was Charles H. Stevenson of the U.S. Fish Commission, who agreed that barren bottoms should be reserved for private cultivation but in other ways challenged what had become the conventional wisdom regarding the Maryland oyster industry.[135]

Stevenson took issue with the 1884 Oyster Commission's methodology, which underpinned Brooks's assessment of the oyster problem. Stevenson argued that it was useless to extrapolate a major trend from only two data sets (the dredge hauls made by Winslow in 1878–79 and by Brooks in 1882–83), a view with which statisticians would agree. At any given time, Stevenson argued, seasonal conditions and the spat attachment rates of the preceding two summers have a great impact on the number of oysters occupying the reefs; thus, several years' worth of information would be needed to assess the fishery's problems and potential solutions. He also took issue with the commission's method of determining oyster abundance. The dredge hauling method lacked legitimacy because the dredge could not possibly catch all oysters in its path as a consequence of such factors as the weather, bottom conditions, vessel form and speed, and the operator's "conscientious ability." In another implicit criticism of Brooks, Stevenson asserted that private ostreiculture's "supposed friends" damaged the cause with their extravagant predictions. The idea that the Chesapeake Bay could be made to produce 500 million bushels a year instead of the present 10 million only inflated the value of barren bottoms and created impossible expectations.[136]

Stevenson also took a much more charitable view of the oystermen. He believed a few reckless dredge captains had ruined the reputation of all, whereas Brooks and other fishery professionals perceived the Oyster Wars as proof of the need for "more efficient control of a class of men who do not hesitate to defy the law and consider themselves the judges of their own rights."[137] Stevenson's attitude was diametrically opposed: "The fishery in Maryland is not, as frequently supposed, a haphazard undertaking conducted by a class of men depending for success on violations of the State laws, but is on a firm, orderly basis, any sudden, revolutionary change in which would work great hardship and distress to the thousands of citizens depending on it for a livelihood." The radical change to which he referred was the state-sanctioned disposal of natural reefs. Northern legislatures shared Stevenson's view that the common fishery should be maintained while encouraging private cultivation of barren bottoms as a "kindred industry," but he went a step further by arguing that the natural beds must be protected through strict enforcement of cull laws and publicly financed reshelling operations.[138] The difficulty and expense of reshelling, however, would lead Marylanders to leave the question of public oyster culture for another generation to implement.

An older contemporary who did not directly critique Brooks but whose work also challenged his assumptions was German zoologist Karl Möbius. In response to fevered 1870s debates about whether Germany's North Sea coast could be transformed using the French system of artificial oyster breeding, Möbius gave a resounding no. The expense of creating and maintaining claires, sea canals, and special spat collectors was prohibitive, as shown by English experiments that amounted to a mind-boggling cost per oyster of between fifty and five hundred pounds. But even unlimited funds could not force every egg to develop to maturity, no matter what Coste and Brooks said. Möbius's analysis of temperature, salinity, and other environmental factors revealed few suitable propagation sites in Germany.

Moreover, Möbius's analysis of the oyster bed as a "social community" showed that external conditions imposed inherent limits on its biological potential. He coined the word *bioconose* from the Greek words for "life" and "having something in common" to convey a new concept regarding the importance of changes in the physical environment to a community of living organisms and vice versa.[139] Möbius's articulation of the bioconose not only provided a conceptual foundation for the fledgling science of ecology but also demonstrated the importance of applied ecological research to natural resource management.[140] As he informed the German agricultural ministry, overfishing had altered the capacity of Europe's oyster reefs by reducing the number of individual bivalves to such an extent that other filter-feeding species, like cockles and mussels, now dominated the food web. Similar shifts in the "biocontoic equilibrium" had occurred in other human-dominated landscapes, most notably the North American prairie, where tame horses and cattle now occupied the niche "where immense throngs of wild buffaloes once ranged in full liberty."[141] But Möbius knew he was outgunned, for the idea that nature could be restocked fit the ethos of scientific agricultural modernization.[142] Not until the late twentieth century would other fishery scholars echo his pragmatic assessment of the ecological and economic limits of private oyster culture.

An Incomplete Revolution

The campaign waged by Brooks and Cowen succeeded, in a way, during the last decade of the nineteenth century – across Maryland's southern border. Like Maryland, Virginia had ante- and postbellum laws on its books allowing individuals to lease small plots for planting oysters, but the private fishery remained undeveloped. Impressed with Brooks's solutions to the problem of declining harvests, Virginia's governor urged the state's 1892 legislature to reform the oyster code. Lawmakers granted many of his wishes, passing a cull law and a ban on exporting seed oysters and making a commitment to hold the natural beds in trust for the people while strengthening private property rights to barren bottom. To that end, the assembly authorized Baylor to conduct the first survey of the commonwealth's oyster waters.[143] But the pro-privatization forces did not seem destined to succeed, since the law authorized the judge of each tidewater county to appoint three men to delineate its natural oyster deposits, where dredging would be prohibited. Accordingly, local tongers exerted a great deal of control over the mapping process, and Baylor considered much of their work exaggerated if not fraudulent: "In some of the counties surveyed . . . the natural oyster beds have been designated as far more extensive than the conditions of the bottoms justified."[144] The public's exclusive right to the beds was even enshrined in the new state constitution of 1902.[145] Given Virginia's strong respect for the common right to the natural beds, how did its extensive system of private oyster culture come to pass?

According to agricultural economist George Santopietro, protecting common fishery rights may have been secondary to encouraging leasing on remaining areas by limiting what tongers could claim as public grounds.[146] Indeed, during the first decade of the twentieth century, the legislature passed several laws strengthening leaseholders' guarantees, culminating in 1910 with the granting of lease rights to corporations. Virginia had by then surpassed Maryland as the leading oyster-producing state. Private grounds generated more than half the commonwealth's harvest, a figure that held until the incursion of oyster pathogens later in the century.[147] Under the Virginia system of private oyster culture, leaseholders followed the Connecticut practice of laying down shell and seed oysters on lots as large as five thousand acres.[148] Moreover, because the state's natural public reefs included the rich seedbeds of the James River, Virginia leaseholders benefited from legislative bans on seed exports, which had enriched northern planters for the better part of a century.[149]

Like their Maryland counterparts, impoverished Virginia oystermen opposed the loss of even part of their domain. Why did they not prevail? Santopietro argues that, among other reasons, Virginia tongers chose not to resist pro-leasing forces as strongly as Marylanders did. Although Virginia tongers opposed leasing in principle, their resistance was "less strenuous" and "less inspired" because the competing interests posed less of a threat for two major reasons. According to Ingersoll's 1881 study of the oyster fisheries, most Virginia planters had no interest in privatizing the natural beds because they sought to maximize profit by growing oysters to their maximum size, which required the less crowded environment of barren bottoms. Moreover, most Virginia leaseholders did not desire to use dredges because of the difficulty of keeping them within property lines and the damage they caused to the expensive shell, which had to be deposited to serve as substrate. Leaseholders therefore personally used tongs or hired tongers, who had to be state residents. Moreover, leaseholders depended on public-domain tongers to provide seed. Thus, Virginia oystermen had less to lose from a privatized fishery than did their Maryland counterparts.[150]

The idea that such employment opportunities muted tongers' resistance to leasing does not explain why the Virginia tongers would not have considered working for private planters as the despised equivalent of "unfree" wage labor. However, three other reasons offered by Santopietro align more closely with my argument regarding the role of political clout because they deal with the coercive forces arrayed against Virginia oystermen. First, Virginia tongers were more subject than were Marylanders to the condign power of the state, to which leaseholders could appeal to punish poachers. Most notably, the 1903 Virginia legislature authorized planters to maintain armed watchtowers over their beds, with the structures becoming "an integral part of the Chesapeake scene in Virginia." Second, Virginia phased in changes to the property rights structure over a relatively long period, thereby increasing economic interest in leaseholding among influential packers. Third, Virginia's higher salinity levels more closely resembled those of northern coastal estuaries than the Maryland portion of the bay. Saltier oysters commanded a higher price up north, which gave Virginia packers more incentive than Marylanders to pressure legislators to liberalize the leasing laws.[151]

Other possible explanations for Virginia's higher degree of privatization pertain to the voting power of the oystermen. Virginia's public-domain tongers did not benefit from malapportionment because the state's inland counties outnumbered the tidewater ones. Moreover, the 1902 poll tax prevented impoverished members of both races from lobbying against existing and proposed leasing laws. As in so many other places where money talks, elite forces played a powerful role in fueling the evolution of private property rights to Virginia's natural resources.

No doubt pleased by Virginia's action on so many of his proposals, Brooks engaged in his last act of advocacy in 1905 by issuing a second edition of *The Oyster*. The previous decade had been one of relative quiet on the Maryland leasing front, with a new leader championing the cause in exclusively economic terms. Baltimore attorney B. Howard Haman had submitted several bills promoting the leasing of barren bottoms as a means of funding road and bridge construction. Although the influential *Baltimore Sun* always supported his efforts, tidewater politicians and citizens derided or, even worse, ignored them. With Brooks's name back in the papers, the controversy reignited, and the *Sun* published an astounding thirty-five editorials promoting Haman's bill in the eleven months leading up to the legislature's 1906 session.[152] The blitzkrieg strategy promising huge revenues to be used for modernizing Maryland's automotive infrastructure apparently worked. The Haman Act allowed individuals but not corporations to lease barren bottoms – up to ten acres in county waters and one hundred acres in the state waters of the bay proper – and authorized a massive survey to distinguish barren grounds from natural bars.

Although oystermen would later consider the Haman Act the opening salvo in a campaign to turn the entire bay over to capitalists, at the time harvests had declined sharply enough (from about 5.7 million bushels in 1900–1901 to 4.5 million in 1904–5) to blunt resistance, and the "friends of oyster culture" had made such major concessions that the prospects for a private fishery might not have seemed terribly threatening. Moreover, harvesters and tidewater legislators may have sought to establish a fixed set of oyster maps because they believed that the natural beds were shrinking. Since there was little incentive to fund a full-scale survey except to distinguish leasable from nonleasable areas, oystermen may have thought that the sooner the most productive reefs were legally codified as forever part of the public domain, the better future aquacultural ambitions could be checked. In other words, tidewater legislators may have signed onto the Haman bill to limit what lessees could claim as leasable.[153]

To oversee the survey and eventual leasing operations, the Haman Act provided for a Shell Fish Commission, and thus Maryland's first permanent resource conservation agency opened for business. Caswell Grave's appointment to the seat reserved for a scientist pleased his former professor, Brooks, who died of heart failure soon thereafter at the age of sixty.[154] As he lay on his deathbed, Brooks may have recalled Coste, who died thirty-five years earlier "at his post, despondent, greatly discouraged, and to the last hour misunderstood by that multitude" of oyster culture skeptics. That quotation, from an 1875 French study, so intrigued Brooks that he had included it in his commission's report.[155] A wave of relief at escaping Coste's sad fate must have washed over him when news of the Haman Act and his protégé's new position arrived.

⌒

The Shell Fish Commission's first task was an overwhelming one: to chart the entire state's oyster grounds to distinguish the natural bars from leasable barren bottoms.[156] Such an extensive oyster survey was unprecedented. The job took six years, and its effects extended far into the future. The charts constructed by engineer Charles Yates and his team provided crucial information for managing the public and private sectors of the fishery. Moreover, although the reefs had already been subjected to decades of dredging and tonging, the maps provided a valuable baseline against which to measure subsequent change.[157]

The Yates Survey seemed to represent a major advance in the scientific dream of controlling the oyster resource, though the effort privileged watermen's understanding of productive grounds. The Haman Act required the surveying party to confer with guides familiar with each county commons regime, making the survey boats "the subject of constant visitation from the local oystermen." Another legislative provision designed to protect watermen's access to fruitful reefs required that each chart be filed in the appropriate county court so that "citizens dissatisfied with the findings of the survey" could appeal before the results gained official standing. The General Assembly thus sought to ensure that the oyster maps reflected "local sentiment" rather than the imperialist ambitions of lessees who might one day seek to farm more than the bay's least valuable bottoms.[158]

With the survey's completion in 1912, the state seemed poised to enter the age of modern fisheries management. The Yates team classified 216,000 acres as natural oyster bars and 44,000 acres as crabbing and clamming grounds. Of the 760,000 acres of barren bottom subject to lease under the Haman Act, 460,000 were thought to be of doubtful value, but the remaining 300,000 acres were deemed either productive or potentially productive for oyster culture, depending on the local hydrographic and topographic conditions.[159] Because the law prohibited modification of the Yates boundaries after the appeals period passed, potential leaseholders presumed that they could safely proceed.[160]

But just as homesteaders had encountered opposition from ranchers accustomed to grazing their cattle on the public lands of the western range, would-be aquaculturists collided with oystermen who began to perceive the threat to their local commons regimes.[161] Despite the Haman Act's inherent limitations, the rationale of codifying natural beds that had seemed to be diminishing was undercut by an ensuing "phenomenal" catch of spat. Landings increased, thereby renewing faith in barren grounds' ability to regenerate on their own. Moreover, as "they saw the ground on which they had been oystering in recent years enclosed within the stakes of private owners," some harvesters protested that they had missed the opportunity to appeal the Yates Survey (fig. 10). Discontent increased further as oystermen from different counties organized a statewide protective association.[162] In response, tidewater legislators drafted a 1914 bill, the Shepherd Act, to resurvey the beds based on the 1881 Goldsborough definition of a natural bar, which the General Assembly had neglected to include in the 1906 act.[163] The *Sun* was so outraged that the day before the final vote on the 1914 measure, the

Oyster bed fence.
San Francisco Bay.
Cal.
Oct 1889.

Fig. 10. The enclosure of the oyster commons, San Francisco Bay, California, ca. 1889. Although entrepreneurs began staking off oyster beds along the Northeast and Pacific coasts in the nineteenth century, Maryland watermen used their disproportionate clout to resist such incursions on their commons. (Photo by Stefan Claesson. Courtesy of National Archives and Historic Fisheries Collection, National Oceanic and Atmospheric Administration.)

paper devoted an entire page to the pro-leasing comments of bankers, businessmen, and social leaders whom it deemed to hold no financial interest in the oyster problem.[164] But it was too late.

Oystermen reasserted their rejection of private oyster culture via the Shepherd Act. Under the new law, three or more state citizens could protest any existing or proposed leasehold by filing suit in their county's circuit court. If the judge decided that the area in question was a natural oyster bar, the leasehold would be seized or the application denied, and the area would be reclassified on the official charts. Finding credible witnesses to testify that they had obtained oysters from the disputed spot during the previous five years was never a problem. As the head of Shell Fish Commission's successor agency complained to the governor in 1927, leasing applications, which had to be advertised in local newspapers, almost always led to lawsuits. Because the state agency was the defendant, it had to pay for the court cases, which in 1926 amounted to a steep $638 for two counties alone. Winning was all but impossible because "a number of oystermen will get up in court and swear that they have caught oysters during a period within five years from the ground that is being applied for, regardless of the facts."[165] Consequently, between 1914 and 1963, the acreage of natural oyster bars rose from 270,000 to 285,000, an increase that represented not a miraculous gift of Nature but rather "a by-product of unsuccessful efforts to acquire leases."[166]

As a strategy for checking the rise of the nascent aquaculture industry, the Shepherd Act worked brilliantly. Would-be cultivators had little incentive to invest in application fees, let alone the needed supplies and equipment, since even if they obtained lots, they could be seized at any time. Oystermen had flexed their political muscle to ensure that their definition of a natural oyster bar would trump scientific criteria in the courtroom long into the twentieth century, making the judicial branch an important adjunct to the advantage offered by legislative malapportionment.

As Arthur McEvoy shows in his studies of the California fisheries, scientific descriptions and baselines necessary for effective natural resource management emerge out of complex interactions among resource ecology, economic production, and the legal system. Both science and lawmaking involve struggles for authority – between scientists and citizens over what counts as reality and between people seeking to allocate access to resources for specific uses, respectively. Production depends on technology, resource availability, the sociology of resource user groups, and the structure of legal entitlements to access. Finally, the sociology and the legal structure of the market help determine the human effects on the ecological system in question.[167] McEvoy's schematic demonstrates that Brooks and his allies neglected to integrate the forces of ecology, production, and lawmaking into their plan for restructuring and managing Maryland's oyster commons – or, more accurately, its patchwork of county-based commons regimes. Each of these forces warrants analysis.

Scientific knowledge regarding the Chesapeake Bay in the late nineteenth century was embryonic, not advanced enough to provide insight into resource management. Even so, Brooks and his allies assumed that science as a way of knowing was superior to the watermen's knowledge base. As a morphologist, Brooks could correct misunderstandings of oyster anatomy and physiology. But because neither he nor ecologists (with the notable exception of Möbius) had spent much time investigating the interactions of physical and biological estuarine forces, Brooks was not justified in rejecting the watermen's observational claims about the workings of nature, such as their contention that oyster abundance could vary dramatically from year to year. Brooks's dismissal insulted precisely the group whose support he needed and established a pattern of mutual suspicion between the two bay stakeholders.

Brooks and his supporters also overlooked broader relations underlying economic production. Brooks cared deeply about improving tidewater communities' financial lot, but his enthusiasm for private oyster culture blinded him to the powerful local facets of human culture aligned against such a system. Just because watermen and their families lacked wealth did not mean they were dissatisfied with their way of life. Money was not a prime motivator for most watermen, as contemporary accounts by anthropologists have shown. His assumption that destitute oystermen would trade self-employment for wage work on corporate oyster farms overlooked the fact that most watermen had already rejected the other major occupation available in tidewater Maryland – that is, the full-time farming of tobacco, grain, or fruits and vegetables. And few of whatever entrepreneurial individuals might have been intrigued by the potential profits of shellfish cultivation could have afforded the startup costs. Harvesting wild oysters required a cheap pair of tongs and a small homemade boat, whereas cultivation required substantial capital, patience, and business sense. Brooks's inattention to the mores and material circumstances of the tidewater world reinforced the watermen's image of scientists as arrogant and out of touch.

Finally, even after three decades of advocacy, Brooks failed to realize that demonstrating the efficacy of oyster culture was not enough and that resource management involved sustained negotiation with all stakeholder groups and careful attention to the political process. But Brooks was not alone in his flawed assumptions, as revealed by the stories of successive scientists who remained convinced that only private enterprise aligned with biological expertise could solve the interconnected problems of limited supply, common ownership, and overexploitation.

State Farming under the Chesapeake

3

Interwar Oyster Conservation, Science, and Politics

From today's vantage point, the Chesapeake Bay's ecological demise appears to date to the decades following the turn of twentieth century, when the first symptoms of systemwide deterioration became apparent. For more than two hundred years, inputs of nitrogen and other nutrient pollutants had escalated, first via intensive agriculture and then through untreated urban sewage. A seemingly passive entity, however, may have mitigated the estuarine impact of antebellum development. As discussed in chapter 1, the bay's molluscan denizens may have suppressed the onset of eutrophication by filtering the increased organic matter from the water column. But the intensification of commercial fishing after the Civil War accelerated the loss of oysters along with their biofiltration services. As biologists, paleoecologists, and archaeologists have observed in recent years, the overlap between the peak period of oyster harvesting, the first recorded hypoxia events, and other acute signs of the bay's reduced vigor suggests a key correlation between the two trends.[1]

While that link is visible now that more is known about the oyster's ecological functions, it was not apparent even to the few who first noticed that the bay no longer appeared as capable of assimilating anthropogenic wastes.[2] Oysters were valued as the commercial products of an immense protein factory, yet they possessed a status unlike other resource commodities. As a treasured food, they held cultural resonance for the millions who savored them each winter. While consumption peaked around Thanksgiving, Christmas, and Lent, Americans served by the railroads grew accustomed in the second half of the nineteenth century to enjoying them from September through April (the R months). Inexpensive, convenient, and protein rich, bivalves on the half shell gained a reputation as "perhaps the closest thing to a classless food."[3] As an English visitor observed in 1859, "The rich consume oysters and Champagne; the poorer classes consume oysters and *Lager bier,* and that is one of the principal social differences between the two sections of the community."[4] Whether raw, fried, or pickled, in soup, stuffing, or pie, served at home, the saloon, or a political fund-raiser, oysters became an American culinary tradition (fig. 11).

Oysters retained their honored status only until they started killing consumers. Sporadic outbreaks of oyster-borne typhoid fever in the 1890s and early 1900s revealed the organism's vulnerability to the sewage flows inundating the northeastern seaboard. Although no tainted specimens were traced back to the Chesapeake, the Maryland industry could not afford even the perception of unwholesomeness.[5] Legislative malapportionment enabled tidewater representatives to force Baltimore City to treat its sewage before dumping it into the Chesapeake Bay, a much more expensive option than the popular "dilution solution" of piping raw waste far downstream.[6] While Baltimore completed the nation's most advanced wastewater treatment plant in 1912, other states allowed untreated sewage to contaminate their coastlines. Even the influential packers who had convinced lawmakers to privatize parts of the oyster commons were no match for municipal polluters. Within a decade of securing their tenure on barren bottoms, Virginia oyster planters suffered the indignity of court rulings asserting that the right of cities to use the Chesapeake as a sewer surpassed leaseholders' rights.[7] Maryland's oystermen, by contrast, possessed the power to compel the state to protect water quality as well as their access to the entire estuarine commons. Yet Maryland suffered as much as its sister states in 1924, when hundreds of people fell ill after eating bad bivalves that probably originated in New York waters. Despite the hasty enforcement of stricter standards for oyster beds, boats, and plants, demand plummeted, leveling out far below the consumption rates of the Gilded Age.

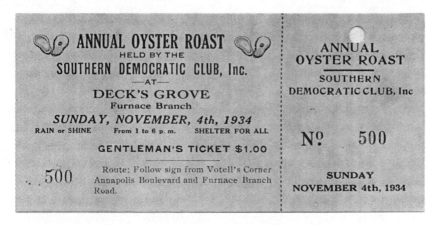

Fig. 11. Fund-raisers featuring the region's most prized seafood testified to the culinary and political importance of oysters in the early and mid–twentieth century. (Courtesy of Special Collections Department, University of Maryland Libraries.)

Amazingly, consumer backlash did little to demoralize Maryland's pro-leasing forces. Eager to increase the size of Chesapeakes and buoyed by the bay's immense capacity to absorb the pollutants hurting north-eastern oysters, privatization proponents pressed on with campaigns in 1927, 1935, and 1937. A new generation of scientist-advocates epitomized by Reginald Truitt led the efforts to liberalize the leasing laws, first in the context of decreased postwar harvests and then as part of a comprehensive conservation program for Depression-era Maryland. Truitt emphasized the value of biological and ecological research for managing seafood species as efficiently as possible. As in William K. Brooks's day, oystermen retained their disproportionate clout, distrust of monopolies, and fear of overproduction, the last of which gained new significance during the depression. However, prolonged depletion softened resistance to conservation measures that went beyond regulating access to the commons, and legislators thus embraced a solution that Truitt proposed as a supplemental means of maintaining the natural beds. Publicly funded oyster repletion, though enacted in the late 1920s, became entrenched during the 1930s because it combined work relief with the underwater equivalent of infrastructure building. Like the federal public works projects that paid jobless citizens to implement resource management, from the Civilian Conservation Corps to the Tennessee Valley Authority, oyster "rehabilitation" provided direct and indirect benefits to industry members by increasing the amounts of money and shellfish in circulation. The ways in which Maryland's famously independent watermen adapted to the crisis of resource depletion illuminate an unappreciated feature of interwar conservation policy, the implementation of large-scale environmental planning, especially at the state rather than federal level.[8]

Another aspect of New Deal conservation reforms – the clash between scientific prescriptions and political realities – was also apparent in public oyster repletion. As director of the Chesapeake Biological Laboratory, the struggling scientific wing of Maryland's besieged conservation agency, Truitt experienced constant frustration about the rehabilitation program's administration. Local oystermen's committees decided when and where to plant shells and seed, not unlike the western rancher-controlled grazing districts and farmer-controlled soil conservation districts established by New Deal policies. By insisting on the superiority of secular science over tidewater attitudes regarding nature, Truitt reinforced the negative view of researchers spawned a generation earlier. Yet he also broke new ground by persuading oystermen and their political allies that scientific expertise deserved a toehold in the emerging edifice of state-supported conservation. How legislators reconciled common-use rights to the fishery with scientific prescriptions for rational conservation sheds light on the development of resource management in states where rural minorities held the balance of power. This chapter deals with three interlocking themes of Maryland oyster conservation during the 1920s and 1930s: the rise of public repletion, the persistence of leasing advocacy, and the difficulties of institutionalizing science-based conservation at the state level.

Consumption and Coastal Contamination

Overconsumption, to which Brooks had attributed the tragedy of the oyster commons, ceased to be a problem in the early twentieth century as pollution helped tip the demand-supply imbalance the other way. From 1880 to 1910, national per capita consumption of oysters fell by a stunning 40 percent, from 3.09 pounds to 1.88.[9] Consumers lost their appetite as turn-of-the-century typhoid outbreaks shone light on the unsanitary conditions in which shellfish sometimes found themselves, from the reef to the packinghouse. The 1906 Pure Food and Drug

Act aimed to stem the spread of *Salmonella typhi* by setting the first national regulations for seafood processors.[10] However, neither prices nor
consumer confidence in what newspapers sensationalized as the "death-
laden luxury" rebounded.[11] To combat what it considered the tide of
unfair publicity – after all, any food could breed bacteria if mishandled –
larger packing firms established the National Oyster Growers and Dealers Association in 1908. The organization touted the mollusk's nutri-
tional benefits in a major advertising campaign, but it remained "the
food that has not gone up," in the words of the U.S. Bureau of Fisheries, the successor to the U.S. Fish Commission.[12] The national launch of
Prohibition a few years later reinforced the bivalve's passé reputation.
Alcohol – beer or champagne, depending on one's degree of affluence –
was a time-honored accompaniment for oysters on the half shell.[13] Dealers could not bring back saloons or unpolluted coastlines, but they could
embrace science-based sanitation.

Packers and leaseholders looked to state health departments and the
U.S. Public Health Service to develop simple methods of purifying contaminated product. This approach complemented that of Progressive
Era public health advocates, who implemented bacteriological standards and disinfection protocols for drinking-water supplies. While such
technocratic techniques aimed only to manage pollutants at the end of
the pipeline rather than to reduce the toxic inputs fueling the industrial economy, they did save many lives.[14] In 1920, William Firth Wells
of the New York Conservation Commission likewise proposed that the
best way "to put the oyster back on the bill of fare in the proud position which it formerly enjoyed" was by transferring suspect shellfish to
chlorinated tanks, where they could filter out harmful microbes. Doing
so posed an expensive logistical challenge, however, for even with multiple changes of water, the cleansing rate of tanks lagged far behind that
of natural tidal flows.[15] And even the priciest, most prolonged purification processes became moot as new problems facing the oyster became
evident.

After the Civil War, oyster populations had experienced enormous
pressure as harvesters and processors sought to feed demand and as
ever greater loads of urban sewage and agricultural runoff gushed into
East Coast estuaries. Fecal bacteria had alarming infectious properties,
but Maryland's expensive solution – state-of-the-art sewage-treatment
technology – was atypical. This approach also failed to address another

threat that escalated during World War I. Industrial wastes had fouled pockets of the seaboard for decades, but never in concentrations high enough to coat entire harbors, rivers, and beaches with ugly slicks of oily muck. Beginning around 1916, oyster larvae failed to mature in many New York, New Jersey, Connecticut, and Rhode Island bays for several years, bringing those states' fisheries to a standstill. Industry members blamed the calamity on wartime wastes, especially shipborne oil slicks, which scientists confirmed killed the floating spawn and spat.[16]

So desperate was New Jersey to restore its oyster productivity that it broke with the revered tradition of prohibiting private property in natural beds. In 1917, legislators privatized the natural reefs of Raritan Bay, the befouled estuary south of New York City over which New York and New Jersey shared jurisdiction. Just as earlier analysts had predicted, resistance to private oyster culture broke down only when extinction loomed.[17] But it was too late for the leaseholders, since larvae could no longer reach viability. New Jersey prohibited all oystering in its half of the befouled Raritan in 1921; New York followed a few years later.[18]

Oil pollution also caused great concern in the Chesapeake, though not enough to nullify the sacred status of the oyster commons. Baltimore's steelmaking and shipbuilding industries built and serviced fleets of tankers that emptied oil sludge from their bilges into the Great Shellfish Bay.[19] Factories and other point sources of pollution also raised concern.[20] The "flood of poisonous industrial wastes" led a New Jersey biologist, Thurlow C. Nelson, to argue that much more than oysters were at stake. Trade wastes also threatened to destroy what he called the biological machine, the ecological complex of bacteria, plants, and animals responsible for "the self purification of our streams and coastal waters." Nelson called for a diverse group of professionals – physicians, health officers, engineers, biologists, commercial fishermen, oyster growers, and coastal property owners – to work out a rational solution aimed at curtailing the industrial and hazardous waste stream.[21] He might also have appealed to sportsmen and bird lovers, who decried the ease with which oil encrusted the wings of waterfowl, and insurance companies, which paid dearly for fires sparked by oil floating atop the harbors of Baltimore and New Orleans in 1920.[22] Nelson warned that without decisive action, the East Coast would soon be "cradled in a septic tank" of toxins.[23]

Nelson's article, published in the *American Journal of Public Health,* reached a mere fraction of the key stakeholders, but what attracted nationwide attention was an oil fire that could have killed the president. After Warren Harding's yacht narrowly escaped a New York conflagration in May 1921, a New Jersey congressman familiar with Nelson's research seized the opportunity to reintroduce a bill banning the discharge of oil wastes into harbors and streams.[24] The subsequent hearings, which provided the first national forum on industrial pollution, featured testimony by Maryland conservation commissioner Swepson Earle and officials from other states regarding the need to protect fish and shellfish from tankers and oil-burning steamships.[25] Proponents justified pollution control in economic terms, a stance consistent with the logic of utilitarian conservationism. However, the strategy left them vulnerable to counterarguments about costs and benefits.[26] Maryland's oystermen possessed the clout to compel the state to protect their economic mainstay, but most commercial fisheries were no match for the corporate industrial polluters driving the regional and national economy.

As congressional debate continued, the National Coast Anti-Pollution League took matters into its own hands. The new organization asked the Commerce Department whether states could pass protective laws governing waters under their own jurisdiction. After receiving a positive response, Earle proposed joint Maryland-Virginia legislation prohibiting ships from flushing oily ballast into the bay.[27] But before the bay states could act, Congress passed the Oil Pollution Control Act of 1924, which banned the discharge of oily water within three miles of shore. A more effective though informal international agreement negotiated two years later encouraged captains to discharge at least fifty miles away, which improved coastal water quality enough to undercut pressure for strong federal laws limiting pollution.[28] By then, the reformist zeal of the Progressive Era had crested, and not until after World War II did the federal government assume a greater role in water pollution control.[29] Most state and federal legislators joined big business leaders in continuing to view environmental degradation as "a necessary by-product of urban and industrial growth."[30] With no mandate to stem the tide of trade wastes, cash-strapped state health departments could protect the public only by condemning oyster beds in ever larger swaths along the New England seaboard.

The nation's public health establishment received a shocking reminder of the harmful impact of biological as opposed to chemical wastes just before the 1924 Christmas holiday, when typhoid fever broke out in Chicago, New York, Washington, and elsewhere. The U.S. Public Health Service traced many of the fifteen hundred cases (about 10 percent of which resulted in death) to a large shipment of oysters infected with the bacterium.[31] Although they probably originated in Raritan Bay, the health commissioner of Illinois criminalized the consumption of all raw oysters, regardless of the source. An economic and public relations disaster struck the Chesapeake oyster industry, the nation's largest. Demand fell by 85 percent as newspapers published cartoons of skull-laden oysters, throwing thousands of cannery workers, shuckers, and oystermen out of work. Crisfield packers, who blamed both inland merchants for increasing oysters' volume by bloating them with contaminated local water supplies and Maryland officials for failing to enforce sanitary standards, demanded to know how government bureaucrats proposed to save the industry.[32] Maryland health and conservation authorities launched a multimedia blitz. Radio broadcasts, telegrams, and tabloids proclaimed "A Square Deal for the Baltimore Oyster," and a movie reel showed Chicago's public health director slurping raw oysters onboard the fishery force's flagship.[33] All the publicity highlighted the state's tough new sanitary standards for boats, processing plants, and more than two thousand square miles of reefs as well as the U.S. Public Health Service's new Shellfish Sanitation Program.[34] Within a year, health officers around the country knew exactly which of the hundreds of packinghouses had been certified.[35] As in other aspects of modern America, it took an emergency to compel strong government oversight of potentially harmful economic activities.[36]

Pressure to pass pollution-control laws in the Chesapeake region diminished after the mid-1920s, when the number of dramatic oil spills decreased and scientists concluded that industrial waste posed an insignificant threat to seafood species. The bay's huge volume of water dissipated the fuel residues discharged by ships and powerboats, and even Baltimore's toxic hotspot, the Patapsco River, became diluted enough that "scarcely a trace" of its contaminants could be detected in adjacent bay waters. Overall, water quality appeared as good as it had been during the peak oyster harvests of the previous century.[37] Not until the late 1930s, when fish kills increased, did scientists question the bay's

assimilative powers and take a deeper look at the negative effects of pollutants on benthic oxygen levels and other murky aspects of the bay ecosystem.[38] The Conservation Department signaled a significant change
in 1940 by announcing plans to examine the "possible accumulative
effect" of pollutants on the "delicate biological balance of Bay waters
and the relationship of these changes to conservation."[39] But even then,
the waters above most overworked reefs remained "physically and biologically suited to oyster propagation" and thus subject to rehabilitative
measures.[40] Scientists considered overharvesting and failure to reshell
depleted beds far greater threats than sewage or chemical pollutants, and
the question of whether overfishing or pollution bore the lion's share of
the blame for the oyster fishery's apparent decline did not reemerge for
several decades.

Paths toward Public Oyster Culture and Institutionalized Conservation

As pollution shut down East Coast oyster beds, efforts to cultivate the
organism in artificial settings escalated after decades of quiet. While state
and federal fish hatcheries had for decades been breeding fry with which
to restock depleted waterways, no comparable development took place
in the oyster industry. Leaseholders had no need to rely on expensive
laboratory methods when they could acquire cheap seed oysters from
natural beds down south or closer to home. That changed when pollution ruined setting areas and southern states banned seed exports. Wells
played a major role not only in developing the means of purifying market oysters but also in reviving the artificial propagation experiments
initiated by Brooks four decades earlier. Corporate, state, and federal
aid enabled him to reexamine the question that had vexed Brooks and
others: how to rear larvae in the laboratory during the free-swimming
stage – that is, the two weeks or so preceding spat attachment. With
every change of water, even the finest straining cloth allowed larvae to
escape. Wells solved the problem using a cream separator as a primitive
centrifuge. Five years later, he served the world's first artificially propa-
gated oysters, complete with birth certificates, an event covered in the
New York Times as an "epoch in the history of the oyster."[41] Wells argued
that science could now play as significant a role in shellfish culture as in
agriculture as long as adequate state support was forthcoming.[42]

Nelson did not share Wells's excitement. Not "until oysters become a far more expensive commodity" would hatcheries become profitable, meaning that efforts to increase the supply would have to remain focused on developing spawning and setting grounds "through intelligent cooperation with natural forces."[43] After several years, Wells admitted as much and left state science for more lucrative opportunities in the Ivy League.[44] Even with the reduction in supply brought about by the closure of polluted beds, market prices remained too low to justify the commercial application of Wells's results. The dream of growing oysters without relying on nature would not come to fruition until later in the century, when the shellfish disease MSX stimulated unprecedented support for molluscan research.

Rather than investing in hatcheries, private oyster growers in northern states either abandoned their leaseholds or hoped for the best as they continued planting shells and seed oysters. When finances permitted, fish commissioners provided assistance by returning shells to public natural reefs and maintaining them as seedbeds. The New York and New Jersey commissions also conducted extensive research on shellfish biology and reproduction. New Jersey's system of science-based oyster conservation began in 1888 when Julius Nelson, who had completed his doctorate under Brooks, established the Department of Oyster Culture at Rutgers University. The department operated as part of the state system of agricultural experiment stations, which aimed to help farmers become more efficient by applying the latest scientific and technological knowledge. Soon after Thurlow Nelson succeeded his father in 1916, he discovered that spawning could be predicted ten days in advance, a crucial managerial insight.[45] However, New Jersey biologists "did not play an explicit role in oyster management until after World War II" and thus shared many of the frustrations of their Maryland counterparts.[46] Nelson and his successors finally achieved political respect when their long tradition of research enabled them to assume a leading role in the MSX crisis of the 1950s and 1960s.[47]

In Maryland, the institutionalization of scientific oyster conservation proceeded at the pace of another kind of mollusk. Although Brooks died in 1908 believing that his dream of science-based private oyster culture had come to fruition, the 1914 Shepherd Act shot it down by allowing oystermen to redefine barren bottoms as natural, productive beds. Nevertheless, the questions of leasing and scientific cultivation failed to rest. As a *Baltimore Sun* journalist observed in 1916, without "the biennial oyster fight," every session of the General Assembly "would seem unreal."[48] Likewise, conservation commissioner Earle poked fun at the bivalve's political entanglements two decades later:

> Taking the resources of Chesapeake Bay in the order of their importance, we come first to the oyster. This inoffensive bivalve has been the cause of more bitter fights in the legislative halls at Annapolis, more "political football" in the tidewater regions from whence it comes, more dissension and actual bloodshed among the watermen who harvest it than any other resource of our State. Indeed, Helen of Troy wrought no more havoc in her day than has the oyster during the past half century, and even today, when the word is mentioned before the General Assembly of Maryland instant attention is obtained.[49]

Earle had a good sense of humor and thick skin, having begun his career in 1906 as the hydrographic engineer of the Shell Fish Commission, the agency whose massive survey was rendered moot soon thereafter by legislative fiat. A 1915 visit to New Orleans for a fisheries conference deeply impressed Earle, who published an attention-getting article in the *Sun* praising Louisiana for vesting authority for all its natural resources in one agency.[50] When a new efficiency-minded governor persuaded Maryland's 1916 assembly to follow suit, Earle became one of the state Conservation Commission's three leaders.[51] In accordance with the Progressive Era dictate that experts rather than political hacks should run government, commissioners were required to possess "special knowledge" of oysters, clams, fish, crabs, terrapin, wild fowl, birds, or game or fur-bearing animals.[52] Such criteria tended to privilege watermen, seafood packers, and tidewater legislators, but after a 1924 cost-cutting reorganization, Earle became the sole commissioner, a position he held for the next decade.[53] Throughout his tenure, he sparked controversy as he struggled to implement science-based resource management.

Though spared the vast quantities of industrial waste choking off spat sets in New England, Maryland oystermen of the 1910s reaped a less lucrative harvest than had recently been the case. Decades of intensive harvesting had removed the large selects and counts for which purveyors of the raw bar trade paid top dollar. Now dredges and tongs came up with the less valuable standards.[54] Processors consequently looked to the less exploited estuaries of the Deep South and Gulf Coast, especially

Louisiana, for big oysters. The Cajun state had a tradition of locally generated oyster culture dating back to the early 1800s, when Yugoslav immigrants began transplanting flavorless seed oysters from overcrowded beds east of the Mississippi River to the saltier, steadier-flowing west side. In the 1850s, Louisiana's parishes (counties) began leasing barren bottoms for such operations, a function assumed by the state in 1902. As in New England and Virginia, Louisiana's private oyster planters relied on public-domain natural beds for seed.[55] Earle perceived the Louisianans' rapid success as cause for concern: "Unless Maryland improves the product we are sending to the Middle West it will only be a question of time before the South will take a large part of our oyster trade."[56] The Maryland legislature and governor agreed on the need for centralized oversight of oyster protection and repletion but disagreed with Earle's argument for expanded leasing.

Just two years after the Shepherd Act dealt leaseholders a kick in the teeth, a Baltimore City senator made a bold though futile move, offering a bill to lease all oyster bottoms, whether natural or barren. He argued that turning all beds over to capitalists would raise three million dollars a year for the state.[57] The plan's strongest denunciation came from Earle's old colleague, Caswell Grave, the scientific member of the former Shell Fish Commission. The gutting of the 1906 Haman Act still angered Grave, who argued that it would have protected public-domain oystermen while modernizing the fishery. By contrast, privatizing the natural rocks would cause great damage to the tidewater counties: "These communities are in our midst as a natural consequence of the inefficient and unjust policy which we have long tolerated and protected and, for our sins in this matter, we must be willing to pay the price," he told Baltimore's City Club. Despite the glaring need to modernize, Grave asserted, private cultivation "should take its place and grow side by side with the free oyster fishery, so that the oystermen of today may have the opportunity to become the oyster planters of tomorrow."[58] While sharing the assumption that commercial fishermen could be converted into rational aquaculturists, Grave's appeal to look beyond the cold logic of economic efficiency represented an important break with his former professor, Brooks. However, Grave's emphasis on the social dimension of the oyster problem and the state's responsibility for conservation did not receive enough press to counteract the oystermen's negative image of Chesapeake scientists.

Government efforts to replenish the Maryland oyster beds began in the late Progressive Era, several years prior to the program's legal codification in 1927. As early as 1886, the General Assembly appropriated five thousand dollars to the Oyster Navy for shell-planting experiments, probably in an effort to emulate Connecticut planters' success. However, the shells failed to facilitate the growth of new oysters, a problem one scientist attributed to the depositing of shell too late in the spawning season to catch the spat.[59] The 1910 assembly passed a law to reshell depleted bars using funds from a new tax of one cent on every bushel, domestic or imported, sold in Maryland. However, the U.S. Supreme Court declared the import tax unconstitutional, forcing the state to use other revenue streams to buy shells, an expensive endeavor at eleven cents a bushel.[60] In 1914, the state tried another approach, moving seed oysters from overcrowded or freshet-prone beds to protected "reserve areas," where they might grow more quickly and absorb more salt.[61] Packer Thomas B. Webster helped convince the legislature to authorize the plan by offering to assume any financial loss if the state did not recoup the cost of policing the beds via a tax of ten cents per bushel. Webster seems to have anticipated that success would break down tidewater resistance to private planting, but the gamble cost him five thousand dollars, and all four of the major state oyster transplantings from 1914 to 1926 ended with net losses to the state.[62] What had gone wrong?

Both during and after this period, state and federal scientists attributed the economic shortfalls of both shell and seed planting to the chronic failure to observe biological criteria. Time after time, the political appointees of the Fishery Force and their oysterman consultants planted shells or seed at the wrong time, in the wrong place, in the wrong way, or in insufficient quantities. After the first seed-transplanting experiment (1914–16) went awry, Maryland officials appealed to the U.S. Bureau of Fisheries (USBF) for assistance. Federal biologists advised the state that when future seed plantings were undertaken, attention should be paid to water quality, the biological fitness of stock obtained from different regions, and other conditions ascertained through a joint state-federal study.[63] The USBF eventually agreed to contract a zoology graduate student from the University of Maryland to perform the work on behalf of the cash-strapped Conservation Commission.[64] Reginald Truitt spent the next three decades studying the optimal biological and political growing conditions for Chesapeake oysters.

Truitt had come to the attention of fishery officials through his master's thesis work on the oyster industry. Having already served as a tidewater high school principal and World War I army pilot, the twenty-eight-year-old began his graduate studies just as the University of Maryland answered the state Conservation Commission's call to expand the concept of agricultural extension.[65] Three decades after New Jersey had incorporated research on oyster culture and biology into its system of agricultural experiment stations, Maryland pursued a similar path in the hopes of producing more enlightened oystermen. As Earle and the packers on the commission expressed it, the state university should promote "the studies of these water foods, with a view of carrying back to the homes of the young men who might attend school from tidewater the application of scientific knowledge."[66] The first step toward that goal took place in 1919, when Truitt organized a series of free evening lectures on the state's water resources. He hoped to replace "blind trust in nature" with an appreciation for solving the problem of decreased oyster production through "Science, the master key to the realm of the organic and the inorganic, the accepted foundation of mechanics and agriculture."[67] Speakers included several USBF researchers, oyster expert Thurlow Nelson, and Hopkins marine biologist Rheinart P. Cowles, a former student of Brooks's who had initiated a massive federally funded biological survey of the bay.[68] Truitt also put himself on the program, noting his status as "an experienced oysterman biologically trained."[69] It was a cheeky move, for Truitt was the son of prosperous packer-planters from the ocean side of the Eastern Shore, where private oyster culture had generated much less resistance than in the counties bordering the Chesapeake Bay. The extent to which the lecture course influenced any sons of tidewater was probably negligible, since it took place during the winter term (the height of the oyster season), the College Park campus was inaccessible by water, and few tidewater teens felt the need for higher education. But the series did help launch Truitt's long career in state conservation.

Chesapeake Science, Politics, and Truitt

If William Keith Brooks was the midwife to Chesapeake science in the 1880s, Reginald Van Trump Truitt ended a prolonged stage of arrested development by nurturing it through a rough 1920s-era adolescence. Truitt served as the Conservation Department's unpaid biologist for several years while completing his graduate studies on oyster biology and economics.[70] Between researching and writing, he taught at the state university and even found time to coach the lacrosse team to two national championships.[71] He retained a partnership in the family packing business, which had stoked his interest years earlier.[72] Rather than downplaying Truitt's packing connections, an approach that might have seemed prudent given the oystermen's antipathy to seafood dealers, Earle emphasized them in agency publicity as evidence of Truitt's credibility. Truitt even used his family's business stationery to correspond with the governor regarding research and policy recommendations.[73] Though not endearing to the harvesters, Truitt's corporate ties may have provided him opportunities unavailable to most state scientists, including a seat on a 1926 gubernatorial advisory committee of packers. His marriage to Mary Harrington, the daughter of former governor Emerson C. Harrington, also probably did not hurt.

Overall, however, the 1920s were lean years for Truitt and the cause of Chesapeake science. His brief federal study revealed that much more ecological information was needed about bivalve spawning and growth.[74] So each summer he returned to Solomons Island to continue his research. Located on a peninsula at the confluence of the bay and the Patuxent River, eighty-five miles south of Baltimore, Solomons provided easy access to some of the state's richest reefs.[75] Truitt named his venture the Chesapeake Biological Laboratory (CBL) in 1925, when he moved from a shack to a parish house whose lack of running saltwater precluded "experimental work of a high order," as he complained to his stingy state patrons.[76] Though he had not yet completed his doctorate, Truitt became a full professor of "aquiculture" at the University of Maryland the same year and continued his unpaid work for the Conservation Commission in exchange for access to boats and reimbursement of his travel expenses.[77] It was a good deal for the commissioners, who generated positive publicity by featuring CBL efforts to improve harvests in the commission's annual report and in newsletters mailed to licensed watermen. Privately, however, Truitt groused that the agency treated the lab "at best . . . merely as a stepchild," while Earle called Truitt "a fair biologist with a greater knack for getting favorable newspaper publicity than for scientific exactitude."[78] Yet for sixteen years, the two men worked together to systematize conservation, an effort set back by the 1924 typhoid epidemic. A couple of months before the outbreak, Earle tried to obtain funds for his own biologist and bacteriologist to supervise the beds after alarming pink oysters appeared in Annapolis shucking houses.[79] But as health authorities assumed responsibility for monitoring sewage-contaminated waters, the urgency of hiring permanent biologists for the fledgling conservation bureaucracy dissipated.

Truitt's research focused on biology and ecology, but because he used his data to make policy recommendations, he also dealt with the sociology of the water business. The "hard-bitten oldtimers" piloting his boats "laughed, winked and nudged each other when he leaned over the side to draw a few drops from the bay's vast expanse in a medicine dropper," as a journalist described. They did not realize that Truitt was also studying them.[80] His dissertation identified three attitudes among industry members regarding the bay's productivity.[81] Truitt considered only the smallest group amenable to an educational campaign promoting shell return, brood stock protection, and perhaps even leasing, since they considered the bay capable of increased harvests. The others rejected human intervention, though for different reasons. Some believed that divine judgment or pollution had rendered a large portion of the Chesapeake waters "dead" and thus that any rehabilitative endeavor constituted a waste of time and money. A more optimistic group articulated a worldview that has since received much attention from maritime anthropologists.[82] Despite the current debilitation, immense production would recur after the bay had passed through its cyclic downturn. There was no point, therefore, in attempting what nature and God would eventually accomplish.

Faith in natural regenerative powers frustrated Truitt, as shown by his response to a Dorchester County politician's letter published in the *Baltimore Sun*. Delegate Charles Spence urged the state to discontinue its expensive shell-planting operations because the bay's abundance was subject to recurring, unpredictable, and uncontrollable forces: "One year I have seen bars almost barren, and without knowing how or why, the very next season from 30 to 40 bushels daily could be taken from the same bars," he explained. "These beds were seeded by Providence and will likewise be protected by the same source."[83] Biologists knew enough about the influence of certain physical forces (tides and currents, wind and wave action, and sudden weather changes) and human actions (shell and seed planting and intensive dredging) on the abundance and distribution of oyster larvae for Truitt to offer a scientific perspective on the dramatic shifts oystermen observed.[84] Truitt thus derided Spence's "plea for no legislation and 'providential restoration'" as an ignorant response to declining harvests.[85] Although Truitt identified himself in his response as an oyster dealer rather than researcher, he had not yet committed himself to reaching out to skeptics to try to negate the negative image of Chesapeake scientists.

In another risky move, Truitt bit the hand most likely to feed the cause of the Chesapeake science. At a time when many watermen perceived *conservation* as a dirty word, he criticized past legislatures for focusing merely on conserving the industry through restrictive policies rather than on rehabilitating the natural resource.[86] By *rehabilitation,* he meant restoring depleted reefs by returning shells to the bay in a rational manner rather than the more expedient methods used over the past decade. However, his critique overlooked the practical benefit of the oyster laws passed by Maryland legislatures after the Civil War, most of which restricted technological innovation and entry to the commons. Even if legislators intended such policies to promote maximum employment rather than oyster protection per se, and even if the Oyster Navy did not always effectively enforce the laws, they had the positive overall effect of decelerating depletion rates and introducing the concept of a conservation ethic. However, like Brooks before him, Truitt's conviction that the Chesapeake oyster grounds could be refashioned through science-backed corporate efficiency led him to devalue the kinds of remedies that had passed muster with the politically powerful oystermen.

Truitt's critique of the state's unofficial program of reshelling depleted bars rested on three lines of reasoning. One concerned the Conservation Department's practice of hiring watermen to do the work during late March and April, between the oyster and crab seasons. While providing employment during a slack time, it gave the shells weeks to sit on the bay bottom prior to the time of spawning. By then, barnacles and other fouling organisms had colonized the shells, interfering with spat attachment. Truitt thus advised delaying most shell plantings until 1 July, during the height of spawning.[87] Of course, this was easier said than done; by July, many tongers and dredgers had either rigged their boats for crabbing or found work picking tomatoes, cutting corn, or canning vegetables.[88]

An easier problem to solve, from Truitt's perspective, was the agency's excessive reliance on oystermen as consultants. Harvesters who accepted the need to return shell to serve as cultch sought to do so in places that had once yielded oysters. But Truitt pointed out that if no more brood stock remained, no amount of shells could help. Microscopic analysis of larval content, not human memory, should guide such operations, as demonstrated by an unfortunate 1918 experiment. Despite the absence of larvae, the state deposited sixty thousand bushels of shells at the formerly productive Harris's Rock. The failure to generate new oysters not only wasted time and money but "turned observing oystermen from enthusiastic backers into reactionaries," thereby reinforcing the traditional idea that oysters could grow on nothing but a natural bar.[89]

Truitt's third recommendation concerned the quantity of shells deposited. Millions of bushels, not a few thousand here and there, were needed each year.[90] The quantities required posed an enormous obstacle to scientific oyster culture, for the huge piles of shells that accumulated outside shucking houses each season represented a valuable commodity. Shell had been used since the colonial period to build roads, fill in wetlands, and provide lime for mortar; during the early twentieth century, it also became a component of chicken feed.[91] As long as the shells could be diverted back into the bay, Truitt suggested in his 1925 report that the means did not matter. Whether private planters or the state paid, "the fact remains that every shell is needed for restoration purposes."[92] But in other contexts, Truitt left no doubt as to which method he preferred.

Like other prominent fishery experts, Truitt considered privatization of oyster grounds the solution to the industry's decline. Whereas Brooks had extolled the northern oyster-culture states of the late nineteenth century, Truitt pointed to Virginia, which had codified property rights to barren bottoms by 1910. Despite the pollution problems of the Norfolk region, Virginia leaseholders had a rich source of seed oysters from which to draw, the James River. By transplanting the seed to less crowded areas and catching the resulting spat by returning shell to the bottoms, Virginia's oyster output jumped from 1.5 million bushels (versus Maryland's 8 million) in 1912 to 12 million bushels (as opposed to Maryland's 3 million) in 1926.[93] The numbers spoke for themselves. After Baltimore and tidewater newspapers reported the Maryland governor's apparent desire to discontinue any leasing, Truitt expressed his incredulity: "Our work on the Bay, embodying both the practical and the scientific, so distinctly suggest the encouragement of leasing that we hesitate to report for reasons apparent." Governor Albert Ritchie, who responded that "of course" he had been misquoted, would soon incorporate Truitt's pro-leasing proposals into his platform for rehabilitating the industry.[94] But as a master politician, Ritchie couched these ideas in language vague enough to be interpreted as either supporting or opposing the privatization of natural beds.

In the interim, the Conservation Department's record of cultivating oysters elicited mixed reactions from oystermen and packers. Despite Truitt's concern that shoddy shell planting prejudiced watermen against rehabilitative measures, some packers expressed enthusiasm. In 1924, Earle urged Ritchie to expand reshelling operations after Baltimore processors told him "that it was only right for the State to demand their supply of shells from the packers."[95] The Crisfield Oyster, Fish, and Crab Association agreed: "Our packers would be willing for the State to take a liberal per cent of all the oyster shells shucked by our people before these shells are sold for other purposes."[96] But none volunteered to give back shells, and neither the legislature nor the governor approved the conservation agency's budget requests, so year after year, insufficient funds prevented officials from planting as much or as efficiently as Truitt desired.[97]

The state also transferred limited quantities of seed to better growing areas. The idea was to move small oysters from places where salinity, pollution, springtime freshets, or winter freezes prevented them from maturing. Because the state often hired dredgers to harvest the resulting bivalves for sale to private planters, some observers felt that the practice benefited Maryland's few leaseholders at the expense of oystermen. As the program's most outspoken critic, Deal Island dredger William C. Todd, told the governor, "Every thing Mr. Earle does is against the oyster beds and for the planter."[98] Even though salinity levels at the head of the bay prevented oysters from growing large, Todd opposed transplanting them: "It looks like the Commissioner and the Committee wants to depleat the oyster beds. . . . So they can lease them out [or] steel them from the public."[99] Removing seed along with old shell destroyed the Upper Bay's natural beds and gave leaseholders an unfair advantage: "You take the Hollands and Kedges Straits operation in 1925[.] Oysters[,] shells and all shoveled and sold to planter that ruines the beds and what was don this spring in appril that is against the oyster beds. . . .

[T]he best bed we have up the bay was shoveled and carried to Western Shore . . . about ten year's ago and there has never been another dayes work on it."[100] Todd lodged these objections even though, according to Earle, the dredger had participated in the operations and been "enthused" to have received a "month's extra employment."[101] Todd may have had an axe to grind, for as a Deal Island constituent informed the governor, "Now it seems that one W. C. Todd is spreading the Report among the voters of this District that you are in favor of Leasing all of the oyster Grounds[.] [I] understand he is very sore on you because he did not get the appointment of Conservation Commissioner."[102] Todd publicized his grievances in the *Baltimore Sun,* asking, "Why destroy the beds that God has put in our care?"[103] In late 1928, having found the Upper Bay reefs in the best condition of the past quarter century, he expressed confidence that the state had nothing to do with their condition. He agreed that the previous summer's floods had killed a third of the oysters and thus left more shell on the beds but attributed the phenomenon to divine intervention: "It therefore seems to me that God, seeing the failure of those in power to replenish the beds, caused the oysters to die in order that the shells might replenish the beds and bring prosperity to the oyster industry."[104] It is difficult to say how many other oystermen agreed with Todd regarding the state's rehabilitative efforts, but even at the height of Earle's unpopularity, dozens petitioned the governor to keep him on the job in gratitude for his efforts in transplanting oysters from unfavorable areas.[105]

The experimental repletion program reignited the leasing question, which had sat on the back burner for a decade. In late 1926, Earle announced what he considered the wonderful results of the planting of 153,000 bushels of shells at the mouth of the Potomac River two years earlier. The five-hundred-acre area, below Cedar Point Hollow, had been kept off-limits to harvesting to allow spat to settle on the shells and mature. Satisfied with their growth, the Conservation Department issued special $1.00 licenses to some ninety dredge boats for the privilege of harvesting part of the reserve and required the buyers to pay an extra tax of ten cents per bushel. In three days, dredgers took forty thousand bushels (far less than the one hundred thousand Earle had predicted), which sold in Crisfield for $1.40 each. Earle enthused that the original shell planting had cost the state $15,000 yet yielded $50,000 to the dredgers.[106] But Governor Ritchie interpreted the operation as a loss because the state received only $4,000 from the bushel tax despite having spent $20,000 on planting and policing. By contrast, he claimed, without citing any evidence, a private individual could have performed the same work for $21,000 and netted a profit of $19,000.[107] Whereas Ritchie based his analysis on the strict dollar output to the government, Earle counted the money that flowed into oystermen's pockets and by extension the tidewater economy, two very different ways of calculating the program's benefits. For decades thereafter, critics of state oyster farming focused on its absolute monetary costs rather than on other measures of value that could not be captured on a spreadsheet. The apparent economic delinquency symbolized by the Cedar Point experiment provided Ritchie and his scientific ally Truitt with the gambit they needed to put leasing back in the spotlight after a decade under wraps.

Return of the Leasing Question

Albert C. Ritchie had every reason to swagger on the opening day of the 1927 General Assembly. Not only was he now the only Maryland governor to serve a third term, but his party dominated both houses and he had just presided over a three-year period without regular legislative sessions, enabling him to consolidate his power.[108] One important change made agencies more responsible to the executive than the legislative branch; in addition, Ritchie spearheaded successful efforts to reduce taxes, trim budgets, build roads, reform education, negotiate with Virginia on legislation protecting the blue crab, and begin to fix the legislative malapportionment and increase Baltimore's representation.[109] Now he turned his attention to the oyster problem, calling it "the most serious consideration of this administration."[110] It was a bold claim given the difficulties Maryland still faced as a small southern state, but reforming the oyster laws in favor of leasing appealed to Ritchie's penchant for "business-modeled" efficiency and economic conservatism.[111] It was no easy task, as a constituent recognized: "How you are going to satisfy the diversified interests and ideas of the Oystermen God only knows and I do not envy the man who undertakes the job."[112]

While running for his third term, Ritchie courted the oyster industry. He convened a 1926 "conservation parley" to which he invited a hundred representatives of the nineteen thousand dredgers, scrapers, tongers, and packers. Five hundred showed up at the statehouse, docking their boats in Annapolis Harbor.[113] Ritchie limited the discussion to the questions of increasing the cull size and limiting the season; he knew better than to raise the leasing specter just yet. The majority of speakers agreed with the idea of increasing the marketable size from 2.5 to 3 inches, a recommendation that Truitt had made to allow oysters an extra season in which to reproduce.[114] The idea appealed to industry members for economic reasons, since they sought to increase the number of valuable selects and counts, a difficult venture when every oysterman scrambled to get the minimum-size specimens before someone else did.[115] At the same time, other attendees argued that there was no use in increasing the cull size when the current law went unenforced – or worse, when inspectors allowed favorites to take undersized oysters.[116] The question of enforcement provoked a flurry of letters to the *Sun,* including Commissioner Earle's impassioned denial of laxity and corruption.[117] Like resource users everywhere, oystermen did not necessarily like laws that restricted their use of the public domain, but the perception of unfairness rankled even more.

The other issue on the agenda also stemmed from a suggestion by Truitt that revealed his sympathy to the interests of the packing industry – eliminating September oystering. Most oyster processors handled agricultural produce in the off-season, and September therefore posed a dilemma. Despite the critical need for workers in the fields and canneries at that time, most of the men departed to dredge or tong, while women left to secure positions as shuckers. Truitt also offered biological reasons for shortening the season. Hot spells during the first R month promoted spoilage, and the bivalves remained watery as a consequence of the energy they expended all summer on spawning. The dredgers attending Ritchie's parley proved much more amenable to eliminating September than did the tongers, probably because the former were less likely to own their own boats, a key factor in the legendary independence associated with working the water.[118] Ritchie's conference ended only with his promise to consider appointing an advisory committee. He ultimately followed through, but the body did not represent the industry's diversity: most members were large processors. Even Truitt, the committee's sole scientist, was identified as a packer.[119] In this context, it is not surprising that Ritchie welcomed the prospect of leasing or that he waited until after winning the election to publicize his plans.

Ritchie's opening address to the 1927 legislature focused on reversing the "gradual extinction of the oyster." Not only had landings dropped to under three million bushels for the first time, but declining quality had weakened the Maryland industry's reputation. To get more big oysters in circulation, he recommended leasing thirty thousand acres of the bay's most depleted bars for five years, using the Upper Bay to propagate seed oysters for transplanting to depleted bars to the south, and enabling tidewater citizens to circumvent local circuit courts to lease depleted bars.[120] Truitt's influence was obvious: he had been suggesting such ideas for years, with Earle's support. Though Ritchie did not use the phrase *natural beds,* leasing them appeared to be his intent. The plan angered many oystermen: "Is it fair to take our oyster rock away from us?" asked Captain Alfred Moss. "That's all right for the capitalists, the fellows who own the packing houses and have a lot of money to plant leased beds, but what are the dredgers and the tongers going to do if all that bottom is taken away from them?" Demanded another man, "How are they going to keep us out of these beds? Each planter will have to keep a battleship to protect his lease when the oystermen get started in the fall." Oystermen's protective associations throughout the state condemned the leasing plan.[121]

The arguments presented at rowdy, well-attended caucuses in Annapolis and tidewater towns echoed those of earlier eras. "As the hearing proceeded time seemed to run back as a scroll and one could close his eyes and imagine himself transported to the early days of this century, when the Haman bill was hammered to death by the oystermen," wrote one *Sun* reporter.[122] But Ritchie also floated a new idea, having processing firms surrender 10 percent of their shucked shells each year to serve as cultch on the bay bottom. Packers had expressed their willingness to do so as far back as 1921, and now that several packers served on Ritchie's advisory committee with Truitt, they agreed to give up a bit of their valuable by-product, presumably because they expected to profit from the concurrent liberalization of the leasing laws.

Legislators also considered several other oyster conservation bills proposed by Ritchie's committee. These measures sought to shorten the season, increase the cull law, limit the maximum dredge size to forty-two inches, provide the conservation commissioner with more discretionary power to open and close reserve areas, and increase license fees and inspection taxes to fund shell planting.[123] A petition from several dozen Solomons Islanders supported reshelling but opposed any other changes: "Please donot limit the size dredge to forty two inches as it will make a hardship for us[.] we cannot operate large boats with that size dredge we just can make a living for our family now and the cull law is allright now if it was enforced. . . . we are satisfied with the law just like it is only add three cents on a bushel [to the inspection tax] for to plant shells with[.] we trust you will consider and give us what we need."[124] The bill to institutionalize shell planting was indeed the most popular one. Despite damaging testimony regarding the Conservation Department's inefficient methods, the oyster industry's branches reached a consensus in favor of more extensive shelling.[125]

By contrast, fear that Ritchie's leasing plan would serve as the opening wedge to corporate raids on the natural reefs washed over the capitol. After several weeks of refusing to compromise, the governor tacitly admitted his miscalculation by claiming that he had not realized that nineteen thousand of the proposed thirty thousand acres to be privatized were still productive and thus not subject to lease under the Haman Law.[126] The *Sun* questioned how such a meticulous administrator could have made such an oversight.[127] But the reversal enabled him to save face and maintain that he had always opposed leasing the natural bars.[128] Early in his career, as a lawyer championing Progressive Era reforms, Ritchie had won a reputation as a friend of the people by securing lower rates from the Baltimore gas and electric utility.[129] Now he appeared the oystermen's defender: wrote one retired dredger, "I feel proud to think that just at the time when the might[y] hand of the rich people were about to swallow us up that we had a man like you to stick buy us[.] they alwas told me the lord would loock out for his people and so have you[.] we are not asking any thing but our free rights to make our livin[.] we are satisfied we are not rich but we are worcking people so iam glad you feel like giving us the chance. . . . dont rob our rocks for seed for private planters."[130] Ritchie remained in office for another seven years and never again mentioned leasing.

The 1927 debate forced oystermen and their legislative allies to acknowledge that greater action was needed to stem the oyster's decline. The assembly increased the minimum marketable size to three inches and established a permanent program of shell and seed planting to be supervised by a salaried three-man commission.[131] The repletion work would be funded by an annual seventy-five-thousand-dollar appropriation, a four-cent gasoline tax on motorized boats, and most importantly, the confiscation of 10 percent of the shells shucked in state – about two hundred thousand bushels – or their cash equivalent.[132] Despite the earlier consensus among packers favoring the shell tax, now that that they had lost the opportunity to expand leasing, some recoiled at what they saw as bankrolling the oystermen by bearing a greater tax burden for rehabilitating the reefs.

Bellevue's William Valliant launched the first shot against the shell tax. As his broadside to the legislature proclaimed, "The packer and the planter has shown a net profit to the State of about $50,000.00 annually, while the natural rock oysterman has shown a loss to the business of about $68,000.00 annually, yet the laws you have under construction were apparently to satisfy the losing customer of the State."[133] Because shell planting had generated such poor economic returns for the state, Valliant asked, "Why should you tax the packer out of business and waste the proceeds and much more of the taxpayers money besides? . . . Had you repealed the Shepperd Act or knocked out some of its teeth . . . and cut September from the season, it would have meant success. What you have done means ruin, at least, to the packer."[134] Weeks before the 1927–28 season opened, the Crisfield-based Tri-State Oyster Packers' Association challenged the constitutionality of the shell tax on the grounds that it deprived them of property without due process.[135] Appellants argued that because they shucked oysters from other states, the shells should not be considered the common property of Maryland.[136] Despite a Court of Appeals ruling upholding the law, Valliant refused to comply until the U.S. Supreme Court weighed in, blocking marine police from his premises. A tense yet nonviolent "shell war" ensued in which another packer had the local sheriff arrest the Oyster Navy commander for taking a few wheelbarrow loads from the packer's shell pile.[137] Valliant took pride in instigating the rebellion, and the Tri-State Association put Earle on the defensive by accusing him of wastefulness and incompetence.[138] The association even attacked Earle for failing to be an oyster conservation innovator, a charge that amused the *Sun,* since "new ideas and original thoughts in this business have invariably met with a merciless bombardment of objections."[139]

Earle won a bittersweet victory after a two-year standoff when the U.S. Supreme Court unanimously upheld the shell act. The justices eviscerated the appellants' case, declaring, "The Federal Constitution may not be successfully invoked by selfish packers who seek to escape an entirely reasonable contribution and thereby to thwart a great conservation measure generally approved."[140] Despite having been raked over the coals, Earle assured resistant packers that their shells would be distributed on nearby beds. Shell nevertheless remained so scarce that it became the limiting factor in repletion efforts, prompting a fifty-year search for alternative cultch sources.[141]

At the same time, other observers argued that lack of shell substrate was the least of the oyster's problems. Packer-planter William Northam had for years ridiculed reshelling on the basis that pollution had destroyed shellfish larvae; Ritchie's support for the program thus pained Northam: "Governor you have been grossly deceived," he wrote, "and I can prove beyond the shaddow of a doubt that every dollar spent for shell planting during your administration has been wasted."[142] Northam subsequently declared that he would refuse to sell any shells beyond the required 10 percent because "the trouble lies not in the scarcity of shells but in the absence of spat," which he blamed on industrial waste. "When our money is spent along the line of trying to find why our oysters are not spawning, we may get somewhere."[143] Pollution greatly concerned Earle, but he dismissed Northam's contentions, asserting that New Jersey, with its far more polluted waters, was planting shells extensively and that "ninety percent of the watermen and the majority of packers believe shellplanting is good."[144] Northam reiterated his points in the *Baltimore Sun;* Earle responded by citing Truitt's research on the need for more shells to which spat could attach rather than the need for more spat per se.[145] The possibility that the waters near Northam's operations in Benedict on the Western Shore's Patuxent River might indeed be contaminated never seemed to occur to Earle or Truitt.

Though disappointed by leasing's failure, Truitt believed that he had convinced decision makers of the value of reshelling beds and increasing the cull size.[146] But the state's willingness to move beyond experimental repletion efforts did not mean that scientists would assume the responsibility. To Truitt's dismay, the Conservation Department continued to broadcast shells when oystermen were available and "where they or their fathers once took quality oysters."[147] He was by no means the only fishery scientist to see his recommendations cast aside. From New Jersey to California, powerful political and economic entities quashed state-employed biologists' hopes that their studies might help regulate overcapitalized fisheries at the breaking point.[148] Maryland's oyster industry had survived primarily because of the persistent use of 1820s technology and the Chesapeake's relative freedom from pollution and disease. But it could not last forever, as thousands of tongs and dredges whittled away at the biological capital on the bay bottoms and as new development patterns threatened to increase inputs of sediment, toxins, and runoff. As Truitt awaited a more opportune time to broach the matter of leasing, he focused on building up the CBL as a first-rate research institution, ready to advise the state if asked.

The Chesapeake Clinic

The year 1929 was not a great one for the scientific equivalent of nation building. Truitt lucked out when, several months before the stock market crash, the Maryland legislature approved funds for a permanent marine laboratory. The *Baltimore Sun* praised the move, proclaiming, "Science can here serve commerce without abandoning its own curiosity as to the laws of social welfare in the oyster world."[149] Political intrigue surrounded the site of the proposed "oyster experiment station." After months of vigorous squabbling among state and federal politicians and local boosters, the town of Solomons won out.[150] At last, Maryland's conservation biologists could conduct their work in a setting more apropos than the parish hall.

Truitt worked his connections to allow construction to proceed despite the onset of the Great Depression. Governor Ritchie squeezed an extra twenty-five thousand dollars from the 1931 state budget for the lab, an impressive concession given his fondness for slashing expenditures. At its completion, the CBL represented the state of the art in marine research. Behind the colonial facade, gas, electricity, compressed air, and saltwater surged to laboratories equipped for studies of biology, biochemistry, and biophysics.[151] Beyond bricks and mortar, the CBL signified a new era in which researchers would extend the reach of the agricultural experiment station to tidewater and riparian America.

Amid ever-worsening economic reports on the national front, officials and residents gathered in June 1932 to dedicate the lab and celebrate applied science (fig. 12). Thanks to the federal largesse that had bankrolled scientific agriculture, stated Lewis Radcliffe of the U.S. Bureau

Fig. 12. R. V. Truitt addressing the crowd at the dedication of the Chesapeake Biological Laboratory, Solomons Island, June 19, 1932. Governor Albert Ritchie is seated behind him. (Courtesy of Chesapeake Biological Laboratory and Marine Biological Laboratory Archives.)

of Fisheries, "the farmer of today knows more science, and makes daily application of it, than the scientist of 50 years ago knew"; commercial fishermen, however, had made no such progress.[152] This was an ironic admission of failure on the part of Radcliffe's own agency, which had erected scores of hatcheries that benefited recreational rather than commercial fishermen and which persisted in funding fish culture despite an astonishing lack of evidence regarding its efficacy.[153] Radcliffe also raised obvious questions when he praised Maryland for "conserving its

God-given resources for its citizens, present and future . . . by not merely locking them up but [making it possible for them] to multiply."[154] Such rhetoric had played well in the Progressive Era, but now it underscored the role of research in fueling agricultural overproduction and thus the depression.[155] While the audience probably took Radcliffe's words at face value on that festive day, the comments of another speaker might have drawn strange looks from local elders. After calling for field laboratories to be built throughout the country to advance both aquatic biology and aquaculture, Cornell University's James Needham invoked Brooks's work a half-century earlier: "It will be well if this laboratory can retain his interest both in pure science and in its applications to human welfare. His most intensive technical undertakings never estranged him from his interest in the practical problems of biology in the Chesapeake."[156] Needham neglected to mention the antagonism that Brooks's advocacy of leasing had provoked, but many more years would pass before tide water audiences disassociated that offensive idea from the broader cause of science-based conservation.

Financial constraints hit the nation's scientific establishment hard in the early 1930s, a problem magnified at the state level. Though Maryland's conservation biologists had a roof over their heads, they could do little with the state's meager annual appropriation of five hundred dollars. Forced to court outside organizations, Truitt convinced the prestigious Carnegie Institution of Washington, D.C., and several area colleges "that the Solomons project held promise for them and the cause of ecology" as a result of its proximity to bay and tributary environments.[157] Each summer from 1933 to 1941, these institutions sent equipment, students, faculty, and funds, making the remote town of Solomons a little like the famous scientific resort of Woods Hole, Massachusetts (fig. 13). Many researchers traveled to the southern Maryland peninsula, including prominent University of Illinois ecologist Victor Shelford, a fact Truitt used in his futile efforts to extract extra funding from the University of Maryland, where he continued teaching.[158] The infusion of talent enabled the laboratory to expand its research far beyond oysters. The earliest attention had gone to commercial organisms, especially the blue crab, rockfish, shad, marlin, croaker, diamondback terrapin, and several kinds of clams. But researchers increasingly turned to less glamorous species such as snails, algae, sea nettles, diatoms, aquatic insects, and boring sponges as well as the complex ecological webs linking life in the

Fig. 13. Biologists R. V. Truitt and Francis Beaven (third and second from right, respectively) with students at the first summer session of the Chesapeake Biological Laboratory, Solomons Island, 1932. (Courtesy of Chesapeake Biological Laboratory and Marine Biological Laboratory Archives.)

bay with physical and chemical forces.[159] By the end of the decade, CBL researchers had conducted groundbreaking studies of estuarine physics and chemistry, thereby setting the stage for the explosive growth of estuarine ecology in later decades.[160]

Industry officials, however, were more interested in how science could address their immediate concerns. "The Chesapeake Biological Laboratory . . . is a very fine thing," wrote a group of packers to the governor soon after its opening, and "biological studies on seafood life are very necessary, as the basis for intelligent conservation." But the industry needed information on "handling and processing the creature of the water after it leaves the water and becomes an article of commerce."[161] Ritchie responded that there was no need for the CBL to duplicate the frozen seafood studies of the Birdseye Biological Lab in Gloucester, Massachusetts.[162] Oysters had made Baltimore the nerve center of the post–Civil War U.S. canning industry, but quick freezing was a new development. Frozen oysters and other fare produced by pioneers such as

Clarence Birdseye were available in a few places by the early 1930s but were luxury items: few stores or consumers owned freezers. Not until after World War II did frozen foods invade the mass market.[163] At that time, Truitt recognized the potential of modern preservation technologies to resolve overproduction, one persistent antileaser fear.[164] Indeed, the postwar Florida citrus industry eliminated surpluses through the "miracle" of frozen concentrated orange juice, a technical advance made possible by state and federal scientists.[165] But Truitt never had any desire to run an industrial research lab, and though he called for better marketing during the 1930s to increase consumer demand, the problem of excess oysters had become almost inconceivable.

To raise the profile of his vision of Chesapeake science, Truitt turned to the *Baltimore Sun,* an old ally in the leasing debates. The paper's weekend magazine featured the lab and its one-thousand-acre aquacultural farm in the context of Truitt's interpretation of the oyster problem: "In spite of the claim of many oystermen that the waters of the Chesapeake are 'dead,' scientific studies . . . showed that this vast body of water is essentially the same today as it was in the glorious eighties, when Maryland dominated the oyster market. . . . To the biologist, the present depletion is not evidence of an angry God, but is rather evidence of the greed of man. Science has established that depleted oyster bars of the Chesapeake can 'come back' if man would only give nature a little assistance."[166] The author—whose status as a CBL staff member was not disclosed—reduced the complex oyster problem to a deceptively straightforward matter. He did not address the support many oystermen expressed for the 1927 repletion law, the huge costs of shell and seed planting, the difficulty of obtaining shells, the state's inattention to biological criteria, or the reality of pollution, however limited. The article's subtle jabs at harvesters' greed and ignorance, combined with the assumption that science had established all the answers, reinforced oystermen's distrust of Chesapeake academics.

Another series of flattering articles on CBL research appeared in the *Baltimore Sunday Sun Magazine* later in the decade under the byline R. L. Carson. Rachel Carson, then in her thirties and an unknown scientist at the U.S. Bureau of Fisheries, had received a master's degree in zoology from Johns Hopkins in 1932, studying under several marine biologists who had worked with Brooks or Truitt. When she turned to professional writing to supplement her government salary and support her family, the

Chesapeake fisheries were an obvious choice. Three of her seven 1937 *Sun* articles dealt with oysters, and she revealed herself an intellectual granddaughter of W. K. Brooks, writing, "Alone of the important oyster-producing States, Maryland clings to her belief in the sanctity of the public beds, and has failed to give active support to a program of private planting." After describing oyster propagation in the eloquent language for which she later became famous and citing Brooks and Truitt, she concluded the article "Farming under the Chesapeake" with an endorsement for leasing from her supervisor at the Bureau of Fisheries, although she did not divulge her connection to the official.[167] Carson had taken for granted scientific experts' economic orthodoxy, an analytical lapse she would not repeat twenty-five years later.[168]

Depression-Era Leasing Debates

As the depression worsened, the state's rehabilitative efforts seemed to be working as evidenced by an increase in oyster landings from 1.8 million bushels in 1930–31 to just over 2 million bushels in 1931–32.[169] But no market for the oysters existed. Prices fell so low in early 1933 that packers stored their stock underwater and harvesters found it more cost-effective to leave bivalves in the bay than expend the energy to extract them.[170] The problem went far beyond the normal lull between the winter holidays and Lent, when Maryland's many Catholics bought extra shellfish as a meat substitute. A banking panic coincided with the start of Lent, dealing the oyster industry a further blow.[171] The sustained lack of demand presented oystermen and processors with their greatest challenge since the 1924 typhoid outbreak. Accordingly, the Oyster Growers and Dealers Association of North America admonished its members to "double the demand for oysters next season or leave the convention with the sure knowledge that all members . . . will swap price punches to the survival of the fittest."[172] Packers often fought to undersell each other, thereby magnifying the problem of low prices fueled by low demand and low-quality product. A more cooperative endeavor, a one-hundred-thousand-dollar national advertising campaign, produced some improvement, but reduced purchasing power served as a powerful disincentive, and cheap imports of frozen oysters from Japan further undercut U.S. firms in the late 1930s.[173] Not until World War II would domestic oyster sales, like the entire economy, rebound.

Oystermen's discontent provided a potent campaign issue for both contenders in the 1934 gubernatorial race. So eager was Albert Ritchie to win a fifth term that he contradicted his well-known stand in favor of states' rights and state responsibility by promising to seek federal funds to employ idle dredgers and tongers in oyster repletion.[174] He also told a Cambridge meeting of three thousand watermen that if reelected, he would repeal the unpopular gasoline tax on workboats, which helped fund shell planting, and reorganize the Conservation Commission, an implicit pledge to fire Earle.[175] The governor had been under pressure to do so for years. As a tonger had warned, "if you retain him you loose thousands of friends . . . give us a practical man and your trouble will be less."[176] When wealthy widow Alice DuPont donated a vessel to the Oyster Navy, it reinforced resentment against Earle for enforcing the conservation laws during hard times: "He lords it and struts like a little bantam anyhow. And to send him in a Pierpont Morgan Yacht is going too far. Sell the boat and let the States business be done in a working boat. Democrats are not used to show of this sort. It is going to hurt us."[177]

Ritchie's challenger, Republican Harry Nice, pounced on Earle's unpopularity. At a mass meeting in the Eastern Shore port of Rock Hall, Nice promised to appoint a three-man Conservation Commission without a "czar." The candidate blamed the industry's desperate condition on several measures, which he neglected to mention had won the approval of oystermen and their representatives in 1927: "The harassing of watermen by burdensome taxes and licenses; the passage of improper legislation regarding barren bottoms at the instance of impracticable theorists, . . . the imposition of an unjust, unnecessary and vicious gasoline tax on work boats and . . . a general refusal to listen to the advice and entreaties of practical watermen until the approach of an election suddenly disclosed to those in power the need to win votes."[178] Although the accusation that Ritchie and Earle had neglected watermen's advice was unfair, the idea of politicians invoking the oyster problem when they needed votes held a grain of truth; allegations had circulated for years that the marine police stopped enforcing conservation laws in the weeks leading up to Election Day.[179] Nice played on this idea as well as on the long-standing resentment of the "impracticable theorists" who advocated leasing. He sensed the opportunity to win the governor's seat, which he had lost to Ritchie in 1919 by a galling 165 votes.[180]

While the electioneering regarding conservation leadership revealed genuine concern over the fishery's future, it masked an ugly open secret of tidewater Maryland. Ritchie was vulnerable not only because he had outworn his welcome after four terms but also because he had enraged rural whites by calling out the National Guard following several brutal Eastern Shore lynchings of African Americans.[181] Both candidates perceived the oyster problem as the key to capturing the shore vote, though the Republican won the traditionally Democratic region. Thus ended Ritchie's remarkable fifteen-year tenure, during which he "brought Maryland into the twentieth century" by strengthening support for conservation, among other important advances.[182] Earle's long career with the state also came to a close, and with the elimination of Ritchie's packer-dominated Oyster Advisory Board, a new era in which watermen exerted even more control over oyster management appeared imminent.[183]

At the same time, new developments on the national stage indicated the possibility of expanding oyster privatization. Convinced that the path to economic and social stability lay in fostering cooperation among professionals from the public and private sectors, President Franklin Roosevelt's administration established the National Resources Planning Board in 1933 to advise policymakers on public works projects, compensatory spending, executive branch reorganization, and the creation of regional and state planning boards.[184] The resultant Maryland State Planning Commission charged its members with outlining a ten-year plan for improving the state's highways, schools, public health, taxation, agriculture, land and water use, and seafood conservation.[185] The commission's director, sanitary engineer Abel Wolman, shared Truitt's conviction that instituting an extensive system of private production would restore Maryland's dominance in the seafood sector. Because Truitt headed the conservation subcommittee, which focused on oysters and included several packers, it seemed that the new context of economic planning might be the perfect venue for promoting elite prescriptions for oyster conservation.

Wolman had begun his career with Maryland's health department, where in 1919 he codiscovered a water-chlorination process ultimately responsible for saving countless lives. After the typhoid outbreak, he helped the U.S. Public Health Service develop new bacteriological standards for oyster processing.[186] By the 1930s, Wolman held a professorship at Johns Hopkins University and played strategic roles in multiple state and federal agencies concerned with public health, water resources, and sanitation, making him "Maryland's number one jobholder."[187] Throughout his seventy-five-year career as one of the century's public health luminaries, world leaders called on Wolman to implement systems designed "to interrupt the hitherto successful link between the diseased and healthy individual," as he defined the role of the sanitary engineer.[188] One biographer argues that because Wolman made a point of promoting projects that did not "oppose the hygienic cultures of communities in which he worked," he resolved the "central paradox of reform groups" regarding whether to impose foreign practices on entrenched cultures or to respect those practices despite their ignorance and obsolescence.[189] But his advocacy of oyster leasing calls this idea into question, since private aquaculture represented an alien undertaking to the oystermen. Wolman also decided early in his career never to endorse political candidates to ensure his security as a public employee in an era when civil service jobs could be reassigned at any moment.[190] His refusal to give endorsements gave him an aura of objectivity, leading many governors to seek his advice even on issues unrelated to his field of expertise.[191] Yet even Wolman's immense clout could not convince leaders to espouse the political hot potato of oyster privatization, and his participation in the Depression-era leasing debates calls into question his political savvy.

By the mid-1930s, despite the ominous changes in the Conservation Department, Truitt and Wolman believed the economic and political climate had changed enough to bring about a bold break. Between 1927 and 1933, the number of licensed tongers dropped from 4,874 to 4,163, dredgers from 282 to 62, and packers from 206 to 165, while the closure of Eastern Shore and Baltimore packinghouses threw hundreds of shuckers out of work.[192] While admitting that something needed to be done to increase consumption rates, which had fallen by 77 percent in fifty years despite a 145 percent increase in the U.S. population, the Planning Commission's conservation subcommittee focused on restoring Maryland's oyster bars "to the high degree of productiveness they once enjoyed."[193] Arguing that the state's rehabilitative efforts were too limited to check the overall downward trend in productivity, the subcommittee recommended developing the oyster fishery along the lines of Virginia's system, in which corporations could lease up to 250 acres of barren bottom and leaseholders could obtain seed oysters from in-state public beds. Public shell and seed planting should be continued, but

not using the present inefficient methods, and the conservation authorities needed to be vested with greater discretionary powers. The proposal did not support the leasing of natural beds but did call for a resurvey of the oyster grounds to distinguish productive from nonproductive
areas.[194] When Truitt and Wolman presented their ideas to the 1935 assembly, they convinced legislators to expand leasing in Calvert County,
home of the CBL, but Governor Nice vetoed the bill after dozens of oystermen descended on Annapolis in protest.[195] The two scientists hun-
kered down and began to prepare for another assault on the next legislative session, two years hence, with Wolman arguing their case in a
Saturday night radio broadcast.[196] Governor Nice expressed his assent,
but during the 1937 session, rural representatives warned that any leasing changes would cause bloodshed.[197]

Beyond the time-honored arguments against oyster privatization, the
question of consumer demand occupied center stage. As a tidewater
delegate asked in disgust after Wolman and Truitt raised the possibility
of regaining the phenomenal harvest levels of the 1880s, "Why must we
bring our people down here year after year to oppose legislation that is
theoretical, hypothetical and impractical? Maryland is raising more oysters now than we can find sale for. What would be the good of ten million to fifteen million bushels of oysters a year if we couldn't sell them at
a fair price?"[198] The prospect of huge harvests made little sense when national agricultural policies aimed to raise commodity prices by reducing
crop surpluses. The notion of developing barren bottoms also contradicted the New Deal strategy of taking submarginal lands out of agricultural production and of closing the arid western range to homesteading
in favor of federally managed grazing districts, as intended by the Taylor
Grazing Act of 1934.[199] Wolman and Truitt published their recommendations for the Planning Commission but did not again push the state to
implement their public-private strategy for oyster rehabilitation.

The idea that a privatized aquaculture industry could thrive only after
the Chesapeake had yielded its last oyster became axiomatic for a new
generation, as expressed by a Baltimorean who signed his 1939 letter to
the *Sun* "Tidewater Man." Having observed the industry for forty years,
he mourned the disappearance of the schooners "lined five and six and
seven deep" unloading cargo at the Inner Harbor, the closing of the
shops on every business block that had sold "a dozen fried" for thirty-
five cents, and the loss of restaurants specializing in "oysters in every

style." The writer blamed the oystermen and tidewater people for mobilizing to defeat every effort to protect the Chesapeake Bay's resources, implying that they were stupid: "Whenever conservation measures were brought up they wanted them administered by 'practical' men, meaning men like themselves. Yet some years ago I heard one of these 'practical' men solemnly testify before a legislative committee at Annapolis that oysters were migratory, that they moved about, that sometimes you found them in one place and sometimes in another!" "Tidewater Man" proposed removing all harvesting restrictions so that within a few years the bay and tributaries would be scraped clean. Only then would it be politically possible to expand the leasing laws, heralding the reappearance of decent bivalves "in about a generation."[200] But the writer overlooked other important factors beyond overharvesting, not the least of which was consumer disinterest in a product highly susceptible to the pollutants clogging the nation's coastlines.

The Entrenchment of State Oyster Farming

The 1930s-era leasing campaigns also failed because state repletion efforts had come to resemble watermen's subsidies rather than conservation measures. Just as the New Deal administration spent millions of dollars on public works projects to provide employment and stimulate spending, shell- and seed-planting operations paid watermen to keep them busy and generate oyster currency. After harvesters realized that public culture was not a prelude to privatization and that the state and packers bore most of the costs, any residual hostility melted into acceptance and expectancy. Noting the legislature's increase in the planting appropriation from $10,000 for 1932 to $125,000 for 1938, a *Baltimore Sun* editorial outlined the policy's benefits: "After the oysterman has spent the winter season dredging oysters from the bars planted a year or two ago and selling them, he leases his boat, his services and equipment to the Conservation Commission and is given employment dredging the seed oysters, replanting them, or hauling shells and replanting them. Thus his working season is lengthened and his crop for the future is prepared." From the oysterman's perspective, "this system must be well-nigh perfect."[201] Indeed, dredgers wrote the governor indignant letters demanding their fair share of the work.[202]

The spring 1934 seed-planting activities demonstrate how the Conservation Department treated oyster repletion as a relief project designed to appease potential subversives, not unlike the projects of the Public Works Administration and other federal agencies. Between 23 April and 10 May, the department hired twenty-six dredge boats and ten run boats, manned by 120 to 150 oystermen from Dorchester, Somerset, and Talbot Counties, to gather 38,037 bushels of Upper Bay seed oysters. After paying the oystermen ten cents for harvesting and five cents for freighting each bushel, the state sold the catch to leaseholders for fifteen cents a bushel. In the second phase, the agency hired the dredgers to catch another 107,402 bushels of seed for transplanting to public bars. Again, the dredgers received five cents for gathering each bushel and three to five cents for delivering and distributing them on five depleted public beds chosen in consultation with local watermen's committees. The department's magazine, *Maryland Fisheries,* proclaimed that the enterprise netted the captains nearly sixteen thousand dollars, money that aided their families and local businesses.[203] The program also provided less tangible benefits, especially the sense of earning a livelihood on one's own terms, which watermen have often valued more than money.[204] Nevertheless, because the financial returns of repletion rarely exceeded the cost to the state, critics for decades thereafter derided the program as a "dredgers' dole."[205]

While public repletion won the oystermen's support, the Conservation Department's efforts to limit access to beds undergoing rehabilitation remained contentious. In late 1938, when asked to open a restricted area in Tangier Sound that had been seeded the previous spring, officials refused on the grounds that prices were too low to justify flooding the market with still more mollusks. Incensed at what they perceived as the state's insulting paternalism or simply desperate to catch whatever they could, eighteen dredge boat captains ignored the decree. Argued one of the alleged poachers,

> The Conservation Commission has been closing different rocks each year for the past eight years. They have been planting six or seven thousand oysters on them until now we have practically no bottom to work on. For instance, Great Rock, where we were arrested today – the first time in my life – is a rock containing 500 acres. They planted 6,000 bushels on fifty acres in 1935 and closed the entire rock. . . . We decided that [the commissioner] had control

long enough and we opened it ourselves today. We found oysters practically all over the rock. They were natural-growth oysters, not oysters that had been planted by the commission. I caught 150 bushels.

Standing up for principle was less important to the other arrestees, who testified to the poor returns of oystering during the depression. Jail would at least provide a decent meal and place to sleep, if not the dignity of providing for one's family: "It cost me $500 to equip my boat to dredge this season, and so far I've made about $200. I owe the entire amount to people who trusted me. Santa Claus is coming to other homes but it don't look as though he will come to mine."[206] The dredgers at least had the law on their side. Within days, a Crisfield magistrate dismissed the charges on the grounds that the area in question had been closed longer than the two-year period required by law.[207] Tidewater judges and juries rarely ruled against accused violators.

But thanks to glutted markets, oyster crime no longer paid very well. The enormous demand stoked by the transcontinental railroad seven decades earlier had long since slacked off, the victim of typhoid scares, Prohibition, and reduced purchasing power. Food historians conclude that because Americans of all economic classes had lost the habit of eating oysters, "the great century of the oyster" ended in the early twentieth century.[208] The industry persevered, though on very different terms. Now, as former federal fisheries official Radcliffe complained, "The great trouble is that oysters have been planted all along the Atlantic, hundreds of thousands of them, and nobody has bothered to find a market for them."[209] Radcliffe, now with the Oyster Institute of North America, again drew ironic attention to officials' ill-fated advocacy of private oyster culture.[210] Now that packers were fighting each other to undersell their stockpiles, a practice that hurt harvesters most of all, he asserted, "The first job is to provide watermen a decent living for their work. Then we can worry about increasing production."[211] Of course, enabling oystermen to gain their livelihood from the bay rather than the welfare office was exactly what the Maryland legislature intended via the public-domain repletion program.

The leasing debates subsided in the wake of the military mobilization, during which many watermen entered the armed services or worked in Baltimore's shipbuilding, steelmaking, and munitions industries. Unlike farmers, commercial fishermen received no draft exemptions, and the government requisitioned many fishermen's boats. Maryland limited the number of oyster licenses, and mine testing restricted access to many parts of the bay. Although naval activities destroyed seven hundred acres of public oyster bars, reduced harvesting pressure gave other reefs a chance to recover. Wartime meat rationing made the limited oystering that did occur very profitable.[212] The war not only revived the national economy but also offered new hope to both watermen and pro-privatization scientists for the oyster industry's postwar prospects.

In the U.S. political system, crisis situations often mobilize support for major reforms that otherwise would have little chance of passing. From the corruption of the Gilded Age to the tragedy of September 11, massive failures of the American order have stimulated sweeping structural changes, many involving vast expansions of governmental powers. Some of the most important U.S. political, economic, and social transformations occurred in response to the Great Depression. The unprecedented magnitude of the 1929 stock market crash overwhelmed the ability of even the most self-sufficient communities to care for their own. To effect economic recovery and preempt a possible uprising, Roosevelt's New Deal policies broke the lingering laissez-faire links to the past by extending the reach of the federal government into everyday life. Agriculture was particularly affected. Newly awakened to the evils of crop surpluses and other forms of overproduction, Americans accepted the administration's solution of direct government intervention in agricultural markets, even though such actions did not address the root problems of overcapitalization and mechanization. Though intended as stopgaps, programs such as acreage reduction and price stabilization subsidies acquired permanency as successive congressional sessions made incremental amendments to the original legislation. Through such means, the New Deal launched the American welfare state.[213]

Late nineteenth-century fishery experts had predicted that a similar pattern of crisis and responsive reform would soon hit the Maryland oyster industry. As soon as overharvesting drove oysters to their inevitable extinction, the political climate would shift in favor of privately funded cultivation. Steep production declines indeed emboldened efficiency-oriented scientists, who considered leasing the only permanent solution to saving the estuarine commons from biological ruin.

But occasional harvest upticks confirmed the tidewater sense of cyclical decline and renewal, thereby undermining the legitimacy of scientific claims that the Maryland oyster faced imminent destruction. Moreover, the undeniable impact of coastal pollution made the oyster appear the antithesis of health food, altering the market to such an extent that scarcity of supply seemed the least of the industry's problems.

And yet the oyster industry survived. Maryland still played a leading role in U.S. and worldwide landings in the 1920s, though the quality of its product declined. Restrictive laws had prevented exhaustion for six decades, but the need for more active manipulation of the resource became evident. Other oyster states had improved quality and quantity by allocating barren bottoms to entrepreneurs who assumed the cost and risk of culturing. But leasing remained politically impossible in the Old Line State because oystermen retained their enormous reserve of political capital, even after Baltimore City won a few more seats in the legislature in the early 1920s.

Legislators responded by adopting the compromise measure of public oyster culture as a relatively low-cost, low-level technology that would maintain production with minimal social disruption. Public shell and seed planting sustained the beds and maintained oystermen's access except for limited, temporary closures. Although harvesters had long insisted that humans could not improve on natural oyster growth, repletion became increasingly attractive as economic conditions worsened and ultimately transformed oystermen's attitudes toward both nature and work. Reaping the benefits of rehabilitated beds facilitated oystermen's acceptance of both interfering with natural cycles and accepting indirect state assistance while allowing them to retain their autonomous status. Watermen, who personified individualism and other hallowed nineteenth-century values, thus evolved into defenders of the state-run put-and-take fishery, derided by later critics as "collective farming on the bay."[214]

Yet oyster culture in Maryland bore no resemblance to the true collective farms established around the same time on the other side of the globe. The interwar oyster conservation program offers an important example of state/society collaboration on behalf on nonelites, unlike the idealistic yet disastrous agricultural projects imposed by Stalinist Russia and Maoist China. Those projects failed not only because they forced impossible production goals on the people and the land but also because they elevated modernist faith over local practices.[215] By contrast, Maryland conservation officers sought to help oystermen earn their living in the tradition of their fathers and grandfathers to the greatest extent possible. No attempt was ever made to mold tidewater society and family life to the dictates of technocratic five-year plans. Instead, the repletion program resembled the nascent American model of state-sponsored planning as epitomized by the economic policies of the Roosevelt administration. The New Deal approach to the devastation of the Great Depression was not to replace capitalism but rather to mitigate its worst flaws and secure economic recovery through institutional reform, business-government cooperation, and large-scale public works projects. Likewise, the measures adopted by Maryland's political establishment during the late 1920s and 1930s sought to provide relief and to stabilize rather than restructure the oyster-based economy. Public oyster culture represented a compromise intended to reconcile the conflicting demands of science-based conservation and democratic decision making, particularly in a state with a rural bias.

The public oystering subsidies echoed those granted by the federal government to more powerful, agriculturally oriented interest groups. Landowners in the South, the country's least mechanized farming area, benefited from agricultural subsidies that enabled them to invest in modern equipment and thus throw thousands of sharecroppers and tenants off the land.[216] Western farmers reaped a windfall from the cheap water provided by federal dams, which despite their personification of New Deal efficiency and equity failed to generate enough revenue to offset the costs of irrigating arid farmland for the fortunate few.[217] And organized ranchers often clashed with the federal government over relatively low grazing fees, which reflected broader debates over the "political meaning" of the public-domain lands withdrawn by the Taylor Grazing Act.[218] For all these groups, after the immediate depression crisis passed, the public subsidies remained in place, enabling beneficiaries to consolidate their control of the economy's agricultural and natural resource sectors.

But a key difference between Maryland oystermen and other groups that profited from New Deal subsidies concerned their economic status. Watermen lacked large assets yet expressed little interest in gaining them, setting themselves apart from the capitalist ethos of American business. However, they sought to control and maintain the commons and thus became adept at organizing and deploying their clout – in this case to compel the packers to shell out for repletion activities. Contrary to other stories in the history of U.S. conservation, this was not a case in which economic elites exercised decision-making authority by virtue of their alliances with the state interests charged with regulating them.

An interrelated way in which this story challenges a major historio-graphical theme of government-sponsored conservation is that the scientists in question had great difficulty convincing decision makers and stakeholders to respect scientific expertise. Scholars have documented the role of technical experts in serving corporate interests and thereby legitimating efficiency-oriented, "elite-dominated resource management regimes."[219] Wealthy interests did not co-opt Maryland's conservation administration, which focused almost exclusively on the oyster from its inception in the 1860s through the 1930s. Although packers, the affluent industry members who joined biologists in supporting privatization, gained some authority as gubernatorial consultants following the passage of the 1927 shell law, they were soon booted out, and in later years they remained a muted force for leasing. Biologists struggled to assert their authority as local, county-based groups of oystermen chose where, when, and how reefs would be replenished.

The conservation reforms of the interwar period opened the door – just barely – to greater scientific involvement in resource administration. Biologists gained a literal place in the state's managerial setup when politicians funded the CBL as one of the earliest state-supported (as opposed to federal or private) marine research facilities. Maryland officials thus acknowledged scientific research, if not administrative authority, as a necessary component of fisheries management.

The interwar repletion activities mitigated watermen's misgivings about science-based conservation, though not necessarily about scientists. Shell and seed replenishment represented a chance to integrate informal local knowledge and formal scientific data to bridge the chasm not only between the two stakeholder groups but also between what one scholar calls "knowledge needed to use the resource in the short term and knowledge needed to sustain the resource over the long term."[220] Important aspects of this information gap involved the immediate question of how long to leave treated areas off limits and the more basic issue of where to concentrate repletion efforts. Truitt despaired at the biological inefficiency of relying on oral tradition regarding optimal oystering spots. Granted, years of intensive dredging and tonging had compromised the reefs' structural integrity, but that development did not render valueless the watermen's knowledge base. In the Maryland oyster fishery, as in any extractive industry that privileges artisanal skills over mechanization, one who is not good at observing and remembering changes in the environment cannot last long. And Truitt's research regarding favorable salinity, temperature, and light levels – plus the bad experiences of postbellum leaseholders – revealed that not just any estuarine bottom could produce oysters. Both researchers and oystermen could have benefited from collaborative fieldwork featuring, for example, the use of the microscope to evaluate traditional knowledge claims.[221] But oystermen enjoyed the control they exerted and thus felt no pressure to lobby legislators to fund such work, and scientists saw little value in tapping the experiential insights of uneducated resource users, however influential. The mutual suspicion lingering from the leasing debates permeated the new era of public oyster culture, thereby limiting the program's effectiveness.

Nevertheless, the interwar oyster conservation policies broached a crucial reconciliation between scientific and folkways of knowing. Recent anthropological work illuminates the ways in which Chesapeake harvesters reconcile potentially opposing views regarding religion, nature, and science. Watermen resist regulations and scientific recommendations that prohibit the harvesting of crabs because a much higher authority – God – has provisioned the creatures for their use. At the same time, however, they support rules and science that improve on the bounty provided by God and nature.[222] Faced with falling production levels and refusing to accept privatization, interwar Maryland harvesters modified their belief that interfering with natural, God-given cycles of oyster decline and abundance was futile when they realized that public cultivation sustained their way of life. These attitudes and the scientist-waterman relationship continued to evolve in the decades surrounding the century's midpoint, especially as new bay stakeholders challenged the Old Line State's long-standing equation of conservation with the oyster.

Postwar Pressures

4

The Improbable Persistence of the
Oyster Commons

By the early twentieth century, the idea that scientific knowledge could solve social and economic problems had become an article of faith among urban intellectuals. Bacteriology and sanitary engineering would end the disease outbreaks that could bring commerce to
a sudden standstill. Scientific forestry would provide the greatest good
for the greatest number by replacing the wasteful logging practices that
produced only short-term takings for the lucky few. The social sciences
would rationalize corrupt economic and political systems through efficient, expert planning. And so on. But what if society failed to appreciate and apply such insights? On the eve of World War II, academic and
corporate observers of Maryland's Chesapeake oyster fishery could not
believe it still embraced preindustrial work patterns and business models,
a stark contrast to the mechanization and consolidation of capital that had
transformed agriculture and other labor-intensive natural-resource-based
industries. Even the Deep South was finally modernizing its economic
base. Yet efforts to reform the Free State's system of oyster production
beyond state-funded seed and shell planting had as yet come to naught.

Three major postwar political developments crystallized the tensions
between tradition and modernity that had long marked the Maryland

oyster industry. First, members of a new interest group, citizen conservationists, joined watermen and scientists in debates about professionalizing fishery management. Although this new constituency, mainly sport fishermen, lacked power because of its geographical base in the underrepresented cities and budding suburbs, it helped frame the oft-interlinked debates over privatizing and administering the oyster commons and provided a precedent for the growth of environmentalism as a political force after reapportionment. Pro-leasers seized episodes of dramatic harvest downturns to push their cause in 1947, 1948, 1953, 1961, and 1988, capping a century of ill-starred attempts to transform the Old Line State's system of estuarine property rights. More successful, incremental efforts to depoliticize and scientize the conservation bureaucracy occurred in 1938, 1941, 1948, and 1961, culminating in the 1969 creation of the modern Department of Natural Resources (DNR). Even though scientists and sport fishermen finally became major players in estuarine policymaking, in the late twentieth century the oyster resource remained a state enterprise subject to a significant degree of tidewater control.

A second potential threat to the oyster commons came from watermen themselves. In the 1940s and 1950s, a few localized groups of harvesters conducted innovative leasing experiments in the Maryland Chesapeake. These high-profile cooperatives showed that oystermen recognized the need to join on a collective basis to protect their livelihood, contrary to the assumptions of the "tragedy of the commons" thesis applied so often to the fishery. Despite substantial assistance from state officials and researchers, however, the co-ops failed within less than a decade. The enormous cost of raising oysters in a culture where few respected them as private property served for many tidewater constituents as but the latest instance of the futility of farming under the sea.

A third agent of political change emanated from the highest court of the nation. Although Maryland's malapportionment was extreme, it was not the only state that gave disproportionate weight to the votes of its rural residents. Metropolitan activists from the South in particular launched a series of legal challenges that caused the U.S. Supreme Court to declare unconstitutional the unequal apportionment of state legislatures. Defenders of tidewater traditions mourned the loss of their geographical advantage, fearing that with the shift of power to the booming, affluent, and well-educated suburbs, the conservation interests that had long sought to impose efficiency on the oyster hunt now had the clout to do so. The new suburban politicians implemented major policy changes reflecting environmentalist concerns, yet the system of state oyster farming established in the first third of the twentieth century survived into the twenty-first.

While political developments threatened the common-property status of the Maryland oyster grounds, the ecological capacity of the resource base to sustain economic health ultimately shaped the political landscape. As in previous decades, instances of severe depletion, as indicated by falling harvests, drove postwar leasing campaigns. Though stakeholders continued to debate the extent to which overharvesting, pollution, mismanagement, and divine providence contributed to localized declines, new agents of undeniable destruction came onto the scene. After decimating oysters along the northern Atlantic coast, the disease parasites Dermo and MSX invaded the Lower Chesapeake in 1949 and 1959, respectively. The mysterious microbes, which may have hitchhiked with nonnative oysters planted by researchers or private growers, led state and federal politicians to turn to scientists for answers. Together with other perceived threats to the nation's estuaries, the disease crisis resulted in record amounts of funding and prestige for estuarine research. Fortunately for Maryland watermen, the Upper Chesapeake's low salinity levels impeded the parasites, and the 1959 discovery of vast deposits of fossil shell enabled the state to ramp up the repletion program, thereby engineering another quarter century of relative prosperity. But changed environmental conditions associated with global warming trends in the 1980s finally enabled the pathogens to wreak havoc on the Maryland fishery, prompting the last privatization debate of the twentieth century. Oyster diseases thus posed both perils and opportunities for the bay's diverse stakeholders, and the inscrutable mix of natural and unnatural causes responsible for their entrenchment further complicated the search for solutions.

By the early 1980s, just a few years before disease hit the Upper Bay, Maryland's several thousand oystermen still fished for the most part as their grandfathers had, in handcrafted sailboats on a regulated commons. That is not to say the industry remained a complete relic. A 1971 court ruling eliminated the long-standing law limiting tongers to their own county waters, thereby providing unprecedented mobility and weakening the concept of local commons regimes. Around the same time, the adoption of citizens band radio gave harvesters greater control in negotiating prices with packers, and a few labor-saving devices such as electronic depth finders eased the job somewhat.[1] However, the venerable laws limiting technological efficiency, in concert with the success of the state repletion program, made the Maryland oyster fishery appear relatively impervious to change. How did the oyster commons endure the enormous economic, political, social, and environmental pressures brought to bear between the 1940s and 1980s? In particular, if legislative malapportionment was the key to the system's survival in earlier decades in the face of otherwise influential stakeholders, how did that system withstand the reapportionment revolution?

The Sporting Critique of Maryland Conservation

The oyster question received national exposure in April 1940 when political geographer Isaiah Bowman discussed it in the lead article of the *Scientific Monthly*. Bowman commanded significant influence as a foreign-policy adviser to Presidents Woodrow Wilson and Franklin D. Roosevelt and as the fifth president of Johns Hopkins University, for which he graced the cover of *Time Magazine* in 1936. Bowman's article, "Science and Social Effects: Three Failures," reflected his wide-ranging interests and experience: tropical soil erosion, which he witnessed early in the century as a self-styled "geographical explorer" in South America; global peacemaking, which he tried to achieve as "chief territorial specialist" to the U.S. delegation at the Paris Peace Conference of 1919; and the Maryland oyster fishery, which seized his attention while he headed a 1938 gubernatorial commission to modernize state government.[2] For Bowman, the oyster situation epitomized the idiocy of ignoring scientists such as W. K. Brooks: "The fatal evolution of the industry in the past half century is one of the most remarkable validations of scientific method which we know." To Bowman's dismay, legislature after legislature since the 1880s had acceded to oystermen's wishes: "Lay opinion was substituted for scientific opinion, the profits of the moment for continuing profits. Compromise of conflicting interests in the bay region were sought to provide a form of democratic control with little regard for the substance of the problem." Bowman concluded that scientific solutions could not be compromised and that the only way to implement them while maintaining the democratic process was through better education of constituents.[3] Chesapeake Biological Laboratory (CBL) director Reginald Truitt, who by then had spent almost twenty years trying to implement his vision of rational oyster management, took comfort in his contemporary's assessment.[4]

Bowman's assumption that scientists had all the answers echoed the elitist outlook of other leaders in the movements for both resource conservation and scientific agriculture. Disgust at the oystermen and legislators who rejected Brooks's vision of science serving the industrial order blinded Bowman to the extent to which scientists had reformed some aspects of oyster management. Oyster culture advocates had prompted the General Assembly to move beyond its long-standing focus on gear and season restrictions toward new kinds of regulations governing the Chesapeake commons, especially the 1890 ban against harvesting immature bivalves and the 1927 implementation of reshelling. Despite severe localized declines, relatively stable baywide Maryland harvests of two to three million bushels per year resulted, at the very least alleviating the oystermen's fear of overproduction. At a time when typhoid outbreaks and the increasing availability of other protein sources had curbed the public's appetite for oysters, it made no sense to the harvesters, whom Bowman derided as "so-called 'practical' oystermen," to bring back the record-breaking harvests of the Gilded Age.[5] Yet long after Brooks's basic rationale for private cultivation – insufficient supply – ceased to be a problem because of the shrinking market for the mollusk, modernizers continued to view the northern Chesapeake oyster grounds as a tragically fallow field. Private enterprise would restore multi-million-bushel yields, and all that was needed to reawaken consumer interest was better advertising. The twin goals of increased output and efficiency reflected broader trends, as "inadequate utilization" remained a shibboleth of the science-based conservation and agricultural reform movements.[6] But whereas federal leaders of those initiatives enjoyed great success in the postwar era, especially with respect to the transformation of southern agriculture, Bowman and his fellow oyster culture boosters were stymied time and again by the poor rural workers who stood to lose the most in the transition to mechanized, capital-intensive cultivation.

Conservationists between the end of World War I and 1950 attacked the oyster question not only via leasing campaigns, as in previous decades, but also by trying to overhaul the state's natural resources agencies. The issue attracted a new constituency: vocal citizen conservationists, a group dominated by urban recreational fishermen. Though their political influence did not become key until reapportionment and environmentalism gained traction later in the century, Maryland's outdoor life groups provided an important stimulus in the debates from the late 1930s through midcentury via their innovative use of the referendum and through the gubernatorial appointments of a few sportsmen as tidewater fishery commissioners.

U.S. environmental historians have long recognized the formative role of sportsmen in promoting conservation during and preceding the Progressive Era. Recognizing the need to preserve their favorite game species, wealthy hunters and anglers used their clout to convince New England and later federal legislators to pass the nation's first laws establishing restocking programs, wilderness areas, restrictions on commercial and subsistence hunting and fishing, and antipollution measures.[7] At the same time, such policies reified unequal human relationships by robbing indigent resource users of their traditional access to natural resources, from Native Americans on the western plains to Italian immigrants in the Adirondacks.[8] The Chesapeake region had its share of affluent sportsmen who likewise sought to preserve choice environs for their exclusive use. New York, Philadelphia, and Baltimore captains of industry began laying claim to the best "gunning shores" as early as 1830 and by the turn of the century had convinced Maryland legislators to pass a variety of laws restricting duck hunting.[9]

Sustained efforts by sport fishermen to influence estuarine policymaking in the Old Line State began after World War I. Groups such as the Izaak Walton League's urban and suburban chapters scored a major victory in 1932 by convincing legislators to ban purse netting of finfish. Nevertheless, other efforts, such as limiting commercial harvests of black bass, failed repeatedly, and challenging the conventional wisdom that bay issues fell under the purview of the seafood industry and tidewater delegation remained difficult for Maryland's outdoor-life enthusiasts.[10] In the Chesapeake, unlike much of the rest of the United States, urban conservation and recreational interests failed markedly in their efforts to wrest control over the commons from locals.

The election of a reform-minded governor in 1938 heartened conservationists who seethed at the political control wielded by tidewater interests. The conservationists had suffered a legislative rebuke three years earlier with the ousting of longtime conservation commissioner Swepson

Earle, whose strict enforcement of the harvesting and shell-confiscation laws and efforts to ban purse, drift, and pound nets helped unite the oft-feuding branches of the seafood industries. Critics charged that the 1935 act replacing Earle with a three-person council had achieved little, since Governor Harry Nice used the council as a "roosting place" for political favorites.[11] The new governor, former attorney general Herbert R. O'Conor, defeated the one-term incumbent by a wide margin on a pledge to balance the budget and root out political corruption and inefficiency.[12] The Baltimorean solidified tidewater support on the campaign trail by assuring audiences of watermen and their wives of his absolute opposition to oyster leasing, a shrewd move even though memories of Governor Ritchie's disastrous privatization campaign were so fresh that a journalist opined, "No politician is likely to suggest it in a long time."[13] Pro-leasers probably laid low in the hope that O'Conor's plan to modernize the state's antiquated administrative and judicial systems would pave the way for an overhaul of the commons-oriented oyster code.

Recognizing the impossibility of getting the county-dominated legislature to confront the archaisms of its own micromanaged bureaucracy, the governor-elect cajoled several "experts and outstanding citizens" into serving on a commission to investigate the state government.[14] Chaired by Bowman, the commission included other members who could be expected to recommend major changes, including a state senator from the growing District of Columbia suburb of Prince George's County, lawyer and U.S. treasury undersecretary Dean Acheson, and airplane manufacturer and waterfowl enthusiast Glenn Martin, who later funded an organization of Maryland sportsmen.[15] Laboring under what Bowman called "incredible pressure," the group issued its report within weeks, just before O'Conor took office.[16] Though the proposals should have contained no surprises given the watermen's history of conflict with reformers, the Bowman Commission's recommendations for restructuring natural resource management plunged the young governor into what his biographer called a "baptism of fire (and water)."[17]

The commission interpreted its modernization mission in the context of broader New Deal efforts to address economic and ecological problems. The desire to resolve both agricultural overproduction and soil erosion stimulated the Roosevelt administration to promote land-use planning, which entailed centralized oversight of public-domain resources, most notably the vast grazing lands and national forests of the

West.[18] Likewise, Bowman's group sought to improve commons management by integrating efforts to control soil erosion, stream pollution, and crab and oyster depletion. The proposed system of "coordinated conservation" called for replacing the fishing-oriented Conservation Commission and the lesser-known forestry, geology, and weather bureaus with a centralized DNR. Such a setup, which recognized links between such problems as piedmont deforestation and the silting over of oyster bars, echoed proposals by renowned conservationists. Wildlife biologist Aldo Leopold argued that each state should establish a unified conservation department in place of the wasteful, competitive agencies that existed in many states, a problem ecologist Victor Shelford attributed to rural-dominated state legislatures.[19] At the federal level, secretary of the interior Harold Ickes tried to consolidate all resource management activities under a single Department of Conservation but was ultimately unsuccessful.[20]

In Maryland, two other groups endorsed the Bowman Commission's call for a centralized conservation agency to be headed by an expert. One was the State Planning Commission under Abel Wolman and Truitt. The other was the new Outdoor Life Federation (OLF), an alliance of forty sportsmen's leagues, garden clubs, granges, and other civic associations. But while the sportsmen leaders squabbled over whether the new agency's director should be a political appointee – a development they feared would perpetuate the excessive influence of commercial fishermen – oystermen worked the halls of the statehouse to kill all "coordinated conservation" bills on the table.[21]

In the midst of the worst dredging season in Maryland history, dredgers and tongers joined forces in 1939 in a front so successful that Governor O'Conor abandoned the Bowman bill in favor of a plan that did anything but unify the administration of Maryland's natural resources.[22] The "split-control" system worked out with tidewater politicians proposed two agencies, one for managing the commercial fisheries and the other for game and inland fishing. Though many other states, including Virginia, New Jersey, and Connecticut, had such arrangements, national conservation reformers decried the separate management of species for commercial and recreational ends.[23] But doing so served Maryland's purposes. As the relieved chairman of the House committee responsible for bay legislation announced, "Now we have something that we can work on. Up to this time we have had the watermen on our neck protesting that they did not want a lot of sportsmen up in Baltimore telling them how to run their business."[24] While commercial fishermen around the country felt likewise about rich angling outsiders, few had the means to command attention at the highest levels of state government.

Rather than effecting fundamental change, the reorganization plan reasserted venerable perceptions about conservation in the Old Line State. It focused on fish and shellfish to the exclusion of broader resource issues involving soil, forests, and climate; it also clarified who held the upper hand in natural resource policymaking. Whereas the agency dedicated to commercial fishing would be headed by a salaried body of "well-qualified and practical men who have had experience in the handling of sea food and who have absorbed knowledge from actual contact and study of various phases of this question," the game bureau would be directed by uncompensated sportsmen.[25] Even Earle, whose outlook often aligned with that of recreational fishermen, favored the separate administration of bay and inland resources and criticized OLF leaders for getting involved in what he felt was "not a proper subject for experimentation by a group of amateurs who are chiefly associated with sportsmen's activities."[26] By heeding Earle's advice, the governor earned the wrath of the *Baltimore Evening Sun* for producing "a surrender to a political pressure group" and the praise of the *Crisfield Times* for developing a "sensible conservation program."[27] Caught in an embarrassing about-face, given his pledge to depoliticize the running of government, O'Conor took to the radio to present the split-control plan as a compromise needed "to save the whole idea of conservation for this session."[28] The General Assembly passed the bill, but the governor's baptism by fire was far from over, as sportsmen regrouped to reassert their vision of conservation (fig. 14).

Outraged by the failure to wrest control of fisheries management from watermen, a group calling itself the Maryland Citizens' Conservation League split off from the OLF to pursue a more aggressive tack. Although the 1915 state constitution authorized direct popular votes on bills passed by the legislature or governor, conservationists had never used that proviso.[29] Advertising executive H. Lee Hoffman led a campaign to collect ten thousand signatures, half from Baltimore City and half from the counties. Hoffman's involvement in conservation issues dated to the late-1920s effort to ban purse netting in the Chesapeake Bay. In succeeding years, he organized several Outdoor Life Shows at

Lay That Pistol Down!

Fig. 14. The *Baltimore Sun*'s editorial board often championed private oyster leasing as the only feasible antidote to what board members perceived as watermen's rapaciousness and helpless gubernatorial regimes. (Drawing by Richard Q. Yardley, *Baltimore Sun,* 5 Jan. 1944, © 1944 The Baltimore Sun Company. All rights reserved. Used by permission and protected by the copyright laws of the United States. The printing, copying, redistribution, or retransmission of the material without express written permission is prohibited.)

the Baltimore Armory, attracting thousands of sports and gardening fans and giving rise to the Maryland OLF. Just a year after the group's founding, Hoffman and other OLF leaders convinced the 1935 General Assembly to provide ten thousand dollars for research on two species of commercial and recreational importance, rockfish and shad, by the CBL, a remarkable achievement given the dire economic situation and tenuous status of state fisheries science.[30] Earle privately accused Hoffman of leading the 1939 initiative for a DNR headed by an expert chosen by an advisory council rather than the governor on the grounds that Hoffman sought the position for himself, deriding him as "an advertising man . . . interested in game fishing and hunting [who] knows nothing about the commercial fisheries of the Bay."[31] In 1941, Governor O'Conor appointed Hoffman to another conservation restructuring committee, and Ickes selected Hoffman to serve on the National Fisheries Advisory Committee.[32] With such a leader, Maryland's sportsmen seemed poised finally to become a significant political lobby.

Whether or not he wanted the natural resources directorship, Hoffman evinced a sharp though biased understanding of the role of sportsmen in the U.S. conservation movement. The Baltimorean, who spent his boyhood summers working on his father's farm in landlocked Howard County, drew attention in a 1939 report to "far-seeing" sportsmen of the late nineteenth century who recognized that game- and fish-restocking programs failed to address the root causes of species decline, which included not just overhunting and overfishing but also pollution, soil erosion, and deforestation. But he did not consider all recreational hunters and fishermen so enlightened: "Unfortunately, there are still too many sportsmen in our State with the same provincial sectional attitude so evident on the part of some watermen and commercial interests."[33] His ally the *Baltimore Sun* ridiculed one such reader who urged fellow "hunters and fishermen who enjoy the privilege of outdoor life" to oppose Hoffman's organization and support the governor for appointing nonpolitical experts to the restructuring commission.[34] The *Sun*'s mocking response echoed Hoffman's call for a more integrated approach to managing diverse resources: "Conservation efforts in Maryland are not likely to produce results until those in authority at Annapolis get beyond the stage of counting bunny rabbits and turn their attention to the soil, the forests and the silted and polluted waters of the State."[35] Convincing Marylanders of the ecological links between problems such as upland deforestation and estuarine sedimentation remained a challenge; as a tidewater politician asserted after hearing testimony by Hoffman and Truitt, "I still think Western Maryland and the Chesapeake Bay are as far apart as night and day."[36] But at a time when ecology lacked stature within the scientific community, let alone outside it, assuming that all resource users in such a topographically diverse state should grasp such relationships was rather unfair.[37]

Hoffman's referendum defeated the effort to replace the Conservation Commission, but the measure garnered unexpected support. Marylanders rejected the governor's split-control system in November 1940 by a margin of 91,021 to 22,728, no doubt influenced by the heavy editorial backing of the Baltimore newspapers.[38] However, the breakdown did not follow the expected urban-rural divide, for all the tidewater counties voted against abolishing the existing Conservation Commission and only the District of Columbia suburbs of Montgomery and Prince George's Counties defied the *Sun* and Citizens' Conservation League. The surprising result might have involved the ballot's "very confusing" language, as a Baltimorean complained to the *Sun*.[39] Conversely, tidewater voters who understood the question probably feared that any reform would mark the opening salvo in a battle that would end with their eventual loss of control over fisheries management. Such thinking always drove harvesters to oppose even modest oyster-leasing bills that elevated watermen over corporate interests. Suburban voters likely approved of split-control conservation because they considered the prospect of imbuing sportsmen with even a slight degree of managerial responsibility a harbinger of eventual dominance.

Maryland sportsmen thus played an ambiguous role in modernizing the state's post-Depression system of natural resource management. Interpreting the referendum result as a mandate for coordinated conservation, Governor O'Conor appointed yet another committee to set forth a new restructuring plan for the 1941 General Assembly.[40] Though the commission included Truitt and more sportsmen than seafood industry representatives, its recommendations reflected a compromise that tilted toward the latter.[41] The final bill approved by the legislature and governor established the Board of Natural Resources with five component departments: tidewater fisheries; game and inland fish; forests and parks; geology, mines, and water resources; and research and education.[42] The setup appeared to embody coordinated conservation, but as a mere advisory body, the board had no authority to coordinate the activities of the subdepartments. The real power base lay in the Department of Tidewater Fisheries (DTF), which enjoyed the largest appropriation and whose director also served as chair of the entire board. Conservation in Maryland thus continued to revolve around the oyster, which remained the Chesapeake's dominant resource despite acute localized declines (especially in the dredging areas of the bay proper, as opposed to the tributary tonging grounds).[43] Another sign that the new system represented continuity more than change involved the absence of the State Soil Conservation Committee from the board despite citizen conservationists' ongoing efforts to link oyster management with erosion control.[44] Politicians thereby burnished the conservation bureaucracy with the patina of modernity rather than reconstituting the whole system.

Tidewater interests' victory over sportsmen and their metropolitan ilk was not complete, however. The first chair of the Tidewater Fisheries Commission (the three-person, policy-oriented leadership of the DTF) and thus of the entire Board of Natural Resources embodied the antithesis of the watermen's ethos. Edwin Warfield Jr. was a gentleman farmer from an inland county; a former director of the OLF; a banker and publisher of Baltimore's legal newspaper, the *Daily Record;* and the son of a former governor. Appointed conservation commissioner by O'Conor in 1939, Warfield remained in charge after the agency reorganization. With his fellow commissioners – both of them oyster packers, another traditional adversary of the oystermen – Warfield instituted important changes in the oyster repletion program. Under his direction, the state began planting shells closer to the spawning period to provide clean cultch for spat and keeping records of the resulting spat attachment rates, thereby providing an indispensable baseline for assessing the program's efficacy.[45] He also heeded scientific advice regarding opening parts of the Upper Bay seed areas to limited dredging, decisions that infuriated sportsmen, oystermen, and packers alike.[46] Though rocky, Warfield's tenure from 1939 to 1947 somewhat improved the status of science in Maryland's resource management regime.

However, the question of oyster leasing ended Warfield's career in conservation. In a major reversal involving a lawsuit over an eight-acre lease granted by the fisheries department in Anne Arundel County's Rhode River, the Maryland Court of Appeals ruled in 1946 that the state possessed the authority to resurvey and reclassify depleted natural oyster beds as barren bottoms, thereby making them subject to lease.[47] Expecting the 1947 General Assembly to pass a law affirming the judgment, dozens of private planters and packers applied to lease more than twenty-eight thousand acres that had not yet officially been reclassified as barren. Some of the applicants applied in family units as a way of amassing large holdings and thereby subverting the ban against corporations – exactly what the watermen feared. Tidewater senators exposed the list as evidence of the DTF's malfeasance, prompting Warfield to return the deposits and deny any illegal intent. However, empowered by the recent Court of Appeals decision, Warfield obtained Truitt's help and within weeks issued a report outlining a plan for leasing depleted natural bars in the bay dredging areas. Though oriented toward individual oystermen rather than corporate cartels, the proposal sparked more than twenty crowded, impassioned hearings at the statehouse and a measure to replace Warfield and the two packers with what Calvert County senator Louis Goldstein called "a practical commission . . . that will enforce the present laws instead of spending all its time thinking up ways it can turn the bay over to private oyster planters."[48] An Eastern Shore resident who "made his bread and Butter out of the water" urged Governor William Preston Lane to follow suit: "Please help to abblosh the present tide water cominission. Mr Warfield is a verry fine gentleman but as Mr Warfield says his self he dont know about orysters or fish and has made a failure of it so please as Governor of md help to save the god given rights of the watermen and do not let them lese the bottoms of chespeak Bay[.] [I] am a waterman oyster fish and crab and have been for forty nine years and i know the present Cominisson has been a failure."[49] Although the "ripper bill" died, Warfield resigned.[50]

Rod-and-reel anglers fired one last round in the immediate-postwar debates regarding the meaning of oyster conservation. After allegations of corruption, secret leasing plans, and favorable treatment of packers reignited resentment against the tidewater fisheries agency, the General Assembly convened a 1948 special session, setting off months of discussion on the ideal system of resource administration. In the end, the Citizens' Conservation League's threat to petition for a referendum on bills awaiting the governor's signature – which banned reclassification of natural bay bars for leasing and ensured that tidewater-county residents would hold four of the five new appointments to the Tidewater Fisheries Commission – reminded politicians of the power of the popular will. Faced with an ominous referendum in the midst of a tough reelection campaign, Governor Lane vetoed the bills in spite of his earlier support for them.[51]

Yet as in the earlier referendum initiative, conservation advocates' victory was not clear-cut. Although Lane lost the 1950 election, he negotiated a last-minute deal with the incoming administration to replace the chair of the Tidewater Fisheries Commission and thus the Board of Natural Resources. In place of the first biologist to hold the position, the state's motor vehicles commissioner, Arthur Brice, assumed control. Despite earlier efforts to depoliticize "the most important policy-making position in the State of Maryland," an unusual coalition of sportsmen, urban and tidewater politicians, and other opponents failed to stop the appointment.[52] Only after four scandal-ridden years did Brice lose his job after federal wildlife agents caught him in a baited duck blind, an illegal act that tarnished the images of both the state agency and recreational hunters.[53] On a symbolic though equally embarrassing level, Hoffman's campaign to erect a memorial to oyster conservationists on the bay bridge – in a spot of high visibility to tidewater legislators en route to the capital – came to nothing.[54] Sportsmen and other metropolitan conservationists would have to wait to become a full-fledged partner in estuarine policymaking.

Cooperative Farming on the Oyster Frontier

While the interwar and postwar efforts to centralize Maryland's resource administration mirrored national trends, the contemporaneous oyster privatization initiatives flew in the face of a milestone decision regarding federal land management. To address economic and ecological problems associated with the unregulated use of western rangelands, the Taylor Grazing Act of 1934 ended the long-standing policy of selling off the public domain for homesteading. Henceforth, stockmen, miners, lumberjacks, and other users of the remaining 140 million acres of public lands would be subject to permits, rental fees, and other means of federal control.[55] Yet more than a decade after Congress moved to arrest overgrazing and stabilize the livestock industry by reasserting federal ownership of the range, Maryland's oyster conservationists remained committed to dismantling the regulated estuarine commons.

Privatization advocates continued to interpret the investiture of property rights in the natural oyster bars as a win-win situation. Not only would the state shed the tax burden of rehabilitating the resource, but oystermen would gain an amazing opportunity for wealth creation. A 1947 *Baltimore Sun* editorial interpreted the proposal as an exciting extension of the legendary yet defunct Homesteading Act:

> By proposing to lease the bay beds to tongers and dredgers, Mr. Warfield and his commission are actually proposing to provide practically free farms for the oystermen. Who said that the day of the pioneer is over – the day when a man might go forth, stake out his claim and gain a livelihood proportionate to the effort expended on it[?] True, Mr. Warfield and his commission are talking about water, not land. But they are offering to the dredgers and tongers of the bay an opportunity not greatly different from that which confronted the pioneers in the days when the rich lands of the West were being opened for settlement.[56]

The rhetoric of the frontier cut both ways, as a tidewater resident articulated, asserting that "the citizens of Maryland should be grateful to" the politicians who had exposed the fisheries department's list of monopolistic lease applicants "for their effort to preserve for us and our posterity our last frontier – the Chesapeake Bay."[57] By "frontier" the writer did not mean a raw wilderness, for the oyster reefs had long since become enmeshed in regulatory frameworks that protected common-use rights. Rather, he seemed to invoke Frederick Jackson Turner's concept of a place at the edge of civilization. The Turnerian frontier was a space essential to the American experience of freedom, democracy, and individualism, still open and public, not privatized and modernized.[58] In this sense, Maryland oystermen functioned like contemporary organized ranchers who viewed the West's public lands as crucial to their economic survival and thus within their rights to use against competing interests and with minimal government interference.[59] Both the "public land question" and the oyster controversies illustrate the complex ways in which nonagricultural resource users related to the public domain and the state entities responsible for managing those resources.

Had the *Sun*'s editors taken a close look at the Taylor Grazing Act, they might have perceived that their rationale overlooked an important reason for the demise of western homesteading: much of the land, despite its fabled fertility, "did not produce enough to be owned."[60] The droughts of the 1930s demonstrated conclusively that the arid and semiarid public range was not arable, at least not without massive irrigation subsidies. Within prescribed limits, ranching came to be seen as a better resource strategy, even though cattlemen had inspired derision for failing to improve – to cultivate – the public lands on which they grazed their animals.[61] Maryland conservationists saw watermen as occupying the same shameful niche because they too took from the public domain without imposing greater order on it (except when the state paid them to engage in repletion activities). But the only politically feasible efforts to establish the estuarine equivalent of homesteading on the Maryland Chesapeake frontier failed to encourage oystermen to clamor for "free farms."

The repeated failure of privatization initiatives suggests that the postwar commons supplied all of Maryland's oysters. In reality, however, leased grounds supplied nearly 20 percent of the state's total output by 1946.[62] Granted, that number paled beside Virginia's rate of 65 percent, and most of Maryland's privately bedded bivalves came from outside the Chesapeake. Barely nine thousand of the Chesapeake Bay's eighty thousand acres of barren bottom were under lease to fewer than one thousand leaseholders at midcentury. Most leased grounds were in the highly saline Sinepuxent and Chincoteague Bays, along the Atlantic, close to where Truitt had come of age around 1900.[63] As he neared retirement, having waged several high-profile campaigns to liberalize the leasing laws governing the vast Chesapeake oyster grounds, Truitt witnessed and encouraged a new approach to the leasing question: efforts by watermen and their legislative allies to sustain local commons regimes through collective yet capitalist means – cooperative leasing.

The concept of the cooperatively owned business organization had gained popularity among small farmers, dairy producers, and fruit growers in the late nineteenth century as a way to reap the benefits of economies of scale and market products to expanding urban populations without sacrificing independence.[64] Congress provided legal protection and financial assistance to farmer co-ops during the interwar agricultural depression and in 1934 gave fishermen and aquaculture growers the same rights as farmers to organize marketing co-ops. However, a subsequent effort to provide the kinds of federal loans available to farmer cooperatives failed, thereby making it much more difficult for fishery cooperatives to obtain access to credit than for their agrarian counterparts to do so.[65] Despite the resource-intensive nature of oyster farming, midcentury privatization advocates sought to overcome resistance by promoting oystermen-owned leasing co-ops in the Maryland portion of the Chesapeake.

The most surprising ally in this endeavor was Senator Louis Goldstein, who had helped engineer Warfield's downfall. The 1947 leasing controversy provided Goldstein with statewide exposure, and his political fortunes rose with his appointment to the prestigious Legislative Council, which prepared bills for the General Assembly.[66] So high was his popularity that his proposals could "usually be taken as the party line or the soon-to-be party line of the commercial fishing interests in the bay area," according to the *Sun*.[67] Therefore, his suggestion that a group of Calvert County harvesters form an experimental leasing cooperative to cultivate oysters on nearby natural bars appeared to constitute an about-face. Goldstein couched his plan as a way to "enable oystermen to keep the bay from getting out of their hands."[68] Goldstein envisioned a program

in which members would finance planting, harvesting, and marketing operations, while the state would provide the acreage, police protection, and if desired, scientific assistance.[69] An Annapolis newspaper
praised his efforts to work out "what might in the end, be the salvation
of our once bounteous Chesapeake oyster beds," thereby signifying "a
man who is in the making as one of the real statesmen of Maryland."[70]
Whoever could solve the intractable oyster problem would be a king-
pin indeed.

Goldstein became one of Maryland's most impressive politicians, rising to serve as Senate president and a record ten terms as comptroller of
the treasury, but he never transformed oystering.[71] After county watermen split on the issue and the local newspaper called him a communist,
Goldstein dropped the cooperative idea.[72] The United States and other
capitalist nations had long featured agricultural cooperatives, however,
and Goldstein had sought to emulate the Sunkist organization, which
had evolved over several decades as a consequence of California citrus
growers' and shippers' efforts to more efficiently produce and market
their fruits.[73] He envisioned a system in which "the working oystermen
would have had a proprietary interest in the program and in the marketing of the oysters after they were caught."[74] While far from collective
farming, Goldstein's plan, with its reliance on indirect subsidies, hardly
exemplified laissez-faire free enterprise. Given his previous opposition to
leasing as the opening wedge to corporate control of the oyster grounds,
he may have been more interested in using the scheme to convince state
officials to open a specific area in Calvert waters that had remained
closed to harvesting since the war. Indeed, Calvert County oystermen,
whose full-time numbers had dropped since 1910 from 40 to 0 dredgers
and 537 to 51 tongers, had long sought to reopen the 660-acre Flag Pond
Oyster Rock.[75] But the communism charge made proceeding dangerous,
and differentiating ideas about public and private control of the Maryland oyster grounds remained a vexing problem.[76]

While Goldstein was still making his case for cooperative oyster leasing in Calvert County, his constituents at the CBL conducted an innovative experiment with a younger audience.[77] In the 1939 government
reorganization, the laboratory had acquired a more independent status
than it had possessed under the old Conservation Commission. It now
functioned along with the state weather service as part of the Department
of Research and Education, one of the five administrative units under

the nominal authority of the Board of Natural Resources. Truitt served as the department's director and struggled for funds throughout the 1940s. After two years without any direct appropriations, he squeezed $56,000 from the governor and legislature for the 1943–44 fiscal year, a pittance compared to the $222,800 earmarked for the DTF.[78] Nevertheless, by 1950 the laboratory employed a staff of fifteen on projects of basic and practical importance.[79] Despite the CBL's financial constraints and its growing reputation as "a sort of Mecca for the world of marine scientists," the lab took a special interest in working with the local high school, attempting to demonstrate the financial rewards of oyster farming to watermen's sons.[80]

Like the Future Farmers of America, 4-H Clubs, and other agricultural extension programs, the Calvert County high school's Student Marine Conservation Society sought to imbue rural youngsters with an appreciation for science-based reforms and more efficient crop-growing techniques, thereby mediating between researchers and resistant parents.[81] The CBL advised twenty participating boys and their teachers on the principles of oyster growth and marketing and worked with the DTF to acquire leases to small plots for the teenagers' use in the nearby Patuxent River and Chesapeake Bay. The experiment was a relatively long-term investment, for the students would not experience their first harvest until two and a half years after they began planting seed oysters.[82] Organizers hoped that the program would not only instill respect for the idea of private aquaculture but also persuade young people not to forsake their heritage for higher-paying city jobs.[83] Rural outmigration, which had escalated during the war as watermen left for military service or work in the Baltimore shipyards, was indeed increasing. Of the six Eastern Shore oyster-producing counties bordering the Chesapeake Bay, five experienced population declines as high as 27 percent between 1900 and 1950.[84] The three Western Shore bay oyster counties, by contrast, gained residents, ranging from Calvert's 18 percent growth rate to Anne Arundel's 200 percent spike (table 1). The race was on to convince two audiences – young men who would choose to work the water regardless of outside economic opportunities as well as those who saw few prospects at home – of the value of underwater farming.

One way to do so was by demonstrating the economic benefits of aquaculture. Though slim, the returns on the students' first harvest, in 1950, were good enough to induce the 1951 General Assembly to enact

Table 1. Population Changes in Maryland's Oyster-Producing Counties
Bordering the Chesapeake Bay, 1900–1950

County	1900	1950	Change (%)
Western Shore			
Anne Arundel	39,620	117,392	+196
Calvert	10,223	12,100	+18
St. Mary's	17,182	29,111	+69
Eastern Shore			
Dorchester	27,962	27,815	−1
Kent	18,786	13,677	−27
Queen Anne's	18,364	14,579	−21
Somerset	25,923	20,745	−20
Talbot	20,342	19,428	−4
Wicomico	22,852	39,641	+73

Source: Historical Census Browser, University of Virginia Library, http://fisher.lib
.virginia.edu/collections/stats/histcensus/ (accessed 25 June 2008).

a law authorizing the DTF to set aside a five-acre tract for each public
tidewater high school for experimental oyster farming.[85] The high school
of Somerset County's Deal Island, one of the poorest tidewater communities, established its Future Watermen's club soon thereafter. Assisted
by a prominent CBL biologist, G. Francis Beaven, and an outspoken
pro-leasing packer, Richard Webster, who planted twenty-five thousand
bushels of shell cultch and promised not to charge the club if oysters did
not grow, the students monitored spat catch, water conditions, parasite
growth, and oyster development through two plantings over the course
of six years.[86] The club netted $1,417 after the first harvest and a bit less
following the second growing cycle, when the students sold the product for $7,826 after spending $6,501.[87] While their profit margin represented about a year's salary for the average oysterman, no tidewater
school could carry out such a project without sustained financial and
technical support. Even the Calvert County effort in the CBL's back-
yard folded after a few years. The high investments of labor, time, and
capital required for oyster culture probably did little to persuade tidewater teens that their parents were wrong to oppose leasing.

An uncommon confluence of actors and circumstances brought about
the most significant experiment encouraging private oyster farming on a

cooperative basis.[88] It involved the oystermen of Smith Island, an iconic Chesapeake Bay fishing community "where independence is valued nearly to the point of anarchy."[89] Situated nine miles from the mainland, along the state's southern border, Smith Island boasted "the most watermanly of watermen, far removed from the taint of big money," in the words of the *Baltimore Sun.*[90] Given their work ethic and relatively strong commitment to capitalist accumulation, values both reinforced and moderated by the community's central institution, the Methodist Church, it is not terribly surprising that such an obvious threat to the idea of public-domain oystering developed there. But it was never inevitable, for pro-leasing officials played a large role in the initiative, which served purposes other than cultivation and which collapsed within a decade despite state support.

As the mainland high schoolers conducted their adventures in aquaculture, a most unusual fisheries official presented a plan of far greater scope to the men of Smith Island. Despite the recent controversy regarding Commissioner Warfield's leasing aspirations, another privatization advocate now held the position. David Wallace was also a scientist, and he intended to win over the watermen and thus the legislature. Wallace initially received the post for only two months when the Senate rejected Governor Lane's nominee but became the permanent officeholder when the governor, fearing citizen conservationists' threatened referendum, vetoed the 1949 "ripper bill" to reorganize the commission.[91] Wallace had begun working for the CBL in 1936 as Truitt's graduate assistant, later embarking on a career in fisheries administration and marine law enforcement. With Wallace's unexpected promotion to the state's highest natural resource management position, Maryland conservationists looked forward to implementing their oyster agenda, for Wallace shared his mentor's conviction that private cultivation constituted the most sensible plan for utilizing the resource.[92]

Smith Islanders appeared amenable to radical change at midcentury because of the desperate state of the oyster bars that fell within their local resource regime – the tonging grounds of the Potomac River to the west and the dredging areas of Tangier Sound to the east.[93] Illegal dredging in the Potomac by both Marylanders and Virginians had become a serious problem with the postwar lifting of price controls. The Maryland legislature's determination to rout the dredgers to preclude Virginia's efforts to expand its jurisdiction over the Potomac (part of a complicated boundary dispute dating to the colonial era) led to major reforms of the marine police force.[94] Smith Islanders who had grown accustomed to pirating oysters with illegal dredges and the small motorized boats permitted only for crabbing resented the crackdown, blaming their "very acute" economic situation on "rigid law enforcement."[95] Following several arrests of Smith Island oystermen, Wallace began meeting with community representatives and their lawyer in late 1949 to discuss solutions. Though Wallace denied their request to dredge under power rather than sail in Tangier Sound, the historically rich grounds that had attracted hundreds of armed vessels during the frenzied exploitation of the late nineteenth century, he noted that leaseholders could use any tool they wanted to harvest their oysters.[96] At the same time, Wallace denied rumors that the department's strict enforcement of the oyster laws aimed to impose such severe hardships that oystermen would be forced to accept private leasing. Wallace also denied that "the Commission intends to give the Smith Islanders the best bottoms in Tangier Sound."[97] In public, he simply said that it was no longer possible "to make a livelihood from legal oyster operations" around the island, a diplomatic concession that obscured the context of conflict.[98]

Wallace's public pronouncements about the January 1950 formation of the Smith Island Oyster Cooperative concealed the state fisheries agency's role in promoting the plan. To journalists he enthused, "This is the first concerted effort by any group of Maryland watermen to go into oyster farming for themselves."[99] But as Wallace had explained two months earlier behind closed doors, "Expediting the program will be primarily the responsibility of you gentlemen present from Smith Island. Active participation by the Commission at this time conceivably could be interpreted incorrectly. We do not wish to appear anxious, but we'll be glad to help wherever we can." When one of the commissioners, a pro-leasing packer, responded to a question about financial aid by offering to allow lease payments to fall in arrears, as the agency had done during the Depression, Wallace interjected that "collection could be deferred rather than waived." But otherwise he offered generous sweeteners, starting with legal assistance for the inevitable court challenge the lease applications would provoke. Because the law allowed the leasing of only barren bottoms, Wallace told the group that the DTF would "survey the area in question and testify in Court that it isn't natural rock." One islander winked that if informed in advance, "We can guarantee the bottom will be as bare as a pool table."[100] Such eleventh-hour dredging would not have affected the legal definition of a natural bar, which was still covered by the Goldsborough rule, but the offer revealed the sense of collusion involved.

The watermen recognized a good deal when they saw one, and as their attorney declared after the negotiations, "If this arrangement won't work on the Island it won't work anywhere."[101] For one thing, the community was extremely close-knit. As one resident explained, the only "foreigners" (whites who had grown up elsewhere), were the doctor and preacher.[102] The thousand inhabitants, who shared a few dozen surnames, revered their independence yet also engaged in collaborative behaviors that facilitated survival in the remote community, which had just gained electricity and still lacked phone service to the mainland.[103] When Wallace asked how the proposed co-op would impact resident harvesters who chose not to join, one representative asserted, "Everyone will get into it eventually."[104] In fact, several islanders had already gained experience running a small-scale cooperative for the marketing of crabs.[105] Moreover, the Smith Islanders had at least one regional precedent. In 1947, a group of Virginia fishermen in the Hampton/Norfolk area had established the Baysea Cooperative Association to try to obtain higher prices from dealers; having achieved their goal, they disbanded by 1952.[106] When pushed, Chesapeake watermen could be as adept at economic organizing as at political rallying.

The islanders developed a vision of cooperative oyster leasing that did not match that of the scientists and conservationists who had long sought to overcome what they considered the inevitable, tragic results of common-pool resource regimes. The state's proposal appealed to the watermen because it offered a way to get immediate relief by decriminalizing the use of efficient harvesting tools, as opposed to a get-rich-eventually scheme entailing capital-intensive aquaculture. As one negotiator said of the proposed leaseholds in Tangier Sound, "We could make a living from that area and get through the winter without starving our children."[107] Since even the most well-off tidewater communities barely met mainstream standards of living, it is not surprising that short-term subsistence goals dominated their outlook.

Illegal fishing thrived under such circumstances, and the group's attorney, a former waterman, thus interpreted the planned cooperative as a way to head off conflicts with the trigger-happy police fleets of both

Maryland and Virginia: "A serious situation resulting in trouble between the Islanders and law enforcement personnel may develop unless preventative action is taken; the oyster cooperative may be the solution."[108] After a fatal 1949 shooting, Wallace got rid of the Oyster Navy's machine guns but not its sidearms. From time to time over the ensuing decade, "bullets whistled on the Potomac within a two-hour drive of the nation's capital as the marine police of the Tidewater Fisheries Commission sought to end poaching and impose Maryland's authority on the river."[109] Becoming lessees enabled Smith Islanders to use labor-saving equipment in broad daylight without getting shot. That development, along with the assurance that big interests would not be granted the same privileges, paved the way for Maryland's first aquacultural cooperative.

While the prospect of producing more oysters through artificial means was incidental to the goal of allowing islanders to "dredge legal," the Smith Island Oyster Cooperative also addressed the fiscal challenge of shellfish culture. Purchasing the bare minimum of shell and seed (fifty thousand bushels of each) during the spring of 1950 would cost more than twenty-five thousand dollars, a staggering amount for men who might make eighteen hundred dollars in a good year.[110] Even if all the island's two hundred watermen participated, their sixty-dollar annual dues would fall far short. The co-op's attorney warned that without outside financing, the enterprise "must necessarily fail."[111] But even the Baltimore Federal Bank for Cooperatives backed off from advancing the big bucks needed. Although Congress had established lending institutions to aid agricultural cooperatives during the Depression, the Baltimore bank president deemed oyster farming too risky.[112] He had a point, for the islanders had no experience in culturing the mollusk, a precarious three-year process. And while Wallace assured the members that the Farm Credit Administration, which ran the banks for cooperatives, had made loans for oyster farming elsewhere, he did not elaborate.[113] The Smith Island Oyster Cooperative's lawyer wrote to the secretary of agriculture explaining the situation but probably did not worry too much about raising funds for seed and shell given the state's promise of assistance and the primary rationale of decriminalizing power dredging in Tangier Sound.[114]

Moreover, the question of finances remained moot as the case wound through the courts. Although trouble had arisen after would-be lessees applied with family members to amass large holdings, the island co-op likewise evaded the anticorporate spirit of the leasing laws by having 30 members apply for twenty-five acres each in Tangier Sound. Each of the co-op's 123 members paid $7.50 to finance the application fees and advertisements, which by law ran in local newspapers for four weeks. With their access to the local commons regime at risk, three watermen from the mainland portion of the county filed suit. Although the Yates inspectors had not charted the oyster grounds in question as natural during the 1906–12 survey, the plaintiffs argued that the reefs were productive and thus not subject to lease.[115]

More than three hundred industry members packed the county courthouse for the trial, which examined only one of the applications because the parties involved agreed that the jury's decision would apply to all of the applications. During the three days of testimony, several harvesters swore that they had seen others take bivalves from the disputed twenty-five-acre site within the past five years, and a few dredgers even brought in bushels they claimed to have hauled from the area earlier that morning.[116] On behalf of the defendants, the CBL's Beaven countered that the bottoms were barren for all practical purposes, though his testimony carried little weight since the legal definition of a natural oyster bar made no reference to biological criteria such as spawning or setting rates. Instead, the 1947 legislature had reaffirmed the Goldsborough standard. Although the state's assistant attorney general argued that the oysters must have come from elsewhere, the jury took just thirty minutes to deem the bottoms active natural bars and thus off limits to leasing.[117] Identical verdicts had led to the reclassification of thousands of acres of barren bottom as natural bars since 1914.[118] On this occasion, the county courts again acted in concert with legislative malapportionment to check efforts to privatize the Maryland oyster commons.

But in "a big test case for the bay, whether oysters could be farmed instead of wild-harvested," an extraordinary decision from higher up the judicial chain came down several months later.[119] Wallace and his fellow commissioners appealed the verdict, and the Maryland Court of Appeals unanimously overruled the Somerset jury. The judges dismissed the Somerset oystermen's testimony that they had seen others oystering in the vicinity as legally insufficient and ruled the evidence of the freshly dredged oysters inadmissible because the act of harvesting did not fall within the five-year statutory period prior to the lease application.[120]

Privatization advocates hailed *Department of Tidewater Fisheries v. Catlin* as a turning point. Thrilled that the appellate judges reflected "none of the tidewater bugaboos about leasing which have influenced tidewater juries," the *Baltimore Sun* waxed lyrical that the Smith Island lessees could now "show that the conservationists are on the side of the watermen, and have been all along." With each acre potentially capable of producing in three years a hundred bushels selling at between three and five dollars each, the island co-op presented the perfect demonstration project.[121]

Yet the newspaper made the illogical assumption that inexperienced, impoverished operators could succeed where the fisheries agency had failed. "The State has done what it could, spending $125,000 a year in tax moneys on oyster cultivation, but the job is too big for the State." Continued the editorialists without apparent irony, "The job should properly be done by the people of Maryland who are closest to the situation, the watermen themselves, who can farm an oyster rock with the same care that a dirt farmer gives to his choicest acres of bottom land."[122] But lessees could gain control only of the least productive grounds; *Department of Tidewater Fisheries v. Catlin* deemed the disputed Tangier beds barren. The answer to the *Sun*'s earlier question, "Who wouldn't like to be given a free farm?" should have been clear from the homesteading experience, for cultivating barren oyster beds was like trying to farm the semiarid lands of the Great Plains – difficult and expensive. But on the Chesapeake frontier, the agrarian ideal still resonated among conservation-minded modernizers, blinding them to the obvious: If the state, with its access to tax revenues and technical knowledge, could not bring back sufficient numbers of bivalves, how could fishermen scraping by from day to day, men whose expertise revolved around hunting rather than culturing organisms, do any better?

Nonetheless, the Smith Island Oyster Cooperative commenced operations in 1951 with significant subsidies. Although Wallace regretted that the state could not provide direct financial aid via a crop mortgage, the DTF outfitted a special boat for surveying and marking leaseholds and stepped up efforts to protect against poaching. Most important, the state sold to the co-op immature oysters grown via the repletion program. Because the average private planter had to hire guards and import seed, these were major benefits, as the department admitted in its 1951 annual report: "These new services were no doubt instrumental in persuading a group of residents of Smith Island to lease last year in one block approximately 1,500 acres of barren bottom for the cultivation of oysters."[123] This is not to say that the co-op failed to provide an "outstanding example of self-reliance and private initiative," as the *Sun* had hoped.[124] During the project's first two years, the members raised about fifteen thousand dollars through their five-dollar monthly dues and a 10 percent tax on their total sales, using these funds to buy and plant sixty-five thousand bushels of shell as cultch. Even president and founding member Shafter Corbin seemed to have accepted the co-op as more than a means of "dredging legal"; as he told a reporter in 1952, "The planters tell us that in a few years each and every one of us can, if he's of a mind to, own a Cadillac."[125]

The co-op's financial success did not result from aquaculture, however. Power dredging, within agreed-upon limits, sent the average member's annual income soaring to five thousand dollars.[126] As Corbin explained, dredging leased waters enabled watermen from the tiny Smith Island community of Tylerton to make seven thousand dollars a week for three consecutive weeks – more than one hundred dollars a week for each of the village's sixty-some families. By contrast, "If we hadn't had the co-op, the whole community wouldn't have had $300 – legally."[127] By 1954, the islanders had dredged enough of the existing oysters on their leaseholds to provide their three best years on record. Resentful oystermen from elsewhere, however, accused the Smith Island men of drifting onto public beds, actions that resulted in the arrests of at least three co-op members.[128] And though the leaders had expressed excitement about harvesting their first crop in 1954, the endeavor did not go well, and a year later, the board of directors announced plans to fold. In 1958, a majority of the co-op's members voted to surrender all their leaseholds, many of which the state had already canceled for failure to pay rent.[129] The newspapers blamed the co-op's collapse on financial problems, especially the cost of immature seed oysters.[130] Prices indeed soared after Maryland's seedbeds encountered poor sets for several years and the Virginia Commission of Fisheries prohibited seed exports, a decision that caused havoc for oyster planters along the entire eastern seaboard.[131] Even the pro-leasing *Sun* featured sober exposés of the hazards of farming under the sea.[132]

An insider confided decades later another reason for the co-op's downfall, affirming the worst assumptions of the tragedy-of-the-commons argument. One of the island's oldest men said that "there wasn't enough marine police in the world to watch that leased bottom. He said – and he put himself right with the rest – that there was such stealing from one another and selfishness and taking the little oysters before they was legal size that it caused the co-op to collapse. He felt maybe there is just something in us against putting a lot of rules and regulations on ourselves."[133]

While the oystermen must be held accountable for their rapaciousness, the state in the form of the Tidewater Fisheries Commission also deserves some blame for the oyster co-op's washout. Expecting people accustomed to a subsistence ethic to run a risky, capital-intensive business without sustained assistance on a massive scale was naive at best.[134] Furthermore, promoting the project as a pioneering venture in aquaculture rather than a way for the lucky few to fudge the laws against efficient technology was no way to persuade a critical mass of watermen of the benefits of private oyster culture.

If anything, the endeavor set back the cause of leasing. Opponents adopted a new strategy of banning privatization initiatives on a county-by-county basis, starting with the home of Smith Island. In 1953, even as the islanders were reaping their best results ever thanks to their status as lessees, Somerset County senator Harry Phoebus convinced his colleagues and the governor to prohibit further leasing of oyster bars there.[135] During the same legislative session, when Baltimore delegates introduced a bill to make seed available on credit to small oyster-farming groups, 350 Eastern Shore residents stormed the statehouse in a scene reminiscent of the 1880s. Unmoved by the example of the islanders, Cambridge attorney Emerson Harrington Jr., who as Truitt's brother-in-law knew all the privatizers' arguments, declared, "The watermen of this State always have and always will oppose leasing." The bill's quick death silenced leasing advocates for years thereafter.[136]

Yet with the 1959 appointment of a maverick fan of leasing cooperatives as the commissioner of tidewater fisheries, a figure who seemed capable of forging a compromise took the center stage of Maryland oyster conservation politics.[137] Harry Clifton "Curley" Byrd, the son of an Eastern Shore seafood packer, had built a statewide reputation running for governor after steering the University of Maryland through a tremendous growth spurt through shrewd and successful lobbying for public funds.[138] The *Baltimore Sun's* editors, who had opposed Byrd on many fronts over the years and recalled his history of sparring with Truitt, viewed his appointment to the fisheries commission by the governor, fellow Eastern Shoreman J. Millard Tawes, as a disaster.[139] Yet the *Crisfield Times,* the newspaper of the self-anointed "seafood capital of the world" considered Byrd the perfect choice, asserting that only such a charismatic figure could effect radical change: "Watermen are not dumb, but they need to be told a lot of present day truths. We believe they will accept this from Dr. Byrd."[140] Byrd agreed, comparing his new job to his earlier work in providing agricultural extension services to Maryland farmers.[141]

Perhaps still harboring political aspirations, Byrd took immediate steps to broaden the appeal of the fisheries commission. After an officer killed a Virginian caught dredging in a restricted area, Byrd completely disarmed the fisheries force, one of several changes that helped bring the Potomac River Oyster Wars to an end.[142] He also embarked on a fact-finding tour among the tidewater counties.[143] Recognizing efforts by other oyster-producing states to mine old shell for use as cultch, one of the persistent limiting factors in the public repletion program, Byrd also authorized fossil shell explorations in the Chesapeake Bay.[144] And he appeased sportsmen who had spent years trying to limit commercial fishing by assuring them, "Politics no longer runs this department."[145]

Success bred recklessness, which the seventy-year-old flashed by ignoring the only warning he had received from his boss, Governor Tawes: "Stay away from private planting." Despite this caveat and the recent demise of the Smith Island Oyster Cooperative, Byrd declared his intention to promote more such groups. A visit to California convinced him that a great market existed in the Far West for Maryland oysters and that Marylanders merely had to "produce in large quantities" to take advantage of that opportunity.[146] Seeking to capitalize on the discontent spawned by the industry's greatest production decline since the early 1930s, Byrd outlined a plan for promoting leasing cooperatives. But the proposal soon foundered.[147] As president of the state university, Byrd had spent years stroking legislators with such tactics as doling out scholarships and alumni mailing lists, but dealing with the General Assembly as head of the natural resource regime was a completely different affair.

Byrd's other efforts to reform oystering also backfired. The 1961 legislature passed his bills to cede greater authority to the Tidewater Fisheries Commission to close oyster bars for rehabilitation or development as seed areas but did so only after altering the measures to grant local

watermen's committees veto power over plans to close bars commissioners deemed unproductive.[148] Another new law gave the official county
oyster committees a greater say in public hearings regarding the distribution of seed oysters among the competing local commons regimes.[149]
In a final blow to privatization advocates, the assembly authorized a bill
to resurvey the bay's oyster beds with the stipulation that no bar designated as natural "shall ever be leased."[150] On the eve of reapportionment, tidewater representatives reasserted their constituents' dominion
over oyster management.

The Suburbanization of Oyster Conservation Politics

The fact that Maryland's baycentric geography and malapportionment
enabled rural tidewater voters to exert disproportionate influence does
not mean that the Eastern Shore and southern Maryland had nothing
in common with the rest of the state. Despite important sectional differences, a "southern segregationist inheritance" still permeated the state's
political and social culture during the mid–twentieth century.[151] Urban
bastions of learning such as Johns Hopkins University upheld discriminatory policies against Jews and African Americans, and Jim Crow laws
prohibiting interracial marriage and equal access to public accommodations prevailed statewide.[152] For historian Richard Hofstadter, who taught
at the University of Maryland at College Park during the Byrd regime
of the 1940s, the region's racism and cultural backwardness exemplified the "parochialness of the Upper South," bolstering "his belief in
the regressive nature of southern society." Hofstadter found refuge at
Columbia University, where he published enormously influential works
in the postwar era on American liberalism, including sharp critiques of
the kinds of anti-intellectualism he had perceived in Maryland.[153]

The worst facet of Maryland's southern outlook gained unwelcome
exposure as officials prepared to show off "the land of gracious living"
to an international audience at the 1964 World's Fair, held in New York
City.[154] The Maryland exhibit was to feature a restaurant serving Chesapeake fare, but civil rights activists revealed the distasteful connections
between the state's culinary and racial landscapes by noting that the eat-
ery would lack authenticity if it failed to enforce the "trespass act against
dark-skinned people." Diners on busy Route 40 outside Baltimore had

refused to serve African diplomats traveling between Washington and the United Nations headquarters in New York, embarrassing the Kennedy administration.[155] If the 1963 Maryland General Assembly failed to mandate equal public accommodations, the Congress of Racial Equality threatened to mobilize a massive picket of the Maryland pavilion.[156] Protests would of course draw attention away from oyster stew, crab cakes, and southern hospitality to the state's de jure racism and intolerance, themes out of sync with the fair's progressive futurism.

By then, almost twenty years after Hofstadter escaped the "provincial dungeons" of central Maryland, waves of white-collar professionals had streamed into the Baltimore-Washington corridor, a hot spot of federal agencies and defense contractors.[157] The new residents transformed the hinterlands through their demands for housing, education, and infrastructure but failed to change the statewide political culture. The 1960 census showed that although the four booming suburban counties of Montgomery, Prince George's, Baltimore, and Anne Arundel now accounted for 45 percent of the state's three million residents, they held only 4 of the 29 Senate seats (14 percent) and 24 of the 123 seats in the House of Delegates (19.5 percent).[158] (Baltimore City and the four suburban counties accounted for 75 percent of the state's population yet held only 34 percent of the Senate seats and 48 percent of those in the House.) Three of the counties bordering the cities had boomed so much that each boasted more residents than all nine counties of the Eastern Shore combined.[159] Suburban reformers argued that each Maryland senator should represent 106,000 people and each delegate 25,000. Yet Somerset County's senator represented 19,375 persons, and each of its three delegates represented 6,458 people, whereas Baltimore County (a separate entity from Baltimore City) had one senator for its 490,201 residents and six delegates, each of whom represented 81,700 inhabitants.[160] Despite the growing disparities, however, rural representatives had no interest in voting themselves out of office, and because declining Baltimore City would also lose out in a population-based legislature, urban and rural delegates and senators joined in defeating numerous 1950s attempts to change the system.[161]

Suburban activists turned therefore to the courts, even though the U.S. Supreme Court had ruled in 1946 that the judicial branch had no business entering the "political thicket" of legislative districting.[162] Rural domination of state legislatures as well as Congress thus remained a national problem, and metropolitan southerners played a crucial role in attacking it.[163] Soon after the Supreme Court ruled in *Baker v. Carr* that the issue was indeed justiciable, an Anne Arundel County Circuit Court judge declared that the membership allocation of the Maryland House of Delegates violated the Fourteenth Amendment's Equal Protection Clause and ordered reconfiguring to end the "invidious discrimination." Governor Tawes, whose halfhearted gestures toward reapportionment had riled his fellow Eastern Shore residents, called a special session of the legislature in May 1962. The assembly acceded only after the governor made an impassioned speech imploring the legislators to act lest the courts do so for them. The stopgap reapportionment added several suburban seats for the four-year terms of office to be elected that fall, with the same number of seats to be subtracted from less populous areas in 1966.[164] Representation of the four booming counties thus increased from 19.5 percent of the assembly to 28 percent, still inequitable but giving urban and suburban delegates a slight edge.[165]

As suburban plaintiffs continued to challenge the makeup of both houses, the enlarged legislature broke precedent. In 1963, after eight years of unsuccessful efforts to abolish the law that allowed hotels, restaurants, theaters, parks, and other places serving the public to discriminate against blacks, Maryland became the first state south of the Mason-Dixon Line to pass a public accommodations law. Although rural conservatives exempted their counties, the new measure suggested that big changes would occur with the increasingly inevitable transfer of power accompanying full-fledged reapportionment.[166]

Since well-heeled urbanites had long tried to impose their conservation philosophy on the commercial fishing lobby, the closing of the estuarine commons began to seem as inescapable to tidewater interests as the dismantling of white supremacy. Somerset senator Phoebus declared that *Baker v. Carr* "means that all our oyster rocks are gone."[167] He and his colleagues had done an excellent job of beating back oyster privatization advocates but also found themselves fighting a resurgence of activism by suburban sportsmen intent on restricting watermen's access to striped bass (also known as rockfish or stripers). Angered by what they considered "the ruinous commercial excesses that threaten the existence of the bay as a natural resource and provider," hook-and-line fishermen sought to ban January and February takings, when the lucrative species schooled in deep waters in a sluggish state, making them easy prey for gill nets.[168] After seeing their bills die in 1953, suburban anglers formed the Maryland Rockfish Protective Association "to carry the torch of conservation to the General Assembly" during the next full session, to be held in 1955.[169] Like the pro-leasers, sport fishermen saw themselves as casting light on the dark stage of tidewater policymaking.

Commercial fishing interests countered with a well-organized campaign, rallying eloquent speakers and hundreds of spectators for the preliminary House hearing on the proposed restrictions. The bills never stood a chance, failing in two attempted House overrides of the decisive committee's unfavorable report.[170] Disappointed sportsmen singled out freshman representative Margaret Collins Schweinhaut, one of the few female members of the assembly, for breaking ranks with her suburban delegation.[171] She later recalled that her critics told her "that there were no watermen in Montgomery County and that I better vote with the sport fishermen."[172] She retorted that supporters had failed to demonstrate the ban's conservation value, a point conceded by the Prince George's County delegate who championed the winter ban.[173] The netters' most effective witness was David Wallace, who since his departure from state employment had presided over a national oyster trade association. Wallace argued that the scientific record did not justify such a drastic measure, for despite heavy harvesting, the bay's striper populations continued to thrive.[174] Indeed, Maryland biologists had for several years credited an innovative 1941 law to limit the number of commercial fishing licenses with producing the largest brood of striped bass in forty years.[175] Although sportsmen were horrified to hear Wallace defend the taking of rockfish prior to the spring spawning season, he was in good company. Fishery biologists around the world were working to advance both science and industry by helping commercial fishing fleets maximize the productivity of the seas, primarily by identifying new stocks and developing new harvest technologies.[176]

But since Maryland biologists had such a long history of opposing commercial fishermen in the name of conservation, the self-styled rockfish protectors were shocked to see the two adversaries in cahoots. Wallace was rumored to have left the fisheries agency in frustration over implementing his reform agenda, and he remained an outspoken advocate of leasing cooperatives and of incorporating more science into the state repletion program.[177] Yet Wallace saw no inconsistency between advocating private oyster culture and intensive public-domain rockfish harvesting in light of data suggesting that salinity fluctuations and other natural factors, rather than fishing intensity, accounted for year-to-year disparities in species abundance. More ecological research was needed to identify environmental limiting factors and thus determine the maximum sustainable yield of each species, as Wallace had argued to fellow scientists eager to develop the seas into the ultimate protein factory. With knowledge of the "biological limitations of the fishery," administrators could focus on new kinds of laws: "Instead of numerous restrictions on catch, imposed as conservation measures by the various states, the marine biologist recommends efficiency in harvesting the crop, with restrictions designed primarily to reduce waste and to take advantage of rapid growth." However, warned Wallace, "This probable environmental relationship has been difficult for the amateur conservationist to accept," given the assumed logic of overfishing as the sole cause of population variability: "Anyone advocating expanded fishing . . . is risking attacks from the very groups who normally are the most ardent supporters of conservation."[178] He knew what was coming when he took the stand at the hearing on winter rockfish takings.

Wallace's testimony caught the sportsmen off guard, however. Convinced that his scientific status gave him special significance in the policymaking realm, the *Washington Post*'s outdoors columnist criticized the former fisheries commissioner for making "deadly" pronouncements "with an air of finality" that "convinces sincere and thoughtful people."[179] The "thoughtful" legislators who most concerned sportsmen were not those of the tidewater counties. The anglers seeking to "rescue the rockfish" in the 1950s expected their more enlightened representatives, along with the state scientists, to agree that commercial fishermen should be prevented from ransacking the estuarine commons. Overlooking their own degree of fishing intensity and unwillingness to participate in efforts to determine their share of the catch, recreational fishermen focused instead on the blows dealt by their presumed allies and "the greedy brethren of the nets."[180] Even though malapportionment gave their opponents an unfair advantage, sportsmen did not put on the best case possible for their conservation ideal.

Schweinhaut remained a stanch defender of winter rockfish gill netting, a stance that helps illuminate later developments regarding watermen's predicted loss of clout under reapportionment. After the 1955 debate the neophyte delegate explained her controversial vote on the grounds that the ban would hurt Marylanders, "while Virginians would make a killing." She later divulged that she had also been moved by the testimony of tidewater women about the hardships of a winter closure on the welfare of their families.[181] Downplaying her gendered sensibilities in the masculine domain of the statehouse, Schweinhaut supported her economic concerns by citing the testimony of L. Eugene Cronin, Truitt's successor as head of the CBL. As she subsequently asserted to her colleagues when the proposed law came up again in 1961, "There are probably more members of the Izaak Walton League in my county than any other and it is very bad politically to be against this bill. But I feel very strongly that to put men out of work is wrong when the top scientist of this state tells us that taking rockfish in January, February, and March has no appreciable effect on the supply."[182] Cronin, an expert on blue crabs, expanded on Wallace's earlier analysis by testifying that year-to-year environmental factors, rather than the winter catch, determined the survival rate of juvenile rockfish.[183] Unable to muster more convincing data, sport fishermen at long last abandoned the dream of a closed commercial season, and winter gill netting remains an important part of the striped bass fishery to this day. Recreational fishermen also increasingly found themselves on the defensive as fishery managers recognized the collective harm inflicted by the hundreds of thousands of anglers crowding the bay and Atlantic coast every weekend.[184] But although sport fishermen (and their environmentalist partners in suburbia) did not acquire a level of influence proportionate to their vast numbers, they benefited enough from changes in the rural/metropolitan makeup of the legislature to emerge later in the century as key stakeholders in Chesapeake resource policymaking.

The rockfish wars of the 1950s and early 1960s helped transform the science-tidewater relationship at a critical point. In the last years of malapportionment, as pressure increased to stamp out the retrogressive remnants of border-state Maryland, tidewater interests learned an important lesson about saving one of their traditions from the reapportionment wrecking ball. In 1961, as the striped bass debates were winding down and suburban demands for fair representation were heating up, reporter Wendell Bradley hinted that the timing was more than coincidental:

> Political scientists, baffled by the inability of state governments to adjust to modern urban life, might well investigate the relationship in Maryland between reapportionment and rockfish. In the Maryland Assembly, the lowly rockfish crops up in debates about Baltimore mass transit. Its silvery green form flits through discussions of welfare measures. It is a standard fixture no matter what the subject – schools or roads or labor – in the frequent tugs-of-war between urban and rural delegates.[185]

As metropolitan legislators had worked for their sportsmen constituents by launching new fronts in the campaign against winter netting, tidewater representatives became more adept at disarming their rivals. The rockfish battles ultimately became much more than a dispute over a particular type of gear and season of capture. At the end of the day, these debates suggested that by deploying scientific expertise on a selective basis and cultivating relationships with sympathetic suburban representatives, the commercial fishing lobby could defend against the estuarine enclosure movement in spite of sweeping shifts in electoral power.

The "reallocation of policy benefits" from rural to metropolitan Marylanders seemed imminent as the most equitable legislature in the state's history convened in 1967.[186] A whirlwind of judicial-legislative wrangling preceded the change. With the 1962 redistribution of House seats, rural state senators had hoped to be let off the hook since the U.S. Constitution authorized representation in one house of Congress based on political jurisdictions. But on 15 June 1964, the Supreme Court delivered a shocking mandate. In what he considered the most important opinion of his tenure, Chief Justice Earl Warren wrote that both houses of all bicameral state legislatures must apportion themselves on the basis of population: "Legislators represent people, not trees or acres."[187] In promulgating the "one person, one vote" principle, the Court rejected the federal analogy argument because the Constitution did not recognize counties as sovereign entities, among other reasons, and ruled that courts could hasten the redistricting process if lawmakers employed the kinds of stalling tactics that had impeded school desegregation since the *Brown v. Board* decision ten years earlier.[188] After many months of bitter debate, the Maryland assembly hammered out a reseating plan for the fall 1966 elections that all but ended rural overrepresentation, although not until 1972 was full population-based apportionment achieved and enshrined in the state constitution.[189] With suburban politicians now laying claim to almost half of each chamber, the postwar demographic revolution finally hit the Annapolis statehouse in January 1967.

While the newly elected assembly's reform agenda seemed fairly obvious, the open governorship raised many unknowns.[190] During the 1966 Democratic gubernatorial primary, the most liberal candidate, a suburban congressman, called for a wide range of changes, including a gradual transition to oyster leasing on the grounds that "misguided public policies" had encouraged "senseless exploitation rather than sensible conservation of our oyster resources."[191] But in a campaign dominated by the issues of open housing and worsening race relations, aquaculture generated little heat. Even so, the Republican nominee, Baltimore County executive Spiro Agnew, took care to distance himself from the oyster question during his few campaign forays into bay country. A moderate Republican who supported new schools and roads, elimination of the flat tax, and pollution control, Agnew represented a new kind of politics far removed from the ethos of the rural conservative Democrats of tidewater Maryland.[192] But he did not write them off and thus relied on perceptive staffers to provide political talking points for Eastern Shore audiences. At the head of the list was "Reassure that reapportionment doesn't mean disenfranchising voter," followed by "STAY AWAY FROM ADVOCATING PRIVATE SEEDING OF OYSTER BEDS!"[193] Agnew still lost the shore vote to his conservative Democratic opponent, George Mahoney, whose single-issue campaign against open housing also attracted many white suburbanites frightened by the crime and decreased property values they associated with black neighbors. But Agnew won the election.[194]

Maryland's first suburban executive and first reapportioned, half-suburban assembly used the 1967 and 1968 sessions to chip away at "the widely held impression of Maryland as a southern backwater state."[195] A tax code overhaul provided one hundred million dollars for public services, the three-hundred-year-old ban on interracial marriages came to an end, and a limited though groundbreaking open housing law was passed, leading the governor to proclaim Maryland "once again in the leadership among Southern states in the enactment of civil rights legislation."[196] Moreover, Agnew's campaign pledge for tougher environmental regulations produced a water-pollution-control program providing $129 million for sewage treatment upgrades, ending the still widespread practice of spewing raw sewage into bay tributaries.[197] Agnew's vow to make Maryland "one of the Nation's leaders in water quality control" thus brought together two broad movements, suburbanites' growing interest in environmental quality, and national recognition of the threats rampant coastal development posed to estuaries and tidal wetlands.[198]

A myriad of newly perceived threats to the bay in the late 1960s and 1970s displaced Maryland conservationists' traditional focus on oysters. The negative environmental effects of the "march of progress" consumed scientists and the public, especially as they perceived the disconnect between the bay's image as a cherished part of the state's identity and its use as a dump (fig. 15). Controversies brewed over complex issues both old (the disposal of sediments dislodged by harbor channel dredging) and new (siting of the state's first nuclear reactor).[199] The singular focus on seafood harvesting that had long dominated the idea of Chesapeake conservation also waned as Congress developed a sense of ownership vis-à-vis the nation's largest estuary. Representatives of Maryland and Virginia increasingly sought federal funds to study the "queen of bays," culminating in the construction of a huge hydraulic model by the Army Corps of Engineers and a separate six-year analysis by the Environmental Protection Agency (fig. 16).[200] These and other scientific results drove later policymaking initiatives made possible by the suburbanization of politics.

Despite the many stresses on the bay ecosystem, the Maryland oyster industry enjoyed relative prosperity for almost two decades following reapportionment, which provides another explanation for leasing's failure to take root. The 1959 discovery of vast deposits of ancient shell beneath the bay remedied the problem of the lack of cultch for spat attachment that had bedeviled the repletion program. The subsequent massive expansion of reshelling activities had a phenomenal impact. From 1960 to 1967, production doubled to around 3 million bushels per year, the highest level in twenty-six years, and Maryland regained its place as the nation's leading oyster-producing state for the first time since 1950.[201] Flush with cheap dredged shell, fishery managers refocused their efforts on "revitalizing a potentially valuable industry" rather than trying to "cushion the fall of a collapsing industry." Convinced that the market could absorb no more than 2.5 million bushels annually, officials seeking to assure high prices for watermen grappled with the specter of overproduction, a climate unripe for leasing advocacy.[202] Despite increasing operating expenses, intraindustry gear conflicts, tensions over opportunistic part-timers, and the damage wrought by Hurricane Agnes (which dumped tons of freshwater, silt, and pollutants into the bay in

Our Heritage

Fig. 15. By the late 1960s, after a century of intensive use as a sewer and industrial waste site, the bay no longer seemed capable of absorbing the endless by-products of "progress." (Drawing by Richard Q. Yardley, *Baltimore Sun,* 11 May 1969, © 1969 The Baltimore Sun Company. All rights reserved. Used by permission and protected by the copyright laws of the United States. The printing, copying, redistribution, or retransmission of the material without express written permission is prohibited.)

1972), oystermen of the 1970s reported satisfaction with their line of work. In 1978, a dredger who had worked the water for five decades called the most recent five years "the best time to be a waterman." Most tellingly, many young local men entered the fishery.[203] The predicted closing of the tidewater frontier, it seemed, had been premature.

Fig. 16. U.S. senator Charles Mathias (third from left), chatting with Maryland watermen during his 1973 fact-finding tour of bay country. Alarmed by the declines in environmental quality he perceived, Mathias convinced his colleagues to authorize the Environmental Protection Agency to coordinate what became a six-year, twenty-seven-million-dollar endeavor involving more than a hundred researchers. The results spurred Governor Harry Hughes to initiate the Save the Bay campaign. (Courtesy of Senator Mathias and Charles McC. Mathias Papers, MS 105, Special Collections, Sheridan Libraries, Johns Hopkins University.)

It was no coincidence that seafood festivals, maritime museums, and other efforts to preserve the heritage of the Chesapeake emerged in the early 1960s just as the watermen's way of life seemed destined for oblivion. Skipjack races had once allowed oystermen to escape the daily routine in a masculine display of sailing prowess, but the practice died out during the Great Depression. After a thirty-year lapse, yacht clubs began holding races in cooperation with the state departments of tidewater fisheries and economic development. Explained an official, "If the West can make a big thing over rodeos, we can call attention to the Skipjack."[204] As the country's last commercial sailing craft, the Maryland dredge boats made good copy. Newspaper and magazine articles alerted readers of the fleeting chance to experience the "last link we have with the Nation's maritime past" aboard one of the forty-two remaining skipjacks.[205] Day-trippers and tourists were hooked, and in 1968, twelve thousand specta-tors crowded the beach at Sandy Point State Park, near the western ter-minus of the Chesapeake Bay Bridge, on a brisk October afternoon for the fourth annual Chesapeake Appreciation Day race.[206] Such celebra-tions helped crystallize regional identity and consciousness as identical suburbs sprawled across central Maryland and the rest of the country.[207] If suburbanization was "an escape from ethnicity into cultural homoge-neity," skipjack festivals and cruises offered the crabgrass frontiersmen and their families a physical and symbolic getaway to the Chesapeake version of Disneyland's Main Street.[208]

As outsiders embraced the charming anachronisms of tidewater Mary-land, they rejected the long-standing insistence that the oyster industry become as efficient as possible, a final reason why leasing did not tri-umph after the demise of malapportionment. Wendell Bradley, who had left the *Washington Post* to sail and study life in the watermen's strong-hold of Tilghman Island, captured part of the unease driving the grow-ing suburban environmentalism, a movement that contrasted in many ways with the older philosophy of utilitarian conservationism. Bradley explained that he "thought it worthwhile to study" the culture of the world's last sailing communities "to find out if what we gained is worth what we lost when we gave up our old relationship to nature in favor of technology." Bradley's answer was a resounding no, and he mourned the loss of coastal peoples whose keen sense of the weather and wind made their dominant technology, the sailboat, perhaps "the only one to play an important part in history without in any way disturbing the natural environment."[209] Bradley understood what it meant to "know nature through labor," a relationship not always appreciated by the new environmentalists, in the view of workers whose livelihoods depend on nature's bounty.[210] Nevertheless, in the transitional period linking the reapportionment and environmental revolutions, the newly empowered suburban elite helped preserve the watermen's foundation – the regu-lated commons – by transforming the focus of conservation from wise use to quality of life.[211]

The ethos of the new conservationism included a very practical ratio-nale for keeping in place the inefficient world of the watermen: corporate consolidation would force many watermen onto welfare, thereby cost-ing the state much more than the annual million-dollar deficit incurred by the repletion program.[212] Oyster privatization not only would not save the state money but would humiliate tidewater communities and rob Maryland of its newfound regional distinctiveness. In this case, efficiency clearly did not pay.

∞

The most obvious expression of the environmental policy impact of reapportionment and of the Chesapeake Bay's image makeover from protein factory to cultural identifier did not materialize until the early 1980s. The worrisome results of a just-completed study by the U.S. Environmental Protection Agency convinced Governor Harry Hughes, then at the start of his second term, to make cleaning up the estuary a top priority. Though a native of the Eastern Shore, Hughes hailed from its only landlocked county and thus took a while to develop an appreciation for the bay, "not only as a traditional place of employment for watermen or as a recreational outlet for hundreds of thousands of sailors and power boaters, but as an intrinsic element of the character of the state."[213] After serving as a legislator and secretary of transportation, Hughes won the governorship in 1978 with a pledge to restore integrity to an office and state disgraced by the bribery indictments of Agnew; Agnew's successor, Marvin Mandel; and other high-level officials. Championing bay restoration provided a way to do something about the Environmental Protection Agency's report rather than filing it away with dozens of other such studies; it also enabled Hughes to rebrand Maryland as a regional environmental leader.[214]

Before approaching the legislature, Hughes and his team spent months selling the public on the idea of a comprehensive, expensive bay cleanup. By the time assembly members convened in 1984, Maryland's 350th anniversary and the Hughes-designated Year of the Bay, he had spearheaded a regional compact outlining a federal/interstate program and engaged a variety of stakeholders to make his vision "very hard for lawmakers to vote against."[215] The controversial centerpiece of his forty-million-dollar initiative was a bill restricting development in a one-thousand-foot buffer zone around the bay's entire shoreline, about 10 percent of the state's land surface. Rural legislators, backed by developers and real estate interests, had long opposed land-use laws as an infringement on local governance and property rights; not surprisingly, therefore, a venerable Eastern Shore legislator, Frederick Malkus, led the opposition.[216] Since losing his position as chair of the influential judicial proceedings committee in the 1966 shakeup, Malkus had remained a bitter foe of the "city boys" who stripped him and his beloved Dorchester County of power.[217] Malkus declared that although he supported efforts to clean up the bay, Hughes's bill would do nothing but "harass the people of the Eastern Shore."[218] But Malkus and his allies had difficulty resisting what the Maryland Watermen's Association called the "Chesapeake cleanup bandwagon . . . set in motion by Harry Hughes, who saw Chesapeake Bay, finally, for what it is – the bloodstream of the state."[219] The governor's strategy of portraying the bill as a touchstone of commitment to the bay worked, and a tidal wave of support overwhelmed the once-powerful rural tidewater senators who tried to mount a filibuster. The passage of laws such as the Critical Area Protection Act of 1984 thus challenges assertions in the political science literature that few measurable policy changes resulted from court-ordered reapportionment and shows the importance of broadening the scale of analysis beyond the years immediately following the power shift.[220]

Of course, Hughes's determination and meticulous maneuvering demonstrated the enormous amount of political will necessary to get even the suburban majority to commit to his vision.[221] Tidewater politicians had predicted in the 1960s that the last oyster-leasing debate of the century would spell disaster for the independent waterman because suburban lawmakers would embrace the rationale of utilitarian conservation and corporate economies of scale at the heart of the oyster privatization argument. But the new power base did not take the efficiency argument for granted and was not easily persuaded to gut a cultural landmark of distinctiveness, as Hughes's successor discovered. William Donald Schaefer, who grew up in Baltimore at a time when streetcars still whisked city dwellers to estuarine oases, had served several terms as the city's charismatic and transformative mayor and won the support of watermen during his 1986 gubernatorial campaign.[222] He surprised them by making aquaculture one of his key initiatives during his second year in office in response to the drastic economic declines brought about by the shellfish disease MSX.[223] With the crippling of the oyster industry, it appeared that economic circumstances had finally worsened enough for Maryland to advance to the next stage on the evolutionary scale of oyster production.

But the Schaefer administration's push to streamline leasing lacked the punch of the previous governor's Save the Bay campaign. The plan to promote cultivation in upstream rivers, where MSX was less likely to flourish, did not feature educational outreach to watermen, who not surprisingly viewed "aquaculture enterprise zones" with suspicion: "The nightmare for most watermen is that one day they [will] be wearing a pair of overalls furnished by a mammoth food corporation as they work the leased bottom for wages," explained an article in the *Waterman's Gazette*.[224] Along these lines, the bill to establish an aquaculture subbureau designated the Department of Agriculture rather than the fisheries-oriented DNR as the lead agency. The bill's backers also failed to enlist prominent allies who might have influenced cosmopolitan legislators, such as Abel Wolman. Not until two months into the legislative session, after Wolman had written to provide a historical perspective on the debate, did a Schaefer aide make a tepid request for Wolman's public support: "A letter to the editor and or to the members of the legislative committees deliberating over our proposal would be most helpful."[225] The ninety-five-year-old sanitarian invoked his policy of eschewing direct lobbying, but it was probably too late anyway.[226] Delegates soon killed the oyster-leasing provisions by a decisive 128 to 1 vote.[227]

The failure of the aquaculture zoning bill provides a cautionary tale for promoting policy, but it is unlikely that even an intense lobbying effort could have persuaded the suburban majority to accept Governor Schaefer's initiative. By then, the Maryland watermen had acquired an immense store of cultural value, not unlike the status conferred on endangered species as their numbers decline. As environmental journalist Tom Horton observed in 1987,

> The existence of watermen is perhaps the most powerful symbol we have that our bay still flourishes. To lose them would be to lose a powerful impetus for maintaining our environmental standards. . . . [T]he waterman is to the rest of us bay dwellers what the canary was to the coal miners, who carried them down the shafts, depending on the bird's exquisite sensitivity to leaking gas to give them an early warning of disaster. If watermen are flourishing, it is a sign that the bay's integrity still holds.[228]

In recognition of watermen's special standing, many inland representatives granted the tiny group high esteem. For example, as the Maryland Watermen's Association noted with pleasure, although only a third of the members of the 1985 House Environmental Matters Committee came from districts bordering the bay, its Baltimore City chair provided "a forum where any waterman's issue could get a fair hearing."

The association, founded in 1973, often expressed gratitude to legislators who, though "swamped with the urban-oriented demands of their heavily-populated districts . . . keep an open ear for issues that concern watermen."[229] The court-ordered demise of malapportionment did not rob watermen of power, as they had feared, but changed the basis of their influence toward a more symbolic form of politics, as demonstrated by the long-term aftermath of the state's 1985 decision to ban the harvesting of rockfish.[230]

This decision was not made by the state per se but rather by the governor and the head of the DNR. With the 1969 creation of the DNR as part of a broad governmental reorganization, the executive agency took on many of the functions formerly performed by the legislature. Conservationists had long sought to escape legislative micromanagement of the oyster fishery; as Wolman argued in 1936, harkening back to Brooks in the 1880s, "Can you imagine what would happen if the State Department of Health, informed of a smallpox epidemic in a Maryland town, had to wait for the Legislature to authorize it to isolate cases and start compulsory vaccination? If an oyster bed is depleted it surely should not be necessary for the State to wait a year – or in this case fifty years – to recognize it and start restocking."[231] Nevertheless, the Board of Natural Resources established in 1941 served only as an advisory body with nominal authority over the tidewater fisheries department, and while fishery commissioners possessed some policymaking influence, they remained hamstrung in many ways, a great inconvenience given the General Assembly's infrequent meetings. When the legislature relinquished many regulatory powers after 1969, resource officials finally gained greater flexibility and insulation from pressure.[232] In the summer of 1984, after the CBL's thirtieth annual young-of-the-year rockfish survey revealed worsening juvenile survival rates, DNR leaders recommended a moratorium. Governor Hughes took the news in stride: "Scientists had been unable to come up with any other answers, so it was the only solution we could think of. I said, 'If that's what we've got to do, let's go ahead and do it.' It was that simple: one meeting and we did it."[233] Closing down an entire fishery had become a straightforward and fairly easy process for a thick-skinned governor, a sharp contrast to the careful strategizing that had been needed to engineer acceptance of the bay cleanup program.

On the heels of the feverish Year of the Bay, watermen and charterboat operators received the governor's announcement with shock: as of

1 January 1985, no rockfish could be taken in Maryland waters, and opponents and their representatives could do nothing to change the situation.[234] The moratorium included provisions to cushion the blow, but harvesters believed that they had been singled out as the easiest target among all the entities responsible for stressing the estuarine ecosystem. Hughes recognized the need to spread the pain at least among fishermen beyond Maryland, since rockfish migrate to the ocean after spawning in the Upper Bay. To address the same point that Schweinhaut had made a generation earlier about Virginia profiting from Maryland's restraint, the governor worked to secure passage of a federal law providing an East Coast fisheries commission with the authority and funds needed to restrict harvesting in all the striped bass states.[235] After five years, DNR biologists lifted the suspension. Stripers now grew so abundant that they seemed to compete with watermen for blue crabs, leading many commercial fishermen to question whether the moratorium had served their interests or those of anglers.[236]

The success in restoring rockfish populations encouraged scientists and environmentalists to call for repeating the experiment with the oyster, but the DNR has never again advised such an unpopular measure. Analysts have concluded that the "story of the rockfish's decline and return . . . holds lessons that apply broadly to stewardship of the Chesapeake's natural resources," especially regarding the need for research funding and enforceable oversight.[237] A more ominous message echoes that of the oyster-leasing debates: whether the watermen's power is real or symbolic, policymakers and conservationists must tread carefully on the commons.

Because the basic system of managing the oyster grounds as a regulated commons remained intact from the 1930s onward, the Maryland oyster industry may appear to have remained static, changing only the scale of production. To some extent, appearances do not deceive. By the early 1980s, the ten thousand or so men who still followed the water shared important socioeconomic, technological, and political commonalities with their great-grandfathers. Whereas capital-intensive industrialization had long since become the norm in agriculture and extractive sectors throughout the rest of the South, the Maryland legal code ensured that the business of oystering remained labor intensive, anticorporate, and minimally profitable – as the watermen wished.

Yet the veil of continuity across the twentieth-century Maryland oyster enterprise conceals forceful efforts to change course. Oystermen fended off campaigns to liberalize the laws permitting private oyster farming but came to defend the subsidized reshelling and seeding operations crucial to maintaining the put-and-take fishery. Oystermen's disproportionate clout also enabled them to resist recreational fishermen's demands to participate in the debates about conserving bay resources. Watermen even defeated state-backed efforts to promote cooperatives featuring the collective harvesting of leased bottoms despite a sustained state-backed effort by a select group of harvesters to use this form of business to reap the technological benefits of leaseholding. In these postwar challenges to the status quo, Chesapeake scientists played a less predictable role than in earlier eras, as debates over estuarine resource policymaking expanded beyond oyster conservation.

Even after the "one person, one vote" Supreme Court decisions ended the tidewater's legislative dominance, a complex of political, socioeconomic, and cultural circumstances kept the regulated commons in place. One important theme was the suburbanization of politics. Agnew's governorship signified a historic shift in U.S. politics, with social issues rather than economic concerns increasingly dominating elections and elections centering on suburban voters.[238] Pro-leasers had always framed their issue as one of economics, especially since the Depression-era entrenchment of state repletion activities. Eliminating the wasteful public expenditures of Maryland's archaic harvest trumped any social dislocations imposed by privatized aquaculture on poor though relatively self-reliant fishing villages. In earlier decades, reformers had dismissed the loss of traditional industries and communities as the price of progress. But at a time when suburbanites enjoyed a high enough level of affluence to accept the greater taxes needed for public education, infrastructure, and other amenities, including environmental well-being, justifying the loss of an increasingly appreciated part of the state's unique cultural landscape in the name of austerity made little sense. Respect for the fishery's unique artisanal status discouraged newly empowered suburban politicians from making radical changes. At the same time, recognition of the Chesapeake as a vulnerable ecological entity that could no longer be taken for granted diverted attention away from shellfish production to estuarine problems perceived as far more pressing by the new conservationists of the 1970s. Accordingly, the suburbanization of Maryland politics both distracted from and helped preserve traditions that had long frustrated efficiency experts.

Another set of factors involved the relative prosperity of the oyster industry and changes in the administration of the fishery. Interest in privatization coalesced during periods of rapid harvest decline, but just the opposite occurred in the years following reapportionment. Two fortuitous features of the bay – its subterranean stock of fossil shell and its disease-inhibiting salinity levels – helped Maryland regain its status as the country's leading oyster producer just as tidewater politicians lost their ability to defend against leasing pressure. By the time harvests crashed almost twenty years later, watermen had cultivated a strong network of sympathetic metropolitan lawmakers. Assessing the policy effects of the late twentieth-century power shifts thus requires attention to a range of circumstances. Much more than "tradition and the indifference of the urban legislators" militated against the privatization of the oyster commons.[239]

Brave New Bay

Bridging Ecology and Economics via Native versus Nonnative Oysters

By the late twentieth century, the Maryland oyster had lost the culinary and political meanings it once held for consumers, scientists, watermen, and elected officials. The blue crab became the region's signature food as watermen derived less and less of their annual income from oystering and as the crab feast replaced the oyster roast as a way for residents and tourists to celebrate Chesapeake heritage. Moreover, the bivalve's significance as an emblem of the difficulties of managing natural resources diminished during the 1960s and 1970s. As oystermen reaped the harvest of the state repletion program and as disease parasites remained confined to Virginia waters, Maryland suburbanites used their newfound influence to draw attention to many other threats facing the Chesapeake Bay, and the oyster question ceased to be the Old Line State's iconic conservation issue.

The 1990s, however, marked the Maryland oyster's political comeback, a development made possible by the fishery's near collapse, new ecological insights, and aquaculture technology. Lethal shellfish pathogens invaded the Upper Bay, besieging watermen's communities and setting off a scramble for new management approaches. Recognition of the oyster's keystone role in improving water quality came just in time, allowing the organism to transcend its status as a commodity to be harvested and either cultivated or allowed to go extinct. Instead, it became seen as a vital player in the overall health of the estuarine system and thus in the political effort to clean up the horrendously polluted bay. Shared understanding of the importance of filter-feeding shellfish challenged age-old assumptions about the negative effects of politics on fishery management. Rather than dividing diverse interest groups that used or viewed the commons in conflicting ways, the bivalve now offered a strategic means of solving both economic and environmental problems. Reconstructing reefs and stocking them with disease-resistant seed produced in high-tech hatcheries – latecomers to the Chesapeake oyster fishery – would transform resource management by utilizing cutting-edge expertise to sustain both human and estuarine communities.

The joint approach to sustaining the seafood industry and cleaning up the bay through oyster restoration was made possible not only by new knowledge but also by a political consensus with a crucial funding partner – the federal government. U.S. government involvement in Chesapeake resource issues stretches back to the beginnings of bay science, when the Coast and Geodetic Survey conducted the nation's first investigation of shellfish decline. Other agencies, including the Bureau of Fisheries, the Atomic Energy Commission, and the Army Corps of Engineers, sponsored studies, but federal commitments increased substantially in the last quarter of the twentieth century. In the 1990s, the Maryland and Virginia congressional delegations secured tens of millions of taxpayer dollars to rebuild and stock reefs, and the 2000 renewal of the regional accord to clean up the bay made restoring oysters a top priority. Federal support for oyster restoration initiatives bolstered the fifteen-year-old cleanup program's sagging reputation as a model of ecosystem management. Yet lurking in the background was the ominous reminder that failure to save the Chesapeake Bay meant there was no hope for resurrecting any other U.S. estuary, for none was as large, valuable, or close to the nation's capital.

The sky-high expectations of the new oyster-management paradigm soon gave way to disillusionment, especially among watermen. Catches remained near all-time lows, the number of skipjacks dropped below ten, and steady paychecks in the construction and prison industries beckoned more than the freedom and insecurity of commercial fishing, stimulating interest in a plan that posed greater ecological risks yet

quicker economic returns than reef restoration. Whereas earlier generations of scientists had sought to conserve the mollusk by transforming
tidewater society, many researchers and environmentalists now found
themselves fending off an equally radical proposal: the deliberate introduction of a nonnative bivalve capable of resisting the disease pathogens
that had invaded the estuary.

Other fisheries around the world had long since revitalized themselves with alien oysters, yet the Chesapeake idea came at a time when
recognition of the harm inflicted by exotic invasive species had reached
unprecedented highs. News media and popular books related many
disastrous examples of intentional and accidental biological introductions, from kudzu to killer bees. Greater awareness of the negative economic, ecological, and public health effects of invasive pests stimulated
new preventative and control efforts at the federal level in the 1990s.[1]

Yet decades before invasive species attracted national attention, Chesapeake stakeholders questioned the wisdom of introducing alien bivalves.
Maryland became the first of several East Coast states to ban aquaculturists from using Japanese oysters in the 1930s, a forgotten controversy
that warrants attention for the ways it illuminates the role of science and
values in environmental policymaking. At a time when Maryland conservation scientists struggled for cultural authority, they achieved success
by framing the ecological threat posed by nonnative species in racist
terms that appealed to rural constituents and legislators. By marshaling
nonscientific criteria and playing on contemporary fears of foreigners,
researchers gained support for an issue that otherwise might not have
attracted interest given the widespread use of nonnative species in other
economic endeavors, especially agriculture. Ironically, this achievement
hindered later researchers' efforts to study the potential benefits of alien
oysters, though not for long.

As native *Crassostrea virginica* populations failed to rebound despite the
intensive restoration efforts of the 1990s, a little-known Chinese species,
C. ariakensis, attracted serious attention as a substitute. The Virginia seafood industry embraced the idea of raising sterile nonnative specimens
in underwater cages, thereby decreasing the ecological threat of escape
but requiring huge capital outlays and constant tending of the crop. Virginia's century-long tradition of oyster privatization made that state better situated to adopt sterile, containerized aquaculture than was Maryland, which showed little interest in either expanding corporate control

of the commons or subsidizing a massive reorientation of the state oyster-farming program. Rather, Maryland watermen and the gubernatorial administration of 2003–7 promoted the controversial choice of permitting foreign bivalves to establish self-sustaining populations in the bay. This framing of the Asian oyster debate deflected attention away from a potential expanded role for private oyster cultivation in the Free State.

Discussion focused instead on the ecological risks of the proposed foreign species and on how much scientific information policymakers needed to make responsible decisions. To minimize the threat of a biological invasion, scientists called for rigorous testing of the organism's environmental impacts. But because so little was known of *C. ariakensis,* researchers had to conduct the kinds of painstaking studies that harked back to the natural history surveys of the eighteenth century. Moreover, because natural and even social scientists benefited from new pools of grant money, desperate industry members accused these researchers of drawing out the assessment process. While respecting the need to evaluate the risks, most watermen disagreed that years of research were required. Thus, despite a narrowing of the gap between watermen's and scientists' worldviews, the two groups retained fundamental differences in expectations for the role of science in policymaking.

The decision-making process was delayed further as other parties demanded a voice. Because an introduced species might escape to other political jurisdictions, the Asian oyster debate attracted attention beyond Maryland and Virginia, making it the most explosive issue involving the Chesapeake around the turn of the millennium. And while scientists tended to reserve judgment pending the completion of extensive studies, many environmentalists opposed the idea from the beginning. Although studies of the sociocultural context of debates over invasive species in other places have ascribed elitist or xenophobic attitudes to those seeking to control such species, such motives do not seem to be at play here.[2] To the extent that concern regarding introducing nonnative oysters to the Chesapeake Bay involves nonecological factors, two purposes appeared to drive anti-*ariakensis* advocates. Giving up on the native oyster in favor of a heartier breed would be the ultimate admission that the broader bay cleanup had failed and would allow an important part of the region's unique biocultural identity to be absorbed into the homogenizing vortex of the global economy.[3]

Filter Feeders to the Rescue

The late 1980s were disastrous years for the Maryland oyster fishery. Prolonged droughts raised salinity levels enough to enable MSX and Dermo, the protozoan disease parasites that entered the Lower Bay in the 1950s, to move northward. Harvests fell from 990,000 bushels during the 1986–87 season to 418,000 in 1990–91. As in previous periods of steep decline, reformers saw a window of opportunity within which to implement their solutions. While scientists and their allies no longer assumed that privatizing the oyster grounds would stimulate conservation – especially after the defeat of the 1988 aquaculture zoning initiative – their new solution generated almost as much anger among watermen. The Chesapeake Bay Foundation, a prominent environmental advocacy group with 80,000 members and 120 employees, proposed reviving the bay's oyster populations via a three-year moratorium on harvesting, during which the state would pay watermen to rebuild degraded oyster bars.[4] But watermen had no interest in such a plan, having just endured the five-year ban on rockfish harvests. In an era in which they could no longer take their political hegemony for granted, watermen countered the proposal with arguments that went beyond the economic and religious. Most notably, they rejected the foundation's scientific rationale that a moratorium would enable more oysters to reach adulthood and thus evolve genetic resistance against disease. Because state surveys indicated that spatfall rates remained high enough to sustain annual harvests of one to two million bushels, the Maryland Watermen's Association argued that rainfall, which reduced salinity, was the most important determinant of oyster survival and maturation. A harvesting ban would also allow reefs to become covered in silt, thereby removing a crucial stewardship service long claimed by dredgers. Far from being greedy despoilers, oystermen considered themselves cooperative and flexible, as shown by their efforts to negotiate new restrictions and a hefty three-hundred-dollar surcharge on the annual fifty-dollar license fee to help fund the shell- and seed-planting program.[5] A ban, they contended, would be both useless and unfair.

Maryland resource officials agreed, and though the moratorium idea receded, watermen's perception of their vulnerability did not.[6] While conceding that the Chesapeake Bay Foundation had done important work on behalf of the bay, President Larry Simns of the Maryland Watermen's Association accused the foundation of ignoring the "real villains" – disease parasites, high salinity, and poor water quality – at the expense of an easy scapegoat: "Like all environmentalists, when they have no where else to turn, they turn on the smallest group, the group that is easiest to regulate – the watermen, in this case."[7] Controlling corporate polluters in the agricultural and waste-management realms and the thousands of nonpoint sources of pollution in the vast watershed, let alone natural forces, indeed overwhelmed the state's regulatory abilities. Yet Maryland's ten thousand watermen still possessed influence out of proportion to their numbers. They had not only defeated the 1988 aquaculture bill but also shot down the moratorium idea before it entered the legislative arena.

Nevertheless, the rapid harvest decline underscored the need for change. The Maryland Department of Natural Resources (DNR) spent $1 million on shell and seed repletion in 1993, while the harvest generated $2.5 million at dockside, a subsidy ratio similar to that of Virginia.[8] Critics decried the low economic returns, especially of Maryland's system of "collective farming on the bay," prompting both states to call for new approaches to the oyster crisis.[9] As Virginia resource officials contemplated a moratorium in that state and funded experiments with Japanese oysters and reef reconstruction, their Maryland counterparts convened forty scientists, watermen, environmentalists, legislators, packers, aquaculturalists – and a mediator – to brainstorm alternative solutions.[10] After six months, during which the harvest limped toward the then-record low of eighty thousand bushels, the group issued its recommendations, none of which involved privatizing the commons or banning harvests.

The Maryland Oyster Roundtable advanced an idea that had deep roots yet was adapted to the peculiar environment of local seafood politics. The members agreed that new aquacultural methods should be tried, but not by private individuals; rather, they advised forming a nonprofit corporation to conduct experiments in rebuilding reefs, growing bivalves at or near the water's surface, and developing "oyster recovery areas" in which disease-free seed produced in hatcheries would be planted under restricted harvesting conditions. The last solution targeted the long-standing practice of transplanting natural seed to more favorable growing areas, a strategy that helped out oystermen in the short run yet facilitated the spread of MSX and Dermo. As a state official acknowledged, "We've moved disease, but we had reason to and the watermen benefited from it."[11] The emphasis on hatcheries also sought to fulfill W. K. Brooks's dream of relying on laboratory science rather than nature to control molluscan breeding, though with a biotechnology tool chest far beyond that of Brooks's watch glass and microscope. The idea of using science-based cultivation to sustain both the watermen and the bay itself marked an exciting new development, the first political recognition of the Chesapeake bivalve's ecological as well as economic importance.[12]

Researchers had drawn attention to the oyster's amazing capacity as a filter feeder in the 1980s, when eutrophication became an issue of international concern. The Chesapeake Bay had become one of the world's most eutrophic estuaries as a consequence of the millions of pounds of nitrogen and phosphorus produced each year by farms, sewage plants, septic tanks, storm-water runoff, and combustion engines. Because oysters, clams, and mussels consume plankton, which grows out of control in the presence of excess nutrients, the idea that molluscan suspension feeders could serve as natural eutrophication controls generated intense scientific interest.[13] Using historical catch records, University of Maryland biologist Roger Newell performed a series of calculations to determine whether the century-long decline of oysters could have exacerbated the negative effects of nutrient enrichment on the bay's water quality. His computations yielded a dramatic insight: whereas oyster populations in the Chesapeake Bay prior to 1870 could filter the entire water column in between 3 and 6 days, the 1988 turnover time was 325 days. Newell concluded that restoration of the bay's once-abundant reefs could complement land-based efforts to improve water quality, such as sewage treatment plant upgrades, tougher regulations on agricultural runoff, and a ban on phosphate laundry detergents.[14] His number crunching attracted immediate press attention.[15] Not only was it easy to grasp, but it suggested a specific policy outcome that offered a rare opportunity to reconcile economic and environmental goals.

The articulation of the oyster's ecological role served an important political function in the early 1990s phase of the oyster question. In any debate, constructive conversation between adversarial interest groups cannot begin unless all participants agree on basic facts and ideas; in controversies involving science, all parties must recognize the credibility of those core ideas.[16] The concept of the oyster as an ecosystem purifier probably derived its trustworthiness from its strong grounding in common sense. No special knowledge is needed to understand the basic link between filter feeding and improved water quality, and although subsequent studies suggested that the phenomenon is more complex than meets the eye, the overall concept falls within the "ordinary knowledge" of laypeople.[17]

The ecological framing of the oyster also helped unite disparate stakeholders at a tense time by offering a politically acceptable way for each party to obtain its ultimate goal. Environmentalists and scientists seeking ecosystem recovery could join hands with watermen desiring to preserve their traditions, packers in search of a steady supply of cheap product, aquacultural entrepreneurs envisioning new markets for immature bivalves, and legislators trying to appease constituents from all of these groups. Over the next several years, state and federal appropriations increased to implement the Oyster Action Plan, culminating in commitments of twenty-five million dollars by Maryland and fifty million dollars by Congress to increase the oyster population tenfold from 2000 to 2010.[18] The U.S. Environmental Protection Agency (EPA), National Oceanic and Atmospheric Administration, and Army Corps of Engineers also oversaw initiatives, as did the Maryland DNR and the Virginia Marine Resources Commission. Federal support also enabled the Oyster Recovery Partnership, the Roundtable's nonprofit aquacultural brainchild, to become a central player in restoration initiatives, a first for a nongovernmental organization.[19] With so much public funding, the eco-oyster idea offered a more direct, feasible way to improve water quality than regulating the manifold sources of pollution enveloping the vast watershed.

Oyster restoration attracted widespread interest and media coverage during the second half of the 1990s. Small- and large-scale projects to increase the number of filter feeders not only promised to improve water quality and watermen's economic viability but also offered opportunities to build new constituencies for environmental reform. Shoreline property owners demonstrated their environmental awareness by hanging mesh bags full of immature oysters from their docks, an expensive hobby publicized as "oyster gardening." The booming construction industry disposed of massive quantities of rubble while claiming credit for creating artificial reefs, a practice that benefited recreational

fishermen by attracting biodiversity. And initiatives that trained students
to cultivate hatchery-produced seed for transplanting to sanctuary reefs
tapped a free labor source while providing hands-on lessons in science
and public service to the next generation of taxpaying voters. Press
accounts of these types of projects offered an upbeat antidote to gloomy
forecasts that the pollution-reduction goals set by the 1987 Chesapeake
Bay Agreement would fall far short of the 2000 deadline.[20]

Public awareness of the links among oysters, water quality, and human
health peaked in 1997, when outbreaks of the toxic aquatic microbe
Pfiesteria piscicida on the Eastern Shore sparked massive media attention. Thousands of fish died, and several fishermen reported rashes,
memory loss, and respiratory problems, prompting the closure of three
waterways. Evidence that decreasing nitrogen and phosphorus inputs
would reduce future *Pfiesteria* events underscored the importance of
restoring the bay's historic oyster populations. As a front-page article
in the *Baltimore Sun* explained, "They remove algae and other microscopic phytoplankton such as *Pfiesteria* – and the nitrogen they contain –
from the water. The oysters' feces are then processed by bacteria in bottom sediments. The bacteria convert the nitrogen to a gas and remove it
from the ecosystem."[21] The editors of *U.S. News and World Report* listed
Chesapeake oyster restoration as one of sixteen solutions for improving
American society in their year-end issue. Revitalize the ailing bay by filtering it with "billions and billions of oysters," read the title.[22]

But restoration was expensive, time consuming, and uncertain. Even
with volunteer labor, the cost of building a reef of shell and live oysters measuring six hundred feet by sixty feet topped four hundred thousand dollars.[23] Between 1995 and 1998, the heyday of restoration enthusiasm, Maryland and Virginia constructed two hundred acres of oyster
habitat, a mere fraction of the hundreds of thousands of acres of once-
productive grounds.[24] Embarrassing snafus also ensued, as when natural
predators gobbled up thousands of baby oysters and when a two-year
effort to apply off-bottom aquacultural techniques yielded just 120,000
adults from a hatchery brood of 14.5 million.[25] Even so, cautious optimism about the intertwined fates of the bay, humans, and oysters prevailed in the policymaking arena as the new millennium approached.
Slight rises in the annual harvests, evidence of increasing disease tolerance, the popularity of oyster gardening, and the continuing influx
of federal, state, and private funds for restoration held together the

tenuous coalition of scientists, watermen, environmentalists, and fishery managers.[26]

Part of the funding went toward developing the infrastructure for a technique crucial to the restoration effort: hatchery production of disease-free spat. Although the state oyster hatchery got its start in the 1970s after Hurricane Agnes dumped loads of smothering silt into the bay, not until the post-Roundtable period did the hatchery begin playing a major role in Maryland oyster management. From 2000 to 2006, hatchery technology enabled nonprofit organizations to increase the number of baby bivalves (known as spat on shell) planted on protected sanctuaries or harvestable bars from 15 million to 350 million.[27] But even that amount could cover only a fraction of the 200,000-acre commons; the practice of planting protected sanctuaries with 2 million spat per acre, for example, translated into only 175 acres.[28] While Maryland moved toward the model of the high-tech West Coast oyster industry, the enterprise still had little entrepreneurial control. The University of Maryland rather than private entrepreneurs operated the hatchery, and officials focused on breeding fertile native oysters in the hopes of jumpstarting a comeback of the wild population rather than on using hatcheries to replace natural production and thereby promoting highly capitalized aquaculture.[29]

The most far-reaching translation of the oyster's new status into public policy came in the 1999 update of the 1987 Chesapeake Bay Agreement. By signing the Chesapeake 2000 (C2K) accord, the governors of Maryland, Virginia, and Pennsylvania; the mayor of Washington, D.C.; the EPA administrator; and the chair of the Chesapeake Bay Commission pledged to restore the bay's water quality by 2010, a court-ordered deadline for removing the bay from the federal listing of impaired waters as required by the Clean Water Act.[30] The first of the hundred goals specified in the C2K document called for increasing native oysters tenfold from their 1994 numbers.[31] Yet no one knew exactly how many bivalves that meant, and biologists had not developed means of quantifying oysters' ecological role that would enable cost-benefit analyses of restoration efforts.[32] The not-so-simple act of determining the required number of oysters—five to six billion for Maryland alone—took two years, one-fifth of the time before the C2K deadline.[33] Moreover, the many ongoing restoration projects lacked coordination and consistent monitoring protocols, casting further doubt on the ability to evaluate success among different sites.[34] The political prominence accorded to oyster restoration thus concealed a significant lack of scientific and managerial certainty.

Nevertheless, elected officials responded to public enthusiasm by appropriating record amounts for oyster restoration. Maryland's environmentalist governor, Parris Glendening, pledged to increase funding to twenty-five million dollars over ten years, more than doubling the one million dollars that Virginia and Maryland had each spent for the previous few years. The federal government pledged fifty million dollars, one-fifth of which Congress allocated during the 1999–2001 fiscal years for projects by the U.S. Army Corps of Engineers, National Oceanic and Atmospheric Administration, and EPA.[35] Given politicians' typical reluctance to take action on long-term, expensive environmental problems, state and federal officials' willingness to embrace oyster restoration after only a few years of experimentation reveals the desperate desire to implement a solution that would appease all the competing parties invested in the oyster problem.

The Eco-Backlash

Yet even before the C2K signing ceremony took place in the summer of 1999, the stakeholder alliance brought about by the ecological understanding of the oyster had begun to corrode. Oystermen felt that harvests had improved enough to drop the eight-year-old emergency regulation limiting them to fifteen bushels a day, a change that the DNR rejected on the grounds that stocks had not sufficiently recovered. In 1999, however, the General Assembly voted to expand motorized dredging in four counties, breaking 132 years of precedent that allowed dredging only under sail for most of the time. Maryland's one thousand licensed watermen thereby revealed their extensive influence in the legislative arena a generation after reapportionment had robbed tidewater senators of their lopsided advantage. The assembly no longer micromanaged the fishery as it had before the 1970s, and the watermen's advocates overcame environmentalist opposition only by authorizing four one-hundred-acre sanctuaries to compensate for the heavier harvesting pressure.[36] But dredgers scored a huge victory four years later, when the DNR stunned environmentalists and scientists by allowing power dredging in almost a third of the bay. The policy change came days after a new Republican governor,

Robert Ehrlich, who had courted the watermen's vote in the 2002 election by promising to relax fishing restrictions, exerted his control over the natural resources agency by firing several top officials. Although Ehrlich stressed his desire to end "us-versus-them" tensions among bay interest groups, resource management remained highly politicized, with oysters again signifying an ideological battleground.[37]

Tension between watermen and scientists had increased as harvests reached their historic nadir and restoration projects failed to produce quick returns. Press reports of poaching in sanctuaries – areas permanently closed to harvesting – revealed frustration on both sides. Researchers who discovered oysters missing from sanctuary reefs stressed the need to protect the experimental organisms for tracking the progression of disease, while watermen rebuffed allegations of stealing.[38] A rare admission of the lure of illegal harvesting came from a tonger who later obtained a DNR position under Ehrlich's 2003–7 administration: "If they're going to do nothing but dump oysters on sanctuaries, we're going to get them. A man who works all day long to pull five bushels off a bar he's allowed to harvest, and then 200 yards away is a bar with beaucoup oysters on them, he's going to get them. They don't have enough marine police to enforce this."[39] Sanctuary poaching generated so much negative publicity that the head of the Maryland Watermen's Association begged his members to observe the laws. One editorial in the *Watermen's Gazette* implored watermen "to be aware that we are outnumbered, outgunned, outfinanced, and most importantly that we cannot keep giving our enemies ammunition by allowing a handful of watermen to abuse the fishery and make the rest of us look bad."[40] Having spent a decade solidifying their status as stewards of the bay and indicators of water quality, watermen could no longer claim the right of free plunder that had once prevailed in tidewater communities.

The issue of protected sanctuaries contributed to the reemerging rift between scientists and watermen. Members of the two groups had agreed in the mid-1990s that restricting harvests on small portions of the public oyster grounds was preferable to shutting down the entire fishery.[41] However, continuing harvest declines prompted two opposing responses: watermen sought greater access to market-sized oysters, which they rationalized would otherwise die of disease, while scientists called for letting more oysters remain in the bay long enough to evolve disease resistance. A few months before the C2K signing, a group of oyster experts from Maryland, Virginia, and North Carolina called for the setting aside of 10 percent of the bay's historic oyster grounds as permanent sanctuaries. The biologists expressed confidence that they had brokered a groundbreaking "technical consensus across state lines" for steering oyster restoration.[42] The 10 percent goal indeed guided many subsequent restoration targets and appeals for federal funding, even though the C2K agreement made no reference to it and many watermen opposed closing off so much of the bay to harvesting.

But an awkward disclosure soon suggested the difficulty of making value-free scientific recommendations. In response to allegations that the researchers had based the goal on factors other than hard data, the Chesapeake Bay Foundation's chief scientist admitted in 2004 that no specific figures on the optimal size or locations of sanctuaries underpinned the consensus statement. Rather, it reflected the scientific community's "best advice" about achieving restoration.[43] The acknowledgment that the "technical consensus" had a less-than-solid technical foundation punctured the aura of scientific objectivity, thereby reinforcing the argument of science studies scholars that when researchers present value judgments as scientific results, they compromise their role in the policymaking process.[44] Indeed, the disclosure provided just the excuse the probusiness governor needed to drop the 10 percent target in accordance with the watermen's wishes. On the tenth anniversary of the Oyster Roundtable agreement, the two sides again struggled to reconcile the ecological and economic benefits of oysters.

Oyster restoration clearly held different meanings for the bay's two historic constituencies. Most scientists saw no point in building new reefs that required continual restocking of hatchery-produced spat: without promoting natural reproduction, such efforts constituted "a useless exercise."[45] Yet because oysters remained an important form of income for many commercial fishermen, they supported the put-and-take approach to maintaining marketable supplies that had underpinned the so-called free fishery since 1927. Scientists and watermen also tended to disagree about how long bivalves should remain in the bay. Watermen contended that disease was so prevalent that oysters should be harvested before lethal parasites could take their toll and render the mollusks worthless. Researchers, in contrast, focused on the mechanics of natural selection, reasoning that even if many individuals succumbed to disease, those possessing genetic traits that enabled them to survive could help propagate the species. Given the two groups' divergent views of molluscan value, it is not surprising that they also applied different metrics of success to restoration efforts. Watermen, along with fishery managers, tracked the abundance of market-size (three-inch) organisms resulting from rebuilt reefs, whereas scientists and their frequent allies, environmentalists, sought to quantify results using more subtle criteria pertaining to water quality. Ironically, however, the persistent lack of quantitative standards for evaluating ecological performance made it difficult to assess the oyster's celebrated value as a purveyor of ecosystem services.[46]

By the turn of the twenty-first century, the ecological significance of oysters no longer appeared as straightforward as it had in the days of the Roundtable. Whereas the 1994 consensus had envisioned oysters as contributors to improved water quality and thus as agents of pollution control, harvesters subsequently articulated almost the reverse idea – that the degraded water quality brought about by pollution and disease precluded the native oyster's comeback. Rather than relying on bivalves to clean up the bay, watermen reiterated their call to target land-based contaminants, a view echoed by several biologists in the national journal *Science* in 2001. A prominent article by nineteen international experts on overfishing linked the historical destruction of Chesapeake oyster bars with the rise in the 1930s of nutrient pollution, hypoxia, and toxic algae blooms. To target those enduring problems, the authors recommended "massive restoration of oyster reefs."[47] But some of the biggest names in Chesapeake biology took issue with the report, countering that although the oyster populations had lost most of their filtration capacity by the 1930s, the "dramatic intensification" of two major symptoms of eutrophication – hypoxia and loss of sea grasses – did not occur until the second half of the twentieth century, when land-based nitrogen inputs more than doubled. Consequently, these scientists concluded, restoring oysters "even to precolonial abundances" was unlikely to eliminate hypoxia and algal blooms in the absence of major efforts to reduce terrestrial nutrient loading.[48] Watermen, who had argued years earlier that oysters could not clean up the bay, no doubt took satisfaction in the biologists' tacit acknowledgment of this insight.

The glowing ecological portrait of the oyster lost more of its luster as new research revealed complex pathways linking the organism with other aspects of its ecosystem. In response to long-standing suspicions that oysters simply recycled back into the water column most of the

nutrients in the algae they consumed, thereby failing to mitigate eutrophication, Newell followed up his groundbreaking 1988 paper with
another study that showed that sediment bacteria remove at least 20 percent of the nitrogen in oyster fecal wastes. Yet while oysters' ability to
promote denitrification reinforced their usefulness as a supplement to
land-based actions to cut nitrogen inputs, oyster restoration was no "silver bullet." Cold temperatures render them dormant, thereby precluding denitrification during the spring freshets that flush heavy loads of
nutrients into the bay. In addition, the bay remained so polluted that it
might compromise the survival of even nonnative oysters, making over-
reliance on any kind of filter feeder a bad bet for pollution control.[49]

Further evidence of the scientific community's retreat from oyster eco-
enthusiasm came in a long-awaited 2003 report by the National Research
Council (NRC) of the National Academy of Sciences on whether the
time had come to replace *C. virginica* with a nonindigenous species. The
authors criticized the C2K goal of increasing oysters tenfold by 2010 as
naive and unrealistic, requiring decades if not centuries to achieve. In
challenging the conventional wisdom that reef restoration would bring
about great improvements in water quality, the authors cited some of
the same reasons long noted by watermen. Sedimentation of prime
oyster settlement areas and mortality from natural predators (along with
intense fishing pressure) limited the oyster's ability to provide ecosystem
services. Moreover, because most remaining populations were located
in the tributaries, they tended to improve water clarity only in shallow
zones rather than the bay's deeper main stem.[50] A computer modeling
study published in 2004 confirmed the idea that oysters repeatedly filter the same parcel of water. Thus, restoring tributary populations would
have little impact on the oxygen-depleted dead zone afflicting deep parts
of the bay each summer.[51]

The NRC report offered an acerbic indictment of the 1990s enthusiasm for reef restoration and restocking: "This myth, though it has served
to make political bedfellows of diverse stakeholders who share the goal
of increasing the oyster population in the bay, should be replaced by the
more realistic assumption that declining water quality results from multiple stressors that cannot be reversed by simply stocking more oysters
in the bay." Increased nutrient runoff, high sediment loads, toxic chemical pollution, and climate shifts had pushed the bay far from the pristine
condition that Captain John Smith had encountered in 1607, and oysters

thus could serve as "only one part of the solution" to the Chesapeake's complex water-quality woes.[52]

Despite its sharp critique of the illusory promise of native oyster restoration, the NRC panel warned against assuming that all such efforts were doomed to fail. Overly optimistic expectations, slowness in breeding and stocking disease-resistant specimens, and the disease-inducing drought and warm winters of 1999–2003 had frustrated recent attempts to bring back the bivalve, but that finding did not mean that all future endeavors would be "entirely ineffectual."[53] The report cautioned against the animosity that revolutions of rising expectations tend to provoke, especially among those with the most to lose.

The Promise and Perils of Exotic Oysters

When Virginia scientists broached the idea of deliberately introducing a nonnative oyster to the Chesapeake Bay in the early 1990s, watermen did not respond as a monolithic group. Some feared that doing so would crowd out the indigenous species, while those on the edge of economic survival saw no harm in trying the new variety.[54] A decade later, however, few held out hope for the native oyster to rebound in polluted waters that no longer resembled those worked by earlier generations of watermen. Nostalgia for traditional work patterns rather than for the bay's "biological heritage" had transformed most watermen into strong supporters of nonnative oysters capable of surviving in the hostile Chesapeake environment.[55] Why scientists and environmentalists focused on the potential negative outcomes rather than the positive economic and ecological effects of expanding the bay's filter feeders puzzled and angered more risk-tolerant, economically disadvantaged oystermen.

Opposition to the plan revealed how much attitudes about improving nature had changed. As in the agricultural realm, other major oyster fisheries had long since revived their fortunes with foreign stock and scientific blessings – most notably, the pioneering aquaculture empire of France under Napoleon III, discussed in chapter 2. Soon after Victor Coste's efforts to cultivate the European flat oyster, *Ostrea edulis,* ended in disappointment in the 1860s, a ship loaded with Portuguese oysters sank at Arcachon in the Bay of Biscay. Supplemented by intentional imports, the Portuguese *Crassostrea angulata* established populations along the

French coast, thereby revitalizing the seafood sector and providing a model for other nations that had overfished their natural reefs.[56]

At the turn of the twentieth century, live iced oysters crisscrossed the globe for introduction to locales far from those in which they had evolved. The confident culturists of the late Victorian age saw no reason to consider the overharvesting of the European flat oyster a tragedy. As one British scientist asserted in the 1890s, "The possible extinction of the unaccommodating 'native' may now be regarded with complete equanimity. Its marsupial habits, so to speak, unfit it for the struggle for existence. . . . Its place will be taken by the less philoprogenitive but not less delicate bivalve of Baltimore or of Portugal."[57] So great was faith in the regenerative power of such "acclimatization" experiments that not until the 1930s, after an astounding seven decades of failure, did attempts to establish *C. virginica* in European waters finally cease.[58]

East Coast oysters also traveled across North America. Displeased with the small size and coppery taste of the local oysters (*Ostrea conchophila* and the more northern Olympia *Ostrea lurida*), San Francisco packers began importing New York seed via the new Transcontinental Railroad around 1870. After pollutants rendered San Francisco Bay unfit for oyster growth, Washington became the center of the Pacific northwestern oyster industry.[59] Frustrated by the decline of Olympia stocks and the failure of East Coast transplants to spawn in the cold northern waters, Washington fish commissioners contacted shellfish experts at the Imperial University of Tokyo in 1899. Several carloads of the Japanese and Korean *Crassostrea gigas* were transplanted into Puget Sound, but the species did not attract major attention until 1922, when the Washington legislature banned noncitizens from owning land. The change forced out of business Japanese nationals who had imported the species for private cultivation. Impressed with the foreign bivalve's rapid growth and large size, the new American owners and fellow aquaculturists increased their orders of Japanese seed, which they marketed under the less provocative name "Pacific oysters." Production of Japanese oysters in Puget Sound alone jumped from 35,000 to 250,000 pounds by 1931, while the native Olympia declined from 500,000 to 300,000 pounds.[60]

In their enthusiasm to improve on nature, aquaculturists of earlier decades had overlooked the environmental changes wrought by their transplantation experiments. But by the 1930s and 1940s, the negative consequences of the half century of global oyster immigration were becoming difficult to ignore.[61] Eagerly awaited barrels and boxcars of foreign oyster stocks often included unwelcome hitchhikers, some of which adapted so well to their new environments that they displaced more prized species. For example, the American East Coast slipper limpet (*Crepidula fornicata*) and oyster drill (*Urosalpinx cinerea*) gained a foothold in Great Britain and California bays after hitchhiking in with the coveted Chesapeake bivalve, decimating the native oysters.[62] Likewise, as imports of Japanese seed to the Pacific Coast states and British Columbia ramped up during the 1920s and 1930s, so did predatory oyster drills (*Tritonalia japonica*). The Washington Department of Fisheries instituted inspection protocols in the mid-1940s to prevent further infestations, but the destructive snail had already ensconced itself in northwestern waters.[63]

Federal and state biologists greeted the discovery of Japanese oyster drills in the Pacific Northwest with alarm. Paul Galtsoff, the director of oyster research for the U.S. Bureau of Fisheries, stressed the importance of taking "precautionary steps" in the form of at least minimal state or federal regulations on live shellfish imports.[64] An immigrant who had carved out a career in the embryonic field of American marine biology after fleeing the Russian Revolution, Galtsoff advised against planting *C. gigas* along the Atlantic Coast, which in the 1930s remained the home of the nation's most valuable oyster fisheries. Doing so might introduce pests that could destroy "our native oysters," which Galtsoff considered superior in appearance and palatability.[65] Japanese oysters also appeared to be much more efficient filter feeders, as shown by studies conducted at the bureau's Milford, Connecticut, laboratory. An adult Japanese oyster could filter sixty-four ounces of water an hour, compared to just ten ounces for the Olympia and thirty ounces for the Chesapeake bivalve. As a *Baltimore Sun* reporter interpreted the results, "Authorities point out that in a struggle for existence food is a prime element, and thus the Chesapeake Bay oyster would be shouldering a great handicap in any such conflict with the Japanese oyster. How, they ask, could the bay oyster survive . . . against . . . its Asiatic kinsman, and especially in seasons when food may be scarce? It is small wonder the native oyster of Puget Sound . . . is slowly but surely being crowded out." Galtsoff's colleague, Lewis Radcliffe, also cautioned against importing "this foreign species which seems to be inferior to our native oyster," as did Virginia's fish commissioner, Robert Armstrong: "If the Japanese oyster is once introduced in our waters it would undoubtedly reseed itself by the thousands. The water temperature in Virginia appears to be just right for its spawning. We would then soon have all the seed we could plant and sell and possibly an overabundance of it."[66] In Depression-era America, the prospect of overproduction provoked great anxiety.

Fearing that the state's few private oyster farmers would be lured into planting cut-rate Japanese seed, Maryland conservation commissioner Swepson Earle convinced the state attorney general to draft a bill prohibiting the practice. Biologist Reginald Truitt conducted experiments in 1932 at the brand-new Chesapeake Biological Laboratory, generating such worrisome results that he terminated the study before its completion. Decades before the development of biosecurity protocols, Truitt minimized the risk of an accidental release by passing the water from the holding tanks through a sewer line into a cesspool and filter basin. Yet even with such precautions, he feared that the foreign bivalve's apparent ability to hybridize with the local species would produce "Jap-Chesapeake" hybrids capable of displacing the native species. Like his federal counterparts, Truitt employed both scientific and nonscientific criteria, criticizing the foreign species for its "inferior" flavor and appearance before concluding that the Japanese oyster could unleash "a genuine 'yellow peril' among native oysters."[67]

Although Truitt had failed to persuade Maryland legislators to expand private leasing of oyster beds or to conduct the public repletion program on a scientific basis, the legislature heeded his warning against Japanese oysters. The 1933 General Assembly made it illegal to cultivate, plant, or introduce into Maryland waters any species of oyster other than the native *C. virginica*.[68] Maryland thus became the first of several Eastern states to prohibit the commercial cultivation of nonnative bivalves.[69] Considering the difficulty encountered by the Conservation Department's scientific consultants in implementing their vision of oyster management, they exerted a remarkable degree of influence over Depression-era discussions regarding the deliberate introduction of a nonnative oyster species. While Chesapeake biologists were out of step with tidewater constituents on the question of oyster privatization, the two groups shared a nativist revulsion against the Japanese bivalve that echoed racist attitudes against Asian Americans and other human minority groups.[70] The scientists were not necessarily xenophobic and did not necessarily oppose all introduced species: not only was Galtsoff an immigrant, but Truitt served as an adviser to a private endeavor that imported nutria to jump-start the Maryland fur industry.[71] However, the 1930s oyster "eco-racism" shows the success scientists could achieve by couching policy goals in a value-laden framework, a strategy for which more recent researchers have come under fire as a consequence of strong public expectations about the objectivity of scientific knowledge.[72]

The Nonnative Counterrevolution

Though rejected by Maryland and other East Coast states, so many nations adopted *C. gigas* that by the 1970s it had become the world's most cultivated oyster species. Thanks to its adaptability and fast growth rate, introduced populations of Japanese oysters thrived in estuaries in the Pacific Northwest, Australia, New Zealand, Great Britain, West Germany, Sweden, Israel, Cyprus, Brazil, the South Pacific, and France, where the Portuguese *Crassostrea angulata* succumbed to gill disease and was replaced by *C. gigas* in 1972.[73] That introduction generated little controversy, but by the decade's end, the ecological and economic risks of exotic species had become too well known for state-supported introductions to take place without extensive discussion, at least in political entities featuring publicly funded research and public interest in environmental affairs.

As pollution and disease battered away at East Coast oyster fisheries, interest in Japanese oysters reawakened. A group of fisheries scientists, aquaculturists, and lawyers met in 1978 at the Woods Hole Oceanographic Institution in Massachusetts to consider the feasibility of future *C. gigas* introductions. After acknowledging that previous introductions had "ranged from good to disastrous," the attendees focused on the latter. To avoid further instances of pest and disease outbreaks and competition and crossbreeding with indigenous oyster species, conference participants called for extreme caution and extensive research involving biologists, economists, lawyers, anthropologists, industry members, and government enforcement agencies. An apparent consensus that the Atlantic oyster industries were not in bad enough shape to warrant such a "drastic," last-resort action and overwhelming research initiative scuttled the idea for more than a decade.[74]

Another likely reason that U.S. East Coast scientists exhibited much greater anxiety about nonnative oysters than their French counterparts involved the story of MSX, the parasite that hit the Delaware Bay and Lower Chesapeake in the late 1950s. Shellfish biologists had for years noted anecdotally that the pattern of MSX infection followed the field experiments of certain researchers, leading to the suspicion that one of their own had inadvertently unleashed the scourge. In the early 1930s, prior to the passage of laws banning nonnative oysters in Atlantic waters, biologist Thurlow C. Nelson planted Japanese oysters in New Jersey's Barnegat Bay. Despite a 1946 warning by the U.S. Fish and Wildlife Service against planting Japanese seed in the Eastern oyster's range, Nelson urged East Coast attendees at that year's conference of the National Shellfisheries Association to experiment with the species, a task taken up by an unknown number of private oyster farmers.[75] From the beginning of the MSX epidemic, attention focused on oyster culturists, and Maryland and other states clamped down on shellfish imports.[76] Molecular biologists finally confirmed in 2000 that MSX had indeed originated in *C. gigas,* but whether the infected oysters arrived via deliberate transplantings or via a less direct route, such as in the hulls or ballast water of Korean War battleships returning to Virginia's James River Reserve Fleet, remains a mystery.[77]

The long-standing hope that the Chesapeake oyster would evolve resistance to MSX and Dermo faded during the late 1980s as the pathogens spread northward, leading some scientists to reconsider solutions dismissed as radical in both the distant and the recent past. After three decades, natural selection had failed to favor the native oyster, either in the wild or the lab. Experts at Rutgers University's Haskin Shellfish Research Laboratory ultimately bred MSX-resistant strains, yet attempts to develop lines resistant to both MSX and Dermo continued to stall.[78] In 1988, Newell concluded that restoring the native variety might be "impossible" because of its stubborn vulnerability to disease and suggested the consideration of a nonnative species.[79] Scientists at the Virginia Institute of Marine Science (VIMS) soon echoed his call.[80]

Virginia researchers played a much greater role than did Marylanders in investigating the feasibility of introducing a more robust oyster to the bay, a reflection of that state's disproportionate decimation by shellfish pathogens. In 1990, the Virginia harvest yielded an all-time low of 135,000 bushels, a fraction of Maryland's take of more than 2,000,000 bushels. The 1995 session of the Virginia legislature authorized VIMS to develop a long-term plan for evaluating nonnative oysters, an action not echoed by the Maryland General Assembly until 2002.[81]

The first alternate species the Virginians considered was *Crassostrea gigas.* The Japanese bivalve had transformed many other oyster industries in concert with a specific set of legal, biological, and technological developments. For the first several decades following the oyster's introduction in Washington state, aquaculturists who took advantage of laws permitting ownership of tidelands relied on regular imports of Japanese seed. They did so because native Olympia stocks remained low and because summertime water temperatures rarely increased enough for the immigrant species to reproduce. The desire to develop domestic seed supplies, combined with a disastrous die-off in the 1950s, led to the rise of hatcheries. West Coast growers implemented another major change in the 1980s, when biologists figured out how to make oysters marketable year-round, not just during the colder winter months, by developing chemically sterilized varieties.[82] Washington biologists also perfected techniques for producing millions of hatchery-raised larvae for cultivation by private entities. Consequently, by the early 1990s, the number of oysters produced in the Pacific Northwest exceeded the Chesapeake output, and other countries that had already embraced the Japanese species clamored for the new technologies.[83] Whereas France and Connecticut had pioneered the adoption of intensive oyster cultivation practices in the mid- to late nineteenth century, Washington now assumed a leading role in the commercial hatchery production of sterile oysters, thereby providing a model for Virginia.

Virginia scientists were intrigued not necessarily by the prospect of introducing another species but rather by the idea of bioengineering a better bivalve. Because *C. gigas* appeared more resistant to the parasites plaguing *C. virginica,* they pondered the idea of developing a hybrid that featured the best qualities of both species.[84] But when VIMS scientists sought to confirm the nonnative oyster's superior disease tolerance by testing sterilized specimens in open water, enormous resistance arose. Regulators and environmentalists feared the potential for genetic contamination of native stocks, as did some other scientists and watermen.[85] Stressing the need to preclude "rogue experiments" by impatient individuals, VIMS leaders finally obtained permission to proceed as long as each organism was certified sterile via time-consuming blood tests.[86] The 1993–94 field tests generated some big surprises. While sterile Japanese oysters met expectations for disease resistance, their slow growth and susceptibility to mud worms cast doubt on their commercial potential.[87]

Moreover, some of the test subjects regained their ability to reproduce, a shock that brought the trial to a sudden end and cast doubt on the technology.[88]

But as the commonwealth's harvest reached rock bottom, the impetus for investigating nonnative species – for use in engineering a hybrid or spearheading a direct introduction – increased. The Virginia legislature agreed to fund a state-of-the-art aquaculture research center, recruiting Stan Allen, a University of Washington–trained pioneer of oyster genetic engineering, to serve as director, and the Virginia Marine Resources Commission voted unanimously in 1995 to authorize a four-year, nine-hundred-thousand-dollar project to test *C. gigas* and lesser-known species.[89] A separate report by University of Maryland analysts concluded that the poor recovery prospects of the native population justified the introduction of *C. gigas* on ecological grounds, but VIMS workers ruled out the Japanese oyster by 1998. It fared well only in the high-salinity waters of the southernmost part of the bay and otherwise failed to perform as well as the native oyster.[90] In its place emerged a new contender, a Southeast Asian variety, *Crassostrea ariakensis*, known in its homeland as the Suminoe and in the United States as the Asian oyster. Field trials of chemically sterilized individuals revealed high disease resistance and a growth rate fast enough to yield two annual harvests.[91] Thus, even as optimism for restoring reefs and developing disease-resistant native stocks blossomed during the mid- to late 1990s, Virginia scientists had primed the pump for debate over a new bivalve.

Survivability, rapid growth, and a taste and appearance similar to the native oyster made *ariakensis* irresistible to the struggling seafood industries of Virginia and Maryland. But many Maryland scientists and fishery managers and environmentalists from both states feared the ecological risks of introducing a species about which scientists knew little. No country had ever used Suminoes for aquaculture, and the specimens used by the VIMS researchers descended from a limited number that had accidentally been imported to Oregon. The Maryland DNR under Governor Parris Glendening resisted consideration of nonindigenous oysters, a stance that could be considered consistent with his proenvironmental policies. While many advocates of Asian oysters derided the Glendening administration as "risk averse," those who sought to slow down the *ariakensis* momentum viewed themselves as adherents of the "precautionary principle," the idea that potentially dangerous activities should cease even when the risks have not been confirmed.[92] Maryland-ers who did not derive their livelihoods from the bay could also afford to be more wary for economic and ecological reasons. As badly as Mary-land's oyster production had declined, it still surpassed Virginia's, which bottomed out at 14,300 bushels during the 1997–98 season, in contrast to the Old Line State's 285,000 bushels. Maryland's salinity regime also made it more likely that native restoration would succeed: fresh-water periodically flushes the Upper Bay, thereby reducing the sever-ity of MSX and Dermo. By contrast, both diseases consistently thrived in Virginia's salty waters, leading to grim predictions that native oysters there could take decades to develop enough disease tolerance to make a comeback.[93]

Yet rapid change in the Maryland seafood sector's most time-honored indicator, the annual harvest, eventually and inevitably drove policy change there, too. The catch dropped to 140,000 bushels during the 2001–2 season, and the number of licensed Maryland oystermen dropped from nine hundred to six hundred in a single year. Glenden-ing could no longer hold back the *ariakensis* momentum. He signed a bill allowing the organism to be studied in state, thereby ending Maryland's six-decade ban on nonnative oysters.[94]

Despite their greater capacity for "risk tolerance," Virginia fishery regulators imposed high biosecurity standards on Suminoe field tests. After two years of pressure from the industry-oriented Virginia Sea-food Council, the regulatory Virginia Marine Resources Commission allowed eight private growers to commence *ariakensis* experiments in 2000. To minimize the chance of an accidental escape, the VIMS scien-tists provided chemically sterilized, second-generation oysters for culti-vation under different salinity conditions. Moreover, test subjects would be contained within cages, checked for sterility every month, removed prior to severe weather, and pulled from the water within a year.[95] The results thrilled the participants so much that the commission extended the experiment for another year and increased the number of test organ-isms to sixty thousand.[96]

Emboldened by its success, the Virginia Seafood Council sought to test one million sterilized Suminoes during the summer of 2002, a pro-posal that raised scientific alarm. VIMS leaders stressed that because the chemical sterilization process was only 99 percent effective, at least ten thousand oysters might be able to reproduce.[97] Instead, the scientists convinced the seafood council to subsidize the more expensive, time-consuming method of genetic sterilization, which would reduce the potential number of fertile individuals to nine hundred.[98] Unwilling to wait for the results of the ongoing study of Asian oysters being conducted by the National Academy of Sciences, the commission allowed the unprecedented experiment to begin in 2003.[99] The "Million Oyster March," as aquaculture geneticist Stan Allen called it, revealed the difficulty of ensuring absolute sterility. A last-minute test protocol of three thousand genetically sterilized *ariakensis* turned up four fertile organisms even before the experiment started, and the ability of sterilized organisms to revert to reproductivity in the wild became apparent at the end of the two-year experiment, when four of the seventy-six hundred oysters examined were found to be fertile.[100] Nevertheless, the seafood council focused on the project's profitability, asserting that each of the eight growers earned between ten thousand and twenty thousand dollars on investments of between three thousand and seventy-five hundred dollars. The council envisioned a new industry based on the cultivation of several million sterile Suminoes a year, a transition that would require large investments in hatchery infrastructure.[101] The Virginia Seafood Council sidestepped the question of maintaining a public fishery based on self-reproducing Asian oysters for watermen not willing or able to make such expenditures. Yet public-domain watermen turned their anger elsewhere.

From Ivory-Tower Theorists to Grant Guzzlers

Scientists who stressed the ecological risks of allowing fecund foreign oysters into the bay infuriated industry members, who felt they had much more to gain than lose. The owner of one of Virginia's last oyster shucking plants captured this perception in a 2001 interview: "With the scientific people, if at the end of the day they don't have any more oysters, they can shrug their shoulders and walk away. I've got families and investments tied up in this business. I've got to either produce or close up. So we don't want this to turn into another 10 years of study and meantime what's left of our industry has collapsed."[102] While the old ivory-tower stereotype no longer prevailed, the idea of shellfish biologists as "grant guzzlers" with a vested interest in prolonging research on

Asian oysters and native restoration gained traction among tidewater fishing communities.[103] An Edgewater resident similarly vented to the *Baltimore Sun,* "We need scientific research to make logical decisions. But what we also need to keep in mind is that a scientist never solves a problem. Scientists always want to continue further research. They live on grant money, and the money does not come in unless there is a problem. That's why they continue to whine about this oyster, which could save our bay. They need problems to keep their grants."[104] Researchers took great offense at such claims. The president of the University of Maryland Center for Environmental Science, Donald Boesch, reminded legislators at a 2005 briefing that Maryland researchers had only begun studying Suminoes the previous year; securing, breeding, and growing the organism was inherently time consuming, and all the Virginia research until then had focused on using *ariakensis* for sterile aquaculture, not on introducing self-replicating populations to the bay. In his three decades on the Chesapeake, Boesch testified, he had never seen his colleagues pursue a topic with such a strong "sense of urgency, openness to collaboration, and serious commitment to objectivity."[105] In addition, although most U.S. researchers depend on grants, public funding is rarely easy to obtain or to sustain indefinitely, and scientists have an interest in solving problems sooner rather than later because that is the route to prestige and career advancement.

The federal government's environmentally oriented agencies defended the need for methodical analysis of the potential risks and benefits of a *C. ariakensis* introduction. Officials from the EPA, Fish and Wildlife Service, and Army Corps of Engineers were among those who pressured the Virginia aquaculturists to scale back the Million Oyster March.[106] The feds even exhorted the bay states to refocus on *C. virginica,* warning in late 2001 that funding for native restoration projects could be jeopardized if Asian oysters became the center of scientific and political attention.[107] Perhaps the least obvious federal partner was the Corps of Engineers, which had become involved in Chesapeake science in the 1960s, when it initiated a comprehensive study of the bay, including the construction of a huge hydraulic model.[108] The corps assumed a major role in native reef restoration during the 1990s and became involved in the Asian oyster debate as a consequence of the agency's responsibility for issuing permits for structures in navigable waterways – in this case, the containers used to secure the sterile experimental Suminoes. Corps officials found themselves pulled in deeper in 2003, when Maryland governor Robert Ehrlich joined his Virginia counterpart, Mark Warner, in asking the corps to conduct an environmental impact study (EIS) on seeding the bay with reproducing Suminoes. Although corps officers demurred on the grounds that they did not consider living organisms "structures," the Virginia and Maryland congressional delegations obtained authorization for the corps to lead the EIS process, an enormous job involving the input of several state and federal agencies. The bay state governors, who sought to finish the EIS within a year, agreed to match the two-hundred-thousand-dollar appropriation while asserting their authority to make the final decision about introducing nonnative oysters.[109] But the EIS took much longer to complete, and the governors' jurisdictional authority proved far murkier.

By the time Congress authorized the EIS, the NRC had spent months immersed in the Asian oyster question. To overcome the impasse that had entangled the stakeholders by early 2002, the council agreed to weigh in on the ecological and economic advantages and disadvantages of Suminoes. When the group announced its conclusions eighteen months later, the political situation in Maryland had undergone a sea change. Ehrlich had already delivered on campaign promises to watermen by relaxing crabbing restrictions and permitting oyster dredging under power rather than sail in almost a third of the bay.[110] He also sought to expand testing of Asian oysters, confident that the corps could quickly complete the EIS.[111] Although the NRC completed its $315,000 review before either state could take irreversible action, the speed with which the bay governors sought to act stood in sharp contrast to the scientific academy's goal of providing a deliberative analysis for use in political decision making.

Perhaps not surprisingly given the lack of information on *C. ariakensis*, the NRC panel proposed a middle path. The committee's marine biologists, aquaculture specialists, economists, anthropologist, and legal scholar began by ruling out two of the three management options in question. They rejected the idea of introducing fertile Asian oysters because of the high level of uncertainty and irreversibility regarding ecological risks. Yet they feared that closing off that alternative might increase the chances of a dangerous rogue introduction. That left the option of continuing to study sterile oysters for aquaculture, which the group recommended as an interim step to minimize ecological risks,

provide policy-relevant data, and allow time to restore native populations.[112] Press coverage focused on the report's affirmation of the path
on which Virginia had long since begun, and the predictable reactions
of the different stakeholders to the call for at least another five years of
study.[113] A half decade seemed interminable to harvesters and seafood
dealers facing insolvency, but researchers still untangling basic taxonomic questions found that period barely adequate, and tension built.

The NRC panel had more in mind than oyster research, for it asserted
the value of analyzing the human communities at the heart of the plan.
Because an *ariakensis* introduction would likely cause major changes for
fishing communities, they urged the collection of baseline data on sociocultural and economic norms, trends, and outcomes. Otherwise, distinguishing the effects of specific management actions from unrelated
changes in the fishery would be impossible.[114] Though the panel's social
scientists had an undeniable self-interest in calling for sociocultural
data, their point was crucial. Many analysts of the oyster problem from
Brooks onward had overlooked relevant aspects of user-group sociology.
In particular, when Isaiah Bowman used the Maryland oyster fishery in
1940 as a case study of the failure to apply science to social problems,
he never considered that the watermen's worldviews might shed light
on the questions he found so vexing – or, for that matter, why scientific
knowledge could be assumed to hold the answers to social problems.[115]
Years after publicly funded investigations of other fishing peoples commenced, the Chesapeake academic and political establishments recognized the importance of local knowledge by supporting intensive anthropological studies of tidewater communities.[116]

The NRC panel took another sociological tack by exposing what it
considered the misconceptions driving the public discourse on nonnative oysters. In addition to attacking the 1990s-era assumption that
native restoration would dramatically improve water quality, the group
challenged the hype surrounding *C. ariakensis*. Smothering sediments
and climate change could harm Asian oysters just as badly as the native
species, and stakeholders should thus stop assuming that the new species would rapidly populate the bay and revive the industry. Quick fixes
were no substitute for long-term, systematic commitments to addressing
the bay's complex problems.[117]

Furthermore, even as "myths" had guided the public debate, the
panel exposed what it considered a worrisome fact that had escaped

discussion: a Suminoe launch required no federal regulatory approval. Because a new species might cross political borders, the panel advised that a regional body such as the EPA's Chesapeake Bay Program receive final authority over such a potentially far-reaching decision. The bureau had established a groundbreaking 1993 policy to ensure comprehensive reviews prior to intentional introductions, but its recommendations were nonbinding, and no statutory mechanism existed for resolving differences among states.[118] EPA officials questioned whether fertile Suminoes might constitute a biological pollutant under the Clean Water Act, thereby requiring an EPA discharge permit.[119] And after neighboring states expressed alarm that the Maryland and Virginia governors possessed the sole decision-making power to proceed with an introduction, the Maryland General Assembly stepped in by requiring legislative approval of any Suminoe introduction, thereby upping the ante over jurisdictional authority.[120]

Hopes that the NRC report would cut through the haze of oyster politics by providing a clear assessment of risks and benefits thus died hard. The harvest season following the report's publication was the worst in Maryland history, yielding just 26,500 bushels, and although harvests topped 150,000 bushels in 2005–6 and 2006–7, the jump reflected the state's expansion of power dredging rather than a biological comeback.[121] As oystermen struggled to make a living and to understand why scientists focused on the negatives rather than the positives of a nonnative oyster overrunning the Chesapeake, complex questions regarding Suminoe biology, jurisdictional authority, the costs of invasive species, and the value of native versus nonnative approaches caused the EIS to stretch months and then years beyond the original cutoff date.

One sticking point involved the genetic fitness of the organisms that would build the new oyster economy. Proponents of Suminoes invested their hopes in the "Oregon strain" on the rationale that it had been raised in that state's waters without incident for thirty years.[122] However, researchers noted that no self-sustaining populations of *C. ariakensis* had ever become established in the wild in the Pacific Northwest, even after being accidentally introduced with another Asian oyster during the 1970s, and that it had never become an important part of the aquaculture industry there. In the early 1990s, Rutgers University researchers imported the first Oregon Suminoes to the East Coast, inbreeding them before shipping their progeny to the VIMS team. As a result, the brood stocks used in the Chesapeake (about one thousand oysters) exhibited low genetic diversity, having stemmed from a founder population of fewer than ten males and ten females. By contrast, argued geneticists, more than a hundred unrelated individuals would be needed to initiate a stocking program. But obtaining new specimens from Asia, quarantining them for at least two generations, and breeding them for a large-scale introduction could take another six to seven years. Suminoe proponents' unabated insistence on the sufficiency of the Oregon strain frustrated scientists, who stressed the irresponsibility of relying on such an inbred population.[123]

New insights into the ecology and natural history of *C. ariakensis* also raised more issues than they resolved. When researchers began studying the species in its indigenous environment, they discovered that contrary to the Chesapeake experiments, in which Suminoes grew faster in high-salinity waters, the opposite seemed to be true in southern China, where the oyster thrived in low-salinity areas and took three to five years to reach market size.[124] Experiments in North Carolina waters undermined the idea of Suminoe imperviousness by revealing its susceptibility to a previously unknown local protozoan parasite.[125] Adding to the confusion, taxonomic studies suggested that oysters previously identified as *Crassostrea ariakensis* consisted of two or more distinct species.[126] Thanks to an unprecedented two-million-dollar grant from the National Oceanic and Atmospheric Administration, U.S. and Chinese scientists made several discoveries that challenged the optimistic findings of the Virginia Suminoe experiments. Preliminary results suggested that fertile Suminoes that escaped to warmer southern waters could crowd out the native *C. virginica* and could become infected with the Dermo parasite without dying, thereby serving as a disease reservoir. Moreover, Suminoes seemed inferior to the native Eastern oyster with respect to building reefs, tolerating low dissolved oxygen levels, and surviving mud crab predation.[127] Conceding that their plans for a rapid introduction had been unrealistic, Ehrlich administration officials backed off from their aggressive timetable.[128] At the same time, a short-lived effort by environmentalists to list the Eastern oyster as an endangered species drew attention to the native but otherwise only angered oystermen and seafood processors from Maine to Louisiana.[129]

Completing the dozens of Suminoe research projects under way slowed down the evaluation process, as did the time needed for meetings and reviews by the many state, federal, and academic participants. The EIS process outlasted the Ehrlich administration. Top-down pressure for introducing fertile *ariakensis* to Maryland tidal waters stalled in late 2006, when Ehrlich lost his reelection bid to Martin O'Malley, a Democrat who supported native restoration and who returned control of the DNR to the director who had overseen implementation of the Roundtable initiatives in the 1990s.[130] By the time of the gubernatorial shakeup, the EIS had taken on a life of its own. The survey was very ambitious, seeking to assess the impact not only of establishing naturalized Suminoe populations in Maryland and Virginia tidal waters but also of eight other actions designed to replicate the harvest levels reached between 1920 and 1970, a tacit admission of the success of the public repletion program. Potential alternatives included the loaded issues of implementing a harvest moratorium or aquaculture operations using either the native or sterile nonnative species. Furthermore, analyzing each idea required the development of complex predictive tools, including computer models measuring oyster demography, larval transport, water quality, and socioeconomic projections.[131] While the delay frustrated those expecting quick results, it showed that Chesapeake scientists and fellow oyster reformers had moved far beyond the one-solution-fits-all ideal of their pro-leasing forebears.

The changing priorities of the 1990s and early 2000s highlighted three long-term trends in oyster management: the entrenched relationship between oysters and Maryland politics, the shift of decision-making power from the legislature to the governor in the wake of reapportionment, and the continuing importance of fishery issues to the state's cultural identity despite the tiny number of individuals who still followed the water.

∞

Recognition of the oyster's ecosystem services brokered a truce between watermen and scientists late in the twentieth century, but reef restoration's inability to deliver quick results has engendered what appears to be the final phase of the contentious oyster question. Seeking to re-create the consensus-driven Roundtable of diverse interests that brokered the oyster recovery approaches of the mid-1990s, the O'Malley administration prevailed on the General Assembly to convene a special group in the fall of 2007. Announced the new governor, "We are clearly running out of time to save a species that is of immeasurable value to the Bay's ecosystem, the seafood industry, and our culture as Marylanders. We are challenging our new Oyster Advisory Commissioners – scientists and stakeholders alike – to work together, to move beyond traditional thinking, and to give us some new ideas for giving our native oyster a new lease on life." Chair William Eichbaum, an architect of the 1980s-era bay cleanup framework, reiterated the governor's renewed focus on the indigenous oyster while stressing the desire to continue linking ecological and economic aims: "We are at a crossroads with oyster management and this new Commission may represent our final opportunity to restore the ecological role of native oysters and assure an economically appropriate and viable industry in the Chesapeake Bay."[132]

Both native oysters and oystermen have teetered near extinction for years. The oyster population remains at just 1 percent of its nineteenth-century levels, and only a handful of the five hundred Marylanders who bought oyster licenses during the 2006–7 season used them to earn a livelihood.[133] Most of the oystering infrastructure has also disappeared. Shucking houses have long since shut down, forcing the few remaining processors to import product. Perhaps more important, tidewater communities have gentrified into waterfront retreats where the "money people" have no interest in the early-morning racket or late-afternoon aroma of workboats.[134] Most Marylanders lost the taste for oysters long ago yet love the romantic symbolism of the skipjack, which was featured on stamps honoring the state issued by the U.S. Postal Service in 1988 and 2002. However, few people outside the waning tidewater communities seem interested in continuing the eighty-year commitment of public funds to the put-and-take fishery. Recent audits of the reef restoration initiatives reflect a growing impatience with the watermen's subsidies.[135] Indeed, the Oyster Advisory Commission began its 2007 deliberations by announcing that the industry should eventually yield to full privatization.[136] Given the current worldwide movement to privatize resources once considered communal, from drinking water to social security, it seems unlikely that Maryland's watermen will emerge unscathed in the aftermath of this latest call to close the oyster commons.

Today's cultural and literal landscape has ruled out the previous century's actions to manage the vast "collective farm" of public oyster bars. Seed transplanting fell out of scientific and regulatory favor in the 1990s because of its role in spreading the disease parasites now endemic in the bay. More recently, the state suspended most shell-planting operations after recreational fishermen argued that the dredging of old shell from beneath the bay damaged fish spawning grounds. Watermen bitterly oppose the termination of the repletion programs, rejecting the argument that ecological conditions have made it unwise to continue such efforts.[137]

But the state has also broken with past management practices in ways that harvesters approve, such as by relaxing the rules on dredging under sail. Power dredgers compare their work to agricultural tilling, arguing that oyster bars must be worked over to prevent the buildup of smothering sediments.[138] Power dredging also enables larger numbers of oysters to be removed more quickly, as evidenced by production increases since the policy change. Because the adoption of more efficient technology always increases harvest pressure, scientists and environmentalists decried the expansion of power dredging.[139] Accordingly, the Oyster Advisory Commission's call to envision a "shift in paradigms" that rejects the policies of the past overlooks important changes that have already occurred.[140]

Those changes include the two hundred or so exotic species that have adapted to Chesapeake waters. Although the MSX parasite has arguably caused the greatest economic and ecological harm, other damaging invaders include nutria and mute swans, which gorge on the bay's seagrass meadows, destroying food and habitat for many creatures. At the same time, many of the apparent invaders have attracted little attention, and some have proved popular, such as sport fish including the largemouth bass.[141] Some exotic species have even been correlated with positive environmental changes: filter-feeding Asiatic clams, for example, may have triggered a resurgence of submerged aquatic grasses after an absence of fifty years.[142]

The intense pushback from ecologically oriented stakeholders against the Asian oyster thus seems to involve motives related to sociocultural factors and human values. Contrary to the findings of other analysts of debates regarding introduced species, however, these motivations show no evidence of xenophobia or nativism. The Asian oyster debate may have evoked such strong reactions among environmentalists because a deliberate nonnative introduction would force the acknowledgment that we – all of us – have failed to achieve the ambitious goals for mitigating our negative effects on the Chesapeake Bay. Despite some progress over the past three decades, the estuary remains under assault by pollution, human population growth, and rising temperatures and sea levels. The watery ecosystem in which oysters evolved has itself undergone a tremendous transformation, and efforts to restore oysters without also reducing anthropogenic inputs are thus likely to fail, a point on which watermen and scientists have found common ground.

Another explanation for the explosiveness of the Asian oyster debate is that Suminoe opponents view the native oyster as a means of maintaining Maryland's regional and biocultural identity. Journalist Eugene Meyer concluded from his travels during the 1980s, when state officials began leading the regional effort to clean up the bay, that despite the rise of seafood festivals and other markers of cultural distinctiveness two decades earlier, the state still lacked a cohesive identity: "The fact is that many Marylanders have little sense of place about their state outside of their own geographical areas."[143] Although the mitigation program failed to achieve many of its aggressive goals in the ensuing quarter century, it did help Maryland solidify its baycentric status among residents and visitors. Newspapers now provide heavy coverage of bay pollution, license plates carry the command "Treasure the Chesapeake," and road signs far from the shore alert drivers to the watershed's broad boundaries. In the late twentieth century, Maryland built up a reputation based on its unique relationship with the Chesapeake Bay, and the prospect of alien oysters jeopardized that uniqueness.

As is true in so many other locales, the distinctiveness of the Old Line State is also under siege from the creeping spread of corporatization and globalization. Many of the oysters sold in Maryland now come from the Gulf Coast, and in the late 1990s, the state's major processor of blue crabs began relying on imports from Thailand.[144] Yet the idea of an estuary full of Asian oysters would break the sense of place unique to the Chesapeake landmass. And even though many people living within a 150-mile radius of the bay are themselves relative newcomers, a Maryland oyster industry based on nonnatives would destroy the illusion of rootedness craved by so many members of our modern, mobile society.

Cultural geographers have shown how the surging popularity of microbreweries and farmers' markets since the 1990s reflects "the desire of people to break away from the smothering homogeneity of popular, national culture, and to reestablish connections with local communities, settings, and economies," a movement termed neolocalism.[145] A similar

dynamic seems to underlie the resistance to introducing nonnative oysters to the Chesapeake Bay. Opposition is greatest among more affluent stakeholders who do not derive their income from the bay and who
show no interest in connecting with the wild estuarine environment in
the intimate, dangerous ways that watermen do. The neolocalism of
most suburban environmentalists embodies a relationship with the bay
that gets no closer than the occasional sailing jaunt or crab feast. Nor
does it feature passionate support for subsidizing the oystermen to the
tune of millions of dollars, especially amid the 2008 crisis of the nation's
economy. The environmentalist preference for restoring native oyster
populations suggests a strong neolocal desire to preserve the ecological
uniqueness of a most uncommon place if not its irreplaceable traditions
of human capital.

Epilogue
Toward a Protein Factory Farm

While images of the Chesapeake watermen have filled shelves of books, they have rarely caught Hollywood's eye, with one notable exception. The gritty 1990s police drama *Homicide* departed from its Baltimore setting for "The Last of the Watermen," a work of art that personifies the stereotype of the waterman-scientist relationship. The episode features a detective seeking to escape "the stench of urban decay" by returning to her Eastern Shore hometown. Her oysterman father has sold his boat to escape being "regulated to death." Then, after her oysterman brother and crew spend an arduous day dredging, the marine police and a state biologist accuse them of using illegal gear and dump their catch back into the bay, precipitating a fight. That night, the detective witnesses a fierce quarrel in the local bar after the biologist shows up. One of the dredgers claims that the biologist has destroyed his livelihood through conservation measures, while the scientist blames the waterman for overharvesting the resource. When the biologist says that the oyster is practically an endangered species, the waterman exclaims, "*We're* the endangered species – not the friggin' oyster." Hours later, the biologist's body is found behind the bar, the victim of multiple stab wounds from an oyster knife.[1]

In reality, no scientist ever lost his or her life to a waterman (though watermen were killed by resource officers), and by the time the episode aired, the two groups had joined other stakeholders in the historic series of meetings that produced the Oyster Roundtable Action Plan. The groundbreaking effort to drive ecological and economic recovery through reef restoration and other taxpayer-funded techniques, however, failed to engineer a rapid increase in the number of marketable bivalves, shredding the fragile veil of harmony. In the opening years of the twenty-first century, tension flared again over the meaning of oyster conservation. The Oyster Wars no longer feature the violence of the late 1800s but do involve frequent volleys of misinformation and oversimplification, which take root most readily without an appreciation of the multiple layers of complexity underlying the problem.

In contrast to the conventional wisdom, the Maryland oyster fishery does not epitomize the tragedy of the commons, and overfishing, mismanagement, and the failure to privatize do not account first and foremost for the long-term decline in landings (fig. 17).[2] Although many oystermen violated conservation laws, sharp localized declines occurred, and dredging altered the physical structure of the reefs for the worse, an overweening focus on resource-user greed and managerial incompetence obscures the state's crucial actions for more than a century to reduce harvest pressure. Restrictions on gear, season and size of capture, and entry to the fishery date to the end of the Civil War. Bloody battles followed as the state tried to protect the resource for its citizens. The majority of oystermen were poor and thus in most places in Gilded Age America could not have overcome the concurrent demands to enclose the oyster beds for hyperefficient aquaculture. Maryland's political geography enabled commercial fishermen to resist privatization, but no free-for-all prevailed after the Oyster Wars subsided.

Under the guidance of tidewater legislators, the oyster commons evolved to include scientific prescriptions for sustainability. The 1927 compromise of public reshelling and reseeding established a put-and-take fishery that maintained relatively stable overall harvests for decades thereafter. The state repletion program enabled thousands of oystermen to feed their families and feel a sense of independence, at least until disease sent the industry into its relentless tailspin in the late 1980s.

Nonetheless, on the eve of that disaster, one of the state's leading chroniclers insisted on the horrible example provided by Maryland:

Fig. 17. By 2006, members of the Chesapeake Bay community recognized the ecological importance of oysters but still clung to the long-held belief that overharvesting played the dominant role in the species' decline. (Toles © 2006 The Washington Post. Reprinted with permission of Universal Press Syndicate. All rights reserved.)

"Local economic interests prevailed over conservation controls, and so the greedy destroyed their own livelihood and much of their folk culture. The oyster story is a lesson in needless resource depletion that should frighten a world facing more portentous losses of food and fuel."[3] This has been the prevailing narrative, but it is not accurate. Scientists, watermen, and policymakers worked together to create a unique system, a regulated commons that balanced science-based conservation and dignified self-employment. The history of the oyster commons has not been a simple conservation failure; to the contrary, it has served as a positive, if imperfect, model for a world undergoing increased corporate control of natural and cultural resources.

The charge that the fisheries agency sowed the seeds of the disease disaster is another part of the conventional wisdom that contains a kernel of truth but must not be used to indict the state for malfeasance. A variety of human activities facilitated the spread of shellfish pathogens. The microbes entered the mouth of the Chesapeake Bay at midcentury by hitchhiking within foreign mollusks, which arrived either via the experimental plantings of researchers and growers or in the ballast and on the hulls of transoceanic ships. Over the next three decades, spikes in human population growth, agricultural and industrial pollutants, and nonnative predators stressed the ecosystem, weakening the bay's ability to endure environmental shocks. Against this backdrop of rapid land-use change, fishery managers continued the practice of transplanting immature seed oysters to satisfy watermen of northern counties whose less salty waters impeded growth. The prolonged drought conditions associated with anthropogenic climate change created salinity levels favorable to the lethal parasites in the 1980s. As in other resource debates, the complex interactions among multiple disturbance factors hinder efforts to pinpoint a primary cause for these disease outbreaks and demonstrate the high degree of uncertainty involved in the remediation of an ecosystem as complex as the Chesapeake Bay.[4]

Another important though misunderstood aspect of the story of Maryland oyster politics concerns the role of malapportionment in preserving the regulated estuarine commons against enclosure. When wealthy and culturally dominant interests threatened their way of life, oystermen overcame intraindustry conflicts to make the most of their collective clout. In so doing, they flouted the assumption that individuals, even those in tight-knit communities, exploit common-pool resources without regard to fellow users. Maryland and many other states featured legislatures dominated by rural minorities, and this phenomenon consequently deserves much more attention from historians of U.S. conservation policymaking and natural resource management. Environmental historians' disproportionate focus on federal rather than state-level initiatives and on moneyed stakeholders' ability to co-opt the administrative bodies charged with regulating them has obscured recognition of the role of rural-dominated legislatures in safeguarding the interests of nonelite resource users prior to the court-ordered structural changes of the 1960s.

Despite the lack of attention to the environmental policy consequences of malapportionment, a few scholars have drawn attention to the overlapping of the reapportionment and environmental revolutions. As Samuel Hays and Barbara Hays write in their influential study of postwar environmental politics, "A determining factor in the emergence of environmental affairs was the timing of the rise of the city to a significant

role in state politics, and this was closely connected to legislative reapportionment." Equal representation for "the middle-class suburbs –
precisely those places where environmental attitudes were strongest" by
1970 "added considerably to the strength of environmental objectives in
state as well as national politics."[5] After reapportionment, Maryland suburbanites likewise transformed the focus of conservation policymaking.
They not only recognized the environmental costs of growth as threats
to their quality of life but also viewed the bay's subsistence fishermen as
artisans whose lifeways were worth saving rather than as embarrassing
throwbacks to a preindustrial economy or to the Old Line State's southern roots.

One of the few studies providing empirical evidence for the environmental policy impact of legislative reapportionment pertains to Florida,
another southern state that experienced heavy postwar in-migration.
Despite the demographic shift, rural counties in the Panhandle and older
northern settlements dominated the state's House and Senate prior to
the 1967 reapportionment. Analysis of roll-call votes before and after
the change reveals dramatic shifts in the strengthening of pollution and
land-use planning laws, making Florida a national leader in environmental protection.[6] Perhaps most notably, Floridians facilitated the rise
of the environmental impact statement, for the newly apportioned legislature responded to recreational fishermen's and suburban newcomers'
protests against the destruction of coastal wetlands by requiring wetlands developers to evaluate their projects' potential effects before state
approval would be forthcoming.[7] Two years later, Congress enshrined
the environmental impact statement in federal law for construction projects involving federal agencies via the National Environmental Policy
Act of 1969. Florida's pioneering efforts to safeguard wetlands led Hays
and Hays to cite the Sunshine State as one of the areas from which the
environmental movement "derived special impetus."[8] Sustained analysis of the ways in which the newly empowered suburban voters of the
late 1960s and 1970s liberalized environmental policymaking at the state
level is needed to provide a fuller accounting of the rise of environmentalism in the South and other regions of the United States.

∞

The idea that the history of Maryland oyster politics features the recur-
rent compromise of science has persisted for many years. With the

failure of rebuilt reefs to reverse long-term declines, optimism about reconciling ecological and economic goals waned in the early twenty-first century. The millennial search for new solutions to the oyster problem fixed on the idea of introducing self-sustaining exotic bivalves because doing so appeared to be the only way to enable watermen to work the water without punching time cards for big corporations. Though they no longer enjoyed the ability to control seafood policy, harvesters still possessed influence out of proportion to their numbers. This led some interests to worry that the ultimate decision on *Crassostrea ariakensis* would be driven by political rather than scientific concerns.[9] As the Chesapeake Bay Foundation's lead scientist concluded his testimony at a 2003 congressional hearing on the Asian oyster, during "the history of oyster management, starting with Dr. William Brooks . . . all the way through some of the recent committees during the last decade . . . , in virtually every case, science has in one way or another been compromised. So . . . let's just not let the science be compromised this time and let's see what it can do."[10] Yet in reality, science has not been compromised, especially not in the pejorative sense of scandalous misuse or neglect. Rather, the oyster story supports the argument that no singular scientific solution uncompromised by politics exists.

Compromise is a crucial part of policymaking, and Chesapeake scientists have fared relatively well in influencing many phases of that process over the past eighty years. Several important solutions adopted by Maryland lawmakers to address the oyster problem incorporated scientific advice. Shell planting in particular reconciled scientific prescriptions with political exigencies, a reasonable negotiation given the power and antileasing sentiment of the tidewater counties. Biologists often disagreed with the repletion program's implementation and did not value its ability merely to sustain (rather than greatly increase) harvests. But just because such notable players as William Keith Brooks, Reginald V. Truitt, Abel Wolman, and Isaiah Bowman despaired at the state's refusal to liberalize the leasing laws does not mean that the politics of the oyster question forced science into shameful concessions.

The charge that Chesapeake science has been compromised in recent decades is also suspect. The ecological understanding of the oyster played a key role in negotiating new solutions acceptable to all the stakeholders in the 1990s. Although the failure of ensuing restoration efforts to produce more oysters in the short time frame of ten years provides an important caveat about expecting too much too soon (as ecologists had indeed warned), the harvest decline should not be used to discount that historic consensus. The ecological rationale had another powerful outcome, underpinning calls to consider nonnative oysters following the disease debacle of the 1980s. Scientists – not watermen or fishery managers or even aquaculturists – first suggested that perhaps the Chesapeake bivalve's filtering capacity could be replicated or genetically enhanced by a heartier foreign species. In fact, convincing regulators to allow testing of exotics in tidal waters required reversing laws passed in the wake of the 1930s scientific campaign against immigrant oysters. In the big picture, given the forces allied against it, Chesapeake science has exerted a surprisingly significant influence over estuarine resource policymaking.

The idea of science being compromised throughout the annals of oyster politics implies that the solution advanced by most Chesapeake researchers, at least until the mid–twentieth century, would have solved the problems of conserving the resource. Yet the logic of private cultivation and estuarine enclosure ignored two broader developments in American culture. The first concerned the bivalve's status as something more than a material resource. Prior to the ecological understanding of mollusks as filter-feeding keystone species, scientists and conservationists alike tended to treat oysters like coal, timber, or other carbonaceous forms of wealth. But oysters are also food and thus possess a set of shifting cultural meanings understood by consumers in a more visceral way than other natural resources. While remaining a key ingredient of holiday meals and other special occasions, oysters ceased to be everyday fare as other protein sources offered safer and cheaper sustenance for the majority of Americans.

The persistent desire to increase oyster production not only overlooked the falloff in consumer demand but also brushed aside the "problems of plenty" plaguing U.S. agriculture throughout the twentieth century. Scientific and technological reforms were so efficient that they generated price-reducing crop surpluses, leading more farmers to rely on federal price-support and acreage-reduction policies.[11] Yet even as the nation's shrinking number of farmers belied the principles of the free market by becoming locked into a cycle of governmental dependence, critics decried Maryland's public oyster-repletion program as a wasteful watermen's subsidy. Those who believed that oyster conservation necessitated the adoption of an agronomic business model urged commercial fishermen to trade the inefficiencies of the hunt for the apparently more predictable and profitable rhythms of underwater cultivation. In so doing, reformers neglected broader forces that reinforced the dependency of both independent and corporate farmers on government aid.

The latest blue-ribbon commission charged with solving the oyster problem echoes the agronomic ideal. Although the 2003 congressional hearing included a one-day session on the potential for an aquaculture industry based on the nonnative Suminoe, the proposal by Governor Robert Ehrlich's administration to seed the Maryland half of the bay with self-reproducing Asian oysters shifted the debate away from aquaculture. With the ascendancy of Governor Martin O'Malley in 2007, native oysters once again assumed center stage, though not in the context of the 1990s effort to integrate commercial and ecological goals. The sudden reframing of the debate revealed the extent to which resource policymaking now resided in the cabinet. Both executives' desire to enact bold changes in oyster management, however their visions differed, also demonstrated the range of policy choices now available – options that scientists helped illuminate.

The O'Malley panel, composed of twenty-one diverse stakeholder representatives selected for their lack of investment in historical approaches, soon signaled its unsurprising intent to break with past managerial practices.[12] While waiting for the U.S. Army Corps of Engineers to complete its massive environmental impact statement assessing native versus nonnative restoration alternatives, the new Oyster Advisory Commission sketched out a vision of an industry that "will have evolved through privatization, thereby shifting much of the financial burden from the public to the private sector." Unlike previous generations of pro-leasers who sought immediate taxpayer relief, however, the preliminary report called for "targeted investment by the state in research and technology" on the order of between $41 and $87 million annually during the first ten years.[13] Why the public would agree to spend that much given the current hand-wringing over the $39.7 million in state and federal funds invested in Maryland reef restoration since 1994 (with another $19 million spent in Virginia) was not addressed.[14] Accordingly, the idea of expending ten to twenty times that amount to get the reefs in shape for withdrawal from the public domain seems to undercut the entire rationale of privatization.

After spending five years and $17 million investigating the environmental trade-offs of several policy options regarding the future oyster fishery, the Corps of Engineers issued its long-awaited environmental impact statement in 2009. An earlier one-thousand-page report had contained no specific recommendations. Instead, corps, Maryland, and Virginia officials announced that they would make no decision until hearing from stakeholders at another six public meetings.[15] The response against nonnative oysters was so overwhelming that leaders agreed to abandon them. Four decades after reapportionment, the watermen's political dominance appeared to be over.

Indeed, mounting pressure for privatized aquaculture shows that the dwindling number of Maryland harvesters can take nothing for granted. Small-scale aquaculture initiatives financed jointly by watermen and the state suggest a growing acceptance of the public fishery's inevitable transformation. Watermen stress that efforts to advance the aquaculture industry must guarantee access to good leases, which would likely mean continuing subsidies. A newspaper headline interpreted the Oyster Advisory Commission's interim conclusion with a sense of doom: "To Save Oysters, a Culture May Have to Die."[16] More accurately, the watermen may have to shed their iconic image as independent hunter-gatherers and fully embrace the role toward which they have evolved over the past eight decades: as state-supported cultivators and active manipulators of a human-dominated resource.

Environmental historians often have the depressing job of pointing out past mistakes that current resource managers and stakeholders would do well to avoid. It is equally crucial to recognize the value of what has worked, especially as we enter what may be the final phase of the oyster question. While we cannot implement the specific strategies that succeeded in the bay of the 1930s or 1960s, we must take care not to accept stereotypes and assume that one side or the other was wronged in the process of negotiating those solutions. Maryland's celebrated "middle temperament," balancing the best of Yankee modernity with southern tradition, prevailed in oyster policymaking as well as in other endeavors.[17] Whether the Old Line State can maintain the precarious balance of conflicting interests in the Chesapeake Bay without abandoning the remarkably durable regulated commons is an issue that requires not only economic, ecological, and anthropological insights but also a more inclusive sense of history.

NOTES

Introduction

1. The phrase *culture wars* dates to the 1990s, when it referred to contemporary ideological debates in American society between "traditionalists" and "secular progressives," as first analyzed by James Davison Hunter in *Culture Wars: The Struggle to Define America* (New York: Basic Books, 1991). I have appropriated it to refer to earlier cultural conflicts regarding issues other than abortion, same-sex marriage, gun control, and so on that involved the same broad clash of world-views. The phrase is especially appropriate in the context of this study because it captures both the anthropological and agricultural meanings of the word *culture*.

On these dual connotations, see Joseph E. Taylor III, *Making Salmon: An Environmental History of the Northwest Fisheries Crisis* (Seattle: University of Washington Press, 1999), 7, 10; Philip J. Pauly, *Biologists and the Promise of American Life: From Meriwether Lewis to Alfred Kinsey* (Princeton: Princeton University Press, 2000), 8–9.

2. "The Oyster Front," *Maryland Tidewater News,* Feb. 1951, 1–3; Garrett Power, "More about Oysters Than You Wanted to Know," *Maryland Law Review* 30 (1970): 199–225.

3. Christopher G. Boone, "Obstacles to Infrastructure Provision: The Struggle to Build Comprehensive Sewer Works in Baltimore," *Historical Geography* 31 (2003): 151–68; Steven G. Davison, Jay G. Merwin Jr., John Capper, Garrett Power, and Frank R. Shivers Jr., *Chesapeake Waters: Four Centuries of Controversy, Concern, and Legislation* (1983; Centreville, Md.: Tidewater, 1997), 84–90; Calvin W. Hendrick, "Colossal Work in Baltimore," *National Geographic* 20 (1909): 365–73.

4. William K. Brooks, *The Oyster: A Popular Summary of a Scientific Study* (1891, 1905; Baltimore: Johns Hopkins University Press, 1996), 142.

5. J. Crawford King Jr., "The Closing of the Southern Range: An Exploratory Study," *Journal of Southern History* 48 (1982): 53–70; Stephen Hahn, *The Roots of Southern Populism: Yeoman Farmers and the Transformation of the Georgia Upcountry, 1850–1890* (New York: Oxford University Press, 1983); Shawn Everett Kantor, *Politics and Property Rights: The Closing of the Open Range in the Postbellum South* (Chicago: University of Chicago Press, 1998); Karen R. Merrill, *Public Lands and Political Meaning: Ranchers, the Government, and the Property between Them* (Berkeley: University of California Press, 2002).

6. Brooks, *Oyster,* 5.

7. Analyses employing this framework and/or the related ideas that overfishing, mismanagement, and a lack of private aquacultural enterprise played dominant roles in the Maryland oyster fishery's long-term decline include Isaiah Bowman, "Science and Social Effects: Three Failures," *Scientific Monthly* 50 (1940): 289–98; Francis Taggart Christy Jr., "The Exploitation of a Common Property Natural Resource: The Maryland Oyster Industry" (PhD diss., University of Michigan, 1964); Power, "More about Oysters"; John J. Alford, "The Chesapeake Oyster Fishery," *Annals of the Association of American Geographers* 65 (1975): 229–39; R. J. Agnello and L. P. Donnelley, "Externalities and Property Rights in the Fisheries," *Land Economics* 52 (1976): 518–29; Charles W. Howe, *Natural Resource Economics: Issues, Analysis, and Policy* (New York: Wiley, 1979); Tom Tietenberg, *Environmental and Natural Resource Economics* (Glenview, Ill.: Scott, Foresman, 1984); John R. Wennersten, *The Oyster Wars of Chesapeake Bay* (Centreville, Md.: Tidewater, 1981), 95; Victor S. Kennedy and Linda L. Breisch, "Sixteen Decades of Political Management of the Oyster Fishery in Maryland's Chesapeake Bay," *Journal of Environmental Management* 16 (1983): 153–71; Tom Horton, *Bay Country* (Baltimore: Johns Hopkins University Press, 1987), 198; Wil-

liam J. Hargis Jr. and Dexter S. Haven, "The Precarious State of the Chesapeake Public Oyster Resource," in *Toward a Sustainable Coastal Watershed: The Chesapeake Experiment,* ed. Paula Hill and Steve Nelson (Edgewater, Md.: Chesapeake Research Consortium, 1998), 559–84; Diana Locke, "Oyster Fisheries Management of Maryland's Chesapeake Bay" (PhD diss., Walden University, 1998).

8. Garrett Hardin, "The Tragedy of the Commons," *Science* 162 (1968): 1244, 1248. See also Garrett Hardin, "Extensions of 'The Tragedy of the Commons,'" *Science* 280 (1998): 682–83.

9. Horton, *Bay Country,* 199.

10. Lionel Bennet quoted in Wennersten, *Oyster Wars,* 135.

11. Bonnie J. McCay, *Oyster Wars and the Public Trust: Property, Law, and Ecology in New Jersey History* (Tucson: University of Arizona Press, 1998), 31, 38.

12. Ibid., 45.

13. Ibid., 38, 121–22, 145.

14. Robert J. Brugger, Cynthia Horsburgh Requardt, Robert I. Cottom Jr., and Mary Ellen Hayward, *Maryland: A Middle Temperament, 1634–1980* (Baltimore: Johns Hopkins University Press, 1989), 302, 304.

15. Davison et al., *Chesapeake Waters,* 80; James B. Crooks, *Politics and Progress: The Rise of Urban Progressivism in Baltimore, 1895 to 1911* (Baton Rouge: Louisiana State University Press, 1968), 75; "Cities That Get Justice," *BS,* 22 Dec. 1908, 14; "Senate: Origin and Functions" and "House of Delegates: Origin and Functions," both in Maryland Manual, Maryland State Archives Web site, http://www.mdarchives.state.md.us/msa/mdmanual/05sen/html/senf.html, http://www.mdarchives.state.md.us/msa/mdmanual/06hse/html/hacf.html (accessed 16 July 2006).

16. Harry J. Green, *A Study of the Legislature of the State of Maryland, with Special Reference to the Sessions of 1927 and 1929* (Baltimore: Johns Hopkins University Press, 1930), 25–26.

17. The postbellum Maryland oyster code authorized county commissioners to allow women to tong without a license if they had no visible means of support, but an 1892 report noted that only two or three women did so and that "no special demand existed for this exception to the license regulations" (Charles H. Stevenson, "The Oyster Industry of Maryland," *Bulletin of the U.S. Fish Commission* 12 [1894]: 229). For a more recent study of women in the Chesapeake fisheries, see Lila Line, *Waterwomen* (Queenstown, Md.: Queen Anne, 1982).

18. A similar dynamic prevailed in the American West, where a wide variety of cultures occupied what has often been seen as a great commons. Hispanos, Anglos, and distinct Indian societies used the land in different ways, making the western landscape a series of "numerous local commons regimes, in which local communities defined their own interactions with their natural environments" (Louis S. Warren, *The Hunter's Game: Poachers and Conservationists in Twentieth-Century America* [New Haven: Yale University Press, 1997], 9). See also Arthur F. McEvoy, *The Fisherman's Problem: Law and Ecology in the California Fisheries,*

1850–1980 (New York: Cambridge University Press, 1986); Richard White, *The Organic Machine: The Remaking of the Columbia River* (New York: Hill and Wang, 1995), 38–46.

19. County residency restrictions on oystering and crabbing remained in place until 1971, when the Maryland Court of Appeals declared them unconstitutional in *Bruce v. Director, Department of Chesapeake Bay Affairs.* See Thomas B. Lewis and Ivar E. Strand Jr., "*Douglas v. Seacoast Products, Inc.:* The Legal and Economic Consequences for the Maryland Oyster Industry," *Maryland Law Review* 38 (1978): 1–36.

20. Harold Anderson, "Slavery, Freedom and the Chesapeake," *Maryland Marine Notes,* Mar.–Apr. 1998, 5.

21. "Oystermen Divided on Ritchie's Plan," *BS,* 10 Jan. 1927, 20.

22. Wennersten, *Oyster Wars,* 122–25.

23. Three management regimes actually govern the Chesapeake oyster grounds: those of Maryland, Virginia, and the Potomac River. Following generations of conflict stemming from the disputed boundaries of the Potomac oyster fishery, federal intervention finally brought peace in the form of the Potomac River Fisheries Commission Act of 1962. This book does not consider the Potomac fishery due to the complications of federal and bistate involvement spanning two hundred years, but the subject is ripe for historical consideration.

24. Christopher L. Dyer and James R. McGoodwin, introduction to *Folk Management in the World's Fisheries: Lessons for Modern Fisheries Management,* ed. Christopher L. Dyer and James R. McGoodwin (Niwot: University Press of Colorado, 1994), 1–15.

25. See, e.g., Evelyn W. Pinkerton, ed., *Co-Operative Management of Local Fisheries: New Directions for Improving Management and Community Development* (Vancouver: University of British Columbia Press, 1989); Susan S. Hanna, "Co-Management," in *Limiting Access to Marine Fisheries: Keeping the Focus on Conservation,* ed. Karyn L. Gimbel (Washington, D.C.: Center for Marine Conservation and World Wildlife Fund, 1994); Susan S. Hanna, "Managing for Human and Ecological Context in the Maine Soft Shell Clam Fishery," in *Linking Social and Ecological Systems: Management Practices and Social Mechanisms for Building Resilience,* ed. Fikret Berkes and Carl Folke (Cambridge: Cambridge University Press, 1998), 190–211; Bonnie J. McCay and James M. Acheson, eds., *The Question of the Commons: The Culture and Ecology of Communal Resources* (Tucson: University of Arizona Press, 1987); James R. McGoodwin, *Crisis in the World's Fisheries: People, Problems, and Policies* (Stanford, Calif.: Stanford University Press, 1990), 189–90.

26. Svein Jentoft and Knut H. Mikalsen, "Regulating Fjord Fisheries: Folk Management or Interest Group Politics?" in *Folk Management,* ed. Dyer and McGoodwin, 288–89.

27. Bowman, "Science and Social Effects," 293.

28. Samuel P. Hays, *Conservation and the Gospel of Efficiency* (Cambridge: Harvard University Press, 1959), 272–75.

29. See McEvoy, *Fisherman's Problem,* esp. chaps. 6–7.

30. Pete Daniel, *Breaking the Land: The Transformation of Cotton, Tobacco, and Rice Cultures since 1880* (Champaign: University of Illinois Press, 1985), 112.

31. A classic case of welfare recipients who do not see themselves as such are the western corporate farmers who rely on irrigation subsidies. See Marc Reisner, *Cadillac Desert: The American West and its Disappearing Water* (1986; New York: Penguin, 1993).

32. Daniel, *Breaking the Land,* 176, 156. See also Jack Temple Kirby, *Rural Worlds Lost: The American South, 1920–1960* (Baton Rouge: Louisiana State University Press, 1987).

33. Carolyn Ellis, *Fisher Folk: Two Communities on Chesapeake Bay* (Lexington: University Press of Kentucky, 1986), 159.

34. William I. Tawes, *God, Man, Salt Water and the Eastern Shore* (1967; Cambridge, Md.: Tidewater, 1977), 25.

35. See Horton, *Bay Country,* 220. Books on Chesapeake watermen and their tools include Gladys Ione Harper, ed., *My Years before the Mast: Memoirs of Chesapeake Bay Waterman William T. Hooper* (n.p., [ca. 1970]); Robert de Gast, *The Oystermen of the Chesapeake* (Camden, Me.: International Marine, 1970); William W. Warner, *Beautiful Swimmers: Watermen, Crabs and the Chesapeake Bay* (1976; Boston: Little, Brown, 1994); James A. Michener, *Chesapeake* (New York: Fawcett Crest, 1978); Randall S. Peffer, *Watermen* (Baltimore: Johns Hopkins University Press, 1979); John Hart Whitehead III, *The Watermen of the Chesapeake Bay* (Alexandria, Va.: Stephenson, 1979); Line, *Waterwomen;* Larry S. Chowning, *Barcat Skipper: Tales of a Tangier Island Waterman* (Centreville, Md.: Tidewater, 1983); Eugene L. Meyer, "The World of the Watermen," in *Maryland Lost and Found: People and Places from Chesapeake to Appalachia* (Baltimore: Johns Hopkins University Press, 1986), 51–64; Bernard Wolf, *Amazing Grace: Smith Island and the Chesapeake Watermen* (New York: Macmillan, 1986); Robert A. Hedeen, *The Oyster: The Life and Lore of the Celebrated Bivalve* (Centreville, Md.: Tidewater, 1986); Mick Blackistone, *Sunup to Sundown: Watermen of the Chesapeake* (Washington, D.C.: Acropolis, 1988); Paula J. Johnson, ed., *Working the Water: The Commercial Fisheries of Maryland's Patuxent River* (Charlottesville: University Press of Virginia, 1988); Glenn Lawson, *The Last Waterman* (Crisfield, Md.: Crisfield, 1988); Susan Brait, *Chesapeake Gold: Man and Oyster on the Bay* (Lexington: University Press of Kentucky, 1990); Mark E. Jacoby, *Working the Chesapeake: Watermen on the Bay* (College Park: University of Maryland Sea Grant College, 1991); Pat Vojtech, *Chesapeake Bay Skipjacks* (Centreville, Md.: Tidewater, 1993); Larry S. Chowning, *Chesapeake Legacy: Tools and Traditions* (Centreville, Md.: Tidewater, 1995); Paula J. Johnson, *The Workboats of Smith Island* (Baltimore: Johns Hopkins University Press, 1997); Vincent O. Leggett, *Blacks of the Chesapeake: An Integral Part of Maritime History* (Annapolis: Leggett, 1997); Vincent O. Leggett, *The Chesapeake Bay through Ebony Eyes* (Arnold, Md.: Bay Media, 1999); Tim Junkin, *The Waterman: A Novel of the Chesapeake Bay* (Chapel Hill, N.C.: Algonquin, 1999);

James Parker, *Kissed by a Minnow, Pinched by a Crab: A Visually Unique Perspective on the Human Nature of the Chesapeake Bay* (Severna Park, Md.: Parker Photography, 2000); Mick Blackistone, *Dancing with the Tide: Watermen of the Chesapeake* (Centreville, Md.: Tidewater, 2001); A. M. Foley, *Having My Say: Conversations with Chesapeake Bay Waterman Wylie "Gator" Abbott* (Elliott Island, Md.: Dogwood Ridge, 2006).

36. Books on Chesapeake culture include Gilbert Byron, *The Lord's Oysters* (1957; Baltimore: Johns Hopkins University Press, 1977); Hulbert Footner, *Maryland Main and the Eastern Shore* (1942; Hatboro, Pa.: Tradition, 1967); Phillip J. Wingate, *Before the Bridge* (Centreville, Md.: Tidewater, 1985); Frances W. Dize, *Smith Island, Chesapeake Bay* (Centreville, Md.: Tidewater, 1990); Lucian Niemeyer and Eugene L. Meyer, *Chesapeake Country* (New York: Abbeville, 1990); John R. Wennersten, *Maryland's Eastern Shore: A Journey in Time and Place* (Centreville, Md.: Tidewater, 1992); Marion E. Warren and Mame Warren, *Bringing Back the Bay: The Chesapeake in the Photographs of Marion Warren and the Voices of Its People* (Baltimore: Johns Hopkins University Press, 1994); John Sherwood, *Maryland's Vanishing Lives* (Baltimore: Johns Hopkins University Press, 1994); Tom Horton, *An Island Out of Time: A Memoir of Smith Island in the Chesapeake* (New York: Norton, 1996); Ed Okonowicz, *Disappearing Delmarva: Portraits of the Peninsula People* (Elkton, Md.: Myst and Lace, 1997); Peter Svenson, *Green Shingles: At the Edge of Chesapeake Bay* (Baltimore: Johns Hopkins University Press, 1999); Janet Freedman, *Kent Island: The Land That Once Was Eden* (Baltimore: Maryland Historical Society, 2005); William B. Cronin, *The Disappearing Islands of the Chesapeake* (Baltimore: Johns Hopkins University Press, 2005).

Books on the Chesapeake Bay ecosystem and/or cleanup efforts include Gilbert C. Klingel, *The Bay* (1951; Baltimore: Johns Hopkins University Press, 1994); Carvel Hall Blair and Willits Dyer Ansel, *Chesapeake Bay: Notes and Sketches* (Cambridge, Md.: Tidewater, 1970); Arthur W. Sherwood, *Understanding the Chesapeake: A Layman's Guide* (Centreville, Md.: Tidewater, 1973); Environmental Protection Agency, *Chesapeake Bay: Introduction to an Ecosystem* (Washington, D.C.: U.S. Government Printing Office, 1982); Environmental Protection Agency, *Chesapeake Bay: A Framework for Action* (Washington, D.C.: U.S. Government Printing Office, 1983); Davison et al., *Chesapeake Waters;* Alice Jane Lippson and Robert L. Lippson, *Life in the Chesapeake Bay* (Baltimore: Johns Hopkins University Press, 1984); J. R. Schubel, *The Life and Death of the Chesapeake Bay* (College Park: University of Maryland Sea Grant College, 1986); Christopher P. White, *Chesapeake Bay: Nature of the Estuary, a Field Guide* (Centreville, Md.: Tidewater, 1989); Tom Horton, *Turning the Tide: Saving the Chesapeake Bay* (1991; Washington, D.C.: Island, 2003); Gerald L. Baliles, *Preserving the Chesapeake Bay* (Martinsville: Virginia Museum of Natural History Foundation, 1995); John R. Wennersten, *Chesapeake: An Environmental Biography* (Baltimore: Maryland Historical Society, 2001); Philip D. Curtin, Grace S. Brush, and George W. Fisher, eds., *Discovering the Chesapeake: The History of an Ecosystem* (Baltimore: Johns Hopkins University Press, 2001); Pat Vojtech, *Chesapeake Wildlife: Stories of Survival and Loss* (Centreville, Md.: Tidewater, 2001); Wendy Mitman Clarke, *Window on the Chesapeake: The Bay, Its People and Places* (Newport News, Va.: Mariners' Museum, 2002); Howard R. Ernst, *Chesapeake Bay Blues: Science, Politics, and the Struggle to Save the Bay* (Lanham, Md.: Rowman and Littlefield, 2003); Michael Paolisso, *Chesapeake Environmentalism: Rethinking Culture to Strengthen Restoration and Resource Management* (College Park: University of Maryland Sea Grant College, 2006); Tom Horton and Ian Plant, *Chesapeake, Bay of Light: An Exploration of the Chesapeake Bay's Wild and Forgotten Places* (Johnson City, Tenn.: Mountain Trail, 2007).

37. John Barth, "Goose Art: The Aesthetic Ecology of Chesapeake Bay," *Washington Post Magazine,* 9 Aug. 1992, W15.

38. Richard W. Judd and Christopher S. Beach, *Natural States: The Environmental Imagination in Maine, Oregon, and the Nation* (Washington, D.C.: Resources for the Future, 2003), x.

39. William Cronon, *Nature's Metropolis: Chicago and the Great West* (New York: Norton, 1991), 220.

40. See, e.g., R. Douglas Hurt, *Indian Agriculture in America: Prehistory to the Present* (Lawrence: University Press of Kansas, 1987), chaps. 8–10.

41. Mart A. Stewart, "If John Muir Had Been an Agrarian: American Environmental History West and South," *Environment and History* 11 (2005): 152; Richard W. Judd, "Writing Environmental History from East to West," in *Reconstructing Conservation: Finding Common Ground,* ed. Ben A. Minteer and Robert E. Manning (Washington, D.C.: Island, 2003), 21.

42. Judd, "Writing Environmental History," 23, 26; Richard W. Judd, *Common Lands, Common People: The Origins of Conservation in Northern New England* (Cambridge: Harvard University Press, 2000).

43. Stewart, "If John Muir," 140, 141; Mart A. Stewart, "Southern Environmental History," in *A Companion to the American South,* ed. John B. Boles (Malden, Mass.: Blackwell, 2002), 415. See also Ira Berlin and Philip D. Morgan, eds., *Cultivation and Culture: Labor and the Shaping of Slave Life in the Americas* (Charlottesville: University Press of Virginia, 1993); Mart A. Stewart, *"What Nature Suffers to Groe": Life, Labor, and Landscape on the Georgia Coast, 1680 to 1920* (Athens: University of Georgia Press, 1996).

44. H. L. Mencken, *Happy Days, 1880–1892* (New York: Knopf, 1940), 55; Stewart, "If John Muir," 142–43.

45. Quoted in Meyer, *Maryland Lost and Found,* 6–7.

46. Introduction to *Encyclopedia of Southern Culture,* ed. Charles Reagan Wilson and William Ferris (Chapel Hill: University of North Carolina Press, 1989), xv; Brugger et al., *Maryland,* 187.

47. Brugger et al., *Maryland,* 217, 219; Elizabeth Sanders, *Roots of Reform: Farmers, Workers, and the American State, 1877–1917* (Chicago: University of Chicago Press, 1999), 14.

246 Notes to Introduction

48. By 1850, more free blacks resided in Maryland than anywhere else in the country, and it became the only slave state with roughly equal numbers of enslaved and free blacks (Brugger et al., *Maryland,* 248, 264–66, 268).

49. Maryland supplied troops to both sides, and although it became the first slave state enact abolition, it did so under pressure from outside Unionists (Brugger et al., *Maryland,* 274–79, 285–86, 297).

50. Eastern Shore loyalists made their most recent threat to secede from Maryland in the 1990s after the state imposed new pollution regulations (Michael Dresser, "Saying So Long to City Bullies," *BS,* 11 Feb. 1998, 1B; Wennersten, *Maryland's Eastern Shore,* 11).

51. Wennersten, *Maryland's Eastern Shore,* back cover; William Faulkner, *Requiem for a Nun* (New York: Random House, 1951), 92.

52. Because disenfranchisement efforts targeted the Republican Party as much as African Americans per se in the Democratic-dominated state, "the failure of disenfranchisement was a victory for the two-party system, not for racial justice" (James B. Crooks, "Maryland Progressivism," in *Maryland: A History, 1632–1974,* ed. Richard Walsh and William Lloyd Fox [Baltimore: Maryland Historical Society, 1974), 610–14, 661, 663]).

53. Margaret Law Callcott, *The Negro in Maryland Politics, 1870–1912* (Baltimore: Johns Hopkins University Press, 1969), 120; "The Negro versus the Oyster," *BS,* 18 Mar. 1904.

54. Sanders, *Roots of Reform,* 25.

55. In 1920, Baltimore City's 733,826 residents accounted for 51 percent of the state's population (U.S. Department of Commerce, *Statistical Abstract of the United States, 1920* [Washington, D.C.: U.S. Government Printing Office, 1921], 49, 52).

56. Kirby, *Rural Worlds Lost,* 27, 49–50; Daniel, *Breaking the Land;* Kantor, *Politics and Property Rights.*

57. See, e.g., Alford, "Chesapeake Oyster Fishery," 235; Kennedy and Breisch, "Sixteen Decades"; Davison et al., *Chesapeake Waters,* 80.

58. Sanders, *Roots of Reform,* 389, 3.

59. Ibid., 159–60, 7.

60. Karl Jacoby, "Class and Environmental History: Lessons from 'The War in the Adirondacks,'" *Environmental History* 2 (1997): 326; Karl Jacoby, *Crimes against Nature: Squatters, Poachers, Thieves, and the Hidden History of American Conservation* (Berkeley: University of California Press, 2001). See also Louis S. Warren, *Hunter's Game;* McEvoy, *Fisherman's Problem;* Mark David Spence, *Dispossessing the Wilderness: Indian Removal and the Making of National Parks* (New York: Oxford University Press, 1999).

61. Exceptions include Judd and Beach, *Natural States;* Thomas R. Huffman, *Protectors of the Land and Water: Environmentalism in Wisconsin, 1961–1968* (Chapel Hill: University of North Carolina Press, 1994); Robert J. Spear, *The Great Gypsy*

Moth War: The History of the First Campaign in Massachusetts to Eradicate the Gypsy Moth, 1890–1901 (Amherst: University of Massachusetts Press, 2005).

62. Sanders, *Roots of Reform,* 9, 16.

63. Green, *Study,* 26.

64. Robert H. Connery, *Governmental Problems in Wild Life Conservation* (1935; New York: AMS, 1968), 177.

65. Helen M. Rozwadowski, *The Sea Knows No Boundaries: A Century of Marine Science under ICES* (Seattle: University of Washington Press and International Council for the Exploration of the Sea, 2002), 5; W. Jeffrey Bolster, "Opportunities in Marine Environmental History," *Environmental History* 11 (2006): 567–97.

66. McEvoy, *Fisherman's Problem;* Richard White, *Organic Machine;* Taylor, *Making Salmon;* Margaret Beattie Bogue, *Fishing the Great Lakes: An Environmental History, 1783–1933* (Madison: University of Wisconsin Press, 2000); Helen M. Rozwadowski and David K. van Keuren, eds., *The Machine in Neptune's Garden: Historical Perspectives on Technology and the Marine Environment* (Sagamore Beach, Mass.: Science History, 2004), xxv n.8; Matthew Morse Booker, "Real Estate and Refuge: An Environmental History of San Francisco Bay's Tidal Wetlands, 1846–1972" (PhD diss., Stanford University, 2005); Matthew Morse Booker, "Oyster Growers and Oyster Pirates in San Francisco Bay," *Pacific Historical Review* 75 (2006): 63–88; Jack Temple Kirby, *Poquosin: A Study of Rural Landscape and Society* (Chapel Hill: University of North Carolina Press, 1995).

67. A. F. Chestnut quoted in Melbourne R. Carriker, *Taming of the Oyster: A History of Evolving Shellfisheries and the National Shellfisheries Association* (Hanover, Penn: Sheridan Press and National Shellfisheries Association, 2004), 8.

68. Joel B. Hagen, *An Entangled Bank: The Origins of Ecosystem Ecology* (New Brunswick, N.J.: Rutgers University Press, 1992); Frank Benjamin Golley, *A History of the Ecosystem Concept in Ecology: More Than the Sum of the Parts* (New Haven: Yale University Press, 1993).

69. Donald S. McLusky, *Ecology of Estuaries* (London: Heinemann, 1971), 103.

70. Donald W. Pritchard, "What Is an Estuary: Physical Viewpoint," in *Estuaries,* ed. G. H. Lauff (Washington, D.C.: American Association for the Advancement of Science, 1967), 3–5; L. Eugene Cronin, "The Role of Man in Estuarine Processes," in *Estuaries,* ed. Lauff, 687.

71. L. Eugene Cronin quoted in Michael Wright, "The Changing Chesapeake," *NYT,* 10 July 1983, SM24.

72. Jeremy C. B. Jackson, Michael X. Kirby, Wolfgang H. Berger, Karen A. Bjorndal, Louis W. Botsford, Bruce J. Bourque, Roger H. Bradbury, Richard Cooke, Jon Erlandson, James A. Estes, Terence P. Hughes, Susan Kidwell, Carina B. Lange, Hunter S. Lenihan, John M. Pandolfi, Charles H. Peterson, Robert S. Steneck, Mia J. Tegner, and Robert R. Warner, "Historical Overfishing and the Recent Collapse of Coastal Ecosystems," *Science* 293 (2001): 629, 636.

73. The idea of labor linking culture and nature is from Richard White, *Organic Machine;* Richard White, "'Are You an Environmentalist or Do You Work for a Living?': Work and Nature," in *Uncommon Ground: Rethinking the Human Place in Nature,* ed. William Cronon (New York: Norton, 1996), 171–85. See also Kevin Dann and Gregg Mitman, "Essay Review: Exploring the Borders of Environmental History and the History of Ecology," *Journal of the History of Biology* 30 (1997): 301.

Chapter 1. Chesapeake Bay

1. On the links between nature and culture, see, among others, Richard W. Judd, "Writing Environmental History from East to West," in *Reconstructing Conservation: Finding Common Ground,* ed. Ben A. Minteer and Robert E. Manning (Washington, D.C.: Island, 2003), 28; Donald Worster, "The Two Cultures Revisited: Environmental History and the Environmental Sciences," *Environment and History* 2 (1996): 3–14. For an analysis of the Chesapeake by a master environmental historian, see William Cronon, "Reading the Palimpsest," in *Discovering the Chesapeake: The History of an Ecosystem,* ed. Philip D. Curtin, Grace S. Brush, and George W. Fisher (Baltimore: Johns Hopkins University Press, 2001), 355–73; the idea of inscribing the landscape with new cultural practices and meanings comes from p. 364. Henry M. Miller articulates the bay's connection with human history and prehistory in "Living along the 'Great Shellfish Bay': The Relationship between Prehistoric Peoples and the Chesapeake," in *Discovering the Chesapeake,* ed. Curtin, Brush, and Fisher, 109–26.

2. Alice Jane Lippson and Robert L. Lippson, *Life in the Chesapeake Bay* (Baltimore: Johns Hopkins University Press, 1984), 4. Some sources say the shoreline covers nine thousand miles; on the difficulties of measuring the bay, see Steven G. Davison, Jay G. Merwin Jr., John Capper, Garrett Power, and Frank R. Shivers Jr., *Chesapeake Waters: Four Centuries of Controversy, Concern, and Legislation* (1983; Centreville, Md.: Tidewater, 1997), 11–14.

3. On the bay's physical and biological features, see Davison et al., *Chesapeake Waters,* 10–201; Lippson and Lippson, *Life;* Donald W. Pritchard and Jerry R. Schubel, "Human Influences on the Physical Characteristics of the Chesapeake Bay," in *Discovering the Chesapeake,* ed. Curtin, Brush, and Fisher, 60–82.

4. William K. Brooks, *The Oyster: A Popular Summary of a Scientific Study* (1891, 1905; Baltimore: Johns Hopkins University Press, 1996), 10.

5. Lippson and Lippson, *Life,* viii, 7–8, 135.

6. H. L. Mencken, *Happy Days, 1880–1892* (New York: Knopf, 1940), 55.

7. Miller, "Living along the 'Great Shellfish Bay,'" 114, 123; Thomas R. Whyte, "Fish and Shellfish Use in the Woodland Period on the Virginia Coast," *Journal of Middle Atlantic Archaeology* 4 (1988): 102–20; John R. Wennersten, *The Oyster Wars*

of Chesapeake Bay (Centreville, Md.: Tidewater, 1981), 5; Bruce Smith, *Rivers of Change: Essays on Early Agriculture in Eastern North America* (Washington, D.C.: Smithsonian Institution Press, 1992).

8. Lippson and Lippson, *Life,* 169–72; Victor S. Kennedy, "Biology of Larvae and Spat," in *The Eastern Oyster: Crassostrea Virginica,* ed. Victor S. Kennedy, Roger I. E. Newell, and Albert F. Eble (College Park: Maryland Sea Grant College, 1996), chap. 10.

9. Lippson and Lippson, *Life,* 177.

10. Filtration takes place mainly during the summer because cold temperatures render oysters dormant. See R. Dame, R. Zingmark, H. Stevenson, and D. Nelson, "Filter Feeding Coupling between the Estuarine Water Column and Benthic Substrates," in *Estuarine Perspectives,* ed. Victor S. Kennedy (New York: Academic, 1980), 521–26; R. F. Dame, R. G. Zingmark, and E. Haskin, "Oyster Reefs as Processors of Estuarine Materials," *Journal of Experimental Marine Biology and Ecology* 83 (1984): 239–47.

11. Roger I. E. Newell and Evamaria W. Koch, "Modeling Seagrass Density and Distribution in Response to Changes in Turbidity Stemming from Bivalve Filtration and Seagrass Sediment Stabilization," *Estuaries* 27 (2004): 793–806.

12. Roger I. E. Newell, "Ecological Changes in Chesapeake Bay: Are They the Result of Overharvesting the American Oyster, *Crassostrea Virginica?*" in *Understanding the Estuary: Advances in Chesapeake Bay Research,* ed. Maurice P. Lynch and Elizabeth C. Krome (Solomons, Md.: Chesapeake Research Consortium, 1988), 539.

13. On the ecosystem engineering concept, see Clive G. Jones, John H. Lawton, and Moshe Shachak, "Organisms as Ecosystem Engineers," *Oikos* 69 (1994): 373–86; Justin P. Wright and Clive G. Jones, "The Concept of Organisms as Ecosystem Engineers Ten Years On: Progress, Limitations, and Challenges," *BioScience* 56 (2006): 203–9. On oysters as ecosystem engineers, see Denise L. Breitburg, "Are Three Dimensional Structures and Healthy Oyster Populations the Keys to an Ecologically Interesting and Important Fish Community?" in *Oyster Reef Habitat Restoration: A Synopsis and Synthesis of Approaches,* ed. Mark W. Luckenbach, Roger Mann, and James A. Wesson (Gloucester Point, Va.: VIMS, 1999), 239–50; J. L. Gutiérrez, C. G. Jones, D. L. Strayer, and O. O. Iribarne, "Mollusks as Ecosystem Engineers: The Role of Shell Production in Aquatic Habitats," *Oikos* 101 (2003): 79–90.

14. Mary E. Power, David Tilman, James A. Estes, Bruce A. Menge, William J. Bond, L. Scott Mills, Gretchen Daily, Juan Carlos Castilla, Jane Lubchenco, and Robert T. Paine, "Challenges in the Quest for Keystones," *BioScience* 46 (1996): 609–20; Victor S. Kennedy, "The Ecological Role of the Eastern Oyster, *Crassostrea Virginica,* with Remarks on Disease," *JSR* 13 (1996): 177–83. For an example of suggested experimental approaches to oyster ecology, see Elka T. Porter, Jeffrey C. Cornwell, and Lawrence P. Sanford, "Effect of Oysters *Crassostrea*

Virginica and Bottom Shear Velocity on Benthic-Pelagic Coupling and Estuarine Water Quality," *Marine Ecology Progress Series* 271 (2004): 61–75.

15. To protect the interests of Virginia oyster leaseholders, the state legislature banned the export of seed oysters at various times during the twentieth century. The bans further constrained the development of a private oyster-planting industry in Maryland (George Santopietro, "The Evolution of Property Rights to a Natural Resource: The Oyster Grounds of the Chesapeake Bay" [PhD diss., Virginia Tech, 1986], 268, 279).

16. Ibid., 287, 291.

17. Jay D. Andrews and John L. Wood, "Oyster Mortality Studies in Virginia: VI: History and Distribution of *Minchinia Nelsoni,* a Pathogen of Oysters, in Virginia," *Chesapeake Science* 8 (1967): 1–13; Jay D. Andrews, "History of *Perkinsus Marinus,* a Pathogen of Oysters in Chesapeake Bay, 1950–1984," *JSR* 15 (1996): 13–16.

18. John J. Alford, "The Chesapeake Oyster Fishery," *Annals of the Association of American Geographers* 65 (1975): 232.

19. Ibid., 234.

20. Andrews, "History of *Perkinsus Marinus*"; B. Drummond Ayres Jr., "Mystery Disease Ravages Oysters and Way of Life," *NYT,* 11 Sept. 1987, A14.

21. T. Cook, M. Folli, J. Klinck, S. Ford, and J. Miller, "The Relationship between Increasing Sea-Surface Temperature and the Northward Spread of *Perkinsus Marinus* (Dermo) Disease Epizootics in Oysters," *Estuarine Coastal and Shelf Science* 46 (1998): 587–97; E. Hofmann, S. Ford, E. Powell, and J. Klinck, "Modeling Studies of the Effect of Climate Variability on MSX Disease in Eastern Oyster (*Crassostrea Virginica*) Populations," *Hydrobiologia* 460 (2001): 195–212.

22. Quoted in James Wharton, *The Bounty of the Chesapeake: Fishing in Colonial Virginia* (Charlottesville: University Press of Virginia, 1957), 37.

23. Victor S. Kennedy and Kent Mountford, "Human Influences on Aquatic Resources in the Chesapeake Bay Watershed," in *Discovering the Chesapeake,* ed. Curtin, Brush, and Fisher, 210.

24. Wennersten, *Oyster Wars,* 7; Bayly Ellen Marks, "Rakes, Nippers, and Tongs: Oystermen in Antebellum St. Mary's County," *Maryland Historical Magazine* 90 (1995): 313–33.

25. Arthur Pierce Middleton, *Tobacco Coast: A Maritime History of the Chesapeake Bay in the Colonial Era* (Newport News, Va.: Mariners' Museum, 1953), 30, 50.

26. Henry M. Miller, "Transforming a 'Splendid and Delightsome Land': Colonists and Ecological Change in the Chesapeake, 1607–1820," *Journal of the Washington Academy of Sciences* 76 (1986): 173–87; Lorena S. Walsh, "Land Use, Settlement Patterns, and the Impact of European Agriculture, 1620–1820," in *Discovering the Chesapeake,* ed. Curtin, Brush, and Fisher, 220–48.

27. Carville Earle and Ronald Hoffman, "Genteel Erosion: The Ecological Consequences of Agrarian Reform in the Chesapeake, 1730–1840," in *Discover-*

ing the Chesapeake, ed. Curtin, Brush, and Fisher, 279–303; Carville Earle, "The Myth of the Southern Soil Miner: Macrohistory, Agricultural Innovation, and Environmental Change," in *The Ends of the Earth: Perspectives on Modern Environmental History,* ed. Donald Worster (Cambridge: Cambridge University Press, 1988), 175–210. Pioneering studies of sediment cores have been performed by Grace Brush; see, e.g., Grace Brush, "Geology and Paleoecology of Chesapeake Bay: A Long-Term Monitoring Tool for Management," *Journal of the Washington Academy of Sciences* 76 (1986): 146–60; Grace Brush, "Forests before and after the Colonial Encounter," in *Discovering the Chesapeake,* ed. Curtin, Brush, and Fisher, 40–59.

28. See, e.g., Grace Brush, "Stratigraphic Evidence of Eutrophication in an Estuary," *Water Resources Research* 20 (1984): 531–41; R. J. Orth and K. A. Moore, "Chesapeake Bay: An Unprecedented Decline in Submerged Aquatic Vegetation," *Science* 222 (1984): 51–53.

29. C. B. Officer, R. B. Biggs, J. L. Taft, L. E. Cronin, M. A. Tyler, and W. R. Boynton, "Chesapeake Bay Anoxia: Origin, Development and Significance," *Science* 223 (1984): 22–27; H. H. Sellger, J. A. Boggs, and W. H. Biggley, "Catastrophic Anoxia in the Chesapeake Bay in 1984," *Science* 228 (1985): 70–73; R. B. Jonas, "Bacteria, Dissolved Organics, and Oxygen Consumption in Salinity Stratified Chesapeake Bay: An Anoxia Paradigm," *American Zoologist* 37 (1997): 612–20.

30. Michael X. Kirby and Henry M. Miller, "Response of a Benthic Suspension Feeder (*Crassostrea Virginica* Gmelin) to Three Centuries of Anthropogenic Eutrophication in Chesapeake Bay," *Estuarine, Coastal, and Shelf Science* 62 (2005): 682.

31. Brush, "Geology and Paleoecology"; Kennedy and Mountford, "Human Influences," 192–95.

32. Davison et al., *Chesapeake Waters,* 30–33, 46–49; Robert J. Brugger, Cynthia Horsburgh Requardt, Robert I. Cottom Jr., and Mary Ellen Hayward, *Maryland, a Middle Temperament, 1634–1980* (Baltimore: Johns Hopkins University Press, 1989), 789; Calvin W. Hendrick, "Colossal Work in Baltimore," *National Geographic* 20 (1909): 365–73.

33. H. F. Moore, "Volumetric Studies of the Food and Feeding of Oysters," *Proceedings of the Fourth International Fishery Congress, Bulletin of the U.S. Bureau of Fisheries* 28 (1908): 1298.

34. Michael X. Kirby and Miller, "Response of a Benthic Suspension Feeder," 684, 687.

35. J. E. Cloern, "Does the Benthos Control Phytoplankton Biomass in South San Francisco Bay?" *Marine Ecology Progress Series* 9 (1981): 191–202; C. B. Officer, T. J. Smayda, and R. Mann, "Benthic Filter Feeding: A Natural Eutrophication Control," *Marine Ecology Progress Series* 9 (1982): 203–10; R. R. H. Cohen, P. V. Dresler, E. J. P. Philips, and R. L. Cory, "The Effect of the Asiatic Clam,

Corbicula Fluminea, on Phytoplankton of the Potomac River, Maryland," *Limnology and Oceanography* 29 (1984): 170–80; Jeremy C. B. Jackson et al., "Historical Overfishing and the Recent Collapse of Coastal Ecosystems," *Science* 293 (2001): 629–38; Donald Boesch, Eugene Burreson, William Dennison, Edward Houde, Michael Kemp, Victor Kennedy, Roger Newell, Kennedy Paynter, Robert Orth, and Robert Ulanowicz, "Factors in the Decline of Coastal Ecosystems," *Science* 293 (2001): 1589–90.

36. Wennersten, *Oyster Wars,* 7; Marks, "Rakes, Nippers, and Tongs."

37. Charles H. Stevenson, "The Oyster Industry of Maryland," *Bulletin of the U.S. Fish Commission* 12 (1894): 205–96; Victor S. Kennedy and Linda L. Breisch, "Sixteen Decades of Political Management of the Oyster Fishery in Maryland's Chesapeake Bay," *Journal of Environmental Management* 16 (1983): 157.

38. Clyde L. MacKenzie Jr., "The Molluscan Fisheries of Chesapeake Bay," in *The History, Present Condition, and Future of the Molluscan Fisheries of North and Central America and Europe,* ed. Clyde L. MacKenzie Jr., Victor G. Burrell Jr., Aaron Rosefield, and Willis L. Hobart (Seattle: U.S. Department of Commerce, 1997), 1:143.

39. A. J. Nichol, *The Oyster-Packing Industry of Baltimore: Its History and Current Problems* (Baltimore: University of Maryland Press, 1937).

40. William Cronon, *Nature's Metropolis: Chicago and the Great West* (New York: Norton, 1991), 233–36.

41. Ernest Ingersoll, *The History and Present Condition of the Fishery Industries: The Oyster-Industry* (Washington, D.C.: U.S. Government Printing Office, 1881), 168. See also W. N. Armstrong, *Remarks on the Oyster Industries of Virginia* (Hampton, Va.: Normal School Press, 1884), 8.

42. Ingersoll, *History and Present Condition,* 167; "The Oyster Trade of Baltimore," *NYT,* 10 Dec. 1867, 2. See also Nichol, *Oyster-Packing Industry;* Caswell Grave, *A Manual of Oyster Culture in Maryland* (Baltimore: King, 1912), 9–10; Kennedy and Breisch, "Sixteen Decades," 160–61.

43. Stevenson, "Oyster Industry," 207.

44. Ibid., 211, 207.

45. Ingersoll, *History and Present Condition,* 159–63; "The Oyster Trade of Baltimore," *Frank Leslie's Illustrated Newspaper,* 11 Oct. 1873, 73–74.

46. On African American watermen of the Chesapeake, see Harold Anderson, "Black Men, Blue Waters: African Americans on the Chesapeake," *Maryland Marine Notes* 16 (Mar.–Apr. 1998): 1–7; Lamont W. Harvey, "Black Oystermen of the Bay Country," *Weather Gauge* 30.1 (1994): 4–13; Greg Toppo, "Black Watermen Survive in 20th Century on Chesapeake Bay," Associated Press, 22 Dec. 1999; Vincent O. Leggett, *Blacks of the Chesapeake: An Integral Part of Maritime History* (Annapolis, Md.: Leggett, 1997); Vincent O. Leggett, *The Chesapeake Bay through Ebony Eyes Curriculum Guide* (Annapolis, Md.: Blacks of the Chesapeake Foundation, 2000). On Eastern Shore race relations, see John R. Wennersten,

Maryland's Eastern Shore: A Journey in Time and Place (Centreville, Md.: Tidewater, 1992), 115–72.

47. Ingersoll, *History and Present Condition,* 169; Stevenson, "Oyster Industry," 266.

48. Of the 8,639 shuckers employed by packinghouses in 1879–80, 71.5 percent (6,179) were men, about three-quarters of them black. An additional 220 shuckers worked on a freelance basis (Ingersoll, *History and Present Condition,* 169). On African American oyster shuckers, see Richard J. S. Dodds, "Black Pioneers of Seafood Packing," *Weather Gauge* 22.1 (1986): 4; John E. Aliyetti, "The Bellevue Seafood Company," *Weather Gauge* 33.2 (1997): 4. On women shuckers, see Roderick N. Ryon, "'Human Creatures' Lives': Baltimore Women and Work in Factories, 1880–1917," *Maryland Historical Magazine* 83 (1988): 346–64; Paula Susan Haag, "'Commerce in Souls': Vice, Virtue, and Women's Wage Work in Baltimore, 1900–1915," *Maryland Historical Magazine* 86 (1991): 292–308.

49. Quoted in Ingersoll, *History and Present Condition,* 169.

50. Wennersten, *Oyster Wars,* 16–17, 25.

51. For a scientific explanation of the higher spat set, see Stevenson, "Oyster Industry," 214.

52. John Van Camp, "Oystermen Lodge 350 Complaints," *BS,* 25 Feb. 1953, 34.

53. Kennedy and Mountford, "Human Influences," 195–201.

54. G. Terry Sharrer, "Farming, Disease, and Change in the Chesapeake Ecosystem," in *Discovering the Chesapeake,* ed. Curtin, Brush, and Fisher, 313.

55. William H. Killian, "The Aquatic Life of Maryland Waters," in *Third Annual Report of the Conservation Commission of Maryland, 1918* (Baltimore: n.p., 1919), 65–74; *Second Annual Report of the Conservation Commission of Maryland* (Baltimore: Thomas and Evans, 1918), 31; MacKenzie, "Molluscan Fisheries," 143.

56. "State Officials, Watermen Disagree on Cause of Record-Low Oyster Catch," *BJ,* May 1994.

57. M. Estellie Smith compares fishermen's conceptions of the natural world with chaos theory, the idea that the dynamics of complex systems can develop in a manner that is nonrandom yet unpredictable because one can never consider the almost infinite number of small initial conditions possible, any one of which can produce surprising, ever-intensifying effects ("Chaos in Fishery Management," *Maritime Anthropological Studies* 3 [1990]: 4–5).

58. William Ward and Priscilla Weeks, "Resource Managers and Resource Users: Field Biologists and Stewardship," in *Folk Management in the World's Fisheries: Lessons for Modern Fisheries Management,* ed. Christopher L. Dyer and James R. McGoodwin (Niwot: University Press of Colorado, 1994), 103–4. See also Paula J. Johnson, "'The Worst Oyster Season I've Ever Seen': Collecting and Interpreting Data from Watermen," *Journal of the Washington Academy of Sciences* 76 (1986): 199–213; Michael Paolisso, "Blue Crabs and Controversy on the

Chesapeake Bay: A Cultural Model for Understanding Watermen's Reasoning about Blue Crab Management," *Human Organization* 61 (2002): 226–39.

59. Kennedy and Breisch, "Sixteen Decades," 157.

60. As a consequence of their different off-season activities, dredgers often favored (and received) a shortened oyster season, whereas tongers preferred a longer one because of the many days lost to bad weather. See "100 Oystermen Invited to Conservation Parley," *BS,* 6 Feb. 1926, 3; "To Consider Proposals to Increase Oysters' Yield," *BS,* 16 Feb. 1926, 4; "Oyster Parley Terminates in No Agreement," *BS,* 18 Feb. 1926, 24.

61. M. V. Brewington, *Chesapeake Bay: A Pictorial Maritime History* (Cambridge, Md.: Cornell Maritime, 1956), 65–66.

62. Tom Vesey, "Maryland Oystermen Face Troubled Waters," *WP,* 20 Sept. 1987, A11; Eugene L. Meyer, "The Loved Boat at Low Ebb," *WP,* 20 May 1991, B1.

63. Chris Guy, "Helping Skipjacks in Bay Stay Afloat," *BS,* 7 June 2002, 1B.

64. Richard White, *The Organic Machine* (New York: Hill and Wang, 1995), chap. 1; Richard White, "'Are You an Environmentalist or Do You Work for a Living?': Work and Nature," in *Uncommon Ground: Rethinking the Human Place in Nature,* ed. William Cronon (New York: Norton, 1996), 171–85.

65. Larry S. Chowning, *Harvesting the Chesapeake: Tools and Traditions* (Centreville, Md.: Tidewater, 1990), 87–88.

66. Ingersoll, *History and Present Condition,* 163, 249.

67. Chowning, *Harvesting,* 88.

68. "Ice Grips Oyster Beds," *WP,* 19 Feb. 1905, R4.

69. Varley Lang, *Follow the Water* (Winston-Salem, N.C.: Blair, 1961), 34–35.

70. BOARD OF NATURAL RESOURCES (Minutes), book 8, Feb.–Dec. 1947, 12, S1782-8, Maryland State Archives, Annapolis.

71. For a good description of dredging, see Tom Horton, *An Island Out of Time: A Memoir of Smith Island in the Chesapeake* (New York: Norton, 1996), 47–51.

72. Ingersoll, *History and Present Condition,* 79; Stevenson, "Oyster Industry," 244.

73. Ingersoll, *History and Present Condition,* 161.

74. Bradford Botwick and Debra A. McClane, "Landscapes of Resistance: A View of the Nineteenth-Century Chesapeake Bay Oyster Fishery," *Historical Archaeology* 39 (2005): 96–97.

75. Ibid., 95.

76. Edward L. Wilson, "The Biography of the Oyster," *Scribner's Magazine,* Oct. 1891, 481.

77. Vincent Leggett quoted in Toppo, "Black Watermen Survive."

78. Botwick and McClane, "Landscapes," 95.

79. Norman H. Plummer, *Maryland's Oyster Navy: The First Fifty Years* (Chestertown, Md.: Literary House, 1993); Wennersten, *Oyster Wars,* chap. 2; Kennedy

and Breisch, "Sixteen Decades," 157–58; James L. Kellogg, *Shell-Fish Industries* (New York: Holt, 1910), 218; Grave, *Manual,* 11–12; "Our Oyster Navy: Small in Size but Plucky," *BS,* 20 Nov. 1888.

80. Brewington, *Chesapeake Bay,* 173.

81. Pro-leaser B. Howard Haman quoted in "Calls Oyster Plan Robbery," *BS,* 3 Feb. 1916, 11. Earlier in the century, a journalist observed, "For years the oyster navy was a matter of ridicule because it simply supplied berths for county politicians" ("State's Oyster Navy," *WP,* 24 Apr. 1901, 10).

82. For an example of the hundreds of letters dispatched by one commander to his inspectors, see T. C. B. Howard to Jacob S. Tyler, 16 Nov. 1911, BPWL, Oyster and Fish Laws, 1910–14, 168, S40-2.

83. Ingersoll, *History and Present Condition,* 173.

84. The state could hold defendants' boats between the time of arrest and the court date, which prevented the accused violator from oystering but also compounded resentment against the state (Charles Whitelock to Albert C. Ritchie, 28 Dec. 1932, GGF, Confederate Soldiers Home–Conservation, "Conservation – 1932" Folder, S1041-435).

85. Quoted in Ingersoll, *History and Present Condition,* 159. In contrast, Stevenson argued in 1892 that acts of defiance by dredgers "are not so common as is generally supposed, and during the last three or four years the quantity of oysters taken in this manner has probably not been very large" ("Oyster Industry," 233).

86. Wennersten, *Oyster Wars,* 36, 71, 97. See also "State's Oyster Navy," *WP,* 24 Apr. 1901, 10; Horton, *Island Out of Time,* 130 47.

87. Bonnie J. McCay, *Oyster Wars and the Public Trust: Property, Law, and Ecology in New Jersey History* (Tucson: University of Arizona Press, 1998).

88. Wennersten, *Oyster Wars,* 84–87.

89. For exceptions, see ibid., 98.

90. Ingersoll, *History and Present Condition,* 160.

91. Brewington, *Chesapeake Bay,* 172.

92. "Worse than Slave-Drivers," *Chicago Daily Tribune,* 7 Nov. 1886, 26; "Tortured on the Bay," *WP,* 6 Nov. 1897, 9. See also "Tells Tale of Brutality," *WP,* 12 Dec. 1905, 11.

93. "Dredges Are Tied Up," *WP,* 22 Nov. 1906, 5; Sherry H. Olson, *Baltimore: The Building of an American City* (1980; Baltimore: Johns Hopkins University Press, 1997), 201; Wennersten, *Oyster Wars,* 63–64.

94. See, e.g., "The Oyster-Pirates," *Chicago Daily Tribune,* 1 Mar. 1883, 6; "Fighting Oyster Pirates," *Boston Globe,* 8 Dec. 1883, 5; "Daring Oyster Pirates," *NYT,* 8 Dec. 1888, 2.

95. Quoted in Ingersoll, *History and Present Condition,* 160.

96. Ibid., 162.

97. Ibid., 157.

98. Ibid., 163.

99. BPWL, Correspondence and Petitions, 1904–5, 183–87, S40-1.

100. Ibid., 171–73, 182.

101. Lloyd L. Simpkins to J. Millard Tawes, 10 Aug. 1961, GGF, Es–Fl, Folder "Fisheries, Dept. of Tidewater 1961–62," S1041-1459.

102. His frustration is palpable in a 1911 letter to a clueless patrolman: "You are one of the Deputy Commanders of the State Fishery Force, and sworn to do your duty in carrying out the provisions of the Oyster Laws. My advice to you is to study the Law, and do your duty irregardless of friend or foe" (T. C. B. Howard to Jacob S. Tyler, 16 Nov. 1911, BPWL, Oyster and Fish Laws, 1910–14, 168, S40-2).

103. Wennersten, *Oyster Wars*, 125. In 1916, the legislature placed the Oyster Navy under the authority of the new Conservation Commission, which removed the governor's authority to appoint commanders, though it granted the governor responsibility for appointing the conservation commissioners (*Laws of the State of Maryland* [Baltimore: King, 1916], 1545–46).

104. "Oystermen" [Cambridge, Maryland, postmark] to J. Millard Tawes, 2 Oct. 1962, GGF, Es–Fl, Folder Oysters, S1041-1459.

105. N. T. Kenney, "Old, Slow Boats Fight Oyster Poachers," *BES*, 4 Feb. 1947, 34; "Budget Cut May Weaken 'Oyster Law' Enforcement," *BES*, 17 Feb. 1947.

106. Elroy G. Boyer to H. C. Byrd, 10 June 1959, CTFM, 1959–61, 3, 6, S321-4.

107. William H. Williams, *The Garden of American Methodism: The Delmarva Peninsula, 1769–1820* (Wilmington, Del: Scholarly Resources, 1984).

108. William W. Warner, *Beautiful Swimmers: Watermen, Crabs, and the Chesapeake Bay* (1976; Boston: Little, Brown, 1994), 77.

109. Quoted in Robert de Gast, *The Oystermen of the Chesapeake* (Camden, Me.: International Marine, 1970), n.p.

110. Carolyn Ellis, *Fisher Folk: Two Communities on Chesapeake Bay* (Lexington: University Press of Kentucky, 1986), 141. See also Warner, *Beautiful Swimmers*, 89.

111. H. C. Byrd to J. Millard Tawes, 29 Mar. 1961, GGF, Es–Fl, Folder "Oysters," S1041-1459.

112. James Eskridge quoted in Karen Jolly Davis, "Fishing by the Book," *NVP*, 16 Mar. 1998, A1.

113. Quoted in Ingersoll, *History and Present Condition*, 159.

114. Ellis, *Fisher Folk*, 118–23, 140.

115. For a vivid description of the hardships of dredging, see Randall S. Peffer, *Watermen* (1979; Baltimore: Johns Hopkins University Press, 1985), 11–21.

116. Milton Evans quoted in Wennersten, *Oyster Wars*, 129–30.

117. Quoted in de Gast, *Oystermen*, n.p.

118. David S. Cecelski, *The Waterman's Song: Slavery and Freedom in Maritime North Carolina* (Chapel Hill: University of North Carolina Press, 2001), 36.

119. Mark M. Bundy and John B. Williams, eds., *Maryland's Chesapeake Bay Commercial Fisheries* (N.p.: Maryland Department of Natural Resources, 1978), 5; Cecelski, *Waterman's Song,* 81.

120. Lang, *Follow the Water,* 34.

121. Annie R. Carter to Albert C. Ritchie, 28 Feb. 1927, GGF, Conservation, 1920–35, S1041-436.

122. Quoted in Ingersoll, *History and Present Condition,* 162.

123. "Oystermen Gathering," *BS,* 29 Oct. 1915, 10.

124. However, subsistence living provided enough of a cushion against market changes that economic downturns, including the Great Depression, that wreaked catastrophe on the mainstream U.S. economy had relatively little impact on tidewater communities (Ellis, *Fisher Folk,* 129).

125. Crab Reef's thinly veiled identity was confirmed by a waterman's wife interviewed by journalist Tom Horton during his stint as an environmental educator on Smith Island in the late 1980s: "A woman came here once to live, workin' on her degree in sociology, and she wrote a book about communities like ours. She didn't call us Smith Island; she called us Crab Reef. Some of what she put in there was none of her business, but a lot of it was true" (quoted in *Island Out of Time,* 83–84). Horton also discusses important social distinctions between the three villages of greater Smith Island as witnessed in the late 1980s, demonstrating a further degree of variation among Chesapeake tidewater communities. For Ellis's response to the backlash by her research subjects, see Carolyn Ellis, "Emotional and Ethical Quagmires in Returning to the Field," *Journal of Contemporary Ethnography* 24 (1995): 68–98.

126. Ellis, *Fisher Folk,* 129, 92, 112, 118–19, 135.

127. Ibid., 141, 92, 112, 118–19, 135.

128. Botwick and McClane, "Landscapes."

129. Lang, *Follow the Water,* 50. For a rebuttal, see William J. Hargis Jr. and Dexter S. Haven, "Chesapeake Oyster Reefs, Their Importance, Destruction and Guidelines for Restoring Them," in *Oyster Reef Habitat Restoration,* ed. Luckenbach, Mann, and Wesson, 329–58.

130. "Baetjer Outlines Ideas on Oysters," *BS,* 21 Jan. 1944, 4; "Lest We Forget the Chesapeake Bay Oyster," *BS,* 3 Feb. 1948, 10; "Setting the Date for the Oyster Memorial," *BS,* 9 Feb. 1948, 8; "In Memoriam: The Bay Oyster," *BS,* 26 Mar. 1949, 8.

131. See, e.g., N. Marshall, "Changes in the Physiography of Oyster Bars in the James River, Virginia," *Virginia Journal of Science* 5 (1954): 173–81; Newell, "Ecological Changes"; B. J. Rothschild, J. S. Ault, P. Goulletquer, and M. Héral, "Decline of the Chesapeake Bay Oyster Population: A Century of Habitat Destruction and Overfishing," *Marine Ecology Progress Series* 111 (1994): 29–39; Jackson

et al., "Historical Overfishing"; Boesch et al., "Factors," 1589–90; Helen Woods, William J. Hargis Jr., Carl H. Hershner, and Pam Mason, "Disappearance of the Natural Emergent 3-Dimensional Oyster Reef System of the James River, Virginia, 1871–1948," *JSR* 24 (2005): 139–42.

132. Quoted in Ingersoll, *History and Present Condition,* 144.

133. Stevenson, "Oyster Industry," 243.

134. See, e.g., Horton, *Island Out of Time,* 52.

135. Quoted in "Oyster Parley Is Called Off; Tension Grows," *BS,* 9 Dec. 1938, 26.

136. Tom Horton, "State Says Catching Oysters Improves Hatching Oysters," *BS,* 31 Jan. 2003, 1A; Tom Horton, "A Turning Point for Bay Oystering," *BS,* 14 Feb. 2003, 2B; Kent Mountford, "No Matter What Shells Are Fired in Oyster Wars, the Resource Always Loses," *BJ,* Mar. 2003; Karl Blankenship, "MD Enacts Emergency Legislation to Allow Power Dredging," *BJ,* Mar. 2003.

137. Quoted in Ingersoll, *History and Present Condition,* 159. On the impact of European railroads on demand for oysters, see Karl Möbius, "The Oyster and Oyster-Culture," trans. H. J. Rice, in *Report of the U.S. Fish Commission, 1880* (Washington, D.C.: U.S. Government Printing Office, 1883): 730–31.

138. Ellis, *Fisher Folk,* 141.

139. See, e.g., James R. McGoodwin, *Crisis in the World's Fisheries: People, Problems, and Policies* (Stanford, Calif.: Stanford University Press, 1990), chap. 8; Brent W. Stoffle, David B. Halmo, Richard W. Stoffle, and C. Gaye Burpee, "Folk Management and Conservation Ethics among Small-Scale Fishers of Buen Hombre, Dominican Republic," in *Folk Management,* ed. Dyer and McGoodwin, 116–38.

140. White, "'Are You an Environmentalist?'" 182; Tom Horton, *Turning the Tide: Saving the Chesapeake Bay* (1991; Washington, D.C.: Island, 2003), chap. 5; John R. Wennersten, *The Chesapeake: An Environmental Biography* (Baltimore: Maryland Historical Society, 2001), chap. 7.

141. For example, a 1905 petition to the Board of Public Works began, "We, Oystermen, Tax-payers and yeomanry of Somerset County, a body of water contiguous to, and separated only from Va. by a meagre and indefinite line, necessitating and requiring constant and vigilant patroling to protect from poachers and depredations of Virginians . . . ask Your Honorable body that the present Police boat be retained for the patroling of the waters of the said Pocomoke Sound the entire calendar year" (BPWL, Correspondence and Petitions, 1904–5, 127, S40-1).

142. On the South's postbellum agricultural economy, see Pete Daniel, *Breaking the Land: The Transformation of Cotton, Tobacco, and Rice Cultures since 1880* (Champaign: University of Illinois Press, 1985); Jack Temple Kirby, *Rural Worlds Lost: The American South, 1920–1960* (Baton Rouge: Louisiana State University Press, 1987); Dwight B. Billings, *Planters and the Making of a "New South": Class,*

Politics, and Development in North Carolina, 1865–1900 (Chapel Hill: University of North Carolina Press, 1979).

Chapter 2. Culture Shock

1. This sentence is an homage to Alfred Crosby's account of the encounter between Captain Cook and the Australians of Botany Bay in *Ecological Imperialism: The Biological Expansion of Europe, 900–1900* (Cambridge: Cambridge University Press, 1986), 18.

2. See, e.g., Samuel P. Hays, *The Response to Industrialism, 1885–1914* (Chicago: University of Chicago Press, 1957); Robert Wiebe, *The Search for Order, 1877–1920* (New York: Hill and Wang, 1976).

3. See, e.g., Kathy J. Cooke, "Expertise, Book Farming, and Government Agriculture: The Origins of Agricultural Seed Certification in the United States," *Agricultural History* 73 (2002): 524–45.

4. William K. Brooks, *The Oyster: A Popular Summary of a Scientific Study* (1891, 1905; Baltimore: Johns Hopkins University Press, 1996), xxxiii.

5. Philip J. Pauly, *Biologists and the Promise of American Life: From Meriwether Lewis to Alfred Kinsey* (Princeton: Princeton University Press, 2000), esp. chap. 2.

6. John F. Reiger describes the Gilded Age fish-culture movement as "the very first environmental crusade to capture a significant percentage of the American public" (*American Sportsmen and the Origins of Conservation* [New York: Winchester, 1975], 53), while Donald J. Pisani calls attention to the links between fish culture and early concern regarding water pollution ("Fish Culture and the Dawn of Concern over Water Pollution in the United States," *Environmental Review* 8 [1984]: 117–31). More recently, Richard W. Judd praises New England's state fish commissioners of the 1860s for pioneering "the institutional basis for conservation in America" (*Common Lands, Common People: The Origins of Conservation in Northern New England* [Cambridge: Harvard University Press, 1997], 157).

7. Judd, *Common Lands, Common People*, 149–57.

8. The classic study of the conservation movement, Samuel P. Hays's *Conservation and the Gospel of Efficiency: The Progressive Conservation Movement, 1890–1920* (Cambridge: Harvard University Press, 1959), dates its beginning to 1890 and attributes it to professional scientists in league with natural-resource-based corporations. Reiger, *American Sportsmen*, challenges Hays by presenting a start date of the 1870s and the primacy of elite sportsmen over scientists and resource officials. Judd disputes the conventional wisdom by arguing that "common people" – that is, regular citizens steeped in the traditional culture of northern New England – "participated enthusiastically in early efforts to protect and sustain their natural resources" (*Common Lands, Common People*, 264), a thesis that has important links with my study. For an older study recognizing the pioneering

efforts of a western New Yorker, see Sylvia R. Black, "Seth Green: Father of Fish Culture," *Rochester History* 6 (1944): 1–24.

9. G. Brown Goode, "The First Decade of the United States Fish Commission: Its Plan of Work and Accomplished Results, Scientific and Economical," *Report of the U.S. Fish Commission, 1880* 8 (1883): 61; Hugh M. Smith, "The United States Bureau of Fisheries: Its Establishment, Functions, Organization Resources, Operations, and Achievements," *Bulletin of the U.S. Bureau of Fisheries* 27 (1908): 1367, 1371; Richard H. Stroud, "Fisheries and Aquatic Resources: Lakes, Streams, and Other Inland Waters," in *Origins of American Conservation,* ed. Henry Clepper (New York: Ronald, 1966), 60, 62; Arthur F. McEvoy, *The Fisherman's Problem: Law and Ecology in the California Fisheries, 1850–1980* (New York: Cambridge University Press, 1986), 101–2, 105; Charles R. Berry Jr., "The American Fisheries Society: An AIBS Member Society Promoting Fisheries Science and Education since 1870," *BioScience* 52 (2002): 758–60.

10. McEvoy, *Fisherman's Problem,* 101.

11. G. Brown Goode, "A Review of the Fishery Industries of the United States and the Work of the U.S. Fish Commission," in *Papers of the Conferences held in Connection with the Great International Fisheries Exhibition* (London: Clowes, 1883), 55–56.

12. For example, 101 bills proposing the creation of seventy-four hatcheries and four laboratories in forty-three states and territories were introduced during the 1907–8 session of Congress (Smith, "United States Bureau of Fisheries," 1382).

13. Judd, *Common Lands, Common People,* 147–48.

14. New England fish commissioners supported limited efforts to reduce sawdust pollution and build fishways around dams, as discussed in ibid., 157–68. But the hatchery movement rarely addressed broader environmental concerns, mainly because overcoming the forces of industrialization would have required tremendous reserves of political will, a problem with which environmentalists today are all too familiar.

15. Smith, "United States Bureau of Fisheries," 1401.

16. McEvoy, *Fisherman's Problem,* 108; Joseph E. Taylor III, *Making Salmon: An Environmental History of the Northwest Fisheries Crisis* (Seattle: University of Washington Press, 1999), chap. 3.

17. Historian Conevery Bolton Valenčius conveys the relationship between farming and landownership well: "To farm a piece of land meant taking it over; agriculture yielded not simply crops, fruits, meats, and grains, but also the social, and then legal, prerogatives of ownership" (*The Health of the Country: How American Settlers Understood Themselves and Their Land* [New York: Basic Books, 2002], 194).

18. Ernest Ingersoll, *The History and Present Condition of the Fishery Industries: The Oyster-Industry* (Washington, D.C.: U.S. Government Printing Office, 1881), 23;

M. de Bon, "Report on the Condition of Oyster Culture in 1875," reprinted in *Report of the U.S. Fish Commission, 1880* 8 (1883): 887. See also Bonnie J. McCay, *Oyster Wars and the Public Trust: Property, Law, and Ecology in New Jersey History* (Tucson: University of Arizona Press, 1998), 10–11.

19. Other branches more closely resemble agricultural processes in terms of producing new organisms: the rearing of oysters by use of spat collectors such as shell or tiles (what most commentators meant by "oyster farming" from the 1870s on) and the rearing of oysters from artificially fertilized eggs produced in hatcheries (not prevalent until the 1970s).

20. For an overview of this region, see Clyde L. MacKenzie Jr., "The U.S. Molluscan Fisheries from Massachusetts Bay through Raritan Bay, N.Y. and N.J.," in *The History, Present Condition, and Future of the Molluscan Fisheries of North and Central America and Europe,* ed. Clyde L. MacKenzie Jr., Victor G. Burrell Jr., Aaron Rosefield, and Willis L. Hobart (Seattle: U.S. Department of Commerce, 1997), 87–117.

21. On protests by oystermen, see Ingersoll, *History and Present Condition,* 65, J. W. Collins, "Notes on the Oyster Fishery of Connecticut," *Bulletin of the U.S. Fish Commission* 9 (1889): 469.

22. *Shepard and Layton v. Leverson* (1808); see McCay, *Oyster Wars,* chap. 3.

23. Only two exceptions seem to have occurred. In 1865, Rhode Island allowed the leasing of bottoms whether or not they contained natural beds to private citizens for the high price of ten dollars per acre per year (but many observers argued that the state no longer possessed productive natural beds as a consequence of overharvesting). Ten years later, the Connecticut legislature exempted three towns, including New Haven, from the rule prohibiting the use of natural oyster beds for planting, apparently on the grounds that otherwise "systematic cultivation would have been vastly hindered, if not altogether killed, by thieves and malcontents, so far as New Haven harbor is concerned" (Ingersoll, *History and Present Condition,* 54, 65–66).

24. R. R. Neild, *The English, the French, and the Oyster* (London: Quiller, 1995); Darin Kinsey, "'Seeding the Water as the Earth': The Epicenter and Peripheries of a Western *Aqua*cultural Revolution," *Environmental History* 11 (2006): 527–66.

25. M. Coste, "Report on the Oyster and Mussel Industries of France and Italy," in *Report of the U.S. Fish Commission, 1880* 8 (1883): 829.

26. Ibid., 835.

27. On East River oyster culture, see W. K. Brooks, James I. Waddell, and William Henry Legg, *Report of the Oyster Commission of the State of Maryland* (Annapolis: Young, 1884), 10; Ingersoll, *History and Present Condition,* 95. In 1862, Coste convinced the French government to send a lieutenant to the United States to check out the state oyster industries; the head of the USFC recognized the resulting report as the most thorough study then published on the subject (P. de Broca, "On the Oyster-Industries of the United States," in *Report of the U.S. Fish*

Commission, 1873–74 and 1874–75 3 [1876]: 271–319). On Baird and Goode's late-nineteenth-century snubs of France's pioneering role in aquaculture, see Kinsey, "'Seeding the Water,'" 547–48.

28. Coste, "Report on the Oyster and Mussel Industries," 831. See also M. Coste, "Report to His Majesty the Emperor on the Condition of the Oyster Beds along the Coasts of France and on the Necessity of Restocking Them," Feb. 1858, in *Report of the U.S. Fish Commission, 1880* 8 (1883): 857–65.

29. Coste credited de Bon with suggesting the use of shells (M. Coste, "Report to His Majesty the Emperor on the Artificial Oyster Beds Created in the Bay of Saint-Brieuc," Jan. 1859, in *Report of the U.S. Fish Commission, 1880* 8 [1883]: 867, 868).

30. Concessions immediately adjoined the natural beds, occupying the space between the beds and the shore. Both parks and claires contained sluiceways to the sea, though parks were close enough to receive saltwater with every tide (Félix Fraiche, "A Practical Guide to Oyster-Culture, and the Methods of Rearing and Multiplying Edible Marine Animals," *Report of the U.S. Fish Commission, 1880* 8 [1883]: 764–65).

31. de Bon, "Report," 892, 893, 894.

32. Abraham Flexner, *Daniel Coit Gilman: Creator of the American Type of University* (New York: Harcourt, Brace, 1946), 35.

33. Ibid., 78.

34. Keith Rodney Benson, "William Keith Brooks: A Case Study in Morphology and the Development of American Biology" (PhD diss., Oregon State University, 1979); Keith R. Benson, "American Morphology in the Late Nineteenth Century: The Biology Department at Johns Hopkins University," *Journal of the History of Biology* 18 (1985): 163–205; Keith R. Benson, "H. Newell Martin, W. K. Brooks, and the Reformation of American Biology," *American Zoologist* 27 (1987): 759–71; Jane Maienschein, "H. N. Martin and W. K. Brooks: Exemplars for American Biology?" *American Zoologist* 27 (1987): 773–83; Jane Maienschein, *Transforming Traditions in American Biology, 1880–1915* (Baltimore: Johns Hopkins University Press, 1991).

35. L. Eugene Cronin, "Chesapeake Fisheries and Resource Stress in the 19th Century," *Journal of the Washington Academy of Sciences* 76 (1986): 190.

36. John F. Stover, *History of the Baltimore and Ohio Railroad* (West Lafayette, Ind.: Purdue University Press, 1987), 80; Flexner, *Daniel Coit Gilman,* 32, 35; Hugh Hawkins, *Pioneer: A History of the Johns Hopkins University, 1874–1889* (1960; Baltimore: Johns Hopkins University Press, 1984), 3–5, 316–20.

37. Examples of Brooks's popular articles include "Influences Determining Sex," *Popular Science Monthly,* Jan. 1885, 323–30; "Can Man Be Modified by Selection?" *Popular Science Monthly,* May 1885, 15–25; "The Study of Inheritance," *Popular Science Monthly,* Feb.–Mar. 1896, 480–92, 617–26; "Thoughts about Universities," *Popular Science Monthly,* July 1899, 349–55. On his community involve-

ment, see *Lectures Delivered to the Employes of the Baltimore and Ohio Railroad Company by Prof. H. Newell Martin . . . and Drs. Henry Sewall, Wm. T. Sedgwick and Wm. K. Brooks* (Baltimore: Friedenwald, 1882). On scientific popularization, see John C. Burnham, *How Superstition Won and Science Lost: Popularizing Science and Health in the United States* (New Brunswick, N.J.: Rutgers University Press, 1987), 151–52, 160.

38. E. A. Andrews, "William Keith Brooks," *Science* 28 (1908): 784. On agricultural experiment stations, see, e.g., Charles S. Rosenberg, *No Other Gods: On Science and American Social Thought,* rev. ed. (Baltimore: Johns Hopkins University Press, 1997), chaps. 8–11.

39. John A. Moore, *Science as a Way of Knowing: The Foundations of Modern Biology* (Cambridge: Harvard University Press, 1993), vii.

40. Andrews, "William Keith Brooks," 783.

41. The shellfishery biologists included Robert E. Coker, Caswell Grave, James L. Kellogg, H. McE. Knower, and Julius Nelson (Melbourne R. Carriker, *Taming of the Oyster: A History of Evolving Shellfisheries and the National Shellfisheries Association* [Hanover, Pa.: Sheridan and National Shellfisheries Association, 2004], 8). Brooks's most famous student was Thomas Hunt Morgan, who won the Nobel Prize in 1933 for his studies of fruit fly genetics. Others who entered the university life sciences included Ross Granville Harrison, Edmund Beecher Wilson, Edwin Grant Conklin, and Ethan Allen Andrews. See Ronald Rainger, Keith R. Benson, and Jane Maienschein, eds., *The American Development of Biology* (Philadelphia: University of Pennsylvania Press, 1988).

42. Edwin Grant Conklin, "William Keith Brooks," *National Academy of Science Biographical Memoirs* 8 (1913): 60.

43. Andrews, "William Keith Brooks," 779; Pauly, *Biologists,* 150.

44. Andrews, "William Keith Brooks," 779; Pauly, *Biologists,* 135; Hawkins, *Pioneer,* 49.

45. Dewey W. Grantham, *Southern Progressivism: The Reconciliation of Progress and Tradition* (Knoxville: University of Tennessee Press, 1983).

46. Edward L. Ayers, *The Promise of the New South: Life after Reconstruction* (New York: Oxford University Press, 1992), 423.

47. "Address of Prof. W. K. Brooks," in *Proceedings of the Convention Called to Consider and Discuss the Oyster Question* (Richmond, Va.: Fergusson, 1894), 33; Brooks, Waddell, and Legg, *Report,* 24.

48. See Sally Gregory Kohlstedt, "Nature, Not Books: Scientists and the Origins of the Nature-Study Movement in the 1890s," *Isis* 96 (2005): 324 n.1.

49. Maienschein, *Transforming Traditions,* 49–55.

50. Frank R. Lillie, *The Woods Hole Marine Biological Laboratory* (1944; Chicago: University of Chicago Press, 1988), 15–23; Keith R. Benson, "From Museum Research to Laboratory Research: The Transformation of Natural History into Academic Biology," in *The American Development of Biology,* ed. Rainger, Benson, and

Maienschein, 60. On the role of marine laboratories in academic biology, see Pauly, *Biologists,* chaps. 5–6. For a contemporary look at the CZL, see Sophie B. Herrick, "The Johns Hopkins University," *Scribner's Monthly* 19 (1879): 207.

51. The CZL dissolved when "the University secured for its faculty and students the use of a table in the station of the United States Fish Commission at Woods Hole, Massachusetts" (John C. French, *A History of the University Founded by Johns Hopkins* [Baltimore: Johns Hopkins University Press, 1946], 228). See also W. K. Brooks, "Chesapeake Zoological Laboratory: Report of the Director for Its First Six Years, 1878–83," *Johns Hopkins University Circular* 3 (1884): 91–94.

52. H. J. Rice, "Experiments in Oyster Propagation," *Transactions of the American Fish-Cultural Association* 12 (1883): 49–56; W. K. Brooks, "Abstract of Observations upon the Artificial Fertilization of Oyster Eggs, and on the Embryology of the American Oyster," *American Journal of Science and Arts* 18 (1879): 425–27.

53. W. K. Brooks, "Development of the American Oyster," in *Report of the Commissioners of Fisheries of Maryland* (Annapolis: Iglehart, 1880), 3–4, 39; H. Newell Martin, "The Oyster Question," *Science* 17 (1891): 169.

54. Brooks, Waddell, and Legg, *Report,* 85.

55. Goode, "Review," 83; Charles T. White, "Mr. Oyster Comes to Town," *New York World,* 1 Sept. 1889, 1; Martin, "Oyster Question," 169.

56. Brooks, "Development," 4, 38–39. On the relationship between American nationalism and the life sciences during this period, see Pauly, *Biologists;* Sharon E. Kingsland, *The Evolution of American Ecology, 1890–2000* (Baltimore: Johns Hopkins University Press, 2005).

57. Conklin, "William Keith Brooks," 60; Ingersoll, *History and Present Condition,* 210–19; Benson, "William Keith Brooks," 127. On the Société d'Acclimation, see Kinsey, "'Seeding the Water,'" 536–37.

58. T. B. Ferguson and Thomas Hughlett, *Report of the Commissioners of Fisheries of Maryland* (Annapolis: Iglehart, 1880), lxxiii.

59. J. B. Baylor, "The Oyster Survey – A Legal Boundary Line between Public and Private Rights," in *The Oyster Industry: A Series of Letters Written for the Richmond "Dispatch" and "Times" during the Winter of 1892–'93* (Richmond: Whittet and Shepperson, 1893), 26; C. C. Yates, "U.S. Coast and Geodetic Survey's Oyster Work," *Fishing Gazette,* 1911, 1057–58.

60. Francis Winslow, "Report on the Oyster Beds of the James River, Virginia, and of Tangier and Pocomoke Sounds, Maryland and Virginia," *Report of the U.S. Coast and Geodetic Survey for 1881* (Washington, D.C.: U.S. Government Printing Office, 1882), 344.

61. "The Chesapeake Oyster-Beds," *Science* 2 (1883): 442.

62. Roger Mann, Melissa Southworth, Juliana M. Harding, and James Wesson, "A Comparison of Dredge and Patent Tongs for Estimation of Oyster Populations," *JSR* 23 (2004): 387–90; Stephen J. Jordan, Kelly N. Greenhawk, Carol B. McCollough, Jessica Vanisko, and Mark L. Homer, "Oyster Biomass, Abundance, and Harvest in Northern Chesapeake Bay: Trends and Forecasts," *JSR* 21

(2002): 733–41. See also M. Geraldine McCormick-Ray, "Oyster Reefs in 1878 Seascape Pattern – Winslow Revisited," *Estuaries* 21 (1998): 784–800.

63. Brooks, *Oyster*, 181.

64. Charles C. Yates, *Survey of Oyster Bars of Maryland, 1906–1912* (Washington, D.C.: U.S. Government Printing Office, 1913).

65. Brooks, Waddell, and Legg, *Report*, 5–6, 13, 18.

66. Ibid., 30, 8.

67. The 1867 Five-Acre Law replaced an 1830 law allowing residents one acre. Maryland was one of the first U.S. states to permit the privatization of oyster bottoms (*First Report of the Shell Fish Commission of Maryland* [Baltimore: Sun Job, 1907], 181; Caswell Grave, *A Manual of Oyster Culture in Maryland* [Baltimore: King, 1912], 9, 11, 17).

68. Brooks, Waddell, and Legg, *Report*, 149; Ingersoll, *History and Present Condition*, 64. On Rowe, see John R. Wennersten, *The Oyster Wars of Chesapeake Bay* (Centreville, Md.: Tidewater, 1981), 68–69.

69. Brooks, Waddell, and Legg, *Report*, 24, 131–33.

70. Quoted in William M. Hudson, "The Shell Fisheries of Connecticut," *Transactions of the American Fish-Cultural Association* 13 (1884): 145. See also H. C. Hovey, "Oyster-Farming in Connecticut Waters," *Science* 2 (1883): 376–77; "The Oyster-Fishery in Connecticut," *Science* 5 (1885): 234; "Shell-Fish in Connecticut," *Science* 7 (1886): 59–60; "Propagation of Oysters," *NYT,* 21 Jan. 1889, 3; Collins, "Notes"; Gordon Sweet, "Oyster Conservation in Connecticut: Past and Present," *Geographical Review* 31 (1941): 591–608. On Goode and his influence on American culture, see Pauly, *Biologists,* 65 70. On Goode's dismissal of French precedents in aquaculture, see Kinsey, "'Seeding the Water,'" 547–48.

71. Brooks, Waddell, and Legg, *Report*, 31.

72. In the executive summary, he acknowledged liberal leasing laws' painful impact on tidewater communities but added a qualification: "Such a change . . . cannot be brought about rapidly without causing great hardship; and it is therefore best that it should come slowly; but the common right of all our people to the use of the oyster beds is a very different thing from the right of a portion of our people to exterminate the beds" (Brooks, Waddell, and Legg, *Report,* 11).

73. Ibid., 128, 69.

74. Ibid., 11.

75. Ibid., 69.

76. Hays, *Conservation,* esp. chaps. 3, 13; A. Hunter Dupree, *Science in the Federal Government: A History of Policies and Activities to 1940* (1957; New York: Harper and Row, 1964), chap. 12. See also Stephen Fox, *The American Conservation Movement: John Muir and His Legacy* (Madison: University of Wisconsin Press, 1986); Char Miller, *Gifford Pinchot and the Making of Modern Environmentalism* (Washington, D.C.: Island, 2001).

77. McCay, *Oyster Wars.*

78. Brooks, Waddell, and Legg, *Report,* 131.

79. McCay, *Oyster Wars*.

80. Quoted in Brooks, Waddell, and Legg, *Report,* 132.

81. *Seventh Report of the Shell Fish Commission of Maryland, 1914 and 1915* (Baltimore: Kohn and Pollock, 1916), 17.

82. Collins, "Notes," 474.

83. Brooks, Waddell, and Legg, *Report,* 133, 131.

84. Collins, "Notes," 462, 486.

85. "Address of Henry C. Rowe," in *Proceedings of the Convention,* 23.

86. Brooks, Waddell, and Legg, *Report,* 9, 11, 133.

87. Ibid., 11, 133, 167.

88. "Minority Report of Wm. Henry Legg," in ibid., 139; Victor S. Kennedy and Linda L. Breisch, "Sixteen Decades of Political Management of the Oyster Fishery in Maryland's Chesapeake Bay," *Journal of Environmental Management* 16 (1983): 161.

89. Mark M. Bundy and John B. Williams, eds., Maryland's *Chesapeake Bay Commercial Fisheries* (n.p.: Maryland Department of Natural Resources, 1978), 70–81.

90. Wennersten, *Oyster Wars,* 68–69.

91. Quoted in Margaret Enloe Vivian, "Tilghman Packing Company and the Transformation of Landscape on Avalon Island," *Weather Gauge* 36.1 (2000): 12–23, 34. Tilghman, like other Eastern Shore canneries, paid oyster shuckers and crab pickers with company tokens valid only at the company store. See also R. Lee Burton Jr., *Canneries of the Eastern Shore* (Centreville, Md.: Tidewater, 1986); Ed Kee, *Saving Our Harvest: The Story of the Mid-Atlantic Region's Canning and Freezing Industry* (Timonium, Md.: CTI, 2006).

92. Quoted in John E. Aliyetti, "The Bellevue Seafood Company," *Weather Gauge* 33.2 (1997): 5.

93. Charles H. Stevenson, "The Oyster Industry of Maryland," *Bulletin of the U.S. Fish Commission* 12 (1894): 240.

94. Pat Vojtech, *Chesapeake Bay Skipjacks* (Centreville, Md.: Tidewater, 1993), 112.

95. Carolyn Ellis, *Fisher Folk: Two Communities on Chesapeake Bay* (Lexington: University Press of Kentucky, 1986); Bradford Botwick and Debra A. McClane, "Landscapes of Resistance: A View of the Nineteenth-Century Chesapeake Bay Oyster Fishery," *Historical Archaeology* 39 (2005): 94–112.

96. Aliyetti, "Bellevue Seafood," 10.

97. See, e.g., Robert Higgs, *Crisis and the Leviathan: Critical Episodes in the Growth of American Government* (New York: Oxford University Press, 1987).

98. Kennedy and Breisch, "Sixteen Decades," 160–61.

99. Grave, *Manual,* 13.

100. John K. Cowen, Letter to the Editor, *BS,* 4 Feb. 1889, 1. See also Kennedy and Breisch, "Sixteen Decades."

101. Benson, "William Keith Brooks," 127.

102. G. Bouchon-Brandeley, "Report Relative to the Generation and Artificial Fecundation of Oysters, Addressed to the Minister of the Marine and the Colonies," *Journal Officiel de la Republique Française* (1882): 6762–64, 6778–82.

103. "National Traits in Science," *Science* 2 (1883): 455–57.

104. Brooks, "Chesapeake Zoological Laboratory," 93.

105. W. K. Brooks to Daniel Coit Gilman, 30 Aug. 1885, Series 1, Daniel Coit Gilman Papers, Ms. 1, Special Collections, Milton S. Eisenhower Library, Johns Hopkins University, Baltimore.

106. W. K. Brooks, "On the Artificial Propagation and Cultivation of Oysters in Floats," *Johns Hopkins University Circular* 5 (Oct. 1885): 10; reprinted in *Science* 6 (1885): 437–38.

107. Hawkins, *Pioneer,* 3–5, 316–20.

108. Edward Hungerford, *The Story of the Baltimore and Ohio Railroad, 1827–1927* (New York: Putnam's, 1928), 203; Stover, *History,* 181; Frank Richardson Kent, *The Story of Maryland Politics* [1911; Hatboro, Pa.: Tradition, 1968], 101).

109. Kent, *Story,* 95.

110. Wiebe, *Search for Order,* 53; Stover, *History,* 135–40.

111. Harold A. Williams, *The Baltimore Sun, 1837–1987* (Baltimore: Johns Hopkins University Press, 1987), 73; John K. Cowen, Letter to the Editor, *BS,* 4 Feb. 1889, 1, reprinted as *The Maryland Oyster and His Political Enemies* (Baltimore: Boyle, 1889).

112. John K. Cowen, Letter to the Editor, *BS,* 4 Feb. 1889, 1.

113. Brooks, *Oyster,* 199.

114. Stevenson, "Oyster Industry," 213.

115. "Save the Oyster Beds," *Baltimore American,* 19 Mar. 1891.

116. Edmonds quoted in Ingersoll, *History and Present Condition,* 168

117. T.P.E., "An Oysterman's Views" (Letter to the Editor), *BA,* 23 Dec. 1890.

118. Nathan Fast, "Oyster Production and Cultch Diversion in Nineteenth Century Maryland" (PhD diss., Johns Hopkins University, 1959).

119. "Going to North Carolina," *BA,* 13 Jan. 1891; "Dredgers Feeling Blue," *BA,* 8 Jan. 1891; "The Oyster Problem," *WP,* 19 Mar. 1891, 1.

120. "Is It Reform or Ruin?" *BA,* 9 Jan. 1891. See also "Facts about the Oyster," *BA,* 26 Jan. 1891; W. K. Brooks, "Oyster Farming Needed," *BA,* 13 Jan. 1891; "Captain Thompson's Views," *BA,* 21 Jan. 1891.

121. The two other speakers were state senator Thomas Hodson, who had sponsored oyster-planting bills and toured the Connecticut grounds, and the director of the U.S. Fish Commission, Marshall MacDonald, who plugged the economic fortunes that would accrue to cultivators and their dependents ("Save the Oyster Beds," *BA,* 19 Mar. 1891). See also Thomas S. Hodson, "Private Oyster Beds: Cultivation Needed in Maryland," *BA,* 14 Aug. 1886.

122. French, *History,* 83, 363–64; Francis F. Beirne, *Baltimore . . . A Picture History, 1858–1968* (Baltimore: Maryland Historical Society, 1968), 57.

123. "Save the Oyster Beds," *BA,* 19 Mar. 1891.

124. Thomas Weeks quoted in ibid.

125. Rebecca Edwards, *Angels in the Machinery: Gender in American Party Politics from the Civil War to the Progressive Era* (New York: Oxford University Press, 1997), 168–69.

126. "Save the Oyster Beds," *BA,* 19 Mar. 1891.

127. Ibid. For a scientific explanation of those leasing failures, see Grave, *Manual,* 75.

128. George H. Wrightson, George R. Gaither Jr., and F. H. Deane, *The Oyster Question: "The Common Heritage of All": Address of the Nationalist Club of Baltimore City to the People of Maryland* (Baltimore: n.p., 1891), 3, 11.

129. Stevenson, "Oyster Industry," 244.

130. Brooks, *Oyster,* 205–6.

131. Ibid., 14.

132. Ibid., 13.

133. On the clash between Progressive Era professionals and their rural clients, see, e.g., David B. Danbom, "The Agricultural Experiment Station and Professionalization: Scientists' Goals for Agriculture," *Agricultural History* 60 (1986): 246–55; Michael Paolisso, "Blue Crabs and Controversy on the Chesapeake Bay: A Cultural Model for Understanding Watermen's Reasoning about Blue Crab Management," *Human Organization* 61 (2002): 226–39.

134. All three men published and lectured in support of private oyster culture in the late nineteenth century. See, e.g., their speeches in *Proceedings of the Convention,* 17–22, 24–32. For negative assessments of the U.S. Fish Commission's approach to fish culture under McDonald, see McEvoy, *Fisherman's Problem,* 106–8; Pauly, *Biologists,* 101.

135. Stevenson, "Oyster Industry," 219.

136. Ibid., 219, 294. Brooks made this claim in Brooks, Waddell, and Legg, *Report,* 26.

137. W. K. Brooks and H. McE. Knower, "The Oyster and the Oyster Industry," in *Maryland: Its Resources, Industries and Institutions: Prepared for the Board of World's Fair Managers of Maryland by Members of Johns Hopkins University and Others* (Baltimore: Sun Job, 1893), 308.

138. Stevenson, "Oyster Industry," 291, 260, 293, 296.

139. In his words, "Any change in any of the relative factors of the biocönose produces changes in other factors of the same. If, at any time, one of the external conditions of life should deviate for a long time from its ordinary mean, the entire biocönose, or community, would be transformed. It would also be transformed, if the number of individuals of a particular species increased or diminished through the instrumentality of man, or if one species disappeared from, or a new species entered into the community" (Karl Möbius, "The Oyster and Oyster-Culture," in *Report of the U.S. Fish Commission, 1880* 8 [1883]: 723).

140. Sergej Olenin and Jean-Paul Ducrotoy, "The Concept of Biotope in Marine Ecology and Coastal Management," *Marine Pollution Bulletin* 53 (2006): 21;

David R. Keller and Frank B. Golley, *The Philosophy of Ecology: From Science to Synthesis* (Athens: University of Georgia Press, 2000), 102, 110; Lynn K. Nyhart, "Civic and Economic Zoology in Nineteenth-Century Germany: The 'Living Communities' of Karl Möbius," *Isis* 89 (1998): esp. 609–13.

141. Möbius, "Oyster and Oyster-Culture," 703, 707, 721–29.

142. In the introduction of his pioneering monograph, he conceded that few oyster culture enthusiasts were likely to accept his arguments (Möbius, "Oyster and Oyster-Culture," 684).

143. George Santopietro, "The Evolution of Property Rights to a Natural Resource: The Oyster Grounds of the Chesapeake Bay" (PhD diss., Virginia Tech, 1986), 252–58.

144. Baylor, "Oyster Survey," 28.

145. Santopietro, "Evolution," 263. It was a rather ironic addition, since the framers' main intent was to disenfranchise black voters, who happened to make up a large proportion of the state's tongers, and the new poll tax sometimes also kept poor white oystermen from voting.

146. Ibid.

147. George D. Santopietro and Leonard A. Shabman, "Property Rights to the Chesapeake Bay Oyster Fishery: History and Implications," *Society and Natural Resources* 5 (1992): 172.

148. Lots were limited to three thousand acres in the tributaries and five thousand acres in the bay's open waters (John J. Alford, "The Role of Management in Chesapeake Oyster Production," *Geographical Review* 63 [1973]: 49).

149. Santopietro, "Evolution," 268. See also Dexter Haven, "Virginia Seed Sources," in *Oyster Culture in Maryland '79: A Conference Proceedings*, ed. Donald Webster (Annapolis: University of Maryland Cooperative Extension Service, 1979), 25; John J. Alford, "The Chesapeake Oyster Fishery," *Annals of the Association of American Geographers* 65 (1975): 229–39; J. L. McHugh and Robert S. Bailey, "History of Virginia's Commercial Fisheries," *Virginia Journal of Science* (1957): 42–64.

150. Santopietro, "Evolution," 289–90; Santopietro and Shabman, "Property Rights," 172; Ingersoll, *History and Present Condition,* 180.

151. Santopietro, "Evolution," 240, 264, 265, 287, 454.

152. Health problems kept Brooks out of the fray (Francis Taggart Christy Jr., "The Exploitation of a Common Property Natural Resource: The Maryland Oyster Industry" [PhD diss., University of Michigan, 1964], 88; Benson, "William Keith Brooks," 104; Kennedy and Breisch, "Sixteen Decades," 161–63).

153. For a sharp critique of the ways in which the Haman Act limited the rise of a private aquaculture industry that was probably penned by Brooks protégé Caswell Grave and that includes the shrinking-beds explanation of the oystermen's lack of resistance to the Haman Act, see *Seventh Report,* 13–30.

154. Conklin, "William Keith Brooks," 60. See also Andrews, "William Keith Brooks," 779.

155. "Oyster Culture in Morbihan" quoted in Brooks, Waddell, and Legg, *Report,* 129. Brooks and other pro-leasers quoted this statement specifically to disparage government management in favor of private enterprise: "It is evident to all that, in spite of the scientific knowledge, the zeal and labors of Coste, his attempts, so far as regards commercial results, were radically fruitless. Nevertheless, he had at his disposition [at Saint-Brieuc] apparatus, boats . . . and . . . resources of the public treasury. Still the reason is very simple. That impersonal being, called the State, is incapable of creating any industry." I consider this assessment unfair. As discussed earlier in the chapter, Coste's original proposal to Napoleon III indicated that he intended the publicly financed restocking of Saint-Brieuc Bay as a temporary demonstration project to stimulate, not replace, private enterprise. Furthermore, de Bon pointed out that unfortunate acts of nature and the inexperience of the concessionaires accounted for the failure of Coste's proposed new form of oyster culture to catch on. Möbius echoed the role of these causes as well as the huge costs involved in "Oyster and Oyster-Culture," 698–701. The quotation thus says more about the antistate bias of Brooks and the administration following Napoleon III than about the efficacy of private versus public management.

156. Grave, *Manual,* 14–18.

157. Yates, *Survey,* 10.

158. *Seventh Report,* 18, 20, 23.

159. Yates, *Survey,* 10, 12; Christy, "Exploitation," 89; Grave, *Manual,* 15.

160. In addition, the 1912 legislature passed the Price-Campbell Bill, which increased maximum leaseholds of barren bottoms to thirty acres in the tributaries and five hundred acres in the bay but kept the ban on corporate holdings (*Seventh Report,* 23).

161. Legal scholar Garrett Power made this analogy first but did so in a way that defined the oyster regime as an "open fishery" rather than a regulated commons subject to state and county controls ("More about Oysters Than You Wanted to Know," *Maryland Law Review* 30 [1970]: 213).

162. *Seventh Report,* 26, 27, 41; Grave, *Manual,* 5, 15.

163. On the complex ways that the Shell Fish Commission had endeavored to "translate the Goldsborough definition, suited as it was to the courtroom, into a definition suitable for [surveying] field work," including collecting economic data to determine "what constituted a livelihood" for the average tonger and dredger, see *Seventh Report,* 17–21.

164. "Oyster Culture's Call Comes Clear and Loud," *BS,* 10 Mar. 1914.

165. Swepson Earle to Albert C. Ritchie, 15 Feb. 1927, GGF, Conservation, 1920–35, S1041-436.

166. Christy, "Exploitation," 93; Power, "More about Oysters," 214.

167. Arthur F. McEvoy, "Science, Culture, and Politics in U.S. Natural Resources Management," *Journal of the History of Biology* 25 (1992): 485. For his ex-

tended analysis of the relationships among user-group sociology, resource ecology, and fisheries management, see McEvoy, *Fisherman's Problem.*

Chapter 3. State Farming under the Chesapeake

1. Michael X. Kirby and Henry M. Miller, "Response of a Benthic Suspension Feeder (*Crassostrea Virginica* Gmelin) to Three Centuries of Anthropogenic Eutrophication in Chesapeake Bay," *Estuarine, Coastal and Shelf Science* 62 (2005): 679–89. According to Kirby and Miller, the earliest published observation of Chesapeake hypoxia dates to 1912, which accords with the paleoenvironmental evidence of sediment cores.

2. A strong indication of the failure to perceive the eutrophication of estuarine waters came from chemists who in 1932 advised oyster farmers to deliberately fertilize their underwater lots (H. D. Pease, "The Oyster: Modern Science Comes to the Support of an Ancient Food," *Journal of Chemical Education* 9 [1932]: 1695).

3. Harvey A. Levenstein, *Revolution at the Table: The Transformation of the American Diet* (New York: Oxford University Press, 1988), 12; Joseph Conlin, "Consider the Oyster," *American Heritage,* Feb.–Mar. 1980, 65–66.

4. Charles Mackay, *Life and Liberty in America; or, Sketches of a Tour in the United States and Canada, 1857–8* (London: Smith, Elder, 1859), 1:115.

5. For an example of an early federal study confirming the safety of Chesapeake oysters, see "Local Oysters Pure," *WP,* 19 Feb. 1911, M11.

6. Christopher G. Boone, "Obstacles to Infrastructure Provision: The Struggle to Build Comprehensive Sewer Works in Baltimore," *Historical Geography* 31 (2003): 160–63.

7. George Santopietro, "The Evolution of Property Rights to a Natural Resource: The Oyster Grounds of the Chesapeake Bay" (PhD diss., Virginia Tech, 1986), 273–74; *City of Hampton v. Watson,* 119 Va. 95, 89 SE 91 (1916); *Darling v. City of Newport News,* 123 Va. 95, 96 SE 307 (1918).

8. On this theme, see Paul S. Sutter, "Terra Incognita: The Neglected History of Interwar Environmental Thought and Politics," *Reviews in American History* 29 (2001): 289–97.

9. *Conservation Problems in Maryland* (n.p.: Maryland State Planning Commission, 1936), 51.

10. G. E. Jennings, "Some Changes in the Fish and Oyster Industry, 1892–1930," *Fishing Gazette,* 1930, 117–19; "Plan Boom for Oyster," *BS,* 16 June 1915, 3; "Oysters Adulterated Now," *BS,* 31 Dec. 1915, 2; "Oysters Condemned as Unfit to Eat," *BS,* 10 Nov. 1922, 24; "Oyster Inquiry Clears Packers," *BS,* 12 Nov. 1922, 24.

11. "Typhoid and the Oyster," *WP,* 21 Sept. 1912, 6.

12. H. F. Moore, *Oysters, the Food That Has Not Gone Up* (cookbook), quoted in "Lauds Oysters as Food," *BS,* 30 Aug. 1915, 5; Melbourne R. Carriker, *Taming of the Oyster: A History of Evolving Shellfisheries and the National Shellfisheries Association* (Hanover, Pa.: Sheridan and National Shellfisheries Association, 2004), 13; W. H. Killian, "Twenty-five Years of the Maryland Oyster Industry," *Fishing Gazette,* 1918, 1006–7. For an Oyster Growers and Dealers Association newspaper ad touting the oyster as a perfect food, see *WP,* 13 Oct. 1912, SM16. On oyster nutrition, see W. O. Atwater, "Contributions to the Knowledge of the Chemical Composition and Nutritive Values of American Food Fishes and Invertebrates," *Report of the U.S. Fish Commission, 1883* 11 (1885): 433–500.

13. "The Sociable Oyster Is Losing Caste," *New York Times Magazine,* 26 July 1925, 14.

14. See, e.g., Joel A. Tarr, *The Search for the Ultimate Sink: Urban Pollution in Historical Perspective* (Akron: University of Akron Press, 1996), chap. 6.

15. William Firth Wells, "The Purification of Oysters as a Conservation Measure," *American Journal of Public Health* 10 (1920): 344; William Firth Wells, "Chlorination as a Factor of Safety in Shellfish Production," *American Journal of Public Health* 19 (1929): 72–79. See also Paul S. Galtsoff, "Biology of the Oyster in Relation to Sanitation," *American Journal of Public Health* 26 (1936): 245–47.

16. Thurlow C. Nelson, "Aids to Successful Oyster Culture: I. Procuring the Seed," *Bulletin of the New Jersey Agricultural Experiment Stations* 351 (1921): 40–41; Bonnie J. McCay, *Oyster Wars and the Public Trust: Property, Law, and Ecology in New Jersey History* (Tucson: University of Arizona Press, 1998), 156–57; Clyde L. MacKenzie, *The Fisheries of Raritan Bay* (New Brunswick, N.J.: Rutgers University Press, 1992), 147–48.

17. Charles H. Stevenson, "The Oyster Industry of Maryland," *Bulletin of the U.S. Fish Commission* 12 (1894): 206; James L. Kellogg, *Shell-Fish Industries* (New York: Holt, 1910), 228.

18. McCay, *Oyster Wars,* 157–58; MacKenzie, *Fisheries,* 148. See also Tarr, *Search,* chap. 2.

19. "Growing Oil Business Killing Fish Industry," *BS,* 6 Nov. 1921, 11; Steven G. Davison, Jay G. Merwin Jr., John Capper, Garrett Power, and Frank R. Shivers Jr., *Chesapeake Waters: Four Centuries of Controversy, Concern, and Legislation* (1983; Centreville, Md.: Tidewater, 1997), 113.

20. On early efforts to link illegal discharges by Baltimore chemical and alcohol factories to fish kills in Curtis Bay, see Abel Wolman to Swepson Earle, 15 Sept. 1925, GGF, Conservation–Correspondence Unanswered, 1921–32, "Conservation – 1921–25" Folder, S1041-501.

21. Thurlow C. Nelson, "Some Aspects of Pollution as Affecting Oyster Propagation," *American Journal of Public Health* 11 (1921): 499.

22. Hugh S. Gorman, *Redefining Efficiency: Pollution Concerns, Regulatory Mechanisms, and Technological Change in the U.S. Petroleum Industry* (Akron: University of Akron Press, 2001), 16–17.

23. Thurlow C. Nelson, "Some Aspects," 501.

24. Gorman, *Redefining Efficiency,* 19–20, 22.

25. "Growing Oil Business Killing Fish Industry," *BS,* 6 Nov. 1921, 11; "Maryland Men Urge Oil Anti-Dumping Bill," *BS,* 8 Dec. 1921, 17; Swepson Earle, "The Pollution of Navigable Waters and Effect on Fisheries of Chesapeake Bay," in *Sixth Annual Report of the Conservation Commission of Maryland, 1921* (Baltimore: n.p., 1922), 65–70; House Committee on Rivers and Harbors, *Hearings on Oil Pollution of Navigable Waters,* 67th Cong., 2nd sess., 25 Oct. 1921.

26. Gorman, *Redefining Efficiency,* 22–26. See also Arthur F. McEvoy, *The Fisherman's Problem: Law and Ecology in the California Fisheries, 1850–1980* (New York: Cambridge University Press, 1986), 177; Joseph E. Taylor III, *Making Salmon: An Environmental History of the Northwest Fisheries Crisis* (Seattle: University of Washington Press, 1999), 226.

27. "Legislation Is Proposed to Check Bay Pollution," *BS,* 4 Oct. 1923, 15.

28. Gorman, *Redefining Efficiency,* 28, 132–33; Andrew Hurley, "Creating Ecological Wastelands: Oil Pollution in New York City, 1870–1900," *Journal of Urban History* 20 (1994): 340–64.

29. Martin V. Melosi, *The Sanitary City: Urban Infrastructure from Colonial Times to the Present* (Baltimore: Johns Hopkins University Press, 2000), 315–16. See also Jouni Paavola, "Interstate Water Pollution Problems and Elusive Federal Water Pollution Policy in the United States, 1900–1948," *Environment and History* 12 (2006): 435–65.

30. Robert Gottlieb, *Forcing the Spring: The Transformation of the American Environmental Movement* (Washington, D.C.: Island, 1993), 54.

31. *The Shellfish Sanitation Program of the Public Health Service* (Washington, D.C.: U.S. Department of Health, Education, and Welfare, 1962).

32. Harold Keats, "Eastern Shore Faces Ruin," *WP,* 1 Feb. 1925, SM1; "Earle Defends Oyster Survey," *BS,* 17 Jan. 1925, 20.

33. "Say Oyster Trade Is Hurt," *NYT,* 20 Jan. 1925, 6; "Chicago Health Officer to Eat Oysters," *BS,* 26 Jan. 1925, 16; Swepson Earle, "Illinois Accuses the Oyster," in *Second Annual Report of the Conservation Department of Maryland, 1924* (Baltimore: n.p., 1925), 104–9; Clyde L. MacKenzie Jr., "History of Oystering in the United States and Canada, Featuring the Eight Greatest Oyster Estuaries," *Marine Fisheries Review* 58 (1996): 21. For the "Square Deal" newspapers, see GGF, Conservation, 1920–35, "Conservation – Oyster, Typhoid Fever Scare – 1925" Folder, S1041-436.

34. "Officials Report on Oyster Survey," *BS,* 30 Oct. 1925, 9; "Requires Certified Oysters," *BS,* 8 Jan. 1926, 7; "Oysters Praised Now by Chicagoans," *BS,* 31 Oct. 1926, 13; "Visitors Study State Oyster Law," *BS,* 17 Nov. 1928, 4; Stirling Graham, "The Health Problems of the Oyster," *BSSM,* 25 Sept. 1932, 10; Clyde MacKenzie and Victor Burrell, "Trends and Status of Molluscan Fisheries in North and Central America and Europe – A Synopsis," in *The History, Present Condition, and Future of the Molluscan Fisheries of North and Central America and*

Europe, ed. Clyde MacKenzie Jr., Victor G. Burrell Jr., Aaron Rosefield, and Willis L. Hobart (Seattle: U.S. Department of Commerce, 1997), 4; "History of the National Shellfish Sanitation Program," U.S. Food and Drug Administration Web site, http://www.cfsan.fda.gov/~ear/nss2-9.html (accessed 5 July 2007). The sanitation program remains in effect today and is now administered by the U.S. Food and Drug Administration.

35. Isaac Rawlings to Wallace M. Quinn, 28 Dec. 1925, GGF, Confederate Soldiers Home–Conservation, "Conservation, General" Folder, S1041-435.

36. Robert Higgs, *Crisis and the Leviathan: Critical Episodes in the Growth of American Government* (New York: Oxford University Press, 1987); Stephen Skowronek, *Building a New American State: The Expansion of National Administrative Capacities, 1877–1920* (New York: Cambridge University Press, 1982).

37. Truitt came to this conclusion after monitoring acidity and salinity levels above eighteen major reefs for nine years and heavy metal wastes for three years (R. V. Truitt, "Oyster Problem Inquiry of Chesapeake Bay," in *Sixth Annual Report of the Conservation Department of Maryland, 1928* [Baltimore: Twentieth Century, 1929], 26–27, 39–41). This is not to say that no pollution threats against fish and shellfish were reported between 1925 and 1940. For example, in 1925, the Kent County Watermen's Protective Association accused the Army Corps of Engineers of dumping mud on fishing grounds at Love Point, and Earle received complaints from time to time of fish and crabs dying near Baltimore's sewage and garbage-disposal plants (Charles R. Kerr to Albert C. Ritchie, 10 Mar. 1925, GGF, Conservation–Correspondence Unanswered, 1921–32, "Conservation–1921–25" Folder, S1041-501; Swepson Earle to Albert C. Ritchie, 5 July 1929, GGF, Confederate Soldiers Home–Conservation, "Conservation, General" Folder, S1041-435; Anonymous, Letter to the Editor, *BS,* 22 Sept. 1927, 12).

38. R. V. Truitt, "Report of the Chesapeake Biological Laboratory, 1938," in *Sixteenth Annual Report of the Conservation Department of Maryland, 1938* (Baltimore: n.p., 1939), 56, 62

39. R. V. Truitt, "Report of the Chesapeake Biological Laboratory, 1940," in *Eighteenth Annual Report of the Conservation Department of Maryland, 1940* (Annapolis: n.p., 1941), 59. Davison et al., *Chesapeake Waters,* 111, also draw attention to this sentence as a revolutionary recognition of threats to water quality.

40. R. V. Truitt, "Report of the Chesapeake Biological Laboratory, 1939," in *Seventeenth Annual Report of the Conservation Department of Maryland, 1939,* (Annapolis: n.p., 1940), 50.

41. William Firth Wells, "Artificial Propagation of Oysters," *Transactions of the American Fisheries Society* 50 (1920): 303–5; William Firth Wells, "Studies in Oyster Culture," reprinted in *Early Oyster Culture Investigations by the New York State Conservation Commission (1920–1926)* (New York: State of New York Conservation Department, Division of Marine and Coastal Resources, 1969); "'Synthetic' Oysters Served to Diners," *NYT,* 2 Oct. 1925, 26; "To Give Us More Oys-

ters Than Ever," *BS,* 21 Sept. 1924, 3; "Science Produces the Super-Oyster," *NYT,* 30 Dec. 1926, 4.

42. Wells, *Early Oyster Culture Investigations,* 9, 16, 46, 66, 100, 119.

43. Thurlow C. Nelson, "Aids to Successful Oyster Culture," 45–46.

44. In 1926, Wells informed the New York legislature that his experimental results were worth much more than the actual oysters produced, a tacit admission of their lack of profitability (*Early Oyster Culture Investigations,* 115).

45. Thurlow C. Nelson, "Aids to Successful Oyster Culture," 47–48; Thurlow C. Nelson, "On the Application of Science to the Fishing Industry," *Nature* 113 (1924): 675.

46. McCay, *Oyster Wars,* 123, 165–66; Susan E. Ford, "History and Present Status of Molluscan Shellfisheries from Barnegat Bay to Delaware Bay," in *History, Present Condition, and Future,* ed. MacKenzie et al., 1:122; Kenneth K. Chew, "Delaware Bay Oystering and the Haskin Shellfish Research Lab," *Aquaculture Magazine,* Jan.–Feb. 2001, 59–68.

47. Nelson's protégé, Harold Haskin, conducted pioneering research on the MSX parasite, naming it in his honor (*Haplosporidium nelsoni*). Ironically, Nelson may have helped introduce MSX to the East Coast by experimenting with infected Japanese oysters (*C. gigas*) in Barnegat Bay during the 1930s (Michael W. Fincham, "The Mystery Invasion of Chesapeake Bay," *CQ* 5.2 [2006]: 4–15).

48. "Oyster Fight Looms Big," *BS,* 2 Jan. 1916, 9.

49. Swepson Earle, "Chesapeake Bay Fisheries," *Maryland Fisheries,* Nov. 1934, 9.

50. Swepson Earle, "The Example That Louisiana Is Setting Maryland," *BS,* 11 Apr. 1915, 8A.

51. Both the Republican and Democratic candidates for governor adopted Earle's suggestion. The 1916 reorganization dissolved the Shell Fish Commission and the Eastern and Western Shore fish commissions and placed the Oyster Navy and state game warden under the authority of the conservation commission. The governor appointed the three commissioners, whose duties included the promotion of leasing of barren bottoms for oyster culture, replenishment of depleted natural bars, and enforcement of the oyster laws (*Laws of the State of Maryland* [Baltimore: King, 1916], 1545–49; "Earle Appointed to Vickers' Post," *BS,* 21 Apr. 1924, 18; "Swepson Earle – Pioneer Conservationist," *Maryland Conservationist,* Spring 1944).

52. Annotated Code of Maryland, Article 19–A; W. Thomas Kemp, ed., *Conservation Laws of Maryland* (Baltimore: Conservation Commission of Maryland, 1916), 5.

53. In 1922, the agency's name was officially changed to the Conservation Department, but the name Conservation Commission was still used, and the leader of the Conservation Department was known as the conservation commissioner. Earle lost his job when a new governor took office in 1935 (Swepson

Earle, "Address before Baltimore City Oyster Packers," 4 Oct. 1934, 1, CON-SERVATION COMMISSION [Minutes], MdHR 12,494-1; "Tells of Conserva-tion Plan," *BS*, 24 Feb. 1916, 5; "Conservation Bill Up," *BS*, 30 March 1916, 7; "Reorganization Plans for State Completed," *BS*, 30 July 1921, 18).

54. Counts are so large that fewer than twenty fill a pint, while between twenty-six and thirty-eight selects and thirty-eight and sixty-three standards constitute a pint (Lonnie Williams and Karen Warner, *Oysters: A Connoisseur's Guide and Cook-book* [Berkeley: Ten Speed, 1987], 48). On the low prices commanded by small oysters, see, e.g., "Oyster Tonging Ends Tonight," *BS*, 24 Apr. 1915, 5.

55. Ronald J. Dugas, Edwin A. Joyce, and Mark E. Berrigan, "History and Status of the Oyster, *Crassostrea Virginica*, and Other Molluscan Fisheries of the U.S. Gulf of Mexico," in *History, Present Condition, and Future*, ed. MacKenzie et al., 1:194.

56. Swepson Earle, "The Example That Louisiana Is Setting Maryland," *BS*, 11 Apr. 1915, 8A.

57. "To Lease All Bottoms," *BS*, 2 March 1916, 2.

58. "He Upholds Oystermen," *BS*, 12 March 1916, 5.

59. Stevenson, "Oyster Industry," 260.

60. "Want $40,000 from State," *BS*, 22 Feb. 1916, 7; "Oyster Packers Lose," *BS*, 2 Mar. 1916, 9; Caswell Grave, *A Manual of Oyster Culture in Maryland* (Balti-more: King, 1912), 16.

61. Annotated Code of Maryland, Article 72; Kemp, *Conservation Laws*, 52–57; "What Oyster Culture Can Do," *BS*, 15 Mar. 1916, 3.

62. The experiments took place at Daddie Dare rock in Calvert County waters in 1914, Governor's Run in Calvert waters in 1917, Hog Island–Parker Moore at the mouth of the Patuxent in 1922–23, and Cedar Point Hollow in St. Mary's County waters in 1924 ("Webster Plan of Transplanting Oysters," GGF, Conser-vation, 1920–35 "Conservation, Legislation – 1927" Folder, S1041-436).

63. "Memorandum Concerning a Provisional Plan of Cooperation between the State of Maryland and the Bureau of Fisheries in Experimental Planting of Oysters in Chesapeake Bay," ca. 1917, Folder "Oysters – Chesapeake Bay, 1917," Records of the Division of Scientific Inquiry, Records of the U.S. Fish Commis-sion and Bureau of Fisheries, Records of the U.S. Fish and Wildlife Service, Rec-ord Group 22, National Archives, College Park, Md.

64. CONSERVATION COMMISSION (Minutes), 26 June–8 July 1919, MdHR 12,489-19, 31 July–22 Aug. 1919, MdHR 12489-22; "Outline of Legis-lation Proposed for 1920," *Fourth Annual Report of the Conservation Commission of Maryland, 1919* (Annapolis: Melvin, 1920), 29–30.

65. Reginald Truitt, interview by John R. Wennersten, 1982. I thank Wenner-sten for sharing his interview tapes.

66. CONSERVATION COMMISSION (Minutes), 6–20 June 1918, MdHR 12,489-1.

67. R. V. Truitt, *Maryland's Water Resources* (College Park: Maryland State College, 1919), 5–6.

68. R. P. Cowles, "A Biological Survey of the Offshore Waters of Chesapeake Bay," *Bulletin of the Bureau of Fisheries* 46 (1930): 277–381.

69. Truitt, *Maryland's Water Resources,* 7.

70. Reginald V. Truitt, "Investigation of the Oyster Industry of the Chesapeake Bay" (master's thesis, University of Maryland, 1922); Reginald V. Truitt, "Biological Contributions to the Development of the Oyster Industry in Maryland" (PhD diss., American University, 1929). A large chunk of the dissertation was reprinted in *Sixth Annual Report of the Conservation Department,* 25–63.

71. Bart Barnes, "Reginald Van Trump Truitt, Naturalist, Bay Biologist, Dies," *WP,* 13 Apr. 1991, B4.

72. As a teenager, Truitt asked a group of watermen working for his father "just what an oyster was." One described it as "a freakish sort of thing . . . that accumulated in water – to use his words – 'it forms just like snot in the nose.'" Despite the unappetizing analogy, Truitt "took to the oyster as a study and, of course, a life's work" (Reginald Truitt, interview by Georgina Earle, 16 July 1971, 2, Oral History Collection, OH 8005, H. Furlong Baldwin Library, Maryland Historical Society, Baltimore).

73. See, e.g., R. V. Truitt to Albert C. Ritchie, 29 Sept. 1924, GGF, Conservation–Correspondence Unanswered, 1921–32, "Conservation – 1921–25 Folder," S1041-501.

74. *Fifth Annual Report of the Conservation Commission of Maryland, 1920* (Baltimore: n.p., 1921) contains three articles by Truitt resulting from his work for the Bureau of Fisheries: "Inspection of the State Oyster Bars 1920," 66–69; "Report on Oyster Conditions," 70–80; and "A Policy for the Rehabilitation of the Oyster Industry in Maryland," 81–86.

75. R. V. Truitt, "Oyster Problem Inquiry of Chesapeake Bay," in *Fourth Annual Report of the Conservation Department of the State of Maryland, 1926* (Baltimore: n.p., 1927), 36; R. V. Truitt to Ernest N. Cory, 3 July 1972, 5, Reginald V. Truitt Papers, Box 1, Folder 3, UML.

76. "Dedication of the Chesapeake Biological Laboratory," *Maryland Fisheries,* July 1932, 6; R. V. Truitt and P. V. Mook, "Oyster Problem Inquiry of Chesapeake Bay," in *Third Annual Report of the Conservation Department of Maryland, 1925* (Baltimore: n.p., 1926), 27. On his early experimental work, see CONSERVATION COMMISSION (Minutes), 20 Nov. 1924–8 Jan. 1925, MdHR 12,490-23.

77. See Truitt, "Oyster and the Oyster Industry," 3.

78. R. V. Truitt to Ernest N. Cory, 3 July 1972, 5, Truitt Papers; Swepson Earle to Clarence W. Miles, 4 Dec. 1938, Series VI, Box 9, Folder "Maryland Committee on the Structure of the Maryland State Government, 1938," Isaiah Bowman Papers, Ms. 58, Special Collections, Milton S. Eisenhower Library, Johns Hopkins University, Baltimore.

79. "Pink Oysters Worry Officials until Invading Germ Is Found," *BS,* 21 Oct. 1924, 6; "Steps to Protect Oysters Are Taken," *BS,* 20 Nov. 1924, 6; "New System of Oyster Inspection Is Planned," *BS,* 23 Nov. 1924, 16. The color was later attributed to a harmless bacterium.

80. Frank Henry, "Chesapeake Bay Is His Oyster," *BS,* 6 Aug. 1950, A3.

81. R. V. Truitt, "Oyster Problem Inquiry," 1928, 27–28.

82. On fishermen's cyclical views of nature, see esp. William Ward and Priscilla Weeks, "Resource Managers and Resource Users: Field Biologists and Stewardship," in *Folk Management in the World's Fisheries: Lessons for Modern Fisheries Management,* ed. Christopher L. Dyer and James R. McGoodwin (Niwot: University Press of Colorado, 1994), 92–113.

83. Charles N. Spence, Letter to the Editor, *BS,* 24 Feb. 1924, 6. Three years later, Spence reiterated this idea: "God has taken the oysters away and He brings 'em back, and no man can understand why" (quoted in "Conservation Plan Is Jeered by Oystermen," *BS,* 27 Jan. 1927, 6).

84. See, e.g., Thurlow C. Nelson, "Aids to Successful Oyster Culture," 29–44.

85. R. V. Truitt, Letter to the Editor, *BS,* 4 Mar. 1924, 10.

86. Truitt and Mook, "Oyster Problem Inquiry," 25.

87. Ibid., 53.

88. R. V. Truitt, *Aspects of the Oyster Season in Maryland: Involving Labor Conflicts Detrimental to Both Seafood and Cannery Industries* (n.p.: Conservation Department of Maryland and Maryland Agricultural Experiment Station, 1927), 4–7.

89. Truitt, "Oyster Problem Inquiry," 1926, 30.

90. Truitt and Mook, "Oyster Problem Inquiry," 46–47; Truitt, "Oyster Problem Inquiry," 1926, 28, 30, 38, 52–54.

91. Nathan Fast, "Oyster Production and Cultch Diversion in Nineteenth Century Maryland" (PhD diss., Johns Hopkins University, 1959).

92. Truitt and Mook, "Oyster Problem Inquiry," 47.

93. "Urges Oyster Plan of Sea-Food Group," *BS,* 30 Jan. 1927, 5.

94. R. V. Truitt to Albert C. Ritchie, 29 Sept. 1924, Albert C. Ritchie to R. V. Truitt, 2 Oct. 1924, both in GGF, Conservation–Correspondence Unanswered, 1921–32, "Conservation – 1921–25 Folder," S1041-501.

95. Swepson Earle to Albert C. Ritchie, 2 Dec. 1924, GGF, Conservation–Correspondence Unanswered, 1921–32, "Conservation – 1921–25" Folder, S1041-501.

96. A. W. Tawes to Swepson Earle, 3 Dec. 1924, in ibid.

97. As early as 1921, the Conservation Commission reported that budget constraints kept the commission from meeting demand for planting shells, but the governor and legislature approved only a fraction of the two hundred thousand dollars requested for two years' worth of operations (Harrison Vickers to Albert C. Ritchie, 2 Mar. 1921, in ibid.; "Annual Planting Urged to Save Oyster Beds," *BS,* 2 Dec. 1921, 13; "Asks $100,000 a Year for Planting Oysters," *BS,*

18 Nov. 1921, 17; "Oystermen Protest Proposed New Taxes," *BS,* 22 Feb. 1922, 7; "Oyster Legislation to Come Up Thursday," *BS,* 10 Mar. 1922, 6; "Tidewater Senators Fail to Halt Oyster Tax Bill," *BS,* 30 Mar. 1922, 6; "Oyster Legislation Ready for Governor," *BS,* 1 Apr. 1922, 6).

98. William C. Todd to Albert C. Ritchie, 2 July 1926, GGF, Confederate Soldiers Home–Conservation, "Conservation, General" Folder, S1041-435.

99. William C. Todd to Albert C. Ritchie, 9 May 1928, in ibid.

100. William C. Todd to Albert C. Ritchie, 2 July 1926, in ibid.

101. Swepson Earle to William C. Todd, 15 May 1928, in ibid. Earle informed the governor that "this Bay dredger is very changeable in his views, and his ideas on many phases of the oyster question are not sound, and he is not considered practical by the majority of watermen who make their livelihood from the oyster bars" (Swepson Earle to Albert C. Ritchie, 15 May 1928, GGF, Confederate Soldiers Home–Conservation, "Conservation, General" Folder, S1041-435).

102. Carroll Walters to Albert C. Ritchie, 6 June 1926, GGF, Confederate Soldiers Home–Conservation, "Conservation, General" Folder, S1041-435.

103. W. C. Todd, "Wholesale Slaughter," *BS,* 9 May 1928, 10.

104. William C. Todd, "Why There Are More Oysters," *BS,* 30 Dec. 1928, 8. Another explanation for the increased size of Upper Bay oysters was the recent construction of the sea-level Chesapeake and Delaware Canal, which enabled saltwater from Delaware Bay to flow into the Chesapeake ("Oysters' Growth at Head of Bay Is Laid to Canal," *BS,* 4 Mar. 1928, 6).

105. Petition of St. George's Island Oystermen to Albert C. Ritchie, 23 Oct. 1934, Petition of 136 West River Kent Island Oystermen to Albert C. Ritchie, 26 Oct. 1934, both in GGF, Conservation, 1920–35, "1934 Conservation" Folder, S1041-436.

106. "Pleased by Oyster Growth," *BS,* 29 March 1926, 16; "Earle Reports Oyster Supply as Excellent," *BS,* 3 Oct. 1926, 8; "State Oyster Bed to Be Opened Today," *BS,* 6 Dec. 1926, 3; "Cedar Point Oyster Reserve Is Opened," *BS,* 7 Dec. 1926, 8; "Cedar Point Oyster Area Closed until 1927," *BS,* 10 Dec. 1926, 9.

107. "Governor's Message Answers Questions on Sea-Food Industry," *BS,* 6 Jan. 1927, 6.

108. The legislature did not meet for three years rather than the customary two because of a change in the election laws, which also shortened Ritchie's second term by a year (Harry J. Green, *A Study of the Legislature of the State of Maryland, with Special Reference to the Sessions of 1927 and 1929,* [Baltimore: Johns Hopkins University Press, 1930], 17–18, 98).

109. Joseph B. Chepaitis, "Albert C. Ritchie in Power: 1920–1927," *Maryland Historical Magazine* 68 (1973): 383–404; Dorothy Brown, "The Election of 1934: The 'New Deal' in Maryland," *Maryland Historical Magazine* 68 (1973): 405–21.

110. Ritchie quoted in George H. Callcott, *Maryland and America, 1940 to 1980* (Baltimore: Johns Hopkins University Press, 1985), 262.

111. Chepaitis, "Albert C. Ritchie," 383.

112. John W. Carroll to Albert C. Ritchie, 6 Jan. 1927, GGF, Conservation, 1920–35, "Conservation, Legislation – 1927" Folder, S1041-436.

113. "100 Oystermen Invited to Conservation Parley," *BS,* 6 Feb. 1926, 3; "To Consider Proposals to Increase Oysters' Yield," *BS,* 16 Feb. 1926, 4; "Oyster Parley Terminates," *BS,* 18 Feb. 1926, 24.

114. Truitt and Mook, "Oyster Problem Inquiry," 52, 54.

115. For a letter from a packer supporting the three-inch cull law because "we can put a much better grade of oysters on the market. And we can pay a better price for the oysters," see W. C. Larrimore to Albert C. Ritchie, 26 Oct. 1927, GGF, Confederate Soldiers Home–Conservation, "Conservation, General" Folder, S1041-435.

116. "Oyster Parley Terminates," *BS,* 18 Feb. 1926, 24.

117. Swepson Earle, Letter to the Editor, *BS,* 26 Feb. 1926, 12. See also letters printed in the *Sun* on 19 Feb. 1926, 8; 3 March 1926, 10; 8 March 1926, 8; 10 March 1926, 12; 13 March 1926, 10; 18 March 1926, 10; 19 March 1926, 10; 23 March 1926, 16.

118. Truitt found that tongers tended to hold the "highest and most responsible places" in the canneries during the summer, but that come September, "they simply can not stand the temptation and, especially, the thought that some other fellow is taking the best of the oysters." Presumably, tongers who sought summer employment in canneries lacked the capital assets to rig their boats to catch crabs (Truitt, *Aspects,* 8–9).

119. For an example of Truitt's identification on the committee as a packer rather than biologist, see "Oyster Dredgers Oppose Lease Plan," *BS,* 6 Jan. 1927, 6. For the other packers' names, see "Scores Assertions on Oyster Question," *BS,* 21 Jan. 1927, 5; "Maryland Seafood Committee's Report on Oyster Conservation," *BS,* 21 Jan. 1927, 5.

120. "Governor's Message Answers Questions on Sea-Food Industry," *BS,* 6 Jan. 1927, 6. The thirty thousand acres were located in the area bordered by the Anne Arundel–Calvert County boundary, south Poplar Island, and Dorchester County.

121. "Oyster Dredgers Oppose Lease Plan," *BS,* 6 Jan. 1927, 6; "Oystermen Divided on Ritchie's Plan," *BS,* 10 Jan. 1927, 20.

122. "Fight Is Opened on Ritchie Plan to Save Oyster," *BS,* 20 Jan. 1927, 1.

123. "Conservation Plan Jeered by Oystermen," *BS,* 27 Jan. 1927, 1; "Ritchie Drops Plan for Lease of Oyster Beds," *BS,* 16 Feb. 1927, 1; "Commissioner Prepares for Next Season," *BS,* 4 Aug. 1927, 3.

124. Petition by Fifty-seven Solomons Island Oystermen to Governor Albert C. Ritchie, 17 Feb. 1927, GGF, Conservation, 1920–35, "Conservation, Legislation – 1927" Folder, S1041-436.

125. "Oyster Group Agrees on Plan to Give Relief," *BS,* 10 Feb. 1927, 24.

126. "Ritchie Drops Plan for Lease of Oyster Beds," *BS,* 16 Feb. 1927, 1.

127. "The Oyster Compromise," *BS,* 17 Feb. 1927, 12.

128. For a justification of what he called his "well-known opposition" to leasing natural beds, see Albert C. Ritchie to J. T. Larrimore, 7 Feb. 1930, GGF, Confederate Soldiers Home–Conservation, "Conservation, General" Folder, S1041-435.

129. Chepaitis, "Albert C. Ritchie," 384.

130. S. T. Gladden to Albert C. Ritchie, 19 Feb. 1927, GGF, Conservation, 1920–35, "Conservation, Legislation – 1927" Folder, S1041-436.

131. "Nine Minor Bills Introduced in House within Forty Minutes," *BS,* 26 Feb. 1927, 15; "Members of New Oyster Body Named," *BS,* 12 June 1927, 14.

132. *Conservation Problems,* 7.

133. W. H. Valliant to Maryland Lawmakers, 7 Mar. 1927, GGF, Conservation, 1920–35, "Conservation, Legislation – 1927" Folder, S1041-436. For details on how Valliant derived his figures, see W. H. Valliant, "The State's Oyster Policy," *BS,* 1 Mar. 1927, 12.

134. W. H. Valliant to Maryland Lawmakers, 7 Mar. 1927, GGF, Conservation, 1920–35, "Conservation, Legislation – 1927" Folder, S1041-436. See also W. H. Valliant, "The State's Oyster Policy," *BS,* 1 Mar. 1927, 12.

135. "Advice on Oyster Shell Law Asked," *BS,* 17 Aug. 1927, 22; "Test Begun on Eve of Oyster Season," *BS,* 1 Sept. 1927, 3; "Packers Plan to Test Oyster Shell Statute," *BS,* 16 August 1927, 24.

136. "New Oyster Law Upheld by Court," *BS,* 27 Oct. 1927, 3; "Oyster Shell Law Upheld by Court," *BS,* 20 April 1928, 3.

137. "State to Enforce Oyster Shell Law," *BS,* 3 June 1928, 3; "Packers Told to Bar Shell Collections," *BS,* 4 June 1928, 20; "State Blocked in Attempt to Gather Shells," *BS,* 5 June 1928, 28; "Both Factions Claim Victory in Oyster War," *BS,* 6 June 1928, 28.

138. "Oystermen Lose in Oxford Fight," *BS,* 8 June 1928, 30; "Calls Earle Wasteful and Incompetent," *BS,* 12 June 1928, 28.

139. "The Usual Sequel," *BS,* 13 June 1928, 12.

140. *Leonard v. Earle,* 279 U.S. 392 [1929]; "Oyster Shell Tax Upheld by Court," *BS,* 14 May 1929, 3.

141. See, e.g., "Chesapeake Biological Laboratory," *Maryland Fisheries,* July 1933, 10–11; P. A. Butler, "Selective Setting of Oyster Larvae on Artificial Cultch," *Proceedings of the National Shellfisheries Association* 45 (1955): 95–105; W. N. Shaw, "Seasonal Fouling and Oyster Setting on Asbestos Plates in Broad Creek, Talbot County, Maryland," *Chesapeake Science* 8 (1967): 228–36; V. S. Kennedy, L. L. Smawley, and J. A. Boettger, *Final Report on a Study of Oyster Settlement and Fouling in Broad Creek and Tred Avon River, Maryland, during the Summers of 1977 to 1979* (University of Maryland, Center for Environmental and Estuarine Studies, Ref. No. 79-194, Horn Point Environmental Laboratory).

142. W. E. Northam to Albert C. Ritchie, 31 Jan. 1927, GGF, Conservation, 1920–35, "Conservation, Legislation – 1927" Folder, S1041-436.

143. W. E. Northam to Swepson Earle, 17 June 1928, Folder "N," Chesapeake Biological Laboratory Archives, Solomons, Md.

144. Swepson Earle to R. V. Truitt, 20 June 1928, in ibid.

145. "Shell Law Is Held Useless by Packer," *BS,* 17 June 1928, 3; W. E. Northam, "'Guessing,'" *BS,* 28 June 1928, 14; "Earle Insists Bay Has Oyster Spat," *BS,* 19 June 1928, 9.

146. A eulogist quoted him as saying, "Winning that battle was the beginning of my success. It showed some practicality in the use of science" (Kenneth Tenore, "Dr. Reginald V. Truitt," 1991, Chesapeake Biological Laboratory Web site, http://www.cbl.umces.edu/rvtruitt.html [accessed 11 June 1998]).

147. R. V. Truitt, "Recent Oyster Researches," in *Sixth Annual Report of the Conservation Department,* 4.

148. The most notorious fishery collapse of the first half of the twentieth century was that of the highly mechanized California sardine fishery, which occurred despite the fact that "California had built up the foremost marine research apparatus in the United States" (McEvoy, *Fisherman's Problem,* chaps. 6–7, p. 184).

149. "To Put Marine Laboratory on Chesapeake," *BS,* 28 Apr. 1929, 20; "The Chesapeake Clinic," *BS,* 29 Apr. 1929, 6.

150. For correspondence between state and federal fisheries officials, Maryland's congressional delegation, and local boosters regarding the proposed site, see, e.g., Swepson Earle to Lewis Radcliffe, 3 May 1929, Phillips Lee Goldsborough to Henry O'Malley, 3 Oct. 1929, Millard E. Tydings to Henry O'Malley, 26 May 1930, R. L. Ender to Millard E. Tydings, 26 May 1930, Henry O'Malley to Millard E. Tydings, 29 May 1930, all in Folder "Oysters, 1930," Records of the Division of Scientific Inquiry, Records of the U.S. Fish Commission and Bureau of Fisheries, Records of the U.S. Fish and Wildlife Service. Relevant newspaper articles include "Earle Inspects Site at Solomons," *BS,* 15 Aug. 1929, 4; "Hooper Island Sea-Food Station Is Suggested," *BS,* 27 May 1930, 6; "Groups Studying Oyster and Crab," *BS,* 13 Aug. 1930, 7.

151. Romeo Mansueti, "The Chesapeake Biological Laboratory, Past and Present," 13 June 1956, Chesapeake Biological Laboratory Archives; *Ninth Annual Report of the Conservation Department of Maryland, 1931* (Baltimore: Twentieth Century, 1932), 26.

152. "Dedication of the Chesapeake Biological Laboratory," 12.

153. McEvoy, *Fisherman's Problem,* 105–8; Taylor, *Making Salmon,* 91–98.

154. Quoted in "Dedication of the Chesapeake Biological Laboratory," 12.

155. A. Hunter Dupree, *Science in the Federal Government: A History of Policies and Activities to 1940* (1957; New York: Harper and Row, 1964), 347, 349. Another interpretation, as secretary of agriculture Henry A. Wallace argued, was that although science "turned scarcity into plenty," society should bear the blame for

failing "to apportion production to need and to distribute the fruits of plenty equitably."

156. Quoted in "Dedication of the Chesapeake Biological Laboratory," 15. See also James G. Needham, "The Teaching of Hydrobiology and Aquiculture in American Universities," *Science* 71 (1930): 265–66.

157. R. V. Truitt to Ernest N. Cory, 3 July 1972, 3, R. V. Truitt to H. C. Byrd, 5 Aug. 1935, 1 July 1940, all in Truitt Papers, Box 1, Folder 3.

158. Robert A. Croker, *Pioneer Ecologist: The Life and Work of Victor Ernest Shelford, 1877–1968* (Washington, D.C.: Smithsonian Institution Press, 1991), 105; R. V. Truitt to H. C. Byrd, 5 Aug. 1935, Truitt Papers.

159. R. V. Truitt, "Report of Chesapeake Biological Laboratory, 1937," in *Fifteenth Annual Report of the Conservation Department of Maryland, 1937* (Baltimore: n.p., 1938), 47–67; Truitt, "Report of the Chesapeake Biological Laboratory, 1939," 38–58. See also Romeo Mansueti, *Maryland Natural Resource Bibliography* (Solomons, Md.: Chesapeake Biological Laboratory, 1955); Frank J. Schwartz, *Bibliography of Maryland Fisheries* (Solomons, Md.: Chesapeake Biological Laboratory, 1960).

160. See, e.g., Curtis L. Newcombe and William A. Horne, "Oxygen-Poor Waters of the Chesapeake Bay," *Science* 88 (1938): 80–81; Curtis L. Newcombe and Andrew G. Lang, "The Distribution of Phosphates in the Chesapeake Bay," *Proceedings of the American Philosophical Society* 81 (1939): 393–420; Curtis L. Newcombe, William A. Horne, and Boland B. Shepherd, "Studies on the Physics and Chemistry of Estuarine Waters in Chesapeake Bay," *Journal of Marine Research* 2 (1939): 87–116; Robert A. Littleford, Curtis L. Newcombe, and Boland B. Shepherd, "An Experimental Study of Certain Quantitative Plankton Methods," *Ecology* 21 (1940): 309–22

161. Petition of Forty Members of the South Dorchester Association of Hoopers Island to Albert C. Ritchie, 15 Sept. 1932, GGF, Confederate Soldiers Home–Conservation, "Conservation–1932" Folder, S1041-435.

162. Albert C. Ritchie to South Dorchester Association, 23 Sept. 1932, GGF, Confederate Soldiers Home–Conservation, "Conservation–1932" Folder, S1041-435.

163. Pease, "Oyster," 1706; "Study of Fresh and Frozen Oysters," *Commercial Fisheries Review* 12 (1950): 5; Mary Emily Miller, "The Delaware Oyster Industry," *Delaware History* 14 (1971): 253; Shane Hamilton, "The Economies and Conveniences of Modern-Day Living: Frozen Foods and Mass Marketing, 1945–1965," *Business History Review* 77 (2003): 34.

164. Frank Henry, "Chesapeake Bay Is His Oyster," *BS,* 6 Aug. 1950, A3.

165. Shane Hamilton, "Cold Capitalism: The Political Ecology of Frozen Concentrated Orange Juice," *Agricultural History* 77 (2003): 557–81.

166. George W. Jeffers, "Solving the Secrets of the Bay," *BSSM,* 24 July 1932, 3.

167. R. L. Carson, "Farming under the Chesapeake," *BSSM,* 24 Jan. 1937, 6–7; Linda Lear, *Rachel Carson: Witness for Nature* (New York: Holt, 1997), 73, 79, 83.

168. See Rachel Carson, *Silent Spring* (1962; Boston: Houghton Mifflin, 2002).

169. "Oyster Increase of 250,000 Bushels Predicted by Earle," *BS,* 10 Feb. 1932, 18.

170. "Oyster Market Is Depressed, Earle Reports," *BS,* 5 Feb. 1933, 3.

171. "Fewer Oysters Sold This Season," *BS,* 13 April 1933, 9; Elmus Wicker, *The Banking Panics of the Great Depression* (Cambridge: Cambridge University Press, 1996), 108–50.

172. "Urges Increased Oyster Demand," *BS,* 7 Aug. 1934, 20; "Oyster Growers and Dealers Meet in Baltimore," *Maryland Fisheries,* Sept. 1934, 14–15.

173. Carriker, *Taming,* 66–69. See also "For Oysters . . . Publicity," *BS,* 8 Dec. 1938, 24; "Truitt Would Aim Sales Plans for Oysters at Middle West," *BS,* 10 Dec. 1938, 22; "Oyster Promotion Funds through Taxes Opposed," *BS,* 13 Dec. 1938, 5.

174. Chepaitis, "Albert C. Ritchie," 385. See also Robert J. Brugger, Cynthia Horsburgh Requardt, Robert I. Cottom Jr., and Mary Ellen Hayward, *Maryland: A Middle Temperament, 1634–1980* (Baltimore: Johns Hopkins University Press, 1989), 451–54, 494–500.

175. "Ritchie Promises Gas Tax Rebate for Oystermen," *BS,* 6 Sept. 1934, 4; Louis J. O'Donnell, "Ritchie Gives His Plans to Aid Oystermen," *BS,* 16 Oct. 1934, 24.

176. J. T. Larrimore to Albert C. Ritchie, 21 March 1927, GGF, Confederate Soldiers Home–Conservation, "Conservation, General" Folder, S1041-435.

177. William Moore to Albert C. Ritchie, 19 Sept. 1932, Albert C. Ritchie to William Moore, 23 Sept. 1932, both in GGF, Confederate Soldiers Home–Conservation, "Conservation-1932" Folder, S1041-435.

178. "Watermen's Vote Is Sought by Nice," *BS,* 17 Oct. 1934, 24, 6; G. Ellsworth Leary, Letter to the Editor, *BS,* 4 Jan. 1935, 10.

179. See, e.g., Interested, Letter to the Editor, *BS,* 19 Feb. 1926, 8.

180. Chepaitis, "Albert C. Ritchie," 385.

181. Brown, "Election of 1934," 416; John R. Wennersten, *Maryland's Eastern Shore: A Journey in Time and Place* (Centreville, Md.: Tidewater, 1992), 148–57.

182. Brown, "Election of 1934," 407; Brugger et al., *Maryland,* 510.

183. "300 Watermen Demand Trial for 3 Friends," *BS,* 9 Sept. 1935, 20; "3 of 4 Social Legislation Bills Passed," *BS,* 3 April 1935, 24.

184. Patrick D. Reagan, "Creating the Organizational Nexus for New Deal National Planning," in *Voluntarism, Planning, and the State: The American Planning Experience, 1914–1946,* ed. Jerold E. Brown and Patrick D. Reagan (New York: Greenwood, 1988), 85–104.

185. *Preliminary Report of the Maryland State Planning Commission* (n.p.: Maryland State Planning Commission, 1934); *Five Years of State Planning* (n.p.: Maryland State Planning Commission, 1938), 1; Brugger et al., *Maryland,* 600.

186. Walter Hollander Jr., *Abel Wolman: His Life and Philosophy, an Oral History* (Chapel Hill, N.C.: Universal, 1981), appendix.

187. Lee McCardell, "Maryland's Number One Jobholder: Abel Wolman Maintains Three Offices but Hates to Get Out of Bed," *BSSM,* 26 Apr. 1936, 5.

188. Abel Wolman, *Water, Health and Society,* ed. Gilbert F. White (Bloomington: Indiana University Press, 1969), 358. See also Abel Wolman, "The Training for the Sanitarian of Environment," *American Journal of Public Health* 14 (1924): 472–73; Abel Wolman, "The Public Health Engineer's Work," *American Journal of Public Health* 27 (1937): 329–32.

189. Gary Rubin, "Heir to the Progressives: Public Health through Public Works: Abel Wolman and the Politics of Sanitary Engineering, 1910–1940" (master's thesis, Johns Hopkins University, 1996), 14.

190. Ibid., 11.

191. Despite his aura of objectivity, in the 1970s Wolman presented himself as a pioneering environmental advocate in articles such as "What Became of Sanitary Engineering?" *Journal of the American Water Works Association* 69 (1977): 515 21. For an analysis that challenges Wolman's environmentalism by examining his role as a consultant for a major industrial polluter during the 1940s, see Mark Reutter, *Sparrows Point: Making Steel – The Rise and Ruin of American Industrial Might* (New York: Simon and Schuster, 1988), 336–41, 399–401.

192. *Conservation Problems,* 54; A. J. Nichol, *The Oyster-Packing Industry of Baltimore: Its History and Current Problems* (Baltimore: University of Maryland Press, 1937), 27.

193. *Conservation Problems,* 9, 51.

194. *Conservation Problems of Maryland,* 2nd ed. (Baltimore: Maryland State Planning Commission, 1936), 12–16.

195. "Coad Offers Bill Affecting U.S. Road Work," *BS,* 23 Mar. 1935, 22; "Proposes Change in Oyster Laws," *BS,* 10 Mar. 1935, 22; "Oystermen Ask Nice to Veto Three Bills," *BS,* 6 Apr. 1935, 12.

196. "Maryland's Oyster Policy under Attack," *BS,* 26 Jan. 1936, 18.

197. "Wolman Is Backed by Nice on Oysters," *BS,* 27 Jan. 1936, 16; "Claim Oyster Plan Means Bloodshed," *BS,* 12 Feb. 1937, 24.

198. "Oyster Conservation Bill's Defeat Predicted after House Hearing," *BS,* 5 Mar. 1937, 28.

199. Karen R. Merrill, *Public Lands and Political Meaning: Ranchers, the Government, and the Property between Them* (Berkeley: University of California Press, 2002).

200. Tidewater Man, "Maryland's Oysters," *BS,* 3 Feb. 1939, 12.

201. "Oysters, Off Season," *BS,* 17 May 1938, 10.

202. George W. Jefferson and William Rowe to Albert C. Ritchie, 16 May 1932, GGF, Confederate Soldiers Home–Conservation, "Conservation – 1932" Folder, S1041-435.

203. "Seed Area and Other Spring Oyster Removal Operations in the State," *Maryland Fisheries,* May 1934, 12–14; "A Two-Fold Benefit," *Maryland Fisheries,* May 1934, 11; "Oyster Planting about Completed," *BS,* 11 May 1934, 22.

204. Bundy and Williams, *Maryland's Chesapeake Bay,* 35–36; Santopietro, "Evolution," 379–81; Santopietro and Shabman, "Can Privatization Be Inefficient?" 413.

205. See, e.g., "Necessary Step in the Oyster Program," *BS,* 9 May 1943, 12.

206. Wilbur Marsh and Elwood Johnson quoted in "Writs Issued for 18 Oystermen," *BS,* 8 Dec. 1938, 4.

207. "30 of 40 Oystermen Arrested Are Freed," *BS,* 10 Dec. 1938, 22.

208. Richard J. Hooker, *Food and Drink in America: A History* (Indianapolis: Bobbs-Merrill, 1981), 314.

209. "Oyster-Boosting Gets Support," *BS,* 13 Jan. 1939, 14.

210. For examples of pro-leasing statements by USBF officials, see Elmer Higgins quoted in R. L. Carson, "Farming under the Chesapeake," *BSSM,* 24 Jan. 1937, 7; Robert O. Smith quoted in *Cambridge (Maryland) Democrat and News* clipping, 1933, GGF, Conservation, 1920–35, "Conservation – 1933" Folder, S1041-436.

211. "Oyster-Boosting Gets Support," *BS,* 13 Jan. 1939, 14.

212. "On the Upgrade," *Southern Fisherman's Daily Oysterman,* 7 June 1944; J. W. Schaefer, "Same Old Issue," *BS,* 9 Dec. 1943, 10; "State's Oyster Take Estimated," *BS,* 29 April 1944, 18; R. V. Truitt, "Report of the Department of Research and Education," in *Maryland Board of Natural Resources Annual Report, 1944* (Annapolis: n.p., 1945), 97–98; "Navy Agrees on Oyster Sum," *BS,* 16 July 1944, 7; "Congress to Pay State Oyster Loss," *BS,* 22 June 1951, 10.

213. Higgs, *Crisis,* 20–27, 192; Gary D. Libecap, "The Great Depression and the Regulating State: Federal Government Regulation of Agriculture, 1884–1970," in *The Defining Moment: The Great Depression and the American Economy in the Twentieth Century,* ed. Michael D. Bordo, Claudia Goldin, and Eugene N. White (Chicago: University of Chicago Press, 1998), 214–15.

214. See, e.g., Frank T. Gray, "Collective Farming on the Bay – It Doesn't Work," *BS,* 14 Jan. 1993, 17A.

215. James C. Scott, *Seeing Like a State: How Certain Schemes to Improve the Human Condition Have Failed* (New Haven: Yale University Press, 1998).

216. See, e.g., Pete Daniel, *Breaking the Land: The Transformation of Cotton, Tobacco, and Rice Cultures since 1880* (Urbana: University of Illinois Press, 1985); Jack Temple Kirby, *Rural Worlds Lost: The American South, 1920–1960* (Baton Rouge: Louisiana State University Press, 1987).

217. See, e.g., Clayton R. Koppes, "Efficiency, Equity, Esthetics: Shifting Themes in American Conservation," in *The Ends of the Earth: Perspectives on Modern Environmental History,* ed. Donald Worster (Cambridge: Cambridge University Press, 1988), 241–42; Marc Reisner, *Cadillac Desert: The American West and Its Disappearing Water* (1986; New York: Penguin, 1993); Donald Worster, *Rivers of*

Empire: Water, Aridity, and the Growth of the American West (New York: Pantheon, 1985).

218. Merrill, *Public Lands,* 190–91.

219. Tom Waller, "Expertise, Elites, and Resource Management Reform: Resisting Agricultural Water Conservation in California's Imperial Valley," *Journal of Political Ecology* 1 (1994): 20; Samuel P. Hays, *Conservation and the Gospel of Efficiency* (Cambridge: Harvard University Press, 1959); Worster, *Rivers of Empire.*

220. Susan S. Hanna, "Managing for Human and Ecological Context in the Maine Soft Shell Clam Fishery," in *Linking Social and Ecological Systems: Management Practices and Social Mechanisms for Building Resistance,* ed. Fikret Berkes and Carl Folke (Cambridge: Cambridge University Press, 1998), 208.

221. The fields of "traditional ecological knowledge" and "folk management" have gained a great deal of attention over the past three decades as scientists made the conceptual leap that "primitive" peoples, both Western and non-Western, had much to teach. However, the implementation of effective long-term collaboration between scientists and small-scale resource users still remains the exception rather than the rule. A pioneering work that drew attention to the valuable knowledge of indigenous peoples was R. E. Johannes, *Words of the Lagoon: Fishing and Marine Lore in the Palau District of Micronesia* (Berkeley: University of California Press, 1981). Numerous books and articles by natural and social scientists, especially maritime anthropologists, have since explored how to apply indigenous insights to natural resource management. They argue not only that biologists and fishery managers have a lot to learn from resource users about how nature works but also that collaborative efforts make harvesters feel validated and thus more likely to take responsibility for sustaining the resource in question. See, e.g., Dyer and McGoodwin, *Folk Management;* Berkes and Folke, *Linking Social and Ecological Systems;* Steven Mackinson, "Integrating Local and Scientific Knowledge: An Example in Fisheries Research," *Environmental Management* 27 (2001): 533–45.

222. Michael Paolisso, "Blue Crabs and Controversy on the Chesapeake Bay: A Cultural Model for Understanding Watermen's Reasoning about Blue Crab Management," *Human Organization* 61 (2002): 226–39.

Chapter 4. Postwar Pressures

1. On the effects of *Bruce v. Director, Dept. of Chesapeake Bay Affairs* (1971) and new harvesting technologies of the 1970s, see Mark M. Bundy and John B. Williams, eds., *Maryland's Chesapeake Bay Commercial Fisheries* (n.p.: Maryland Department of Natural Resources, 1978), 50–68.

2. On Bowman's career, see Geoffrey J. Martin, *The Life and Thought of Isaiah Bowman* (Hamden, Conn.: Archon, 1980); Robert Kargon and Elizabeth Hodes, "Karl Compton, Isaiah Bowman, and the Politics of Science in the Great

Depression," *Isis* 76 (1985): 301–18; Neil Smith, *American Empire: Roosevelt's Geographer and the Prelude to Globalization* (Berkeley: University of California Press, 2003), 53, 143.

3. Isaiah Bowman, "Science and Social Effects: Three Failures," *Scientific Monthly* 50 (1940): 293.

4. R. V. Truitt to Isaiah Bowman, 26 Jan. 1944, Series 2, Box 439, Folder "Truitt, R. V., Trujillo, Rafael L., Truman, Harry S.," Isaiah Bowman Papers, Ms. 58, Special Collections, Milton S. Eisenhower Library, Johns Hopkins University, Baltimore.

5. Bowman, "Science and Social Effects," 293.

6. For a contemporary use of this phrase with respect to oysters by a Chesapeake insider, see Curtis L. Newcombe, "The Study of Conservation," *Journal of Higher Education* 16 (1945): 300.

7. John F. Reiger, *American Sportsmen and the Origins of Conservation* (New York: Winchester, 1975); Richard W. Judd, *Common Lands, Common People: The Origins of Conservation in Northern New England* (Cambridge: Harvard University Press, 2000).

8. Mark David Spence, *Dispossessing the Wilderness: Indian Removal and the Making of National Parks* (New York: Oxford University Press, 1999); Louis S. Warren, *The Hunter's Game: Poachers and Conservationists in Twentieth-Century America* (New Haven: Yale University Press, 1997); Karl Jacoby, *Crimes against Nature: Squatters, Poachers, Thieves, and the Hidden History of American Conservation* (Berkeley: University of California Press, 2001).

9. C. John Sullivan, *Waterfowling on the Chesapeake, 1819–1936* (Baltimore: Johns Hopkins University Press, 2003), 3, 73, 83–89; William B. Cronin, *The Disappearing Islands of the Chesapeake* (Baltimore: Johns Hopkins University Press, 2005), 59.

10. Bill Ackerman, "On Fishing," *WP,* 9 Oct. 1938, X6; Robert H. Connery, *Governmental Problems in Wild Life Conservation* (New York: Columbia University Press, 1935), 139.

11. "Promising Suggestion," *BS,* 3 Dec. 1938, 8; "The Good Intentions of Governor Nice," *BS,* 16 Oct. 1938, 8.

12. Harry W. Kirwin, *The Inevitable Success: A Biography of Herbert R. O'Conor* (Westminster, Md.: Newman, 1962), 203, 224, 230.

13. Louis Azrael, *Baltimore News-Post,* 6 Sept. 1938, quoted in Kirwin, *Inevitable Success,* 211.

14. "Good Start for O'Conor," *WP,* 7 Jan. 1939, 5.

15. "Glenn Martin, Air Pioneer, Dead at 69," *WP,* 5 Dec. 1955, 1; "Glenn Martin's League of Sportsmen Folding," *WP,* 16 Nov. 1958, C11.

16. Bowman quoted in "O'Conor Holds Patronage as Assembly Whip," *WP,* 12 Feb. 1939, 12.

17. Kirwin, *Inevitable Success,* 236.

18. See, e.g., Otis L. Graham Jr., *Toward a Planned Society: From Roosevelt to Nixon* (New York: Oxford University Press, 1976), 36–44; Karen R. Merrill, *Public Lands and Political Meaning: Ranchers, the Government, and the Property between Them* (Berkeley: University of California Press, 2002).

19. Aldo Leopold, "Conservation Economics," *Journal of Forestry* 32 (1934): 537–44; V. E. Shelford, "Conservation of Wildlife," in *Our Natural Resources and Their Conservation,* ed. A. E. Parkins and J. R. Whitaker (1939; New York: Wiley, 1949), 479. See also Connery, *Governmental Problems,* esp. 177.

20. Jeanne Nienaber Clarke, *Roosevelt's Warrior: Harold L. Ickes and the New Deal* (Baltimore: Johns Hopkins University Press, 1996), 120–28, 231–34, 268, 372; Neil M. Maher, *Nature's New Deal: The Civilian Conservation Corps and the Roots of the American Environmental Movement* (Oxford: Oxford University Press, 2008), 196–209.

21. See Robert H. Archer, "Conserving the State's Resources," *BS,* 16 Jan. 1939, 8; "Impending Muddle," *BS,* 20 Jan. 1939, 12; Edwin Warfield Jr., "Conservation Legislation," *BS,* 21 Jan. 1939, 10. See also Kirwin, *Inevitable Success,* 235–38.

22. "Oystermen Seek Voice in New Laws," *BS,* 10 Feb. 1939, 6; "Tongers and Dredgers Agree to Work Together," *BS,* 17 Feb. 1939, 4; H.O., "Conservation Unity," *BS,* 23 Feb. 1941, 10; "Recapitulation," *BS,* 2 Mar. 1939, 10.

23. Connery, *Governmental Problems,* 230.

24. P. Elliott Burroughs quoted in Louis J. O'Donnell, "O'Conor Drops Conservation Plan of Board," *BS,* 27 Feb. 1939, 16.

25. O'Conor quoted in ibid., 8.

26. Swepson Earle to Clarence W. Miles, 4 Dec. 1938, Series 6, Box 9, Folder "Maryland Committee on the Structure of the Maryland State Government, 1938," Bowman Papers; Swepson Earle to Herbert R. O'Conor, 1 Mar. 1939, cited in Kirwin, *Inevitable Success,* 240.

27. *BES,* 1 Mar. 1939, and "O'Conor Proposes Sensible Conservation Program," *Crisfield (Maryland) Times,* 3 Mar. 1939, both quoted in Kirwin, *Inevitable Success,* 242–43. For other criticisms of O'Conor, see "Mr. O'Conor Walks Out," *BS,* 28 Feb. 1939, 8; "They Asked for It," *BS,* 3 Mar. 1939, 14; "Long and Expensive Death," *BS,* 9 Mar. 1939, 12.

28. *BS,* 11 Mar. 1939, quoted in Kirwin, *Inevitable Success,* 243; "Bay Conservation Bill Passes House," *BS,* 15 Mar. 1939, 24.

29. Stephen E. Fitzgerald, "Conservationists Split on Plan for Referendum," *BES,* 2 June 1939; "How Conservation Stands," *BES,* 7 Nov. 1940.

30. Harry Haller, "Baltimore's First Outdoor-Life Show," *Baltimore Sunday Sun,* 28 Nov. 1937, 9.

31. Swepson Earle to Clarence W. Miles, 4 Dec. 1938, Series 6, Box, 9, Folder "Maryland Committee on the Structure of the Maryland State Government, 1938," Bowman Papers.

32. H. Lee Hoffman obituary, *BS,* 26 June 1980; "Given Post on U.S. Fisheries Bureau," *BS,* n.d., clipping in Hoffman Collection, Box 2, Folder "Maryland Outdoor Life Federation – Newsclippings (II), 1935–49," Harry Lee Hoffman Jr. Collection, MS 2583, H. Furlong Baldwin Library, Maryland Historical Society, Baltimore.

33. Harry Lee Hoffman, "Annual Report of the President," 31 Mar. 1939, 4, Box 1, Folder 2, Hoffman Collection.

34. Stephen H. Ford, Letter to the Editor, *BS,* 7 June 1940, 16.

35. "First Things First in the Conservation Problem," *BS,* 7 June 1940, 16.

36. Senator Louis N. Phipps quoted in N. T. Kenney, "Dize Blames State for Oyster Fight," *BS,* 13 Mar. 1941, 8.

37. On the slow maturation of interwar ecological science and its struggle "to find its place in American society," see Sharon E. Kingsland, *The Evolution of American Ecology, 1890–2000* (Baltimore: Johns Hopkins University Press, 2005), 154; Donald Worster, *Dust Bowl: The Southern Plains in the 1930s* (New York: Oxford University Press, 1979), chap. 13.

38. "Fisheries Plan Is Rejected by Voters," *BS,* 6 Nov. 1940, 24; "Hoffman Accuses Conservation Foes," *BES,* 3 Dec. 1940. *BS* editorials include: "We Shall Grow Up," 16 Mar. 1939, 12; "One and Inseparable," 21 Mar. 1939, 12; "Mr. Labrot's Chance," 1 Apr. 1939, 8; "Toward Rationality," 8 June 1939, 12. See also "Defeat It," *BES,* 8 Oct. 1940. See also Hoffman Collection, Box 2, Folder "Maryland Outdoor Life Federation – Newsclippings (III), 1935–1949."

39. Edward O'Malley, Letter to the Editor, *BS,* 5 Nov. 1940, 12.

40. "O'Conor Names Group on Conservation Plan," *BS,* 5 Dec. 1940, 7; "Unified Maryland Resources Body Urged," *BES,* 11 Dec. 1940; Peter C. Chambliss, "Fisherman's Luck," *BS,* 23 Feb. 1941, 9.

41. For more details, see Christine Keiner, "Scientists, Oystermen, and Maryland Oyster Conservation Politics, 1880–1969: A Study of Two Cultures" (PhD diss., Johns Hopkins University, 2000), chap. 4.

42. "Conservation Report Sent to Lawmakers," *BS,* 25 Jan. 1941, 22; "Conservation Measure Passed by Senate, 21–6," *BS,* 29 Mar. 1941, 8; "Conservation Bill Passed by House," *BS,* 30 Mar. 1941, 24.

43. H.O., "Conservation Unity: Its Present Status," *BS,* 23 Feb. 1941, 10; Peter C. Chambliss, "Fisherman's Luck," *BS,* 23 Feb. 1941, Sports 9. On the decline of bay (as opposed to tributary) Chesapeake oysters, see "Baetjer Outlines Ideas on Oysters," *BS,* 21 Jan. 1944, 4.

44. *Maryland Board of Natural Resources Twenty-first Annual Report, 1964* (Annapolis: n.p., 1965), 22, 192.

45. *Maryland Board of Natural Resources Annual Report, 1944* (Annapolis: n.p., 1945), 36; *Seventeenth Annual Report of the Conservation Department of Maryland, 1939* (Annapolis: n.p., 1940), 14–15, 133–34.

46. "2 Back Stand in Oyster Bar Dredging Okay," *BS,* 4 Jan. 1944, 8; "Board Renews Dredging Ban at Hodges Bar," *BS,* 5 Jan. 1944, 20; "Baetjer Raps War-

field on Conservation," *BS,* 6 Jan. 1944, 20; "Truitt Holds Flood Caused Oyster Loss," *BS,* 10 Jan. 1944, 16; "Oysters Are Dead on Many Bay Bars," *BS,* 14 Oct. 1946, 26. See also Keiner, "Scientists," chap. 4.

47. *Popham v. Conservation Commission,* Department of Tidewater Fisheries 186 (Md.) 62 (1946); "Appeals Court Hears County Oyster Case," *Annapolis Evening Capital,* 15 Jan. 1946, 1; "State Is Upheld on Oyster Area," *BS,* 16 Mar. 1946, 22; "Some Oystermen Fight in Support of Conservation," *BS,* 26 May 1946, 14.

48. N. T. Kenney, "Fisheries Group Ouster Is Aim," *BES,* 17 Feb. 1947, 32; "Oystermen Meet on Shore," *BS,* 17 Feb. 1947.

49. Oscar L. Dodds to William Preston Lane, 1 Mar. 1947, GGF, Fisheries–Fre, 1947–48, Folder "Legislation Proposed – FISHERIES, 1947," S1041-873.

50. "2 Introduce Oyster Lease," *BS,* 27 Feb. 1947, 8; David Stickle, "Oyster-Rock Bill Is Urged," *BS,* 12 Mar. 1947, 14; "The Protesting Oystermen and the Need for Facts," *BS,* 14 Mar. 1947, 12; "Senate Okays Ripper Bill Abolishing Tidewater Unit," *BES,* 18 Mar. 1947; "Edwin Warfield, Jr.," *BS,* 24 Feb. 1939; "Edwin Warfield, Jr. Dies," *BES,* 20 Nov. 1952. See also Keiner, "Scientists," chaps. 4–5.

51. "Lane Offers Tidewater Proposals," *BS,* 18 Mar. 1949, 38; "Lane's Oyster Plan Assailed," *BS,* 22 Mar. 1949, 15; "Conservation Setback," *BS,* 29 Mar. 1949; "While the Chesapeake Bay's Natural Resources Dwindle," *BS,* 19 Apr. 1949, 14; "Lane Vetoes Tidewater Measure," *Annapolis Evening Capital,* 7 May 1949.

52. Baltimore County state senator John Grason Turnbull quoted in Thomas O'Neill, "Brice Gets Post in Deal with GOP," *BS,* 10 Jan. 1951, 28; "Sportsmen's Club Opposed to Brice," *BS,* 23 Nov. 1950, 11; Thomas O'Neill, "Anti-Brice Revolt Halts Legislature," *BS,* 9 Jan. 1951, 30, "Brice Has 'No Definite Ideas' on State Sea-Food Problems," *BS,* 16 Jan. 1951, 28.

53. Hugh Brannen, "Maryland Wardens Called 'Hamstrung,'" *WP,* 12 Jan. 1955, 28. On Brice's tenure, see Keiner, "Scientists," chap. 6.

54. "In Memoriam: The Bay Oyster," *BS,* 26 Mar. 1949, 8; Deborah B. Morrison, "An Old Waterman Visits the Flower Show," *BS,* 2 Mar. 1951; H. Lee Hoffman to William Bayliff, 9 Aug. 1956, Hoffman Collection, Box 2, Folder "Maryland Conservation Federation – Correspondence 1951–58."

55. See Merrill, *Public Lands,* esp. 257–62.

56. "Who Wouldn't Like to Be Given a Free Farm?" *BS,* 22 Feb. 1947, 6. See also the following *BS* editorials: "The Leasing Program: An Opportunity for the Oystermen," 27 Feb. 1947, 14; "Does Maryland Want a Thriving Oyster Industry," 12 Mar. 1947, 10; "The Protesting Oystermen and the Need for Facts," 14 Mar. 1947, 12; "The Inland Legislators Have a Stake in the Bay," 18 Mar. 1947, 16; "Is the Reward for Duty to Be Political Oblivion?" 19 Mar. 1947, 12.

57. Robert Preston Lambden, Letter to the Editor, *BS,* 22 Feb. 1947, 6.

58. Frederick Jackson Turner, "The Significance of the Frontier in American History," in *Report of the American Historical Association* (1894), 199–227. For helpful definitions of the *frontier* and the Turner thesis, see Edward L. Schapsmeier

and Frederick H. Schapsmeier, *Encyclopedia of American Agricultural History* (Westport, Conn.: Greenwood, 1975), 136, 354.

59. Merrill, *Public Lands,* 176.

60. Ibid., 157.

61. Ibid., 42.

62. A. W. Anderson and E. A. Power, *Fishery Statistics of the United States 1946* (Washington, D.C.: U.S. Government Printing Office, 1950), 135.

63. James P. Connelly, "Oyster Gets a New Lease on Life," *WP,* 17 Dec. 1950, B6.

64. Joseph G. Knapp, *The Rise of American Cooperative Enterprise, 1620–1920* (Danville, Ill.: Interstate, 1969), chap. 5.

65. Joseph G. Knapp, *The Advance of American Cooperative Enterprise, 1920–1945* (Danville, Ill.: Interstate, 1973), 466–67.

66. "A New Role for Senator Goldstein," *BS,* 14 Dec. 1947, 14.

67. "Senator Goldstein's Plan to Save the Bay Oysters," *BS,* 8 Mar. 1948, 10.

68. "Plan Offered for Lease of Oyster Bars," *BS,* 7 Mar. 1948, 28.

69. Ibid.; "Calvert Oystermen Vote to Consider 'Leasing' Program," *Annapolis Southern Maryland Times,* 26 Mar. 1948, 1.

70. R. B. Taney, "Under the Dome of the State House," *Annapolis Southern Maryland Times,* 5 Mar. 1948, 19 Mar. 1948.

71. Louis Goldstein obituary, *BS,* 4 July 1998.

72. The accusation still stung four decades later. See Louis L. Goldstein to Frank T. Gray, 14 Jan. 1993, personal files of Frank T. Gray. I am grateful to Gray for granting permission to quote from this document. On the tendency to conflate cooperatives with socialism and communism, see Gene Ingalsbe and Frank Groves, "Historical Development," in *Cooperatives in Agriculture,* ed. David W. Cobia (Englewood Cliffs, N.J.: Prentice-Hall, 1989), 106–20, 107. On the historical roots of U.S. cooperatives, see Knapp, *Rise.*

73. Louis L. Goldstein to Frank T. Gray, 14 Jan. 1993, personal files of Frank T. Gray. On the rise of Sunkist Growers, see Joseph G. Knapp, *Farmers in Business: Studies in Cooperative Enterprise* (Washington, D.C.: American Institute of Cooperation, 1963), chap. 5; Knapp, *Rise,* chap. 13; Douglas Cazaux Sackman, *Orange Empire: California and the Fruits of Eden* (Berkeley: University of California Press, 2005), chap. 3.

74. Louis L. Goldstein to Frank T. Gray, 14 Jan. 1993, personal files of Frank T. Gray.

75. "Bay Leasing Is Indorsed," *BS,* 25 Feb. 1947. On Goldstein's desire to begin co-op operations on Flag Pond Oyster Rock, see "Plan Offered for Lease of Oyster Bars," *BS,* 7 Mar. 1948, 28; "Calvert Oystermen Vote to Consider 'Leasing' Program," *Annapolis Southern Maryland Times,* 26 Mar. 1948, 1.

76. Merrill, *Public Lands,* analyzes the cyclical debates between the federal government and public-land ranchers over the use of the western range.

77. Although the CBL was located in Goldstein's district, Goldstein and Truitt did not get along, and thus it is likely that they developed their cooperative-leasing initiatives independently. On public feuds between the two men, see "Seeks Answer on Wallace," *BS,* 11 Oct. 1950, 6; "No Privacy for Dr. Truitt," *BS,* 6 Mar. 1952.

78. The DTF's legislative appropriation, which derived from general state taxes, far exceeded that of any of the other four departments under the Board of Natural Resources, and the money collected via license fees, fines, and fishing industry taxes further raised the DTF's available funds to $381,000 ("Research Group's Request Ignored," *BS,* 17 Feb. 1943, 26; *BS,* 5 Apr. 1943, 10; *Maryland Board of Natural Resources Annual Report, 1944,* 117).

79. Examples of the CBL's work during this period, in addition to monitoring oyster spat sets and testing optimal shell-planting periods, included genetic and migratory studies of shad and croaker populations, analyses of marine borers and other pests, evaluations of commercial fish hatcheries, and the development of fish marking methods and techniques for rearing shad in ponds ("Research on the Fisheries," *Maryland Tidewater News* 7 [June 1950]: 1).

80. Frank Henry, "Chesapeake Bay Is His Oyster," *BS,* 6 Aug. 1950, A3.

81. See Wayne D. Rasmussen, *Taking the University to the People: Seventy-five Years of Cooperative Extension* (Ames: Iowa State University Press, 1989), chap. 8; A. B. Graham, "Boys' and Girls' Agricultural Clubs," *Agricultural History* 15.2 (1941): 65–68.

82. "Annual Report, Department of Research and Education," *Maryland Board of Natural Resources Eighth Annual Report, 1951* (Annapolis: n.p., 1952), 168–69.

83. Likewise, the steadfast leasing supporters on the *BS*'s editorial board expressed the hope that the program would give rise to "a more objective and reasoned" generation of watermen who might "voice their indignation over the present folly of oyster operations in the bay and demand their right to farm the bay beds intelligently" ("The Limited Future of Young Oyster Farmers," *BS,* 16 Nov. 1950, 18). On the desire to stem outmigration, see Audrey Bishop, "Calvert County Boys Starting at Bottom," *BS,* 27 Mar. 1949, A5; E.L.J., "Going to School about Oysters," *BS,* 27 Nov. 1951, 16.

84. The exception was Wicomico County, which experienced a 73 percent growth rate thanks to the city of Salisbury, a lumber and agricultural shipping center and home to a state university and medical center (John R. Wennersten, *Maryland's Eastern Shore: A Journey in Time and Place* [Centreville, Md.: Tidewater, 1992], 75–77).

85. "Student Oyster Farming Proposed," *BS,* 10 Feb. 1951, 7; E.L.J., "Going to School about Oysters," *BS,* 27 Nov. 1951, 16).

86. For an example of Webster's pro-leasing activism, see Richard Webster, "The Oyster Packer's Side," *BES,* 6 Mar. 1947.

87. James A. Flood, "Shore Packer Urges Oyster-Farm System," *BES,* 13 Sept. 1956; "Deal Island Pupils Give Oyster Farming Lesson," *BES,* 10 June 1958; S. Russell Bozman, "Young Oyster Farmers," *BS,* 9 Aug. 1958; *Maryland Board of Natural Resources Ninth Annual Report, 1952* (Annapolis: n.p., 1953), 159.

88. On other scattered efforts during the 1950s to establish Chesapeake oyster cooperatives, see Keiner, "Scientists," chap. 5.

89. Tom Horton, *An Island Out of Time: A Memoir of Smith Island in the Chesapeake* (New York: Norton, 1996), 11.

90. "The Smith Islanders Look to Oyster Leasing," *BS,* 31 Jan. 1950, 12.

91. "Clark Is Rejected; Harrison Quits," *BES,* 2 Apr. 1949, 10; "Lane Vetoes Tidewater Measure," *Annapolis Evening Capital,* 7 May 1949.

92. "David H. Wallace Appointed Chairman of Fisheries Group," *BS,* 5 Apr. 1949, 32; Anne W. Hutchinson, "Fisheries' Unit Study Is Asked," *BS,* 28 Mar. 1950, 32.

93. "The Smith Islanders Look to Oyster Leasing," *BS,* 31 Jan. 1950, 12.

94. John R. Wennersten, *The Oyster Wars of Chesapeake Bay* (Centreville, Md.: Tidewater, 1981), 107–9.

95. CTFM, 1947–51, 1 Dec. 1949, 115, S321-1; Janice Marshall quoted in Horton, *Island Out of Time,* 106; James M. Cannon, "Smith Island Oystermen Triple Incomes since Taking Leases," *BS,* 24 Feb. 1952, 32.

96. John Van Camp, "Smith Island Oystermen Plan to Add Bay Acreage in Lease," *BS,* 6 Feb. 1950, 17.

97. CTFM, 1947–51, 1 Dec. 1949, 115, S321-1.

98. Wallace quoted in "Smith Island Starts Oyster Co-op," *BS,* 30 Jan. 1950, 24.

99. Ibid.

100. CTFM, 1947–51, 1 Dec. 1949, 118, S321-1.

101. Ibid., 118.

102. Quoted in John Van Camp, "Smith Islanders Take Co-op Steps," *BS,* 27 Dec. 1950, 4.

103. Horton, *Island Out of Time,* 90.

104. CTFM, 1947–51, 1 Dec. 1949, 117, S321-1.

105. John Van Camp, "Smith Islanders Take Co-op Steps," *BS,* 27 Dec. 1950, 4.

106. Michael K. Orbach, "Fishery Cooperatives on the Chesapeake Bay: Advantage or Anachronism?" *Anthropological Quarterly* 53 (1980): 48–55.

107. CTFM, 1947–51, 1 Dec. 1949, 117, S321-1.

108. Ibid., 115.

109. Wennersten, *Oyster Wars,* 108, 113.

110. "Watermen Ask Oyster Loan," *BS,* 1 Feb. 1950, 20; James M. Cannon, "Smith Island Oystermen Triple Incomes since Taking Leases," *BS,* 24 Feb. 1952, 32.

111. Prentiss W. Evans quoted in John Van Camp, "Oyster Plan Waits Money," *BS,* 7 Feb. 1950, 17.

112. Ibid. On the banks for cooperatives, see Knapp, *Advance,* 253, 403–4.

113. "Smith Island Starts Oyster Co-op," *BS,* 30 Jan. 1950, 24.

114. John Van Camp, "Oyster Plan Waits Money," *BS,* 7 Feb. 1950, 17.

115. John Van Camp, "Smith Island Oystermen Plan to Add Bay Acreage in Lease," *BS,* 6 Feb. 1950, 26.

116. Garrett Power, "More about Oysters Than You Wanted to Know," *Maryland Law Review* 30 (1970): 199–225.

117. "Oyster Co-op Plan Denied," *BS,* 20 Apr. 1950, 38.

118. Power, "More about Oysters," 212.

119. Janice Marshall quoted in Horton, *Island Out of Time,* 106.

120. "Available Oyster Rocks Total 1,000 Acres," *BES,* 9 Dec. 1950; "Court Ruling Aids Plan for Oyster Co-op," *BS,* 9 Dec. 1950, 24, 9; *Department of Tidewater Fisheries v. Catlin,* 196 Md. 530 (1950).

121. "Exciting Prospects for Maryland Watermen," *BS,* 10 Dec. 1950, 16.

122. Ibid.

123. *Maryland Board of Natural Resources Eighth Annual Report, 1951,* 9. In addition to the 750 acres in Tangier Sound, the islanders also obtained leaseholds on the bay side of the island. On the state's inability to set up a crop mortgage agreement, see John Van Camp, "Oyster Plan Waits Money," *BS,* 7 Feb. 1950, 17.

124. "The Smith Islanders Look to Oyster Leasing," *BS,* 31 Jan. 1950, 12.

125. Quoted in James M. Cannon, "Smith Islanders Look to Harvest," *BS,* 25 Feb. 1952, 26.

126. James M. Cannon, "Smith Island Oystermen Triple Incomes since Taking Leases," *BS,* 24 Feb. 1952, 32. Co-op members agreed to take only ten bushels per day and to return shells and undersized oysters to the beds.

127. Corbin quoted in ibid.

128. James A. Flood, "Best Years So Far for Oyster Co-op," *BS,* 18 Jan. 1954, 17; "Oystermen Fined," *WP,* 7 Jan. 1953, 22.

129. CTFM, 1956–59, 4 Feb. 1958, 73, 8 Apr. 1958, 80–82, S321-3.

130. "Cooperative Oyster Farm Venture in Bay Folding Up," *BS,* 24 Jan. 1958; "New Try on Leasing," *BES,* 9 Feb. 1960.

131. James Wharton, "Woes of the Oyster Planter," *BS,* 29 Mar. 1955, A1; James S. Keat, "Watermen Gamble on Oystering," *BS,* 17 July 1958.

132. James S. Keat, "Watermen Gamble on Oystering," *BS,* 17 July 1958.

133. Janice Marshall quoted in Horton, *Island Out of Time,* 106.

134. For analyses of subsistence regimes that call into question mainstream assumptions about what constitutes rational economic behavior, see Arthur J. Vidich and Joseph Bensmen, *Small Town in Mass Society: Class, Power, and Religion in a Rural Community* (Princeton: Princeton University Press, 1958); James C. Scott, *The Moral Economy of the Peasant* (New Haven: Yale University Press, 1976),

which coined the phrase "subsistence ethic." For relevant studies set in the context of Maryland's Eastern Shore from the 1970s through 1990s, see Boyd Gibbons, *Wye Island: Outsiders, Insiders and Change in a Chesapeake Community* (1977; Washington, D.C.: Resources for the Future, 2007); Meredith Ramsay, *Community, Culture, and Economic Development: The Social Roots of Local Action* (Albany: State University of New York Press, 1996).

135. "Oyster-Leasing Ban Sped for Somerset," *BES,* 13 Feb. 1953, 25; "Oyster Leasing Ban Is O.K.'d by M'Keldin," *BES,* 17 Mar. 1953, 14.

136. John Van Camp, "Big Oyster-Law Changes Proposed," *BS,* 31 Jan. 1953, 22; Harrington quoted in John Van Camp, "Oystermen Lodge 350 Complaints," *BS,* 25 Feb. 1953, 34; Charles G. Whiteford, "House Beats Down 'Oyster Farming' Bill," *BS,* 5 Mar. 1953, 36; Charles G. Whiteford, "'Oyster Farm' Measure Dies," *BS,* 7 Mar. 1953, 26.

137. Henry L. Trewhitt, "Byrd as Head of Fisheries Unit," *BS,* 8 May 1959.

138. George H. Calcott, *The University of Maryland at College Park: A History* (Baltimore: Noble House, 2005), 80–81.

139. Ibid., 71; "Not Dr. Byrd," *BS,* 9 May 1959. For the antipathy between Byrd and Truitt, see R. V. Truitt to Ernest N. Cory, 3 July 1972, 5, Reginald V. Truitt Papers, Box 1, Folder 3, UML; R. V. Truitt to H. C. Byrd, 1 July 1940, Truitt Papers, Box 1, Folder 1.

140. "New Tidewater Fisheries Commission Faces a Great Industrial Challenge," *Crisfield (Maryland) Times,* 5 June 1959; "Byrd Should Head Tidewater Fisheries Commission," *Maryland Gazette,* 14 May 1959, Series 4, Box 3, Folder "Clippings 1959," Harry Clifton Byrd Papers, UML.

141. Laurence Stern, "Curly Byrd Makes Big Tracks Again," *WP,* 2 Aug. 1959, E2.

142. J. W. Anderson and Laurence Stern, "Virginian Killed in Oyster Feud," *WP,* 9 Apr. 1959, A1; Laurence Stern, "Curly Byrd Makes Big Tracks Again," *WP,* 2 Aug. 1959, E2. On other police reforms and the creation of the bistate Potomac River Fisheries Commission, see Wennersten, *Oyster Wars,* chap. 6.

143. *Maryland Board of Natural Resources Seventeenth Annual Report, 1960* (Annapolis: n.p., 1961), 25.

144. Henry L. Trewhitt, "Oyster Aid Seen under Bay Floor," *BS,* 25 June 1959, 21. Maryland biologists had long promoted dredging for fossil shell; see, e.g., "New Oyster Shell Source Looms," *BES,* 26 June 1948.

145. "Politics Out, Byrd Says," *BES,* 17 Dec. 1959; Kennedy Ludlam, "Economic Importance of Sports Fishermen Is Becoming Apparent," *WP,* 3 June 1960, C6.

146. H. C. Byrd, Speech, ca. 1960, Series 2, Subseries 2, Box 2, Folder "Speeches," Byrd Papers.

147. Henry L. Trewhitt, "Byrd Admits Oyster Plan Has Hit Rocks," *BS,* 13 Feb. 1960, 17; Henry L. Trewhitt, "Byrd's Unit Retreats on Legislation," *BS,* 16 Feb.

1960, 21; "Byrd Pushes Oyster Plan, Asks Power to Lease Sites," *BS,* 12 Mar. 1960, 18; Henry L. Trewhitt, "Byrd Predicts Assembly Will Enact Seafood Bill," *BS,* 28 Sept. 1960, 40; "Oyster Bed Plan Killed," *BS,* 1 Nov. 1960.

148. "Tawes Releases Oyster Bills Giving TFC More Development Powers," *BES,* 10 Jan. 1961; Henry L. Trewhitt, "Byrd's Oyster Plan Assailed," *BS,* 3 Feb. 1961, 28; "Measures to Curb Wide Agency Power Called Certain," *BES,* 3 Feb. 1961.

149. *Maryland Board of Natural Resources Eighteenth Annual Report, 1961* (Annapolis: n.p., 1962), 124.

150. "Byrd Program: Fisheries Chairman Loses Two of His Three Positions," *BES,* 1 Apr. 1961; Power, "More about Oysters," 215.

151. Kenneth D. Durr, *Behind the Backlash: White Working-Class Politics in Baltimore, 1940–1980* (Chapel Hill: University of North Carolina Press, 2003), 9.

152. On discrimination at Hopkins, see Neil Smith, *American Empire,* 247.

153. David S. Brown, *Richard Hofstadter: An Intellectual Biography* (Chicago: University of Chicago Press, 2006), 39, 47; Richard Hofstadter, *Anti-Intellectualism in American Life* (New York: Vintage, 1962).

154. "Tawes Samples Menu for State's Fair Exhibit," *WP,* 15 June 1962, D3.

155. Barbara Mills, *"Got My Mind Set on Freedom": Maryland's Story of Black and White Activism, 1663–2000* (Bowie, Md.: Heritage, 2002), 232; Calcott, *Maryland and America,* 155.

156. "Picketing of Md. Fair Restaurant Threatened to Spotlight State Bias," *Chicago Daily Defender,* 15 Nov. 1962, 6; Mills, *"Got My Mind,"* 319.

157. Brown, *Richard Hofstadter,* 47.

158. *The Case for Fair Representation in Maryland* (n.p: Maryland Committee for Fair Representation, 1962), Box 1, Folder "Maryland Committee for Fair Representation," Archives of the Montgomery County Committee for Fair Representation, UML.

159. Wendell P. Bradley, "'Shore' Still an Island, Like England," *WP,* 5 Mar. 1961, E2.

160. *Case for Fair Representation,* 2.

161. Ibid.

162. *Colegrove v. Green,* 328 U.S. 549 (1946).

163. The Supreme Court's four landmark reapportionment decisions concerned cases brought by urban southern plaintiffs: Tennessee's *Baker v. Carr* (369 U.S. 186 [1962]), which deemed the question of reapportionment justiciable; Georgia's *Gray v. Sanders* (373 U.S. 368 [1963]), which applied the "one person, one vote" principle to statewide primary elections; *Wesberry v. Sanders* (376 U.S. 1 [1964]), which applied the principle to the U.S. House of Representatives; and Alabama's *Reynolds v. Sims* (377 U.S. 533 [1964]), which applied that principle to bicameral state legislatures. For overviews, see Robert B. McKay, *Reapportionment: The Law and Politics of Equal Representation* (New York: Twentieth Century

Fund, 1965); Richard C. Cortner, *The Apportionment Cases* (Knoxville: University of Tennessee Press, 1970).

164. Wendell P. Bradley, "Legislators Criticize Tawes Bill, Recess," *WP,* 26 May 1962, A1; Wendell P. Bradley, "Apportion Bills Gain in Senate," *WP,* 31 May 1962, A1; Charles Whiteford, "Tawes's Stop-Gap Reapportionment Plan Is Passed," *BS,* 1 June 1962, A1; McKay, *Reapportionment,* 110.

165. *The Unfinished Business of Reapportionment in Maryland*" (n.p.: Maryland Committee for Fair Representation, ca. 1963), Box 1, Folder "Maryland Committee for Fair Representation," Archives of the Montgomery County Committee for Fair Representation.

166. Mills, *"Got My Mind,"* 320.

167. Quoted in James E. Clayton, "Key States' Rural Lawmakers Resist Loss of Power by Reapportionment," *WP,* 4 June 1962, 1.

168. Hugh Brannen, "Time nor Tide Waits on Chesapeake Bay," *WP,* 15 Feb. 1953, C4; Maryland Board of Natural Resources, Department of Research and Education, *The Commercial Fisheries of Maryland* (Solomons Island, Md.: Chesapeake Biological Laboratory, 1953) 20.

169. Hugh Brannen, "Rockfish Protective Association Forms," *WP,* 12 Nov. 1954, 61; Hugh Brannen, "Rockfish Protectors Ready for Battle," *WP,* 7 Jan. 1955, 33.

170. Hugh Brannen, [untitled], *WP,* 17 Feb. 1955, 18; George Bowen, "Rockfish Bill Beaten in House," *WP,* 26 Feb. 1955, 22; Frank R. Kent Jr., "Perkins Cites Trebled Budget," *WP,* 2 Mar. 1955, 18.

171. For the most sustained critique of Schweinhaut's position, see Hugh Brannen, "Marylanders Modest in Rockfish Demands," *WP,* 20 Mar. 1955, C6).

172. Quoted in Jo-Ann Armao, "In Md., a Masterly 34 Years in Politics," *WP,* 20 Mar. 1989, D5.

173. Hugh Brannen, "Marylanders Modest in Rockfish Demands," *WP,* 20 Mar. 1955, C6.

174. Hugh Brannen, [untitled], *WP,* 17 Feb. 1955, 18.

175. Ralph C. Hammer and R. V. Truitt, "Control of Fishing Intensity in Maryland," *Transactions of the American Fisheries Society* 71 (1941): 144–48; R. E. Tiller, *The Maryland Fishery Management Plan* (Solomons Island: Chesapeake Biological Laboratory, 1944); R. E. Tiller, *The Maryland Management Plan and the Rock Industry* (Solomons Island, Chesapeake Biological Laboratory, 1944); *Maryland Board of Natural Resources Fourth Annual Report, 1947* (Annapolis: n.p., 1948), 181; "Wallace Discusses Fish Management Plan in Maryland," *Annapolis Evening Capital,* 13 Feb. 1948; Ralph Murdock, "Fish Conservation Program Paying Off," *WP,* 22 Sept. 1950.

176. Francis T. Christy Jr. and Anthony Scott, *The Common Wealth in Ocean Fisheries: Some Problems of Growth and Economic Allocation* (Baltimore: Johns Hopkins University Press, 1965); Helen M. Rozwadowski, *The Sea Knows No*

Boundaries: A Century of Marine Science under ICES (Seattle: University of Washington Press and International Council for the Exploration of the Sea, 2002), chap. 5; Arthur F. McEvoy, *The Fisherman's Problem: Law and Ecology in the California Fisheries, 1850-1980* (New York: Cambridge University Press, 1986), chaps. 8-9.

177. On Wallace's resignation, see "Seeks Answer on Wallace," *BS,* 11 Oct. 1950, 6; "Wallace Denies Any Politics in Resignation," *BES,* 12 Oct. 1950; "Disconcerting Rumor about the Tidewater Fisheries Post," *BS,* 18 Nov. 1950, 8; Thomas O'Neill, "Brice Gets Post in Deal with GOP," *BS,* 10 Jan. 1951, 30; *Maryland Tidewater News,* Oct. 1950, 3. For Wallace's criticisms of Maryland oyster management, see David H. Wallace, "Ecology, Water Conservation, and the Shellfisheries," *Scientific Monthly* 73 (1951): 352-53; James S. Keat, "Wallace Urges Revision in State Oyster Program," *BS,* 12 Mar. 1958, A13.

178. Wallace, "Ecology," 349-50.

179. Hugh Brannen, "Marylanders Modest in Rockfish Demands," *WP,* 20 Mar. 1955, C6.

180. Aubrey Graves, "10 Less 10 Equals 10, Say Rockfish Hogs," *WP,* 12 Nov. 1957, A23.

181. Hugh Brannen, "Marylanders Modest in Rockfish Demands," *WP,* 20 Mar. 1955, C6; Jo-Ann Armao, "In Md., a Masterly 34 Years in Politics," *WP,* 20 Mar. 1989, D5.

182. Quoted in Wendell P. Bradley, "Maryland Rockfish Mysteriously Angles into Redistricting and Welfare Debates," *WP,* 20 Mar. 1961, B8.

183. Ibid., B8.

184. See, e.g., "Bill Offered to Limit Rockfish Catch by Sports Fishermen," *WP,* 26 Feb. 1967, C8; C. Boyd Pfeiffer, "Time for the Angler to Pay," *WP,* 13 Apr. 1973, D11.

185. Wendell P. Bradley, "Maryland Rockfish Mysteriously Angles into Redistricting and Welfare Debates," *WP,* 20 Mar. 1961, B8.

186. Matthew D. McCubbins and Thomas Schwartz, "Congress, the Courts, and Public Policy: Consequences of the One Man, One Vote Rule," *American Journal of Political Science* 32 (1988): 388.

187. *Christian Science Monitor,* 29 Oct. 1968, B1, summarized in Cortner, *Apportionment Cases,* 253.

188. Robert A. Liston, *Tides of Justice: The Supreme Court and the Constitution in Our Time* (New York: Delacorte, 1966), 135.

189. Alan L. Dessoff, "Maryland Plan Is Bitter Pill to Rural Legislators," *WP,* 17 Oct. 1965, B1; Hughes with Frece, *My Unexpected Journey,* 69-71.

190. Alan L. Dessoff, "Maryland Reform Awaits a Governor," *WP,* 11 Sept. 1966, E1.

191. U.S. Representative Charlton Sickles quoted in Bart Barnes, "Sickles Finds an Oyster Peril in Plan to Revive the Industry," *WP,* 8 Aug. 1966, B1.

192. On the gubernatorial race, see Theo Lippman Jr., *Spiro Agnew's America: The Vice President and the Politics of Suburbia* (New York: Norton, 1972), chap. 6; Justin P. Coffey, "Spiro Agnew and the Suburbanization of American Politics, 1918–1968" (PhD diss., University of Illinois at Chicago, 2003), chap. 4.

193. "General Eastern Shore Issues," "Talbot County Advance Sheet," both in Spiro T. Agnew Papers, Series 2, Subseries 4, Box 2, Folder 14, UML.

194. Alan L. Dessoff, "Transit Pact, Limited Fair Housing Urged by Spiro Agnew in Suburbs," *WP*, 12 July 1966, B3; Coffey, "Spiro Agnew," chap. 4.

195. Coffey, "Spiro Agnew," 118.

196. "Agnew Signs Open Housing, 250 Other Bills," *WP*, 22 Apr. 1967, 18; Lippman, *Spiro Agnew's America,* 90–95; Coffey, "Spiro Agnew," chap. 5.

197. Jack Eisen, "Anti-Pollution Fund Sought," *WP*, 2 Feb. 1968, B3; Eric Wentworth, "Dirty Rivers Are Clean Compared to Estuaries," *WP*, 1 May 1966, E4; "Stickles Stirs Up Storm by Bay Pollution Charge," *WP*, 16 July 1966, B2; "Finan Outlines Drive against Bay Pollution," *WP*, 28 Aug. 1966, B2.

198. Agnew quoted in Richard Hoffman, "Interest Bill Is 1 of 400 Signed by Gov. Agnew," *WP*, 8 May 1968, B2. On the rise of suburban environmentalism, see Samuel P. Hays with Barbara Hays, *Beauty, Health and Permanence: Environmental Politics in the United States, 1955–1985* (Cambridge: Cambridge University Press, 1987); Adam Rome, *The Bulldozer in the Countryside: Suburban Sprawl and the Rise of American Environmentalism* (Cambridge: Cambridge University Press, 2001). On estuarine and wetlands advocacy, see John Teal and Mildred Teal, *Life and Death of the Salt Marsh* (Boston: Little, Brown, 1969); Ann Vileisis, *Discovering the Unknown Landscape: A History of America's Wetlands* (Washington, D.C.: Island, 1997), chap. 11.

199. Constance Holden, "Chesapeake Bay: 'Queen of Bays' Is a Rich Commercial and Recreational Resource, but March of Progress Imperils Her Health," *Science* 172 (1971): 825–27. Examples of press coverage of some of these problems include Robert Herzberg, "Thermal Pollution of Bay Is Studied," *WP*, 24 Dec. 1968, C4; Hal Willard, "Plant's Waste Heat a Major Concern," *WP*, 10 July 1969, G1; "Chesapeake Bay Fights for Its Life," *Business Week,* 7 Mar. 1970, 40–44; Thomas J. Bray, "Chesapeake Area, Fearing a Ruined Bay, Strives to Balance Ecology and Growth," *Wall Street Journal,* 17 Sept. 1975, 42.

200. Christine Keiner, "Modeling Neptune's Garden: The Chesapeake Bay Hydraulic Model, 1965–1984," in *The Machine in Neptune's Garden: Historical Perspectives on Technology and the Marine Environment,* ed. Helen M. Rozwadowski and David K. Van Keuren (Sagamore Beach, Mass.: Science History, 2004), 273–314; Environmental Protection Agency, *Chesapeake Bay: Introduction to an Ecosystem* (Washington, D.C.: U.S. Government Printing Office, 1982); Environmental Protection Agency, *Chesapeake Bay: A Framework for Action* (Washington, D.C.: U.S. Government Printing Office, 1983).

201. John Woodfield, "Maryland Fisheries Sales Set Mark," *WP*, 7 July 1967, A12; "Maryland Leads U.S. in Oyster Production," *WP*, 20 Dec. 1968, C4.

202. M. Gordon Wolman, Russell Dize, Billy Martin, Eamonn McGeady, Roger Newell, John Parran, Lewis R. Riley, Samuel H. Shiver Jr., John F. Slade III, Ivar Strand, *The Role of the State of Maryland in Oyster Fisheries Management: Recommendations of the Governor's Committee to Review State Policy for Funding Maryland's Chesapeake Fisheries* (n.p., 1990). 53, 60.

203. John Larrimore quoted in "Old Skipjacks Reap Rich Oyster Harvest," *NYT,* 18 Mar. 1978, 29; Bundy and Williams, *Maryland's Chesapeake Bay Commercial Fisheries,* 5. For less optimistic takes in the wake of Hurricane Agnes, see B. Drummond Ayres Jr., "Nature and Man Peril Chesapeake Oyster Fleet," *NYT,* 21 Nov. 1973; Bill Richards, "Oystermen in Trouble," *WP,* 26 Sept. 1974, D1.

204. Lester R. Trott quoted in Steve Cady, "The Oysterboats R in Season: Race Tomorrow Will Prove it," *NYT,* 26 Oct. 1962, 54. See also "Bay's Old Workboats to Race Again," *WP,* 26 Aug. 1960, A19.

205. Wendell Bradley, "Skipjack Invites Sailing Parties," *WP,* 16 Aug. 1966, D6. See also Luis Marden, "The Sailing Oystermen of Chesapeake Bay," *National Geographic* 132 (1967): 798–819; Howard I. Chapelle, introduction to Wendell Bradley, *They Live by the Wind: The Lore and Romance of the Last Sailing Workboats* (1966; New York: Knopf, 1969), xv; Bradley, *They Live by the Wind,* chap. 3.

206. Keith Reekie, "Oyster Boats Race Saturday," *WP,* 24 Oct. 1965, B1; "Skipjack Races Set for Saturday," *WP,* 30 Oct. 1969, F5.

207. On the sharpening of "the historical sense of Marylanders – their awareness of belonging to a place through time," see Robert J. Brugger, Cynthia Horsburgh Requardt, Robert I. Cottom Jr., and Mary Ellen Hayward, *Maryland: A Middle Temperament, 1634–1980* (Baltimore: Johns Hopkins University Press, 1989), 654–59. On factors shaping regional consciousness and foodways, see, e.g., Barbara G. Shortridge and James R. Shortridge, eds., *The Taste of American Place: A Reader on Regional and Ethnic Foods* (Lanham, Md.: Rowman and Littlefield, 1998); M. Beth Schlemper, "The Regional Construction of Identity and Scale in Wisconsin's Holyland," *Journal of Cultural Geography* 22 (2004): 51–81.

208. David Broder, *Changing of the Guard: Power and Leadership in America* (New York: Simon and Schuster, 1980), 345. For an up-to-date list of the almost two dozen seafood festivals that now take place each year, see the Web site of the Maryland Department of Agriculture's Seafood Marketing and Aquaculture Development Program, http://www.marylandseafood.org/festivals (accessed 12 October 2008).

209. Bradley, *They Live by the Wind,* 7, 9.

210. Richard White, *The Organic Machine* (New York: Hill and Wang, 1995); Richard White, "'Are You an Environmentalist or Do You Work for a Living?': Work and Nature," in *Uncommon Ground: Rethinking the Human Place in Nature,* ed. William Cronon (New York: Norton, 1996), 171–85.

211. On this shift, see Hays with Hays, *Beauty, Health, and Permanence,* chap. 1; Robert Cameron Mitchell, "From Conservation to Environmental Movement:

The Development of the Modern Environmental Lobbies," in *Government and Environmental Politics: Essays on Historical Developments since World War Two,* ed. Michael J. Lacey (Baltimore: Johns Hopkins University Press, 1989), 81–113. For an interpretation that highlights continuities between the two eras, see Robert Gottlieb, *Forcing the Spring: The Transformation of the American Environmental Movement* (Washington, D.C.: Island, 1993).

212. John J. Alford, "The Chesapeake Oyster Fishery," *Annals of the Association of American Geographers* 65 (1975): 238. See also George D. Santopietro and Leonard A. Shabman, "Can Privatization Be Inefficient? The Case of the Chesapeake Bay Oyster Fishery," *Journal of Economic Issues* 26 (1992): 407–19.

213. Harry Roe Hughes with John W. Frece, *My Unexpected Journey: The Autobiography of Governor Harry Roe Hughes* (Charleston, S.C.: History, 2006), 176–77.

214. See ibid., 177–78, 122, 125; David A. Maranis, "Integrity is the Message, but Message Is Veiled," *WP,* 31 Aug. 1978, B1; Brugger et al., *Maryland,* 651–53.

215. Hughes with Frece, *My Unexpected Journey,* 178.

216. For earlier examples of efforts to pass land-use controls, see Edward Walsh, "Lee Says Md. Land Use Law Could Destroy Local Planning," *WP,* 1 Dec. 1972, B2; Edward Walsh, "Logrolling for Land-Use Bill," *WP,* 24 Mar. 1974, A1.

217. Hughes with Frece, *My Unexpected Journey,* 71–72; William Thomson, "Malkus Plans Memoirs on 48 Years in Assembly," *BS,* 27 Mar. 1994, 1B; "Seed Oyster Bill Withdrawn by Malkus," *WG,* Apr. 1987, 6.

218. Malkus quoted in Saundra Saperstein and Tom Kenworthy, "Assembly Passes Strict Bay Bill," *WP,* 8 Apr. 1984, B1. Environmentalists did not tend to rate Malkus highly because of his stringent defense of owners' right to use their property as they saw fit. However, Malkus and environmentalists at times agreed, as in 1975 when he helped secure passage of a law providing the first long-term containment facility for sediments ("spoils") generated by navigational channel dredging of Baltimore Harbor. Rather than damaging water quality via open-water dumping, the spoils have helped build up the eroded Hart and Miller Islands into a bird refuge (Jefferson Morley, "Dredge Disposal Debate Gets Hot," *WP,* 18 Mar. 1999, M1).

219. Joe Valliant, "Harry Hughes, Watermen, and Chesapeake Bay," *WG,* July 1987, 4, 6.

220. For another analysis linking the bill's passage with reapportionment, see Steven G. Davison, Jay G. Merwin Jr., John Capper, Garrett Power, and Frank R. Shivers Jr., *Chesapeake Waters: Four Centuries of Controversy, Concern, and Legislation* (1983; Centreville, Md.: Tidewater, 1997), 202. For a list of studies published between 1964 and 1973 questioning the policy impact of state and federal reapportionment, see McCubbins and Schwartz, "Congress," 388; for a survey of part of this literature, see Larry M. Schwab, *The Impact of Congressional Reapportionment and Redistricting* (Lanham, Md.: University Press of America,

1988), chap. 1. For a long-term case study that demonstrates important changes in environmental policymaking, see Michael A. Maggiotto, Manning J. Dauer, Steven G. Koven, Joan S. Carver, and Joel Gottlieb, "The Impact of Reapportionment on Public Policy: The Case of Florida, 1960–1980," *American Politics Quarterly* 13 (1985): 101–21.

221. Hughes with Frece, *My Unexpected Journey,* 179–80. For Hughes's use of the phrase *political will,* see Harry R. Hughes and Thomas W. Burke Jr., "The Cleanup of the Nation's Largest Estuary: A Test of Political Will," reprinted in *The Law of Biodiversity and Ecosystem Management,* ed. John Copeland Nagle and J. B. Ruhl (New York: Foundation, 2006), 796–801.

222. C. Fraser Smith, *William Donald Schaefer: A Political Biography* (Baltimore: Johns Hopkins University Press, 1999), 21–22; Joe Valliant, "Sympathetic Governor Great Help to Watermen," *WG,* June 1987, 4.

223. On the frantic Maryland response to MSX in the 1960s, see Keiner, "Scientists," chap. 7.

224. Charles Cohen, "Watermen Worried about Bottom Leasing," *WG,* Feb. 1988, 12; "Aquaculture Bills Seen as Opening Doors to Leasing," *WG,* Mar. 1988, 1–2.

225. Mark Wasserman to Abel Wolman, 3 Mar. 1988, Series 7, Box 7.50, Folder "Md. Environmental Leadership Group, 1988," Abel Wolman Papers, Ms. 105, Special Collections, Milton S. Eisenhower Library, Johns Hopkins University, Baltimore. See also Abel Wolman to Mark Wasserman, 16 Feb. 1988, Wayne A. Cawley Jr. to Abel Wolman, 29 Feb. 1988, both in Wolman Papers.

226. Abel Wolman to Mark Wasserman, 7 Mar. 1988, Wolman Papers.

227. Joe Valliant, "Leasing Dead This Year," *WG,* Apr. 1988, 1; "Aquaculture Bill Passes Legislature Minus Oyster Leasing Provisions," *WG,* June 1988, 2.

228. Tom Horton, *Bay Country* (Baltimore: Johns Hopkins University Press, 1987), 197–98.

229. Joe Valliant, "Environmental Matters Committee Matters to Maryland Watermen," *WG,* Sept. 1986, 4.

230. On this theme, see Murray Edelman, *The Symbolic Uses of Politics* (Urbana: University of Illinois Press, 1967).

231. "Maryland's Oyster Policy under Attack," *BS,* 26 Jan. 1936, 18.

232. Howard R. Ernst, *Chesapeake Bay Blues: Science, Politics, and the Struggle to Save the Bay* (Lanham, Md.: Rowman and Littlefield, 2003), 131.

233. Hughes with Frece, *My Unexpected Journey,* 182.

234. Tom Kenworthy, "Maryland to Ban Fishing for Rockfish after Jan. 1," *WP,* 12 Sept. 1984, A1; Angus Phillips, "Glum Prognosis for Watermen," *WP,* 26 Sept. 1984, C1; Tom Kenworthy, "Governor Tries to Reassure Md. Watermen," *WP,* 27 Sept. 1984, B1.

235. On the savvy backstage efforts to bring about the Atlantic Striped Bass Conservation Act of 1984, which included Hughes reaching out to the

watermen's association and giving an influential U.S. senator a rockfish painting, see Hughes with Frece, *My Unexpected Journey,* 183.

236. See Tom Horton and William M. Eichbaum, *Turning the Tide: Saving the Chesapeake Bay* (Washington, D.C.: Island, 1991), 159–60.

237. Ibid., 153.

238. Coffey, "Spiro Agnew," 139

239. Alford, "Chesapeake Oyster Fishery," 235.

Chapter 5. Brave New Bay

1. U.S. Congress, Office of Technology Assessment, *Harmful Non-Indigenous Species in the United States* (Washington, D.C.: U.S. Government Printing Office, 1993); Don C. Schmitz and Daniel Simberloff, "Biological Invasions: A Growing Threat," *Issues in Science and Technology* 13 (1997): 33–40; Don C. Schmitz and Daniel Simberloff, "Needed: A National Center for Biological Invasions," *Issues in Science and Technology* 17 (2001): 57–62. Popular books on the topic published during this period include Chris Bright, *Life Out of Bounds: Bioinvasion in a Borderless World* (New York: Norton, 1997); Robert S. Devine, *Alien Invasion: America's Battle with Non-native Plants and Animals* (Washington, D.C.: National Geographic Society, 1998); George W. Cox, *Alien Species in North America and Hawaii* (Washington, D.C.: Island, 1999); Jason Van Driesche, *Nature Out of Place: Biological Invasions in the Global Age* (Washington, D.C.: Island, 2000); Kim Todd, *Tinkering with Eden: A Natural History of Exotics in America* (New York: Norton, 2001); Yvonne Baskin. *A Plague of Rats and Rubber-Vines: The Growing Threat of Species Invasions* (Washington, D.C.: Island, 2002).

2. For an argument linking ecological restoration with the desire to reinforce hegemonic social relations, see Jennifer Foster and L. Anders Sandberg, "Friends or Foe? Invasive Species and Public Green Space in Toronto," *Geographical Review* 94 (2004): 178–98; Jennifer Foster, "Restoration of the Don Brick Valley Works: Whose Restoration? Whose Space?" *Journal of Urban Design* 10 (2005): 331–51. Analyses charging xenophobia, racism, and nativism include Jonah H. Peretti, "Nativism and Nature: Rethinking Biological Invasion," *Environmental Values* 7 (1998): 183–92; Mark Sagoff, "What's Wrong with Exotic Species?" *Report from the Institute for Philosophy and Public Policy* 19.4 (1999): 16–23; Banu Subramaniam, "The Aliens Have Landed! Reflections on the Rhetoric of Biological Invasions," *Meridians: Feminism, Race, Transnationalism* 2.1 (2001): 26–40; Gert Gröning and Joachim Wolschke-Bulmahn, "The Native Plant Enthusiasm: Ecological Panacea or Xenophobia?" *Landscape Research* 28 (2003): 75–88. For a critique of these later works that has informed my analysis, see Daniel Simberloff, "Confronting Introduced Species: A Form of Xenophobia?" *Biological Invasions* 5 (2003): 179–92.

3. For an excellent discussion of how "biological nativists' antagonism toward exotics need not be xenophobic . . . and . . . can be justified as a way of preserving the diversity of ecological assemblages from the homogenising forces of globalization," see Ned Hettinger, "Exotic Species, Naturalisation, and Biological Nativism," *Environmental Values* 10 (2001): 219. For an extended analysis of how the "ties between conservation and prejudice, between the desire to preserve an 'American' nature and to defend old-stock America . . . have largely dissolved," see Peter Coates, *American Perceptions of Immigrant and Invasive Species: Strangers on the Land* (Berkeley: University of California Press, 2006), 10.

4. William J. Goldsborough, "Point of No Return: Only Drastic Action Will Save the Oysters of the Chesapeake Bay," *WP*, 28 July 1991, A8; Tom Horton and William M. Eichbaum, *Turning the Tide: Saving the Chesapeake Bay* (Washington, D.C.: Island, 1991), 273.

5. Larry Simns, "A Moratorium Won't Bring Back the Oyster," *WP*, 11 Aug. 1991, C8.

6. "Md. Official Rejects Proposal for Moratorium on Oystering," *WP*, 16 June 1991, C11; Mary Knudson, "State Rejects Push to Ban Bay Oystering," *BS*, 15 June 1991, 14B.

7. Larry Simns, "CBF: Waterman's Friend or Foe?" *WG*, July 1991, 2.

8. D'Vera Cohn, "A Shell Game of Survival," *WP*, 23 May 1993, B3. Virginia's harvest, however, was one-third as large as Maryland's.

9. Frank T. Gray, "Collective Farming on the Bay – It Doesn't Work," *BS*, 14 Jan. 1993, 17A.

10. D'Vera Cohn, "Va. to Consider Canceling Oyster Harvest," *WP*, 25 Aug. 1993, B1.

11. Quoted in Bill Gifford, "Shell Shock," *Washington Post Magazine*, 27 Mar. 1994, W18. See also Kennedy T. Paynter, "Managing around Oyster Diseases in Maryland and Maryland Oyster Roundtable Strategies," in *Oyster Reef Habitat Restoration: A Synopsis and Synthesis of Approaches,* ed. Mark W. Luckenbach, Roger Mann, and James A. Wesson (Gloucester Point, Va.: VIMS Press, 1999), 317–28.

12. Timothy B. Wheeler, "First Session . . . to . . . Resolve the Oyster Crisis," *BS*, 14 July 1993, 5B; "Groups Sign Agreement," *BS*, 2 Dec. 1993, 4B; Karl Blankenship, "Divergent Groups Sign onto MD 'Action Plan,'" *BJ*, Jan.–Feb. 1994.

13. J. E. Cloern, "Does the Benthos Control Phytoplankton Biomass in South San Francisco Bay?" *Marine Ecology Progress Series* 9 (1981): 191–202; C. B. Officer, T. J. Smayda, and R. Mann, "Benthic Filter Feeding: A Natural Eutrophication Control," *Marine Ecology Progress Series* 9 (1982): 203–10; R. R. H. Cohen, P. V. Dresler, E. J. P. Philips, and R. L. Cory, "The Effect of the Asiatic Clam, *Corbicula Fluminea,* on Phytoplankton of the Potomac River, Maryland," *Limnology and Oceanography* 29 (1984): 170–80.

14. Roger I. E. Newell, "Ecological Changes in Chesapeake Bay: Are They the Result of Overharvesting the American Oyster, *Crassostrea Virginica?*" In

Understanding the Estuary: Advances in Chesapeake Bay Research, ed. Maurice P. Lynch and Elizabeth C. Krome (Solomons, Md.: Chesapeake Research Consortium, 1988), 539, 542.

15. "Oysters Could Help Clean Up the Bay," *WP,* 1 Apr. 1988, D5.

16. Stephen Bocking, *Nature's Experts: Science, Politics, and the Environment* (New Brunswick, N.J.: Rutgers University Press, 2004), 165.

17. Charles Lindblom and David Cohen, *Usable Knowledge: Social Science and Social Problem Solving* (New Haven: Yale University Press, 1979), 12, quoted in Frank Fischer, *Citizens, Experts, and the Environment: The Politics of Local Knowledge* (Durham: Duke University Press, 2000), 194; Bocking, *Nature's Experts,* 172. Lindblom and Cohen define "ordinary knowledge" as "knowledge that does not owe its origin, testing, degree of verification, truth, status, or currency to distinctive . . . professional techniques, but rather to common sense, causal empiricism, or thoughtful speculation and analysis."

18. John A. Morris, "Hatchery Project to Boost Ailing Oyster Population," *BS,* 2 June 1994, 6B; Mark Davenport, "State Plans to Replenish Bay Oysters," *AC,* 19 July 1996, B1; Steny Hoyer, "Investing in Programs that Work, Restoring the Oyster Population to Clean up the Bay," 30 June 2005, http://www.hoyer.house .gov/Newsroom/index.asp?ID=432&DocumentType=Op-Ed (accessed 15 July 2005); "Mikulski Announces Grant for Bay Projects," *WP,* 26 Oct. 1998, D3.

19. Robert Wieland, "Managing Oyster Harvests in Maryland's Chesapeake Bay, 2007, 25, http://www.dnr.state.md.us/fisheries/oysters/mtgs/111907/man ageharvests.pdf (accessed 2 July 2008).

20. See, e.g., Carl Schoetler, "As Population of Oysters Drops in Bay, a New Type of Farming Takes Seed," *BS,* 6 July 1995, 1D; Peter S. Goodman, "Sowing Oysters to Reap a Cleaner Chesapeake," *WP,* 21 Aug. 1997, A1; Lyndsey Layton, "Volunteers Find Oyster Mortality Doubled in '98," *WP,* 14 Feb. 1999, M1; Steven Ginsberg, "Students Play Role in Reviving Oysters," *WP,* 20 Aug. 1999, B4. Scientific assessments include Francis X. O'Beirn, "Community Aquaculture in Virginia," in *Proceedings – Delmarva Coastal Bays Conference III: Tri-state Approaches to Preserving Aquatic Resources,* ed. Frederick W. Kutz, Phyllis Koenings, and Laurie Adelhardt (Narragansett, R.I.: U.S. Environmental Protection Agency, 1999), 107–9; R. D. Brumbaugh, L. A. Sorabella, C. Johnson, and W. J. Goldsborough, "Small Scale Aquaculture as a Tool for Oyster Restoration in Chesapeake Bay," *Marine Technology Society Journal* 34 (2000): 79–86; Robert D. Brumbaugh, Laurie A. Sorabella, Carene Oliveras Garcia, William J. Goldsborough, and James A. Wesson, "Making a Case for Community-Based Oyster Restoration: An Example from Hampton Roads, Virginia, USA," *JSR* 19 (2000): 467–72. Overall, only modest gains in restoring water quality and natural resources ensued, and the 2000 deadline for reducing nutrient pollution by 40 percent passed unheeded. For critiques of the bay program, see Howard R. Ernst, *Chesapeake Bay Blues: Science, Politics, and the Struggle to Save the Bay* (Lanham, Md.: Rowman and Littlefield, 2003); Fred Powledge, "Chesapeake Bay Restora-

tion: A Model of What?" *BioScience* 55 (2005): 1032–38; U.S. Government Accountability Office, *Chesapeake Bay Program: Improved Strategies Needed to Better Guide Restoration Efforts* (Washington, D.C.: U.S. Government Printing Office, 2006), http://www.gao.gov/new.items/d06614t.pdf (accessed 2 July 2008).

21. Frank D. Roylance, "Fish Woes Linked to Oysters' Decline," *BS,* 27 Sept. 1997, 1A. See also Tom Horton, "Pfiesteria's Surprising Benefit," *BS,* 5 Dec. 1997, 2B; Joann M. Burkholder and Howard B. Glasgow, "History of Toxic Pfiesteria in North Carolina Estuaries from 1991 to the Present," *BioScience* 51 (2001): 827–41; Ernst, *Chesapeake Bay Blues,* 47; R. E. Magnien, "The Dynamics of Science, Perception, and Policy during the Outbreak of Pfiesteria in the Chesapeake Bay," *BioScience* 51 (2001): 843–52.

22. Tim Zimmerman, "8. How to Revive the Chesapeake Bay: Filter It with Billions and Billions of Oysters," *U.S. News and World Report,* 29 Dec. 1997, 63.

23. Scott Harper, "State Hopes Project Restores Lynnhaven Oysters," *NVP,* 17 July 1997, B5; Scott Harper, "Man-Made Oyster Reefs Beginning to Bear Young," *NVP,* 13 Oct. 1998, B1; Scott Harper, "Pet Oysters Sent into the Wild," *NVP,* 20 May 1998, B1.

24. Tawna Mertz, "Can Bay's Oysters Make a Comeback?" *BJ,* Sept. 1999.

25. Timothy B. Wheeler, "Experiment with Oysters Runs Aground," *BS,* 3 Oct. 1999, 1B.

26. See, e.g., Lawrence Latane III, "Hope Restored for Bay Oysters," *RTD,* 14 Dec. 1997, C1; Patrick Lee Plaisance, "A Year Later, Oysters Return to Elizabeth," *BS,* 28 May 1999, 11B; Joel McCord, "Oyster Yield Likely to Rise," *BS,* 8 June 1999, 1B; Raja Mishra, "Renewing the Oyster Reefs," *WP,* 5 Aug. 1999, 1, 2; Daniel LeDuc, "Bay Health Improving," *WP,* 9 Sept. 1999, B3; Todd Shields, "Beneath the Bay, Signs of Resurgence," *WP,* 18 Jan. 2000, B1.

27. Rona Kobell, "Experts Tie Bay Cleanup to Oyster Recovery Plan," *BS,* 31 Jan. 2007, 5B.

28. Merrill Leffler, "Don Meritt: The Hatchery Connection," *CQ* 1.3 (2002): 11.

29. The Horn Point Laboratory, part of the University of Maryland Center for Environmental Science, produces most of the oyster larvae and spat on shell, but the Department of Natural Resources also maintains a facility at Piney Point (Leffler, "Don Meritt"; Donald Meritt, "Oyster Hatcheries in Maryland," *Maryland Aquafarmer* [Fall 1999]: 1–3; Donald Meritt, "Oyster Production at the Horn Point Laboratory, 1994–2000," *Maryland Aquafarmer* [Fall 2000]: 3; Rona Kobell, "Seeding the Bay," *BS,* 17 Dec. 2006, 1F, 6F; Rona Kobell, "Experts Tie Bay Cleanup to Oyster Recovery Plan," *BS,* 31 Jan. 2007, 5B). On commercial production of triploid Pacific oysters, see, e.g., John A. Nell, "Farming Triploid Oysters," *Aquaculture* 210 (2002): 69–88.

30. If the deadline is not met, a likelihood the EPA conceded in 2006, the EPA may be obliged to require a more formal cleanup program known as a total maximum daily load (Karl Blankenship, "EPA Report Indicates 2010 Cleanup

Deadline Will Not Be Met," *BJ,* Apr. 2006, 1; Karl Blankenship, "Failure to Meet 2010 Cleanup Deadline Will Likely Result in TMDLs," *BJ,* Apr. 2006, 16–17).

31. Chesapeake Bay Program, *Chesapeake 2000,* reprinted in Tom Horton, *Turning the Tide: Saving the Chesapeake Bay* (1991; Washington, D.C.: Island, 2003), 337.

32. Douglas Lipton, "The *Values* of Oysters," *Maryland Aquafarmer,* Fall 1999, 4.

33. Karl Blankenship, "Scientists Figuring Out How to Measure Bay Program Oyster Goal," *BJ,* Sept. 2000; Roger Mann, Melissa Southworth, Juliana M. Harding, and James Wesson, "A Comparison of Dredge and Patent Tongs for Estimation of Oyster Populations," *JSR* 23 (2004): 387–90; Stephen J. Jordan, Kelly N. Greenhawk, Carol B. McCollough, Jessica Vanisko, and Mark L. Homer, "Oyster Biomass, Abundance, and Harvest in Northern Chesapeake Bay: Trends and Forecasts," *JSR* 21 (2002): 733–41.

34. Don Meritt and Merrill Leffler, "Oyster Restoration in the Chesapeake Bay," *Maryland Aquafarmer,* Fall 2000, 1–2.

35. Karl Blankenship, "All Sides Agree Sanctuaries Key to Oysters' Recovery," *BJ,* Apr. 2000; Karessa E. Weir, "Oyster Plans to Get Windfall," *AC,* 17 Jan. 2000, B1; Karl Blankenship, "Congress Gives Oyster Restoration Projects $1.45 Million," *BJ,* Nov. 2000; Geoff Oxnam, "Congress Boosts Bay Oyster Recovery Effort with $5 Million," Chesapeake Bay Foundation Press Release, 15 Nov. 2001, http://www.cbf.org (accessed 7 Aug. 2006).

36. E. Janene Nolan, "Oyster Restrictions Anger Watermen," *AC,* 22 Dec. 1998, C1; Karl Blankenship, "1999 Legislative Roundup for Maryland, Virginia," *BJ,* May 1999.

37. John Biemer, "Ehrlich Should Have Advantage on the Eastern Shore," Associated Press, 25 Sept. 2002; Laura Loh, "Fisheries Chief Fired after Bay Decree," *BS,* 16 Mar. 2003, 3B; Tom Horton, "State Says Catching Oysters Improves Hatching Oysters," *BS,* 31 Jan. 2003, 1A; Tom Horton, "A Turning Point for Bay Oystering," *BS,* 14 Feb. 2003, 2B; Kent Mountford, "No Matter What Shells Are Fired in Oyster Wars, the Resource Always Loses," *BJ,* Mar. 2003; Karl Blankenship, "MD Enacts Emergency Legislation to Allow Power Dredging," *BJ,* Mar. 2003; Anita Huslin, "Watermen Laud DNR Deputy Pick," *WP,* 22 Jan. 2003, B7; Gene Mueller, "New Maryland DNR Brass Form Delicate Balancing Act," *Washington Times,* 30 Jan. 2003, C8.

38. See, e.g., Rona Kobell, "UM Biologist's Work Is Critical to Oyster Debate," *BS,* 7 Mar. 2005, 1A.

39. Kenny Keen quoted in Anita Huslin, "Oysters' Survival May Lie in Sanctuaries," *WP,* 26 Nov. 2000, C1.

40. Larry Simns, "Time Has Come for Watermen to Be More Vigilant," *WG,* Oct. 2007, 2.

41. Robert Wieland, "MD Oyster Management Efforts Are All but Subsidies for Watermen," *BJ,* Oct. 2007, 18–19.

42. Donald Boesch quoted in Tawna Mertz, "Scientists Reach Consensus on Plan to Restore Oyster Populations in Chesapeake Bay," *BJ*, Sept. 1999. See also Tom Horton, "Science May Solve Oyster Problem," *BS*, 17 Mar. 2000, 2B.

43. Chesapeake Bay Foundation scientist William Goldsborough quoted in Karl Blankenship, "10% Oyster Sanctuary Goal Dropped from Management Plan," *BJ*, July–Aug. 2004, 5.

44. See, e.g., David M. Lodge and Kristin Shrader-Frechette, "Nonindigenous Species: Ecological Explanation, Environmental Ethics, and Public Policy," *Conservation Biology* 17 (2003): 32.

45. Stephen Jordan quoted in Anita Huslin, "A Watered-Down Memorial Stadium," *WP*, 16 Sept. 2002, B1.

46. Mark W. Luckenbach, Loren D. Coen, P. G. Ross Jr., and Jessica A. Stephen, "Oyster Reef Habitat Restoration: Relationships between Oyster Abundance and Community Development Based on Two Studies in Virginia and South Carolina," *Journal of Coastal Research* 40 (2005): 76.

47. Jeremy C. B. Jackson et al., "Historical Overfishing and the Recent Collapse of Coastal Ecosystems," *Science* 293 (2001): 636.

48. Donald Boesch, Eugene Burreson, William Dennison, Edward Houde, Michael Kemp, Victor Kennedy, Roger Newell, Kennedy Paynter, Robert Orth, and Robert Ulanowicz, "Factors in the Decline of Coastal Ecosystems," *Science* 293 (2001): 1589–90.

49. Roger I. E. Newell, Jeffrey C. Corwell, and Michael S. Owens, "Influence of Simulated Bivalve Biodeposition and Microphytobenthos on Sediment Nitrogen Dynamics: A Laboratory Study," *Limnology and Oceanography* 47 (2002): 1367–79; Karl Blankenship, "Oysters Will Help Trigger Bay Cleanup, but Are No Silver Bullet," *BJ*, Dec. 2004, 5.

50. Committee on Nonnative Oysters in the Chesapeake Bay, *Nonnative Oysters in the Chesapeake Bay* (Washington, D.C.: National Academies Press, 2004), 237.

51. Carl F. Cerco and Mark R. Noel, "Process-Based Primary Production Modeling in Chesapeake Bay," *Marine Ecology Progress Series* 282 (2004): 45–58.

52. Committee on Nonnative Oysters in the Chesapeake Bay, *Nonnative Oysters,* 238–39.

53. Ibid., 239.

54. D'Vera Cohn, "Plan to Revive Bay's Oysters Creates a Regional Dispute," *WP*, 18 Nov. 1991, A1; Paul Hoversten, "Sides Are Oceans Apart on Oysters," *USA Today,* 29 Nov. 1991, 5A.

55. Schmitz and Simberloff, "Biological Invasions," 33.

56. Charles S. Elton, *The Ecology of Invasions by Animals and Plants* (1958; London: Methuen, 1969), 100; Philippe Goulletquer and Maurice Héral, "Marine Molluscan Production Trends in France: From Fisheries to Aquaculture," in *The History, Present Condition, and Future of the Molluscan Fisheries of North and Central America and Europe,* ed. Clyde MacKenzie Jr., Victor G. Burrell Jr., Aaron

Rosefield, and Willis L. Hobart (Seattle: U.S. Department of Commerce, 1997), 3:139.

57. Quoted in John R. Philpots, *Oysters and All about Them* (London: Richardson, 1891), 2:1145.

58. James T. Carlton and Roger Mann, "Transfers and World-wide Introductions," in *The Eastern Oyster, Crassostrea Virginica,* ed. Victor S. Kennedy, Roger I. E. Newell, and Albert F. Eble (College Park: Maryland Sea Grant College, 1996), 691–706.

59. Paul S. Galtsoff, "Oyster Industry of the Pacific Coast of the United States," in *Report of the U.S. Fish Commission for 1929* (Washington, D.C.: U.S. Government Printing Office, 1930), 368; Ernest Ingersoll, *The History and Present Condition of the Fishery Industries: The Oyster-Industry* (Washington, D.C.: U.S. Government Printing Office, 1881), 202–3; Matthew Morse Booker, "Oyster Growers and Oyster Pirates in San Francisco Bay," *Pacific Historical Review* 75 (2006): 63–88; Mitchell Postel, "A Lost Resource: Shellfish in San Francisco Bay," *California History* 67 (1988): 26–41.

60. Galtsoff, "Oyster Industry," 388–89; Cedric E. Lindsay and Douglas Simons, "The Fisheries for Olympia Oysters . . . Pacific Oysters . . . and Pacific Razor Clams . . . in the State of Washington," in *History, Present Condition, and Future,* ed. MacKenzie et al., 2:97; Alen Lawe, "Closing the Bay to Japanese Oysters," *BSSM,* 5 Mar. 1933, 4.

61. Darin Kinsey, "'Seeding the Water as the Earth': The Epicenter and Peripheries of a Western *Aqua*cultural Revolution," *Environmental History* 11 (2006): 551.

62. Elton, *Ecology,* 100–101; Harvey C. McMillin and Paul Bonnot, "Oyster Pests in California," *California Fish and Game* 18 (1932): 147–48.

63. Lindsay and Simons, "Fisheries," 103; Elton, *Ecology,* 103; "Warning Made by FWS in Planting Japanese Seed Oysters in the Waters of Atlantic and Gulf Coast States," Department of the Interior Information Service Press Release, 21 Jan. 1946, http://www.fws.gov/news/historic/1946/19460121.pdf (accessed 2 July 2008).

64. Galtsoff, "Oyster Industry," 398.

65. Quoted in Swepson Earle, introduction to *Tenth Annual Report of the Conservation Department of Maryland, 1932* (Baltimore: n.p., 1933), 37.

66. Alen Lawe, "Closing the Bay to Japanese Oysters," *BSSM,* 5 Mar. 1933, 14.

67. R. V. Truitt, "Report of the Chesapeake Biological Laboratory, 1932," in *Tenth Annual Report,* 49, 50.

68. *Tenth Annual Report,* 33.

69. Alen Lawe, "Closing the Bay to Japanese Oysters," *BSSM,* 5 Mar. 1933, 4; "Warning Made by FWS in Planting Japanese Seed Oysters in the Waters of Atlantic and Gulf Coast States," Department of the Interior Information Service Press Release, 21 Jan. 1946, http://www.fws.gov/news/historic/1946/19460121 .pdf (accessed 2 July 2008).

70. Philip J. Pauly discusses attitudes toward nonnative species and human immigrants in *Biologists and the Promise of American Life: From Meriwether Lewis to Alfred Kinsey* (Princeton: Princeton University Press, 2000), chap. 3. For an opposing view stressing scientists' ecological concerns, see Simberloff, "Confronting Introduced Species." See also Philip J. Pauly, "The Beauty and Menace of the Japanese Cherry Trees: Conflicting Visions of American Ecological Independence," *Isis* 87 (1996): 51–73, and the exchange with Simberloff in *Isis* 87 (1996): 676–87.

71. Maille Lyons, "Paul S. Galtsoff," *NSA Quarterly Newsletter* (Aug. 2004): 10; Phillip J. Wingate, *Before the Bridge* (Centreville, Md.: Tidewater, 1985), chap. 17.

72. Coates, *American Perceptions,* 187. Analysts of recent debates over invasive species have accused scientists of continuing to pass off value judgments as scientific results. See, e.g., Lodge and Shrader-Frechette, "Nonindigenous Species"; Brendon M. H. Larson, "The War of the Roses: Demilitarizing Invasion Biology," *Frontiers in Ecology and Evolution* 3 (2005): 495–500. On the persistent difficulty of separating science from values and politics despite long-standing views linking scientific knowledge with objectivity, see, e.g., Bocking, *Nature's Experts,* 19, 74.

73. Studies suggested that *C. angulata* and *C. gigas* were actually the same species and that Portuguese sailors introduced the former to Japan either by accident or by design just prior to the start of Japanese oyster culture in the early 1600s (R. W. Menzel, "Portuguese and Japanese Oysters Are the Same Species," *Journal of the Fisheries Research Board of Canada* 31 [1974]: 453–56). See also Goulletquer and Héral, "Marine Molluscan Production," 140; Roger Mann, ed., *Exotic Species in Mariculture: Case Histories of the Japanese Oyster, Crassostrea Gigas (Thunberg), with Implications for Other Fisheries* (Cambridge: MIT Press, 1979), ix; J. D. Andrews, "A Review of Introductions of Exotic Oysters and Biological Planning for New Importations," *Marine Fisheries Review* 42 (1980): 1–11.

74. Jay D. Andrews, "Scenario for Introduction of *Crassostrea Gigas* to the Atlantic Coast of North America," in *Exotic Species,* ed. Mann, 229; Thomas B. Lewis and Garrett Power, "Chesapeake Bay Oysters: Legal Theses on Exotic Species," in *Exotic Species,* ed. Mann, 265–305; Roger Mann, "Exotic Species in Aquaculture," in *Exotic Species,* ed. Mann, 337–38.

75. "Warning Made by FWS in Planting Japanese Seed Oysters in the Waters of Atlantic and Gulf Coast States," Department of the Interior Information Service Press Release, 21 Jan. 1946, http://www.fws.gov/news/historic/1946/19460121.pdf (accessed 2 July 2008); Michael W. Fincham, "The Mystery Invasion of Chesapeake Bay," *CQ* 5.2 (2006): 12.

76. *Maryland Board of Natural Resources Sixteenth Annual Report, 1959* (Annapolis: n.p., 1960) 113. On the MSX epidemic, see Christine Keiner, "Scientists, Oystermen, and Maryland Oyster Conservation Politics, 1880–1969: A Study of Two Cultures" (PhD diss., Johns Hopkins University, 2000), chap. 7.

77. Fincham, "Mystery Invasion," 13–15.

78. S. E. Ford and H. H. Haskin, "Infection and Mortality Patterns in Strains of Oysters *Crassostrea Virginica* Selected for Resistance to the Parasite *Haplosporidium Nelsoni* (MSX)," *Journal of Parasitology* 73 (1987): 368–76.

79. Newell, "Ecological Changes," 543–44.

80. Roger Mann, Eugene M. Burreson, and Patrick K. Baker, "The Decline of the Virginia Oyster Fishery in Chesapeake Bay: Considerations for Introduction of a Non-endemic Species, *Crassostrea Gigas* (Thunberg, 1793)," *JSR* 10 (1991): 379–88.

81. Merrill Leffler, "Does the Bay Need a New Oyster?" *CQ* 1.3 (2002): 8.

82. Adam Woog, *Sexless Oysters and Self-Tipping Hats: 100 Years of Invention in the Pacific Northwest* (Seattle: Sasquatch, 1991), 137–41.

83. Mann, Burreson, and. Baker, "Decline," 382; Lindsay and Simons, "Fisheries," 97–111; Beth Baker, "Building a Better Oyster," *BioScience* 46 (1996): 240–41; Standish K. Allen Jr., Patrick M. Gaffney, and John W. Ewart, *Genetic Improvement of the Eastern Oyster for Growth and Disease Resistance in the Northeast* (North Dartmouth, Mass.: Northeastern Regional Aquacultural Center, 1993]), 1, 4, http://www.aquanic.org/publicat/usda_rac/efs/nrac/nrac210.pdf (accessed 2 July 2008).

84. For comparative studies of the two species with respect to disease resistance, see J. A. Meyers, E. M. Burreson, B. J. Barber, and R. Mann, "Susceptibility of Diploid and Triploid Oysters, *Crassostrea Gigas,* to *Perkinsus Marinus,*" *JSR* 10 (1991): 433–37; B. J. Barber and Roger Mann, "Comparative Physiology of *Crassostrea Virginica* and *Crassostrea Gigas:* Growth, Mortality, and Infection by *Perkinsus Marinus,*" *JSR* 12 (1993): 358; B. J. Barber and Roger Mann, "Growth and Mortality of Eastern Oysters, *Crassostrea Virginica* (Gmelin, 1791), and Pacific Oysters, *Crassostrea Gigas* (Thunberg, 1793) under Challenge from the Parasite *Perkinsus Marinus,*" *JSR* 13 (1994): 109–14; C. A. Farley, D. L. Plutschak, and G. E. Krantz, "*Crassostrea Gigas* Disease Exposure to *Haplosporidium Nelsoni* and *Perkinsus Marinus* in Chesapeake Bay Waters," *JSR* 10 (1991): 306.

85. D'Vera Cohn, "Plan to Revive Bay's Oysters Creates a Regional Dispute," *WP,* 18 Nov. 1991, A1; Paul Hoversten, "Sides Are Oceans Apart on Oysters," *USA Today,* 29 Nov. 1991, 5A; D'Vera Cohn, "Oyster-Planting Proposal Wins Backing of Va. Marine Institute," *WP,* 29 Jan. 1992, D1.

86. Beth Baker, "Botcher of the Bay or Economic Boon?" *BioScience* 42 (1992): 746; "Va. Approves Test Seeding of Foreign Oysters," *WP,* 27 May 1992, D5.

87. Karl Blankenship, "York River Experiment Finds Japanese Oysters Resist Disease," *BJ,* Jan.–Feb. 1994; Karl Blankenship, "Gigas Experiment Bolsters Hopes for Disease-Resistant Oyster," *BJ,* July–Aug. 1994; D'Vera Cohn, "Hardy Japanese Oysters Fail to Thrive in Bay," *WP,* 28 Oct. 1993, C2; Gustavo W. Calvo, Mark W. Luckenbach, Standish K. Allen Jr., and Eugene M. Burreson, "Comparative Field Study of *Crassostrea Gigas* (Thunberg, 1793) and *Crassostrea Virginica* (Gmelin, 1791) in Relation to Salinity in Virginia," *JSR* 18 (1999): 465–73.

88. Karl Blankenship, "Experiment with Japanese Oysters Ends Abruptly," *BJ,* July–Aug. 1994.

89. See Executive Summary, "VIMS Rational Plan for Testing Application of Non-native Oyster Species," 1996, 4, http://web.vims.edu/abc/Rational PlanExecSum.pdf (accessed 2 July 2008); Lawrence Latane III, "VIMS Wants to Try New Experiment with Oysters," *RTD,* 16 Dec. 1995, B1; Scott Harper, "Bay Oyster Experiment to Resume," *NVP,* 20 Dec. 1995, B1; Lawrence Latane III, "VMRC Approves Testing 4 Types of Asian Oysters," *RTD,* 20 Dec. 1995, B4.

90. Sara J. Gottlieb and Mona E. Schweighofer, "Oysters and the Chesapeake Bay Ecosystem: A Case for Exotic Species Introduction to Improve Environmental Quality?" *Estuaries* 19 (1996): 646–47; Scott Harper, "Japanese Oysters Offer No Miracle," *NVP,* 20 Apr. 1998, A1; Richard Stradling, "Researchers End Tests of Japanese Oysters," *Newport News (Virginia) Daily Press,* 5 May 1998.

91. Lawrence Latane III, "Va. Scientists Seek to Create Better Bivalve," *RTD,* 17 Jan. 1999, C1; Gustavo W. Calvo, Mark W. Luckenbach, Standish K. Allen Jr., and Eugene M. Burreson, "Comparative Field Study of *Crassostrea Ariakensis* (Fujita, 1913) and *Crassostrea Virginica* (Gmelin, 1791) in Relation to Salinity in Virginia," *JSR* 20 (2001): 221–29.

92. Kerry H. Whiteside, *Precautionary Politics: Principle and Practice in Confronting Environmental Risk* (Cambridge: MIT Press, 2006).

93. Karl Blankenship, "Expanded Use of Nonnative Oyster Seems Likely in Bay," *BJ,* Nov. 2001; Leffler, "Does the Bay Need a New Oyster?" 8.

94. Heather Dewar, "Md. Oyster Season Is Nearing Dismal End," *BS,* 26 Mar. 2002, 1A; Charles Cohen, "Shell Game," *Baltimore City Paper,* 16 Oct. 2002, 16.

95. Lawrence Latane III, "Funds Pledged to Test New Oyster in Bay," *RTD,* 8 Feb. 2002, B2; Leffler, "Does the Bay Need a New Oyster?" 6.

96. Scott Harper, "New Species Test," *NVP,* 23 May 2001, A1; Karl Blankenship, "Dream Come True or Nightmare?" *BJ,* Sept. 2001; Scott Harper, "Best Hope for the Bay?" *NVP,* 30 July 2002, A1.

97. Lawrence Latane III, "Pacific Oysters Test in Bay Delayed," *RTD,* 18 May 2002, B1; Anita Huslin, "Va.'s Oyster Hopes Held at Bay," *WP,* 19 May 2002, C1.

98. Lawrence Latane III, "Pacific Oysters Test in Bay Delayed," *RTD,* 18 May 2002, B1; Timothy B. Wheeler, "Va. Expected to Introduce Foreign Oyster Species in Bay," *BS,* 25 Feb. 2003, 1A; Lawrence Latane III, "Oyster Test Has Small Risk; Bay Panel Suggests Changes to Proposal," *RTD,* 25 Feb. 2003, B3; Lawrence Latane III, "Oyster Test Gets Nod," *RTD,* 26 Feb. 2003, B2; David Malakoff, "Controversial Oyster Test Approved," *Science Now,* 28 Feb. 2003; Scott Harper, "Asian Oyster to Get Wider Testing in Bay," *NVP,* 26 Feb. 2003, A1.

99. Lawrence Latane III, "Oyster Test Has Small Risk; Bay Panel Suggests Changes to Proposal," *RTD,* 25 Feb. 2003, B3; Lawrence Latane III, "Oyster

Test Gets Nod," *RTD,* 26 Feb. 2003, B2; David Malakoff, "Controversial Oyster Test Approved," *Science Now,* 28 Feb. 2003; Scott Harper, "Asian Oyster to Get Wider Testing in Bay," *NVP,* 26 Feb. 2003, A1.

100. "Report Backs Testing Sterile Asian Oysters in Chesapeake Bay," *BS,* 15 Aug. 2003; Gabriel Baird, "New Safeguards Added to Permit for Foreign Oysters in Chesapeake," *WP,* 2 Apr. 2003, 2B; Gretchen Parker, "U.Md. Scientists Working to Drop Asian Oysters in Chesapeake Bay," Associated Press, 18 Oct. 2003.

101. Karl Blankenship, "Seafood Group Seeks New Tests with Ariakensis," *BJ,* Apr. 2005, 1; Dave Schleck, "Seafood Council Gets OK for Asian Oyster Experiment," *Newport News (Virginia) Daily Press,* 23 Mar. 2005.

102. Tommy Kellum quoted in Anita Huslin, "Pacific Oyster Raises Watermen's Hopes," *WP,* 31 Dec. 2001, B7.

103. Quoted in Kenny Keen, Letter to the Editor, *Bay Weekly,* 11–17 Oct. 2007, reprinted in *WG,* Nov. 2007, 20.

104. Kerry Muse, Letter to the Editor, *BS,* 24 Feb. 2005, 18A.

105. Donald F. Boesch, "Briefing on Asian Oysters," in *Testimony Presented to Transportation and Environment Subcommittee, Appropriations Committee, Maryland House of Delegates, 19 Jan. 2005,* 5, http://ca.umces.edu/2005Session/Boesch%20Asian%20oysters%20Appropriations%20Committee1.pdf (accessed 2 July 2008).

106. Anita Huslin, "Va.'s Oyster Hopes Held at Bay," *WP,* 19 May 2002, C1.

107. Anita Huslin, "Pacific Oyster Raises Watermen's Hopes," *WP,* 31 Dec. 2001, B7; Scott Harper, "U.S. Plan Puts the Bay's Native Oysters First," *NVP,* 23 Dec. 2001, B1.

108. Joseph L. Arnold, *The Baltimore Engineers and the Chesapeake Bay, 1961–1987* (Baltimore: U.S. Army Corps of Engineers, 1988); Christine Keiner, "Modeling Neptune's Garden: The Chesapeake Bay Hydraulic Model, 1965–1984," in *The Machine in Neptune's Garden: Historical Perspectives on Technology and the Marine Environment,* ed. Helen M. Rozwadowski and David K. Van Keuren (Sagamore Beach, Mass.: Science History, 2004), 273–314.

109. Mike Unger, "State to Study Foreign Oysters in Bay," *AC,* 19 June 2003, A1; Karl Blankenship, "Feds May Rule on Introducing Foreign Oysters," *BJ,* Nov. 2003, 1; Karl Blankenship, "State, Federal Roles in Oyster Introduction Pondered," *BJ,* Oct. 2003.

110. John Biemer, "Ehrlich Should Have Advantage on the Eastern Shore," Associated Press, 25 Sept. 2002; Tim Hyland, "Ehrlich Vows Millions for Water Clean-Up," *AC,* 21 Jan. 2003, A1; John Biemer, "Ehrlich Delivers First State of the State Address," Associated Press, 30 Jan. 2003; Tim Hyland, "DNR to Ease Restrictions on Crabbing," *AC,* 14 Mar. 2003, A1; Tim Craig, "Ehrlich's Proposal to Ease Crabbing Limits Toughened," *BS,* 1 Apr. 2003; John Biemer, "DNR Eases Crabbing Restrictions," Associated Press, 14 Mar. 2003; Tom Horton, "Agency in Troubled Waters," *BS,* 21 Mar. 2003, 2B; Tim Hyland, "New DNR Chief Puts Science over Politics," *AC,* 3 Feb. 2003, A1.

111. "Maryland Oyster Study Draws Cheers, Concern," *BS,* 20 June 2003; Anita Huslin, "Experts Shuck Off Ehrlich's Oysters," *WP,* 20 June 2003, B6.

112. Committee on Nonnative Oysters in the Chesapeake Bay, *Nonnative Oysters,* 7, 233–36; Testimony of James L. Anderson in *Efforts to Introduce Non-native Oyster Species to the Chesapeake Bay and the National Research Council's Report Titled "Non-native Oysters in the Chesapeake Bay,"* Oversight Field Hearing before the Subcommittee on Fisheries Conservation, Wildlife, and Oceans of the Committee on Resources, U.S. House of Representatives, 14 Oct. 2003 (Washington, D.C.: U.S. Government Printing Office, 2004), 5, http://www.access.gpo.gov/congress/house (accessed 2 July 2008).

113. Anita Huslin, "Scientists Urge Md. to Continue Studying Asian Oysters' Risks," *WP,* 14 Aug. 2003, B1; "Report Backs Testing Sterile Asian Oysters in Chesapeake Bay," *BS,* 15 Aug. 2003; Karl Blankenship, "State, Federal Roles in Oyster Introduction Pondered," *BJ,* Oct. 2003; Tom Horton, "Introducing Oyster Has Yet to Be Tested," *BS,* 19 Sept. 2003, 2B.

114. Committee on Nonnative Oysters in the Chesapeake Bay, *Nonnative Oysters,* 246–48.

115. Isaiah Bowman, "Science and Social Effects: Three Failures," *Scientific Monthly* 50 (1940): 289–98.

116. Michael Paolisso, Stan Herman, and Nicole Dery, "Cultural Analysis for EIS on Oyster Restoration Alternatives, Including *Crassostrea Ariakensis,*" Preliminary Report Prepared for Maryland Department of Natural Resources, 30 Apr. 2005, http://www.dnr.state.md.us/dnrnews/infocus/cultural_analysis_eis _oyster_restoration.pdf (accessed 2 July 2008). I thank Paolisso for granting permission to cite this source. See also Michael Paolisso, Nicole Dery, and Stan Herman, "Restoration of the Chesapeake Bay Using a Non-native Oyster: Ecological and Fishery Conditions," *Human Organization* 65 (2006): 253–67; Michael Paolisso, "Cultural Models and Cultural Consensus of Chesapeake Bay Blue Crab and Oyster Fisheries," *National Association for the Practice of Anthropology Bulletin* 28 (2007): 123–35; Jack Greer, "A Life among Watermen," *CQ* 2.3 (2003): 3–11; Jack Greer, "An Anthropologist's Journey," *CQ* 2.3 (2003): 12–14.

117. Committee on Nonnative Oysters in the Chesapeake Bay, *Nonnative Oysters,* 236–37, 239–40; Karl Blankenship, "Panel Supports Aquaculture, but Warns against *Ariakensis* in Wild," *BJ,* Sept. 2003.

118. Committee on Nonnative Oysters in the Chesapeake Bay, *Nonnative Oysters,* 245–46; Karl Blankenship, "State, Federal Roles in Oyster Introduction Pondered," *BJ,* Oct. 2003; Karl Blankenship, "Policy Seeks to Control New Species Entering the Bay," *BJ,* Jan.–Feb. 1994.

119. Karl Blankenship, "State, Federal Roles in Oyster Introduction Pondered," *BJ,* Oct. 2003; Testimony of Rebecca Hanmer in *Efforts to Introduce Non-native Oyster Species,* 30.

120. David A. Fahrenthold, "Plan for Asian Oysters Worries Del. and N.J.," *WP,* 30 Dec. 2004, B7; Rona Kobell, "Senate Passes Bill to Slow Timetable for

Introducing Asian Oysters into Bay," *BS,* 18 Mar. 2005, 4B; "Limits OK'd on Putting Asian Oysters in Bay," *BS,* 7 Apr. 2005, 2B.

121. Tom Horton, "It's Not Too Late for Chesapeake Oysters," *BS,* 15 July 2005, 2B; Rona Kobell and Greg Garland, "Oystermen Reap Federal Bounty," *BS,* 1 Apr. 2007, 1A.

122. Testimony of C. Ronald Franks and Larry Simns in *Efforts to Introduce Non-native Oyster Species,* 45, 71.

123. Denise Breitburg, Mark Luckenbach, and Jonathan Kramer, *Identifying and Prioritizing Research Required to Evaluate Ecological Risks and Benefits of Introducing Diploid* Crassostrea Ariakensis *to Restore Oysters to Chesapeake Bay* (Annapolis: Scientific and Technical Advisory Committee of the Chesapeake Bay Program, 2004), 8–9, http://chesapeakebay.net/content/publications/cbp_13328.pdf (accessed 2 July 2008); Karl Blankenship, "Scientists Concerned about Inbreeding in Stocking of *Ariakensis,*" *BJ,* Mar. 2004, 6; Karl Blankenship, "Many Are Called *Ariakensis,* but Only One Oyster Species Will Be the Chosen," *BJ,* Nov. 2004, 1, 14, 15; Rona Kobell and Tom Pelton, "Scientists Say History on Oyster Misleading," *BS,* 19 Feb. 2005, 1B.

124. Karl Blankenship, "Trip to Observe *Ariakensis* in Orient Raises New Questions about Oyster," *BJ,* Oct. 2003.

125. Susan Levine, "Tests Discover Parasite in Asian Oysters," *WP,* 17 Dec. 2003, B3; Howard Libit, "Parasite Kills Asian Oysters in N.C. Test," *BS,* 17 Dec. 2003, 1A.

126. Karl Blankenship, "Many Are Called *Ariakensis,* but Only One Oyster Species Will Be the Chosen," *BJ,* Nov. 2004, 1; Mingfang Zhou and Standish K. Allen Jr., "A Review of Published Work on *Crassostrea Ariakensis,*" *JSR* 22 (2003): 1–20.

127. Karl Blankenship, "NOAA Announces $2 Million to Fund *Ariakensis* Research," *BJ,* Nov. 2004, 15; Karl Blankenship, "Early *Ariakensis* Research Findings Reveal Mixed Results, Surprises," *BJ,* June 2005, 6.

128. EPA, FWS, and National Oceanic and Atmospheric Administration, "Summary of Research Needs for a Defensible EIS on the Non-native Oyster," 31 Aug. 2004, http://chesapeakebay.noaa.gov/docs/EisResearchNeeds.pdf (accessed 2 July 2008); Karl Blankenship, "Federal Agencies Seek 3 Years of Research for *Ariakensis,*" *BJ,* Oct. 2004, 5; Karl Blankenship, "Ehrlich Asks Leavitt to Help Speed up *Ariakensis* Research," *BJ,* Dec. 2004; Tom Pelton, "Md. to Extend Asian Oyster Impact Study by 6 Months," *BS,* 28 June 2005, 2B; Rona Kobell, "Plan on Oysters Delayed Again," *BS,* 16 June 2006, 5B.

129. "Petition Seeks Federal 'Endangered' or 'Threatened' Status for Native Oyster," *BJ,* Mar. 2005, 24; Joshua Partlow, "Dissension on the Chesapeake," *WP,* 4 Aug. 2005, B1.

130. Kristen Wyatt, "Lawmakers Pledge Push to Revive Oysters," *Baltimore Examiner,* 17 Jan. 2007, 10; John Wagner, "O'Malley Pushes Native Oysters," *WP,* 13 Mar. 2007, B2; "Governor-Elect O'Malley Nominates Secretaries for

Planning, Natural Resources," State News Service, 16 Jan. 2007, http://www
.mdp.state.md.us/pdf/sec_hall.pdf (accessed 2 July 2008).

131. Virginia Marine Resources Commission, Maryland Department of Natural Resources, and U.S. Army Corps of Engineers, "Programmatic Environmental Impact Statement for Evaluating Oyster Restoration Alternatives for the Chesapeake Bay, Including the Use of Native and Non-native Oysters: Progress Report, 20 June 2007," http://www.dnr.state.md.us/dnrnews/infocus/Oyster EISProgressReportJune202007.pdf (accessed 2 July 2008).

132. "Maryland Establishes New Oyster Advisory Commission," Maryland Department of Natural Resources Press Release, 18 Sept. 2007, http://www.dnr .state.md.us/dnrnews/pressrelease2007/091807.html (accessed 2 July 2008).

133. Rona Kobell, "Oystermen to Organize," *BS,* 3 Sept. 2007, 5B.

134. Lyndsey Layton, "With Pleasure Craft Displacing Crab Boats, Some Watermen Are Left without a Place to Tie Up and Unload in Calvert County," *WP,* 22 Aug. 1999, C1; Steve Goldstein, "A Bay and a Way of Life Imperiled," *Philadelphia Inquirer,* 5 Sept. 2006, A1.

135. Rona Kobell and Greg Garland, "Oystermen Reap Federal Bounty," *BS,* 1 Apr. 2007, 1A; Robert Wieland, "MD Oyster Management Efforts Are All but Subsidies for Watermen," *BJ,* Oct. 2007, 18–19; David A. Fahrenthold, "Oyster Saving Efforts a Wash in Chesapeake: Fewer Bivalves in the Bay after $58 Million Campaign," *WP,* 2 June 2008, A1.

136. Maryland Oyster Advisory Commission, "2007 Interim Report: Concerning Maryland's Chesapeake Bay Oyster Management Program, Submitted to the Governor and General Assembly, January 4, 2008," 4, 8, http://www.dnr.state .md.us/fisheries/oysters/OAC2007_interim_report.pdf (accessed 2 July 2008).

137. Rona Kobell, "Oystermen to Organize," *BS,* 3 Sept. 2007, 1B, 5B.

138. Shane Jacobus, "Power Dredging Does Much Good for Bay," *WG,* Jan. 2007, 3.

139. Tom Horton, "State Says Catching Oysters Improves Hatching Oysters," *BS,* 31 Jan. 2003, 1A; Tom Horton, "A Turning Point for Bay Oystering," *BS,* 14 Feb. 2003, 2B; Kent Mountford, "No Matter What Shells Are Fired in Oyster Wars, the Resource Always Loses," *BJ,* Mar. 2003; Karl Blankenship, "MD Enacts Emergency Legislation to Allow Power Dredging," *BJ,* Mar. 2003.

140. Maryland Oyster Advisory Commission, "2007 Interim Report," 5.

141. Tom Pelton, "Scientific Sleuths Tail Bay Invaders," *BS,* 23 July 2007.

142. Harriette L. Phelps, "The Asiatic Clam (*Corbicula Fluminea*) Invasion and System-Level Ecological Change in the Potomac River Estuary near Washington, D.C.," *Estuaries* 17 (1994): 614–21.

143. Eugene L. Meyer, *Maryland Lost and Found: People and Places from Chesapeake to Appalachia* (Baltimore: Johns Hopkins University Press, 1986), 2.

144. Michael Paolisso, "Taste the Traditions: Crabs, Crab Cakes, and the Chesapeake Bay Blue Crab Fishery," *American Anthropologist* 109 (2007): 654–65.

145. Steven M. Schnell and Joseph F. Reese, "Microbreweries as Tools of Local Identity," *Journal of Cultural Geography* 21.1 (2003): 46. See also n. 116 and Erve Chambers, *Heritage Matters: Heritage, Culture, History, and Chesapeake Bay* (College Park: University of Maryland Sea Grant College, 2006).

Epilogue

1. "The Last of the Watermen," *Homicide: Life on the Street,* season 3, episode 20, original air date 9 Dec. 1994, written by Henry Bromell and Tom Fontana, directed by Richard Pearce.

2. For recent reassertions of this idea, see Callum Roberts, *The Unnatural History of the Sea* (Washington, D.C.: Island, 2007), chap. 16; Rowan Jacobsen, *A Geography of Oysters: The Connoisseur's Guide to Oyster Eating in America* (New York: Bloomsbury, 2007), 139–40.

3. George H. Callcott, *Maryland and America, 1940–1980* (Baltimore: Johns Hopkins University Press, 1985), 259.

4. For insightful discussions of "people's resistance to acknowledging a more complex history" of other fisheries crises, see Joseph E. Taylor III, *Making Salmon: An Environmental History of the Northwest Fisheries Crisis* (Seattle: University of Washington Press, 1999), chap. 8; Arthur F. McEvoy, *The Fisherman's Problem: Law and Ecology in the California Fisheries, 1850–1980* (New York: Cambridge University Press, 1986), chap. 11.

5. Samuel P. Hays with Barbara Hays, *Beauty, Health, and Permanence: Environmental Politics in the United States, 1955–1985* (Cambridge: Cambridge University Press, 1987), 428–29. For other brief mentions of the impact of reapportionment on environmental politics, see Thomas R. Huffman, *Protectors of the Land and Water: Environmentalism in Wisconsin, 1961–1968* (Chapel Hill: University of North Carolina Press, 1994), 3; Philip Shabecoff, *A Fierce Green Fire: The American Environmental Movement* (New York: Hill and Wang, 1993), 135.

6. Michael A. Maggiotto, Manning J. Dauer, Steven G. Koven, Joan S. Carver, and Joel Gottlieb, "The Impact of Reapportionment on Public Policy: The Case of Florida, 1960–1980," *American Politics Quarterly* 13 (1985): 117.

7. See Luther J. Carter, *The Florida Experience: Land and Water Policy in a Growth State* (Baltimore: Johns Hopkins University Press, 1974), 54; Hays and Hays, *Beauty, Health, and Permanence,* 279.

8. Hays and Hays, *Beauty, Health, and Permanence,* 44. For two recent studies that imply the environmental policy impact of legislative reapportionment in Florida but focus instead on gubernatorial agency, see Bruce Stephenson, "A 'Monstrous Desecration': Dredge and Fill in Boca Ciega Bay," in *Paradise Lost? The Environmental History of Florida,* ed. Jack E. Davis and Raymond Arsenault (Gainesville: University Press of Florida, 2005), 326–49; Gordon E. Harvey, "'We Must Free Ourselves . . . from the Tattered Fetters of the Booster Mental-

ity': Big Cypress Swamp and the Politics of Environmental Protection in 1970s Florida," in *Paradise Lost,* ed. Davis and Arsenault, 350–74.

9. See, e.g., Charles Cohen, "Shell Game," *Baltimore City Paper,* 16 Oct. 2002, 19–20; Timothy B. Wheeler, "Asian Oyster Holds Promise, Risk," *BS,* 9 Oct. 2008, 1A.

10. Testimony of William J. Goldsborough in *Efforts to Introduce Non-native Oyster Species to the Chesapeake Bay and the National Research Council's Report Titled "Non-native Oysters in the Chesapeake Bay,"* Oversight Field Hearing before the Subcommittee on Fisheries Conservation, Wildlife, and Oceans of the Committee on Resources, U.S. House of Representatives, 14 Oct. 2003 (Washington, D.C.: U.S. Government Printing Office, 2004), 90, http://www.access.gpo.gov/congress/house (accessed 2 July 2008).

11. R. Douglas Hurt, *Problems of Plenty: The American Farmer in the Twentieth Century* (Chicago: Dee, 2002).

12. Maryland Oyster Advisory Commission, "2007 Interim Report: Concerning Maryland's Chesapeake Bay Oyster Management Program, Submitted to the Governor and General Assembly, January 4, 2008," 5, http://www.dnr.state.md.us/fisheries/oysters/OAC2007_interim_report.pdf (accessed 2 July 2008).

13. Ibid., 4, 16–17.

14. For recent critiques of the public oyster restoration expenditures, see Rona Kobell and Greg Garland, "Oystermen Reap Federal Bounty," *BS,* 1 Apr. 2007, 1A; Robert Wieland, "MD Oyster Management Efforts Are All but Subsidies for Watermen," *BJ,* Oct. 2007, 18–19; David A. Fahrenthold, "Oyster Saving Efforts a Wash in Chesapeake," *WP,* 2 June 2008, A1.

15. Timothy B. Wheeler, "Asian Oyster Holds Promise, Risk," *BS,* 9 Oct. 2008, 1A; *Draft Programmatic Environmental Impact Statement for Oyster Restoration in Chesapeake Bay Including the Use of a Native and/or Nonnative Oyster* (Norfolk, Va.: U.S. Army Corps of Engineers, 2008), http://www.nao.usace.army.mil/Oyster EIS/ (accessed 30 Oct. 2008); Karl Blankenship, "Introduction of Asian Oysters Too Risky for Bay," *BJ,* May 2009, 1.

16. David A. Fahrenthold, "To Save Oysters, a Culture May Have to Die," *WP,* 16 Jan. 2008, B7; Timothy B. Wheeler, "Farming the Chesapeake: Calvert Watermen's Aquaculture Experiment Could Help Revive Faded Md. Oyster Industry," *BS,* 3 Dec. 2008, 1A; Timothy B. Wheeler, "State Seeks Ways to Back Aquaculture Industry," *BS,* 14 Nov. 2008, 5A.

17. Robert J. Brugger, Cynthia Horsburgh Requardt, Robert I. Cottom Jr., and Mary Ellen Hayward, *Maryland: A Middle Temperament, 1634–1980* (Baltimore: Johns Hopkins University Press, 1988).

Environmental History and the American South

Lynn A. Nelson, *Pharsalia: An Environmental Biography of a Southern Plantation, 1780–1880*

Jack E. Davis, *An Everglades Providence: Marjory Stoneman Douglas and the Environmental Century*

Shepard Krech III, *Spirits of the Air: Birds and American Indians in the South*

Paul S. Sutter and Christopher J. Manganiello, eds., *Environmental History and the American South: A Reader*

Claire Strom, *Making Catfish Bait out of Government Boys: The Fight against Cattle Ticks and the Transformation of the Yeoman South*

Christine Keiner, *The Oyster Question: Scientists, Watermen, and the Maryland Chesapeake Bay since 1880*

LaVergne, TN USA
28 December 2010
210291LV00002B/53/P